BRUCE N. SHORTT

THE HARSH TRUTH ABOUT
PUBLIC SCHOOLS

CHALCEDON FOUNDATION
VALLECITO, CALIFORNIA

Chalcedon
P.O. Box 158
Vallecito, CA 95251
U.S.A.

Library of Congress Cataloging-in-Publication Data

Shortt, Bruce N.
The Harsh Truth About Public Schools
Includes index
ISBN 978-1-891375-23-1

Printed in the United States of America

Reprinted 2007

DEDICATION

To my loving wife, Lan, the sons God has graciously given us,
Hugh, Ian, and Owen, North Oaks Baptist Church,
and Christian children and parents everywhere.

WHAT OTHERS ARE SAYING...

"This book presents an idea whose time has come. Modern public education in America has too often degenerated into indoctrination in secular humanism. This book presents the solution to the problem."

D. James Kennedy
Senior Minister
Coral Ridge Ministries

"Bruce Shortt shows why the public schools are increasingly no longer suitable for Christian children — and why they are not likely to be reformed, owing to the teachers' unions and other secularist influences. We should stop treating the public schools as ends in themselves that always have to be 'preserved.' They are means, not ends; and when we discover that they no longer work, we should try something else. The book is quite readable and I hope it will find the audience it deserves. The subject matter is vast; yet it covers much of the salient material in a way which should open some eyes."

Kenneth D. Whitehead
Assistant Secretary of Education
for Ronald Reagan and George H.W. Bush

"*The Harsh Truth about Public Schools* by Bruce Shortt is a sad book. It is sad that the condition documented in this book actually exists in a nation founded on the principles of religious liberty, but it is even more sorrowful to know that, short of a miracle, the very Christian parents and other Christian leaders who need to read this book the most will probably pass it by. For those, however, with courage and a desire to know the truth this volume will be an incredible blessing."

Paige Patterson, President
Southwestern Baptist Theological Seminary
Fort Worth, Texas

"Everyone truly interested in our children, our homes, and the future of our beloved America should read and study this book."

Chaplain (Col.) E. H. Jim Ammerman
U. S. Army Retired, Endorser for over 500 Chaplains representative to the U. S. Military for over 15 million independent church members.

"Bruce Shortt clearly and forcefully sets forth overwhelming evidence of the anti-Christian bias in parts of our public school system. This book is a must-read for anyone concerned with the future of the United States."

Judge Paul Pressler

"Bruce Shortt's new book, *The Harsh Truth About Public Schools*, is clear evidence that concern over the catastrophic meltdown of public education in the United States is being felt in every segment of American society."

Dr. John C. Lundt
Professor of Education, The University of Montana, and coauthor of *Leaving School: Finding Education*, Matanzas Press, 2004

"All parents are ultimately responsible for how their children are educated. This book not only shows forcefully why Christian parents must revolutionize education through homeschooling and Christian schools, it also helps guide parents on their journey into the adventure of Christian education."

Eric and Joyce Burges
Co-founders of the National Black Home Educators Resource Association

"Bruce Shortt has produced a devastating indictment of our public school system, which he believes is not only destroying the intelligence of our children, but is wreaking havoc with our moral and spiritual future. The book is a veritable encyclopedia of educational failure, corruption, and malfeasance by those who run the system"

Samuel L. Blumenfeld
Author of eight books on education, including *NEA: Trojan Horse in American Education, How to Tutor, Alpha-Phonics: A Primer for Beginning Readers*, and *Homeschooling: A Parents Guide to Teaching Children.*

"Anyone considering the possibility of placing their child
in a government school should read this book first. Anyone who
has already made that choice should read this book and reconsider.
Bruce Shortt has exposed the proverbial elephant in the middle of
the room and we can ignore it no longer."

Dr. Voddie Baucham, Jr
National Bible Teacher
Author of *The Ever-Loving Truth*

"Harsh truths with enough humor to make it a fun read.
Presenting this compelling book in discrete chunks
made it easy to start anywhere."

Marshall Fritz
President, Alliance for Separation of School & State
Founder, GetTheKidsOut.org

"A graphic and well-documented reference source that provides a host
of compelling arguments for taking Christian kids out of public schools.
Dr. Shortt casts no aspersion on the motives of most teachers, but his
examples of destructive practices and curricula nevertheless illustrate that,
indeed, "The road to hell is paved with good intentions.""

Dr. Arnold Burron
Professor Emeritus: University of Northern Colorado

"In a readable and enjoyable fashion Bruce Shortt's book combines
the best Biblical, academic, and social arguments for Christians
to abandon K-12 public schools. The postscript addressed to our
Christian public school teachers is a unique challenge."

E. Ray Moore, Jr.
Chaplain (Lt. Col.) US Army Reserve, Retired
Director and Founder, Exodusmandate.org

CONTENTS

FOREWORD

T.C. Pinckney

Bruce Shortt's book, *The Harsh Truth about Public Schools*, combines a sound Biblical basis, rigorous research, straightforward, easily read language, and eminently sound reasoning. Whether one is a parent or parent-to-be, pastor, church staff member, or educator, this book has much to offer. It is based, first of all, upon a clear understanding of God's educational mandate to parents. Its second foundation is a thoroughly documented description of the inescapably anti-Christian thrust of any governmental school system and the inevitable results: moral relativism (no fixed standards), academic dumbing down, far-left programs, near absence of discipline, and the persistent but pitiable rationalizations offered by government education professionals.

Chapter 6 may prove to be especially enlightening, for it provides a brief review of education in America from Pilgrim days, through founding of the first governmental school system in Massachusetts in the 1830s, up to more recent court decisions, and ends with a demonstration of the hopelessness of even well-meant governmental "school reform" programs.

Chapter 7 effectively explodes the excuses so often given for leaving Christian children in the government's "spiritually, morally, and academically corrosive" schools. It would be helpful to read this chapter at least twice. Odds are you will want to discuss its points with more than one family member and other Christians.

The last chapter discusses the advantages and effectiveness of truly Christian schools and homeschooling, and provides numerous sources of further information, many as convenient as the Internet. By this point Shortt will have piqued your interest in alternatives to government schools, so you will really appreciate this help.

Let me close with a quote from Chapter 6: "A Christian education must impart a Christian worldview in which the sovereignty of God and the central role of Jesus Christ in human history and affairs are understood by every Christian child." Do you really think it is

You should also know that this book doesn't have to be read chapter by chapter from beginning to end. Each chapter can be read on its own. Don't worry that you will lose the continuity of the argument if you choose to begin somewhere other than the beginning. The story can start at almost any point.

As a final word, I should mention that government schools, like all institutions, involve a complex interaction between people, institutional culture, and legal rules. To avoid giving offense, many Christian critics of government schools are reluctant to criticize the "people" side of the problem. I am not. Otherwise, a major part of what is wrong would be withheld from scrutiny. Consequently, within these pages government schoolteachers and administrators, *in general*, come in for some much deserved criticism. Needless to say, however, what is true in general is never true in every particular case. *There is still a sizeable remnant of wonderful teachers and administrators, Christian and otherwise, who struggle daily with the strange and toxic places government schools have become.* Their special burdens and frustrations could be the subject of several books. Moreover, this remnant often provides some of the most trenchant criticism of government schools. For that remnant I have added a brief postscript, but this book throughout remains about our children and what we must do.

INTRODUCTION

"I am afraid that the schools will prove the very gates of hell,
unless they diligently labor in explaining the Holy Scriptures and engraving them in the heart of the youth."

Martin Luther

It's a familiar routine: Roughly 180 days a year millions of Christian families begin their day by waking their children, giving them breakfast, and helping them wash their faces, brush their teeth, get dressed, and collect their schoolbooks. They then deliver their children by car, bus, or foot to a seemingly benign, ubiquitous, and familiar institution: the government school. Today this ritual seems unexceptionable. Most of us, after all, went through it as children. The vast majority of parents do it, and, in the public's mind, attending government schools is virtually synonymous with getting an education.

Yet, this has not always been so. For most of America's history, including the colonial period, education was provided primarily by families and the church. To those earlier Americans, the notion of entrusting their children's education to strangers in a secular institution would have been unthinkable. When the government school movement began to emerge in the middle part of the 19th century, it was strongly resisted by many parents and clergy, enough so that government schools could not fully triumph over America's original educational traditions until the early part of the 20th century. We are now several generations removed from that controversy; and, unfortunately, very few even know it existed or why.

This transformation of American education has had profoundly destructive consequences. The most obvious has been the epidemic spread of ignorance and semi-literacy. Contrary to the happy-talk from the education industry and media that today's children are the best educated ever, few public school children can read or write proficiently, let alone do mathematics or science at an advanced level. Indeed, many schoolchildren would have trouble finding Chicago on a map, and by the 12th grade American children are math and science dunces by international standards.

For Christian parents, however, this is far from the most serious problem with government schools. American education is now aggressively anti-Christian, both spiritually and morally. Government schools have effectively become parochial schools for secular humanism and many varieties of New Age spirituality. Moreover, for decades the unacknowledged moral code of government schools has been moral relativism. While the general cultural toll inflicted by the social and moral values propagated through government schools is reflected in levels of violence, drug use, and sexual immortality that would have been almost unthinkable before the 1960s, the damage to American Christianity has been far more profound.

That damage has occurred primarily because the vast majority of Christian parents permit government schools to "educate" their children. Research by the Nehemiah Institute shows that children from Christian homes who attend government schools are five times more likely to adopt such anti-Christian dogmas as moral relativism than those who attend Christian schools.[1] The damage is also painfully evident from the fact that a substantial majority of children from Christian homes stop attending church within two years after graduating from public high school.[2] In fact, teenagers today are the least likely in twenty years to continue attending church once they leave home.[3] More generally, the number of Americans who identify themselves as Christians dropped from 86% to 76.5% between 1990 and 2001, and by late 2001 only 22% of Americans believed that moral absolute truth exists, down from 38% at the beginning of 2000.[4] None of this bodes well for the future of our children and grandchildren.

At points this book may seem harsh. *If so, it is only because the truth about government schools is harsh.* As you will see, I have drawn upon the research of many authors who have carefully examined such issues as the infiltration of government schools by secular humanists and New Agers, the academic failings of government schools, how government schools have effectively become the nation's largest drug pusher, and how government schools discriminate against boys. I encourage you to go to those sources so that you can draw your own conclusions. But if you do, I think you are likely to conclude that the problems are even more acute than I have described.

The fact is that government schools are killing our children spiritually, morally, and intellectually. But most of us don't even see the problem; we simply assume that all is well with our children's education as long as our children seem untroubled and bring home "My Child is on the Honor Roll" bumper stickers. In essence, we have abdicated our responsibility to educate our children. As a consequence, we have simultaneously put our children in harm's way and have failed to notice that the "little red schoolhouse" has effectively become a pagan seminary nurturing our children in alien creeds and infusing them with false values. This, in turn, is transforming our families, our churches, our culture, and our society.

Are we doing this on purpose? Not really. Most of us attended government schools. They are what we know, and because they are familiar we tend not to think much about them, let alone closely scrutinize what they are doing. Giving our children to "experts" for their education seems to be a reasonable division of labor — an arrangement we are also not prone to question because it is convenient. Frankly, we have been led to think that the education of our children is somehow someone else's responsibility and that, in any event, we aren't quite up to the task ourselves. And, if we are willing to be completely honest, many of us shy away from asking awkward questions about what government schools are doing because we fear the responsibility that knowing more would force upon us.

To some this picture may seem too "dark." After all, aren't there still Christian teachers and administrators in government schools? Of course. But the mere presence of some Christian teachers and administrators doesn't mean that our children are receiving a Christian education. For those who care to look carefully, it is plain that the curricula, the institutional rules, and many of those working within government schools are aggressively promoting anti-Christian values and an anti-Christian worldview. In fact, government schools have become so hostile institutionally to Christianity that Christian teachers and administrators who actively profess their faith within government schools will be dismissed or disciplined if they are "caught." Moreover, the number of good teachers and administrators, whether Christian or not, has been dwindling as a result of retirement, frustration, and an institutional structure that protects incompetence. *The problem we face is not undue pessimism, but complacency and misplaced trust.*

So what is this book about? It is about the many ways in which government schools are hazardous to children, and especially Christian children. Christian parents and grandparents need to see government schools for what they really are, not for what they claim to be or for what they once were. This book is also about why government schools are unreformable — why they cannot and should not be expected to provide the Christian education that the Bible enjoins Christian parents to provide to their children. Finally, this book is about restoring Christian educational traditions through Christian schools and homeschooling. In sum, this book is about the future of our children, our families, our culture, and our faith.

WHY ARE YOU EDUCATING
YOUR CHILDREN AT A PAGAN SEMINARY?

"For as a man thinks, so he is...."
Proverbs 23:7

"[P]ublic education is the parochial education
for scientific humanism."
Joe R. Burnett, an editor of *The Humanist*[1]

You're a Christian; you love your children; you know that the Bible instructs you to raise them in the nurture and admonition of the Lord. Yet, you send them for their education to an institution from which all vestiges of Christianity were driven out long ago – an institution that is also awash in secular humanist and neo-pagan theologies. That institution, of course, is a government school.[2]

Do you really believe that government schools are somehow religiously neutral? Can we honestly think that committing our children from their earliest years to the care and nurture of schools dominated by secular humanism and New Age paganism doesn't harm them spiritually? Do you believe that we are not commanded to give our children an explicitly Christian education? After reading this chapter you will at least know what government schools are doing to our children spiritually.

THE LITTLE RED SCHOOLHOUSE IS NOT WHAT IT USED TO BE

In a time now culturally far distant, Christmas and Easter holidays were a source of anticipation among schoolchildren and were celebrated with programs and pageants in government schools. In fact, for those old enough to remember, Good Friday also received some official recognition from the government schools, even if it was only the small gesture of ending school early in honor of Good Friday so that children could attend a church service or a showing of "The Greatest Story Ever Told" at the local cinema. Bibles then were not considered contraband, and in most schools organized prayer was included as a normal part of the school day. In sum, while government schools were not Christian schools, the government schools at least seemed tolerant of Christianity.

Today, of course, everything has changed. Prayer long ago was driven from government schools through a series of federal court decisions too well known to bother naming here. But eliminating prayer from government schools was just the beginning. Now Christmas carols are treated as if they are "hate speech." Christmas pageants are prohibited. "Christmas vacation" must now be referred to as "Winter break," and "Easter vacation" as "Spring break."[3] Gideons can no longer give away Bibles in government schools. School boards have refused to allow posters bearing the national motto "In God We Trust" for fear of giving offense. Almost incredibly, the ACLU even demanded that a California elementary school take down a sign saying "God Bless America" that the school had put up in the aftermath of the September 11, 2001, terrorist attacks.[4] Examples of this sort abound, and they illustrate how much government schools have changed since today's parents and grandparents attended them.

HE WHO IS NOT WITH ME IS AGAINST ME

As troubling as these issues are, they are the *least* of the problems with the "education" inflicted on Christian children by government schools. In fact, *even if the government schools returned today to the accommodation of a few Christian symbols and rituals, they would still be an unfit place for Christian children*. Why? Because the government schools by legal necessity are committed to a non-Christian worldview.

Virtually every Christian knows that beginning in the 1940s, and especially in the 1960s and 1970s, the Supreme Court created a new jurisprudence of the First Amendment in which the Court sought to create what it termed a "wall of separation" between church and state. The objective of the Court's decisions was to eliminate from government schools the core of the Christian culture that characterized American society since its earliest colonial days. The intent was to transform government schools into what the Court considered religiously neutral, secular institutions.

As a result of federal court rulings over the last six decades on the meaning of the religion clauses of the First Amendment, school districts and administrators have struggled with figuring out what they could lawfully say and do regarding religion. In response, professional organizations and school systems have developed guidelines for teaching about religion.

One of these efforts was a report produced by the Americans United Research Foundation (1988) entitled "Religion in the Public School Curriculum: Questions and Answers." The report suggests the following principles for marking the boundary between teaching about religion, which is Constitutionally permitted, and religious indoctrination, which is not:[5]

- **The school's approach to religion is academic, not devotional.**

- **The school strives for student awareness of religions, but does not press for student acceptance of any one religion.**

- **The school sponsors study about religion, not the practice of religion.**

- **The school exposes students to a diversity of religious views; it does not impose any particular view.**

- **The school educates about all religions; it does not promote or denigrate any religion.**

- **The school informs students about various beliefs; it does not seek to conform students to any particular belief.**

In a very general sense, this set of guidelines fairly summarizes a theory of what the federal courts should permit – *religious indifference*. Mohammed? Zoroaster? Wotan? Christ? Whatever.

INDIFFERENCE AS "PROGRESS"

More recently, the federal Department of Education adopted regulations regarding accommodation of religious speech in government schools. As described by Brian Jones, a DOE attorney, those regulations do not attempt to move beyond the existing case law concerning religious speech in schools: "What we are trying to do… is bring some clarity to the perceived fuzziness in the law by letting districts know exactly what the courts are saying and standardizing that view."[6]

In truth, the regulations are an attempt to rein in the increasingly overt hostility toward Christianity manifested in government schools across the country. Despite not departing from existing law, the Department of Education's new regulations have drawn criticism from liberal groups such as Americans United for Separation of Church and State.[7] In other words, an attempt to return to mere "indifference" toward Christianity is now viewed as controversial by liberals and, *unfortunately*, as progress by Christians.

The new regulations notwithstanding, those within the education establishment who are opposed to Christianity will continue to find ways to make government schools a hostile environment for Christian children, teachers, and administrators. You can count on it.

OUR OBLIGATION TO GIVE OUR CHILDREN A CHRISTIAN EDUCATION AND "THE SILENCE OF THE PASTORS"

Even though the Department of Education's regulations may pass Constitutional muster, they scarcely constitute an acceptable approach to the education of Christian children. Nor, as you will see, do they represent what is *really* happening inside government schools.

Our God is a jealous God. We may not put other gods before Him, and we cannot be double minded in the way we live our lives. As Jesus said in Matthew 12:30, "He who is not with Me is against Me." Plainly, an education that attempts to distance itself from a commitment to Christianity, and to treat all religious beliefs as equal, is profoundly anti-Christian.

The Bible repeatedly indicates that children are to receive a Christian education, and parents are responsible for providing it. *Parents*, for example, are directed to raise their children in the fear and admonition of the Lord (Ephesians 6:4). Moreover, their obligation is not to instruct children in the Word occasionally, but to do so all of the time (Deuteronomy 6:6).[8] Yet, today, most Christian parents behave as if there are passages in the Bible instructing them to give the education of their children over to anti-Christian government schools and telling them that exposing their children to Christianity two or three hours a week is sufficient.

About 85% of Christian children attend government schools, but the message that Christian parents are obligated to provide a Christian education to their children is seldom heard from the pulpit. Can you imagine a similar silence if 85% of a congregation's parents with school-age children had a "drug problem" or an "adultery problem"? For far too long and for far too many Christian parents and churches this has been an area of spiritual blindness. Regrettably, we have failed to give our children a Christian education because we have been *hearers* of the word rather than *doers* of the word (James 1:22-23).

THE THEOLOGIES OF THE GOVERNMENT SCHOOL

Any Christian who believes that government schools operate on religiously neutral principles is deceived. There is no such thing as metaphysical neutrality. If a society or an institution rejects the Bible's teaching about the nature of God, man and the universe, then it necessarily accepts, implicitly or explicitly, some other worldview, whether it be the materialist metaphysics of secular humanism, the cosmic humanism of the New Age religions, or something else. Government schools are no exception.

The net result of the last fifty years or so of Supreme Court rulings on the meaning of the Establishment Clause of the Constitution has not been to create a level playing field for different beliefs, but simply to take all vestiges of Christianity out of government schools. Today, secular humanism, New Age mysticism, and other forms of paganism pervade government schools at all levels. The teachers' unions, such as the NEA, are openly hostile to Christianity and its values, and the curricula of schools of education, from which the overwhelming majority of teachers are drawn, are suffused with a mélange of secular humanist, New Age, and other worldviews. Not surprisingly, textbook publishers accommodate the education establishment's worldview by providing textbooks that conform to the prevailing anti-Christian perspective of the education establishment.

SECULAR HUMANISM AND GOVERNMENT SCHOOLS

For at least the better part of a century a version of humanism,[9] often termed "secular humanism," and Christianity have been the two major contending worldviews in America. At the core of secular humanism is a materialist metaphysics. According to that worldview, matter, energy, and the laws of physics are what ultimately exist, and they can explain everything that happens.

The *Humanist Manifesto* of 1933 was perhaps the first broadly influential and coherent American statement of the tenets of secular humanism.[10] The *Manifesto*'s authors, who included the education theorist John Dewey, explicitly characterized their views as "religious." As they were quick to point out, however, their "religion" was not traditional. Rather, the authors of the *Manifesto* simply stated that the *Manifesto* articulated their philosophical views about "matters of final concern" – *e.g.*, the nature of the universe, what exists, the place of Man in the universe, and so on. Consequently, their project was to set forth a new *secular* view of reality that they believed would better fit the needs of the age.

What exactly is the worldview of the *Humanist Manifesto*? Among other things, Dewey and the other authors:[11]

- Regarded the universe as self-existing and not created.

- Believed that man is a part of nature and that he emerged as a part of a continuous evolutionary process.

- Held an organic view of life and rejected mind/body dualism.

- Rejected as scientifically unacceptable any purported supernatural or cosmic guarantee of human values.

- Were convinced that the time had passed for religious views such as theism and deism.

- Considered the complete realization of human personality to be the purpose of man's life.

- Advocated establishment of a "socialized and cooperative economic order."

- Asserted that the purpose and program of humanism is the intelligent evaluation, transformation, control, and direction of all associations and institutions for the fulfillment of human life.

The extent of the influence of the *Manifesto* itself is a matter for scholarly research. What is certain, however, is that the *ideas* embodied in the *Manifesto* were tremendously influential. Nowhere did those ideas result in a more radical change than in American education.

ESTABLISHING SECULAR HUMANISM

The triumph of secular humanism in American schools has not been the result of legislation or popular clamor; it was imposed by the federal courts. As adopted, the First Amendment to the Constitution prohibits, among other things, both the establishment of religion and interference in the free exercise of religion by the *federal government*. It was *not* a grant of power to Congress or the federal courts authorizing them to involve themselves in state actions touching upon religion. And, indeed, the religion clauses of the First Amendment were not much litigated until after the Supreme Court's decision in *Everson v. Board of Education* in 1947.

EVERSON AND THE TRANSFORMATION OF GOVERNMENT SCHOOLS

In *Everson*, the Supreme Court upheld a New Jersey school board resolution directing that all parents whose children must ride public buses to school be reimbursed for the amount of the fares. *Everson* is typically described as a taxpayer suit in which the plaintiff objected that the reimbursement of bus fare violated the Establishment Clause because some of the parents reimbursed were sending their children to Catholic parochial schools. This much is true. But it should also be pointed out that the plaintiff, Arch Everson, was a member of the New Jersey chapter of the Junior Order of United American Mechanics, a nativist organization that had often allied itself with the Klan.[12] According to legal historian Philip Hamburger: "In the 1930s, after the decline of the Klan, the Junior Order continued to stand 'at the portals of our American public school system to guard it from sectarian and foreign influence.'"[13] In other words, the Junior Order viewed its role in large part as "protecting" government schools from Catholicism. Not surprisingly, although Arch Everson's name was on the pleadings, the Junior Order was the real force behind the case.[14]

Everson reflected a social climate during the decade of the 1940s in which Catholicism continued to be viewed with suspicion by significant parts of American society. As in the past, the nativists were not alone in their hostility towards Catholicism. Many secular liberals were angered by the Catholic Church's opposition to communism, and many "theologically and politically liberal" Protestants and Jews considered Catholicism "divisive."[15] Further, issues touching on education were undoubtedly points of great sensitivity for American liberals and nativists, whose ability to force children into government schools had been foreclosed by the Supreme Court's 1925 ruling in *Pierce v. Society of Sisters.*

While the Supreme Court rejected the argument that the Establishment Clause had been violated, it also for the first time found that the Establishment Clause of the First Amendment applied to the states as a result of the adoption of the 14th Amendment.[16] In his opinion for the Court, Justice Black, a former Democrat Senator from Alabama appointed to the Court by Franklin Delano Roosevelt, also laid down the now well-known doctrine that the purpose of the Establishment Clause is to erect "a wall of separation between church and state."

The subtlety of Justice Black's ruling was lost for a time on the supporters of the plaintiff in *Everson.* Indeed, there was a keen sense of betrayal. Black, after all, had been a member of the Klan who "had long before sworn, under the light of flaming crosses, to preserve 'the sacred constitutional rights' of 'free public schools' and 'separation of church and state.' Subsequently, he had administered this oath to thousands of others in similar ceremonies...."[17] Jim Esdale, a Grand Dragon of the Klan and Klan colleague of Black, had also noted that "Hugo could make the best anti-Catholic speech you ever heard."[18] Of course, when his Klan membership was discovered shortly after his confirmation to the Supreme Court, Black distanced himself from the Klan.[19]

Even though Black had ostensibly retired his sheets by the time he reached the Supreme Court, he continued to feed his Klan-period views of the Catholic Church by reading the "respectable" anti-Catholic writings of the secular humanist and liberal, Paul Blanshard.[20] Thus, it's not surprising that having written an opinion ruling in favor of a state expenditure that indirectly benefited Catholic schools Justice Black was, at least initially, excoriated by liberals and nativists alike.[21]

Black, however, knew what he was about. As noted by Philip Hamburger: "in a conversation with a clerk, he [Black] alluded to it [the *Everson* ruling] as a Pyrrhic victory." This also, in time, was appreciated by at least some supporters of an expansive view of the "separation of church and state."[22] For example, Joseph Martin Dawson, a liberal Baptist leader and supporter of Everson's suit against the New Jersey school board, ultimately declared, "[W]e had lost the battle, but won the war."[23]

It is at least somewhat ironic that an unreconstructed ex-Klansman wrote the opinion in what has proved to be the most important case in Establishment Clause jurisprudence, and that *Everson* was effectively served up to the Supreme Court by an organization that shared the views of the Klan on the issue at stake in that case.[24] We must wonder, too, if the members of the Supreme Court who have subsequently elaborated on the "separation" principle in *Everson* have really understood the origins of the jurisprudence they have been applying.[25]

THE MEANING OF *EVERSON*

As a practical matter, *Everson* made the federal courts the arbiter of what the states could and could not do in the area of religion. Never mind that for the roughly eighty years following the adoption of the 14th Amendment no federal court had claimed or noticed that it had this power. Never mind, also, that a few years after the adoption of the 14th Amendment the Congress rejected a proposed Constitutional amendment known as the Blaine Amendment, which had as its express purpose the application of the religion clauses to the states.[26]

Whatever the reasons given by the Supreme Court for its actions in *Everson*, the truth of the matter is that the Court simply decided that it was time for the federal courts to *force the transformation of American culture and its institutions* – including the government schools. What kind of transformation? A transformation in which Justice Black's "wall of separation" language was to be interpreted eventually as requiring the elimination all traces of a Christian world-view from government schools and, more generally, the public policies of the federal government and the states. In effect, *Everson* made the thorough secularization of government schools a mission of the federal courts. It also placed a powerful weapon in the hands of the enemies of Christianity.

Until the 1970s the public policy battles fought by Christians involving education predominantly concerned religious symbols and observances in schools, aid to religious schools, and the teaching of evolution. Christians lost these battles decisively. The Supreme Court long ago outlawed prayer and other forms of religious observance in government schools. Similarly, the Supreme Court has prohibited aid to religious schools except under very limited circumstances. Darwinian evolution is now well-entrenched dogma in most government schools. In fact, Darwin's theory of evolution even enjoys a measure of legal protection against *competition* as a result of a 1987 Supreme Court decision holding that Louisiana could not mandate the teaching of creationism alongside evolution because creationism, the court claimed, is essentially a religious doctrine.

In another example of the evolution wars, the Kansas State Board of Education in 1999 removed most of the references to Darwin's theory of evolution from the state's educational standards.[27] This had the practical effect of leaving Kansas school districts free to set their own curriculum standards for the teaching of evolution and also assured that evolution would not be tested on new statewide science tests. *No district was prohibited from teaching evolution, and no district was required to teach any competing theory.* Yet even this modest victory was short lived. Two years later, a new school board restored the theory of evolution to the state standards, in effect returning the theory of evolution to its monopoly position within Kansas government schools.[28]

Thus, while Christians have divergent views on matters of origins and creation, it is a measure of the influence of secular humanism in government schools that the education establishment brooks no opposition to the theory of evolution.

THE NEW PAGANISM

In 1973, having enjoyed more success in transforming American culture and education than they could have imagined in 1933, humanists restated and reaffirmed their gospel in the *Humanist Mani-*

festo II. The *Humanist Manifesto II* reiterated the same anti-Christian themes of the original *Manifesto*. But it also discarded the rhetoric of religion contained in the original *Manifesto* and focused far more explicitly on social and moral issues than its predecessor. Its devotees were instructed, for example, that abortion should be legal, nationalism should be rejected, war is obsolete, the earth must be considered a single ecosystem, and "moral values derive their source from human experience. Ethics is autonomous and situational needing no theological or ideological sanction. Ethics stems from human need and interest."[29]

RELIGIOUS HUMANISM AND THE NEW AGE

The publication of the *Humanist Manifesto II* coincided roughly with the high tide of secular humanism's influence within government schools. Beginning in the 1970s, however, new forms of religious humanism based on various neo-pagan, environmental, spiritualist, and other occult beliefs (often loosely labeled as the New Age movement) started infiltrating government schools. In essence, much of the New Age movement incorporates the "transpersonal psychology" that grew out of the work of Carl Rogers and Abraham Maslow in the 1960s, along with various forms of eastern mysticism and the occult. One handbook on cults explicitly describes the New Age movement this way:

> The central vision of the New Age is one of radical mystical transformation on an individual level. It involves an awakening to such new realities as a discovery of psychic abilities, the experience of physical or psychological healing, the emergence of new potentials within oneself… the acceptance of a new picture of the universe. The essence of the New Age is the imposition of that personal vision onto society and the world. Thus, the New Age is ultimately a vision of the world transformed, a heaven on earth, a society in which the problems of today are overcome and a new existence emerges.[30]

New Age spirituality denies the existence of our transcendent God. Instead, it often preaches a kind of pantheism (all is god) or panentheism (all is becoming god).

Over the last thirty years the influence of the New Age movement has perhaps eclipsed secular humanism as the primary agent of anti-Christian influence within government schools. A few examples will illustrate what is going on.

WHAT A FRIEND WE HAVE IN GANESHA

Imagine asking your child some evening what he learned in school and having him respond: "Nothing much. We made images of a Hindu god, Ganesha, and learned that when we remove a plant from the garden or cut down a tree we should pray to Mother Earth to ask her permission. Oh, have you seen this really neat card game with demons and vampires that help me learn math? We get to cast spells and sacrifice people and everything!" Actually, for some of the parents of Bedford Central School District in New York the curriculum included all that and more.

In the late 1990s some parents became concerned about what was being taught in the Bedford Central School District schools when they discovered that their children were playing a card game called "Magic: The Gathering" as part of school-sanctioned extracurricular activities.[31] In the game, players compete by accumulating "mana," which is characterized as "power that comes from the earth." The game also involved casting spells and ritualistic human sacrifice. Moreover, the imagery on the cards was troubling. One card, for example, depicted a frightened woman with a hand holding her head down and a large knife at her throat. Another card showed a man with a knife about to be driven into his heart and was inscribed with the words "Sacrifice one of your creatures to add to your mana pool a number of black mana equal to that creature's casting cost." Further inquiry by the parents uncovered pagan "Earth Day" rituals and other strange practices within the Bedford schools.

As a result of their investigation, these parents filed a lawsuit alleging practices within the school district that in their totality involved "the promotion of Satanism and occultism, pagan religions and a New Age Spirituality." Those practices included, among other things:[32]

- Teachers playing an audio-tape in class called "Listening to Nature" that used a background of forest and ocean sounds to present prayers and invocations reflecting North American Indian animist religious beliefs, such as the following Taos Indian creed: "The Mother of us all is the Earth. The Father is the Sun. The Grandfather is the Creator who bathed us with his mind and gave life to all things. The Brother is the beasts and trees. The Sister is that with wings. We are children of the earth and do it no harm in any way, nor do we offend the Sun by not greeting it at dawn. We praise our Grandfather for his creation. We share the same breath together, the beasts, the trees, the birds and the man."

- An Earth Day ceremony involved the "erection of symbolic structures equal to an altar, and a chorus of drums playing throughout the presentations" and the presentation of gifts to the earth.

- A teacher during the Earth Day ceremony taught that "[w]e came from the earth, we are part of the earth, and we are all involved in this cycle. One day we will become [dead] and then we'll go back to the earth."

- Students were taught how to pray to "Mother Earth."

- A student newspaper reported that teachers urged students to deify the earth and do something that would make Mother Earth smile.

- Teachers had children make "worry dolls," told the children that the dolls had supernatural powers to relieve worry, and taught the children how to use them.

- Teachers had children read about and make images of "Ganesha," an elephant-headed god regarded by Hindus as the personification of the material universe.

The two-week trial included a parade of colorful witnesses including a yogi-numerologist known as the "Yoga Guy," a psychic-telepath, and a mineralogist known as the "Rock Hound."

Two and one-half months after the trial, U.S. District Judge Charles Brieant ruled in favor of the plaintiffs on three of their allegations. The judge noted particularly that some of the aspects of the Earth Day celebrations were "truly bizarre" and had many of the attributes of the worship ceremonies of organized religions. Consequently, Judge Brieant ordered, among other things, that the school district: (1) prevent school sponsorship of earth worship, nature worship, or North American Indian animism, (2) remove worry dolls from the schools and refrain from suggesting that tangible objects have supernatural powers, and (3) prohibit directing students to make graven images or likenesses of gods or religious symbols.

On appeal, however, a panel of the Second Circuit Court of Appeals reversed all of Judge Brieant's findings for the plaintiffs.[33] Although most of the reversals were based on technical grounds, the Court of Appeals, incredibly, found that the Earth Day ceremonies did not violate the Establishment Clause.

YES, BUT THAT'S JUST NEW YORK

Most Christian parents have no idea how far the New Age and related movements have penetrated into government school practices and curricula. Before looking at this issue more broadly, let's consider some examples similar to the Bedford Central School District case.

NEW AGE BUDDHIST CONGA LINES IN UTAH?

The Jefferson 21st Century Institute, a tax exempt organization that promotes the separation of church and state, recently reported on New Age practices in Utah, a state not known for having much in common culturally with New York:[34]

- **Uintah and Duchense School Districts.** Third graders were sent to an Earth Day ceremony "that included prayers by a Ute elder and the Rt. Rev. Carolyn Tanner Irish in which trees were blessed and Mother Earth was praised." The ceremony also included devotional statements instructing the children that the earth and trees are sacred.

- **Grand County and Salt Lake City School Districts.** In the Grand County School District students attended an assembly in which robed Tibetan tantric Buddhist Monks "chanted prayers and danced in front of an altar with smoking incense, a picture of their religious leader, the Dalai Lama, and a large mural of their temple." The same monks were in a Salt Lake City school during school hours for three days performing a mandala construction ceremony in which the monks constructed a sand painting in the form of a circle dedicated to a Buddhist deity. The ceremony, which required several days, began with chants and prayers and ended when the sand painting was destroyed and the earth and its inhabitants reconsecrated by pouring the sand from the mandala into a stream.

- **Park City School District.** The same group of Tibetan Buddhist monks performed their "mandala ceremony" for six full days during school hours in Park City High School. At some point during the ceremony students were dancing in a conga line behind a Buddhist monk.

- **San Juan County School District.** First graders were taken on field trips by a local environmental group, a Forest Service Ranger, and an Americorp volunteer. During the field trip "the children were told to wrap their arms around a tree, smell it, *and feel its spirit.*"

- Various other Utah school districts have allowed "philosophical" schools or associations to teach children "'traditional' Scandinavian or other 'eco-philosophies' which declare nature, land, trees, and the earth are sacred and subject to worship."

- Many Utah schools have illegally sponsored Native American and Gaia religions. For example, many schools use a fourth grade text that declares, "The Earth is Our Mother," "in wilderness is salvation," "animals know best," and other religious principles. Innumerable schools have been decorated with posters espousing similar devotionals.

Interestingly, the performances of the Tibetan Buddhist monks in Utah were part of a 100-city tour in which the monks performed devotional rituals in government schools around the country.

THE WALDORF NEW AGE: LUCIFER AND TEACHER TRAINING

Other government schools have adopted, or have considered adopting, the Waldorf curriculum, which is based on the rather peculiar New Age doctrines of Rudolph Steiner, a 19th century German.[35] Some of the more colorful aspects of the Waldorf method received public attention when two school districts in California that had set up "Waldorf" schools were sued by an organization known as People for Legal and Non-Sectarian Schools.

The lawsuit revealed that one of the school districts used a manual called *The Waldorf Teacher's Survival Guide* to train teachers in Waldorf teaching methods.[36] An examination of the manual made it clear that Waldorf schooling had its roots in Steiner's theology, which is known as "Anthroposophy." Anthroposophy regards Lucifer as the god of light, and his nemesis is Ahriman, the god of darkness. According to Steiner, Christ came to earth as a sun god to balance the forces of light and darkness. These teachings are reflected in *The Waldorf Teacher's Survival Guide*:

> Most of that which contributes to our work as teachers, prepa-
> ration work, artistic work, even meditative work, is *under the*
> *guardianship of Lucifer*. We can become great teachers under his
> supervision, for he is responsible for much that has blossomed
> in the unfolding of the civilization and culture in the past.
> [Emphasis added.] [37]

Anthroposophy also includes some very unusual views concerning race (*e.g.*, it associates intelligence with blondness), medicine (*e.g.*, it views illness as primarily the result of a disturbance of a "vital essence"), and evolution (*e.g.*, animals are believed to be by-products of human development).[38]

The organization that brought the California lawsuit also discovered that school teachers in the Waldorf government schools had been instructed by Anthroposophist trainers from the Rudolph Steiner College to use zodiac signs to categorize children.[39] But it gets even stranger. One parent reviewed the course of study for Waldorf teachers at the Rudolph Steiner College and was stunned to find that it was, in her view, a religious institution:

> When I read what the course of study was for Waldorf teachers,
> I realized right away that it was *a religious seminary*. There's no
> core academic classes in the entire teacher training program....
> The required text for the first year includes occult science, and
> the spiritual hierarchies, spiritual guidance of man...I mean,
> where's the phonics? [Emphasis added.] [40]

WWGD: WHAT WOULD THE GNOME DO?

When questioned about how the exotic doctrines of Anthroposophy get applied in the classroom, Waldorf teachers usually say something along the lines of "Just because Steiner had some odd views, it doesn't mean we can't use his insights" or "Even though we may be trained in Anthroposophy, we don't teach it in the classroom." Waldorf practice, however, doesn't seem to bear this out.

One intrepid Texas reporter, for instance, ventured into the precincts of a newly opened suburban Waldorf private kindergarten.[41] There he found a "TV and computer blackout" based on the Waldorf belief that the dark spirit "Ahriman" lives inside the boxes; gnome dolls in the classroom representing the Anthroposophical belief that there are elemental beings that care for the air, soil, and water; and staff who will tell you that illnesses later in life can be traced to early reading.[42]

Gnomes are important to Waldorf. Think of the gnomes as playing the role of Charlie McCarthy to the teachers' Edgar Bergen. Waldorf teachers "ask" the gnomes questions to teach children the Waldorf way of thinking about things. In addition, the gnomes provide a kind of deniability: the teachers don't teach Anthroposophy, the gnomes do.

The reporter also observed parts of the Waldorf liturgy. Before meals, for example, the children recite the Waldorf version of "grace": "Earth, who gives to us this food, sun who makes it ripe and good. Dear sun, dear earth, by you we live, our loving thanks to you we give."[43] Later, during "music and movement" time, the children walked around a candle chanting in a "spirit recital of mother earth."[44]

Yet, the Waldorf program is widely considered nonsectarian and has been spreading in government schools primarily through the charter school movement.[45]

DON'T WORRY, IT ISN'T REALLY WICCA OR DEEP ECOLOGY

Every school day across America, thousands of children bring home permission slips for mom or dad to sign so that they can participate in some inoffensively described government school sponsored activity or program. So, imagine the surprise of a Michigan mother who decided to attend the first day of an "environmental" program called "Earthkeepers" with her fourth grade daughter only to discover that

Earthkeepers was much more like a three-day introduction to Wicca and Deep Ecology[46] than a program about environmental science.

Wicca is a pagan religion associated with witchcraft, while Deep Ecology is an environmentalist philosophy associated with eco-terrorism that many think has its roots in Wicca. The first principle of Wicca is that "We are all connected – people, plants, and animals." Similarly, Deep Ecologists believe that we are all part of the earth. Deep Ecologists also believe that the population of the earth must be substantially reduced and are supporters of abortion and euthanasia. Significantly, the Earthkeepers curriculum was written by a noted Deep Ecologist, Steve Van Matre, who is also the author of a book, *Earth Education*. In *Earth Education* Van Matre explicitly states that earth education should be about inculcating *all* of the message of Deep Ecology.

So, what does all of this look like when translated into a program targeted at nine-year-olds that allegedly teaches children about the environment? The children begin the Earthkeepers program by forming a circle and joining themselves at the elbows. Next, they are taken into the laboratory of a mysterious "wizard" named "E.M." The laboratory, it turns out, is a dark, candle lit garage decorated with herbs and plants on the wall. Eventually the children are told that "E.M." stands for "energy and materials," "my experience," and "Me."

Part of the Earthkeepers program is devoted to telling children how "specks" – which in Earthkeepers' terminology turn out to be water, soil, air, and energy from the sun – form "trails," *i.e.*, are involved in the transformation of things into other things. The children were also told to choose "magic spots" where they would "reflect" on nature. In addition, the children were instructed to chant in unison the concepts behind the four "keys" of Earthkeepers: "All living things are connected. Getting in touch with the earth is a good feeling. Your actions on the earth make a difference. Helping others improve their relationship with the earth is an urgent task." In all of this the children are helped by Earthkeeper teachers who wear medallions that on one side resemble an astrological chart.

In the beginning, the Michigan mother, who is also a cancer surgeon, was mainly concerned about the program's lack of scientific content and use of unscientific terms such as "specks." As she investigated further, she found that Earthkeepers had numerous obvious parallels with Wicca and ties to Deep Ecology. When she raised her concerns about these parallels she was told that they were just coincidences:

> They are doing things that are very much like things in pagan religions and telling us it doesn't mean anything.... Is it just a coincidence that E.M.'s lab looks like a Witches Cove, coincidence that the specks taught in Earthkeepers are the same as the elements of witchcraft [air, earth, fire, and water], coincidence that the magic spots are similar to pagan meditation, coincidence that the medallion with the symbol has the same shape as the astrological chart?[47]

But this doesn't exhaust the "coincidences." Was it also a coincidence that the circles the children were gathered into were also similar to the circles practitioners of Wicca form to "contain energy flow"? Was it coincidence that the first key concept of Earthkeepers that the children chanted in unison in a dark candle lit room is also a first principle of Wicca? Was it a coincidence that the "E.M." concept as used in Earthkeepers seemed to represent, as the Michigan mother concluded, the principle from Deep Ecology and Wicca that everything on earth, including people, is connected? Finally, was it a coincidence that all of these coincidences just happen to be part of a curriculum written by a Deep Ecologist?

By the way, Earthkeepers is used not only in Michigan, *but also in 30 other states* and in some foreign countries.

FROM SEA TO SHINING SEA

Far from being isolated events, the incidents described above are a reflection of American primary and secondary schools being awash in non-Christian worldviews. These are most commonly found in transpersonal and humanistic curricula. Humanistic education typically involves training children in values clarification and emphasizes the importance of developing self-esteem.[48] Humanistic approaches to education may also involve hypnosis or other psychotherapeutic techniques. Unlike humanistic education, which tends to have a secular focus, transpersonal education is just New Age religion in drag. It is, therefore, more obviously essentially religious. Moreover, because humanistic and transpersonal approaches to education are not mutually exclusive, they often show up in combination.

While "humanistic education" and "transpersonal education" may not be familiar terms, if a school-age child has ever told you "What's right for you is not necessarily right for me," the odds are that he's been through a humanistic values clarification curriculum teaching situational ethics in at least one of the schools he has attended. Similarly, if you have heard terms such as "guided imagery," "centering," "inner guides," "left/right brain equilibrium," "visualization," or "human potential" from a child or anyone else connected with a primary or secondary school, or if you have seen them in a student's handouts or textbooks, you are seeing evidence of the presence of transpersonal education in your schools. But even if you haven't seen or heard any of these things, you should not assume that they are not in your public schools because, as we will see below, concealing what is going on from parents has been an accepted tactic among transpersonal and humanistic educators for years.

In their important and wide-ranging study of the influence of humanistic and transpersonal curricula in schools, John Ankerberg, John Weldon, and Craig Branch observed in 1993:

> It can be demonstrated that there are many educators and curriculum developers who are either personally involved in the New Age perspective or have accepted the practices, techniques, and theories *without knowledge of their source*.... It can be demonstrated that the adoption of New Age/occultic ideology and practices *is not just sporadic and random*... these beliefs tend to enter through counseling; self-esteem, stress reduction, health, and gifted programs; creative writing classes; some

global education courses; and some literature curricula....The usual form these programs take is in deep breathing relaxation or progressive relaxation exercises, guided imagery, and visualization. These are sometimes associated with inappropriate and ineffective value-free or affective learning programs. [Emphasis added.][49]

Moreover, the authors of the study found that these curricula are based on Eastern and other mystical traditions:

The techniques and the presuppositions on which such programs are based are intrinsic to Eastern and other mystical religious traditions and practices (such as Hinduism and meditation). Further, they are frequently synonymous with the techniques of hypnosis and trance induction. Unfortunately, *often these techniques are disguised to project a secular appearance.* [Emphasis added.][50]

Obviously, there is plenty of religion in government schools. It's just not Christianity.

THE NEW AGE MOVEMENT AND EVANGELIZING BY STEALTH

The practical insight of Proverbs 22:6 – "Train up a child in the way he should go; and when he is old, he will not depart from it" – has been well understood by "progressive" educators who have been busily re-making government schools and children in their own image. In one of John Dewey's earlier writings, "My Pedagogic Creed,"[51] Dewey recognizes that if you systematically change what goes on in classrooms you can reshape children and, ultimately, society. His goal, of course, was to use government schools to reshape society in ways agreeable to the progressives of his era. Those who today dominate the education establishment – the devotees of humanistic psychology, the New Agers, and the secular humanists – also understand that the classroom is the key to cultural supremacy, and they have not been shy about saying so.

Writing in *The Humanist* magazine, John Dunphy, a much-quoted figure from the humanist movement, urged:

> [T]he battle for humankind's future must be waged and won *in the public school classrooms* by teachers who correctly perceive their role as proselytizers of a new faith: a religion of humanity ....These teachers must embody the same selfless dedication as the most rabid fundamentalist preachers. The classroom must and will become an arena of conflict between the old and new – the rotting corpse of Christianity, together with all its adjacent evils and misery, and the new faith.... [Emphasis added.][52]

Marilyn Ferguson, a prominent New Age guru, makes the same point in her highly influential book, *The Aquarian Conspiracy*:

> You can only have a new society... if you change the education of the younger generation.... Of the Aquarian Conspirators surveyed, *more were involved in education than in any other single category of work*. They were the teachers, administrators, policy makers, educational psychologists.... Only a new perspective can generate a new curriculum.... [Emphasis added.][53]

So, what is the "new perspective" that Ferguson's "Aquarian Conspirators" are looking to inject into the classroom? According to Ferguson, the perspective of the Aquarian Conspiracy is:

> [A] constellation of techniques and concepts sometimes called transpersonal education. The name derives from a branch of psychology that focuses on the transcendent capabilities of human beings.... [T]he deliberate use of consciousness expanding techniques in education, only recently well under way, is new in mass schooling.... Altered states of consciousness are taken seriously: "centering" exercises, meditation, relaxation, and fantasy are used to keep the intuitive pathways open. These are techniques to encourage this awareness: deep breathing, relaxation, yoga movement, biofeedback....[54]

These influences are widespread in government schools. By the early 1990s just one of the many curricula based on the use of "transpersonal" techniques, "Pumsy," was used in 40% of the nation's elementary schools.[55]

Of course, parents often object if they understand what is actually happening in government schools. This has led, on occasion, to lawsuits and legislation[56] in attempts to restrict the use of curricula based on transpersonal and humanistic theories of education. So, if you are a highly trained education professional trying to remake society in your own image, and parents and the law are getting in the way, what are you going to do?

"KEEP IT SUBTLE, KEEP IT QUIET, OR THE PARENTS WILL REALLY GET UPSET."[57]

The basic tactic for smuggling New Age religious concepts and practices into classrooms is to *deceive* parents simply by changing terminology. As Dick Sutphen, a prominent New Ager, has written:

> One of the biggest advantages we have as New Agers is, once the occult, metaphysical and New Age terminology is removed, we have concepts and techniques that are very acceptable to the general public. So we can change the names and demonstrate the power. In so doing, we open the New Age door to millions who would not be receptive.[58]

Consequently, New Age educators will introduce children to "imaginary guides" rather than "spirit guides," "centering" or "relaxation" rather than meditation or hypnosis, and so on. Nevertheless, the techniques and objectives remain the same.

This sort of deliberate deception is not something invented by Sutphen. In the late 1960s nuns belonging to the Sisters of the Immaculate Heart of Mary invited Carl Rogers, the father of the humanistic psychology and the human potential movements, to apply his theories to their religious community using "encounter groups" in a two-year experiment.[59] The result was the destruction of the order. When Rogers and his team later met to review the tragic consequences of the application of their theories and whether they would undertake a similar project in the future, the consensus was that they wouldn't, *or at least they would not use the term "encounter groups."* [60] In fact, Rogers cynically quipped: "I'd change the name just as fast as needed to keep ahead of the critics."[61]

Changing the name to stay ahead of critics is exactly how so many failed educational theories manage to cheat a well-deserved death. It is also exactly how many New Age and other theologies manage to infiltrate and survive in government schools.

Occasionally, the promoters of Eastern religions and the occult get caught doing this and are stopped. For example, in the 1970s certain schools in New Jersey introduced the "Science of Creative Intelligence" into their curricula. The Science of Creative Intelligence, it turned out, was just a repackaged version of a Hindu religious practice known more widely as Transcendental Meditation. In a lawsuit brought to enjoin the teaching of the Science of Creative Intelligence in New Jersey schools on Establishment Clause grounds, the plaintiffs were able to expose the sham and obtain an injunction.[62] Unfortunately, New Age practices that have been successfully objected to often reappear in new guises.[63] Moreover, the Bedford Central School District case demonstrates that some federal judges on important courts are willing to ignore the blatantly religious nature of New Age curricula.[64]

THE ABC PRINCIPLE (ANYTHING BUT CHRISTIANITY)

Legal positivists used to quip cynically that the Constitution means what the cop-on-the-beat says it means. That is not a widely held view today. But if you are wondering how our government "educators" seem to wink at the presence of all of the non-Christian religions in government schools today, you need to understand that for many of those in charge of government schools the "wall of separation" is really a "wall of separation" between the *Christian* church and the state.

A 1995 incident in an Ohio high school involving a class assignment illustrates what the "wall of separation" actually means in the minds of many government school educators.[65] An English teacher assigned sophomores the task of writing and *signing* a contract with the Devil, Satan, Lucifer, a genie, a witch, or a warlock. The contract was to specify what the students wanted from Satan, for example, and three things they were willing to give up in return.

When some parents questioned the appropriateness of the assignment, the teacher told the parents that she recognized that the assignment might be sensitive, and that was why she gave students several options concerning with whom to make the contract. After the parents pointed out that all of the choices were demonic, the discussion moved to the high school principal.

The principal defended the teacher as having merely made a mistake. When the principal was asked, however, what he would do if the assignment had been to write a contract with God, Christ, Jesus, the Lord, the Savior, or the Holy Spirit, he *immediately* responded that it wouldn't be permitted because of the separation of church and state. Ultimately, the school board apologized on behalf of the school district and repudiated what the teacher had done.

The point here is not so much the inappropriateness of the assignment, although having children *sign* their "contracts" certainly raises questions regarding the teacher's judgment. Instead, what is illuminating is the response of the principal. While he evidently saw no Establishment Clause issue in what the teacher had done, his immediate reaction to the parents' hypothetical assignment was that it would violate the separation of church and state. Obviously, what *Everson* meant to him was simply that Christianity must be kept out of the high school. This is the sort of mentality that accounts for school administrators banning Christmas carols while at the same time permitting earth worship ceremonies in school.

NEWS FLASH FROM OHIO: JESUS CHRIST NOT A REAL PERSON

The Brookfield School District in Ohio was sued for violating the First Amendment rights of a Christian middle schooler.[66] Phillip M. Vaccaro, a 14-year-old described as "educationally challenged," was given an assignment to write an essay about someone who has influenced his life. Because Vaccaro had used his faith to overcome many of his problems in school, he wrote about Jesus Christ. *His teacher, however, advised him that Jesus was not a real person* and told Vaccaro to chose someone else. When Vaccaro's mother contacted school administrators about the unusual historical views of her son's teacher, the school officials backed the teacher. It's also rumored, by the way, that Brookfield school district officials may announce any day that Julius Caesar, Saul of Tarsus, and Abraham Lincoln were not real persons. Stay tuned.

Ohio does not, of course, have a corner on anti-Christian zeal in the heartland. Evidently concerned that there might be an outbreak of reading among students in the district, a Wayland, Michigan, school superintendent ordered Gideons International to stop its annual practice of handing out Bibles to 5th graders.[67] Not to be outdone by Michiganders, a school district in Davenport, Iowa, banned students from giving away Bibles and passing out church-event fliers on school grounds even when classes were *not* in session.[68] According to one student who was a plaintiff in a lawsuit against the school district over the incident, "It's pretty bizarre how we have to go and pull teeth to do this…. They told us we couldn't do it because it was religious."[69]

Anti-Christian animus also thrives in government schools in the "Bible Belt." Many districts refuse to allow ministers to have lunch with students or meet with them on campus. In 2004, for example, Kentucky's Bullitt County School Board banned ministers from their campuses.[70] The ministers were not praying or evangelizing during their lunch-time visits, but were instead just talking about problems and giving advice to students whom they knew.[71] The only explanation from the school administration was that the visits were against district policy. This sort of "policy" is not that unusual in school districts from Texas to Georgia. Not surprisingly, these same school districts that are terrified that some adult might mention the name of Jesus on campus often allow purveyors of earth-worship and other religions access to students through "environmental," "diversity," or "safe schools" programs and curricula.

CHRISTMAS: THE HOLIDAY THAT DARE NOT SPEAK ITS NAME

Now that Christians with children in government schools have become desensitized to "Christmas vacation" being replaced by "Winter break" or "Winter vacation" and Christmas carols being banished, courageous anti-Christians are moving on to the next frontier – banning the word "Christmas" entirely. For example, in Colorado, the Ayatollahs of the ACLU threatened to sue a school if any reference to Christmas was made during the 2003 "holiday program."[72] The ACLU also insisted that singing "Jingle Bells" be banned, evidently confusing it with a song of invitation or an altar call.

Also in the vanguard of the movement to protect children against the horrors of hearing the word "Christmas" is a principal in an elementary school in Sacramento, California, who met with three first-grade teachers to instruct them that the spoken or written use of the word "Christmas" in school was now prohibited.[73]

Of the three teachers in the meeting, one disagreed with the ban, but was willing to go along with it, and a second thought the ban was just fine. The third, a twenty-four year education veteran, was of a different mind: "People need to stand up to all these wackos. It's nuts."[74] Nuts? Yes, but don't expect many of our highly trained education professionals to get out of their chairs to do something about it – or many Christian parents, for that matter.

By the way, a junior high school principal in Abington, Pennsylvania, seems to be contesting the Sacramento principal for the honor of having the most avant-garde anti-Christian position. When a mother questioned the principal's refusal to allow her honor student son to wear a pro-life t-shirt at school, the principal told her that "the shirt and the message were the equivalent of a swastika being displayed on the shirt."[75] The principal's position, however, proved a bit too advanced, at least for the moment, and the school district relented when faced with a lawsuit.

Where do government schools find these principals? Try your local university's school of education. But that is a story for Chapter 5.

DANGEROUS CONTRABAND: "CHRISTIAN" CANDY CANES

No trifle seems to escape the gaze of the anti-Christian zealots in government schools. Several high school students in Massachusetts were suspended from school for giving other students candy canes with a Christian message just before Christmas.[76] In Reno, Nevada, high school students were allowed to distribute Christmas candy canes with the message "Jesus Loves You" only after the school was threatened with a lawsuit. In Oregon, the Gresham-Barlow school district was sued over prohibiting a six-year-old from handing out Christmas cards because the cards mentioned Jesus.[77]

In a similar attempt by school officials to prevent Christian students from privately sharing their faith, a Pennsylvania school prohibited a student from giving away pencils bearing the message "Jesus loves the little children." Of course, handing out condoms is probably just okey-dokey in these schools.

PERSECUTION OF CHRISTIAN TEACHERS AND COUNSELORS: A FEW EXAMPLES

Christian teachers and counselors are not immune from the anti-Christian jihad being waged in government schools. In North Carolina, for example, a high school dropout prevention counselor was suspended while she was investigated for allegedly giving a student religious advice.[78] The counselor, Beth Pinto, had been approached by a student fighting homosexual urges, and the student asked what the Bible taught about homosexuality. Mrs. Pinto responded by sharing some relevant passages from Scripture. Evidently, a third party overheard the conversation and told an administrator, which resulted in Pinto's suspension and the investigation. Although Mrs. Pinto was eventually reinstated, the district officials took the opportunity to warn school employees that they must not commit the high crime and misdemeanor of giving students "religious advice." In a similar display of intolerance, public education officials in Pennsylvania suspended a teacher's aide for one year without pay for wearing a one and one-quarter inch cross pendant on a necklace.[79]

As should be evident, we are long past the point where the controversy in government schools is over Bible reading or prayer. Now the anti-Christian bigots are attempting to intimidate Christians into complete, cowering silence by using even the slightest pretexts to harass them. Answering a student's question, wearing "inappropriate"jewelry, and gift giving among children is the new line in the sand being drawn by those who control government schools. And if you don't like it, they will do what they can to make your life miserable.

GOVERNMENT SCHOOL MOSQUES AND MUSLIM PRAYER WARRIORS

Some highly publicized incidents involving religions other than Christianity drive home the extent to which government school officials tend to understand the "wall of separation" as nothing more than a tool for separating Christianity from schools. Following the terrorist attacks of September 11, 2001, the Chancellor of New York City's government school system publicly announced that New York schools would set aside special classrooms where Muslim students could pray during school through the month of Ramadan.[80] In fact, the Chancellor's policy of allowing Muslims to assemble and worship publicly in schools had been quietly in place for some time.[81]

Evidently, the Chancellor decided to go public with the policy as a gesture of reassurance to Muslims in New York schools in the aftermath of the terrorist attacks. When the Catholic League praised the policy and asked that the same level of accommodation be shown Christians, the Chancellor immediately reversed his decision.[82] Thus, in the end it appears that reassuring Muslim students was less important to the Chancellor than keeping Christianity out of New York schools.

The principal of a Flushing, New York, magnet school was even more blatant in her anti-Christian bias.[83] Prior to Christmas 2001, the principal issued a memo to teachers urging them to bring to school religious symbols representing the Muslim, Kwanzaa,[84] and Jewish religions. Although the memo didn't mention Christianity, someone put up a Christmas tree in the school. The principal immediately ordered the tree taken down claiming that it was too large when compared to the menorah, crescent, and star. Obviously, Christianity was the only religion unwelcome in this Flushing school.

This sort of thing is not limited to the Northeast. For example, a Missouri high school principal was embarrassed when a school employee let the press know that Muslim students were allowed to set up a mosque within the school.[85] Evidently, the school provided Muslim students a room to use for prayer during the school day. A sign stating that the room was the "Muslim Prayer Room" identified the room. Inside was a sign asking visitors to "remove shoes when entering the mosque." As might be expected, once the story broke the principal denied that the school intended to allow the room to become a mosque. Needless to say, however, no room within the school had inadvertently been set aside as a church for Christian students to use during the day.

"ASSALAM ALEIKOOM, FELLOW MUSLIMS"

In California, many 7th grade students are taking an intensive three-week course on Islam. As part of the course the children memorize verses from the Koran, adopt a Muslim name, dress as Muslims, learn the tenets of Islam and the important figures in the history of Islam, and are taught to pray "in the name of Allah, the Compassionate, the Merciful" and to chant "Praise to Allah, Lord of Creation."[86] Students are also taught to greet one another with the pious Muslim greeting "Assalam aleikoom, fellow Muslims," and pronounce the Muslim war cry "Allahu Akbar." [87] Just to show which side the schools are on, students who are unwilling to wear Muslim dress have to sit in the back of the classrooms.[88] Best of all, however, the children get to conduct a mock "jihad" using a dice game.[89] Do you suppose that California schools are also requiring 7th graders to memorize Bible verses or to pray in the name of Jesus?

In Syracuse, New York, the principal and staff of H.W. Smith Elementary claimed to want "to make sure the school respects all the varied traditions" of the immigrant children in the school.[90] In practice, this meant that at Thanksgiving the traditional school Thanksgiving feast was cancelled. Why? Because some of the children in the school were Muslim, and Thanksgiving fell within the month of Ramadan, a time during which Muslims are expected to fast. You see, allowing students the traditional Thanksgiving turkey dinner just wouldn't do if at the same time Muslim students were *choosing* to fast. Do you suppose the school also serves only fish on Fridays out of concern for the sensibilities of the children from Catholic families?

Anti-Christian Logic: No Words, But Too "Preachy"

Recently, Huron High School officials in Ann Arbor, Michigan, asked student organizations to provide skits and videos for the school's "Multicultural Show."[91] Students from a Christian club submitted a four-minute video consisting of clips from the film "Jesus of Nazareth" set to music – none of the dialogue from the movie was included, just music. The Christian students were told they could not show their video because it was too "preachy." No words? Too "preachy"? Four minutes? Videos from the Islamic Student Union and the Gay/Straight Alliance were, of course, permitted.

Fortunately for the Huron High Christian students, the Thomas More Law Center had a few words with the government school administrators, who subsequently decided that the wordless video wasn't too "preachy" after all.

As surprising as it may seem, these are far from isolated incidents. *Education Week* reports that government schools are working hard at accommodating Islam.[92] Menus, testing schedules, P.E. requirements, and many other aspects of school life are being adjusted around the country to make government schools Islam-friendly. At Robert E. Lee High School in suburban Virginia, for example, the principal read a statement noting the commencement of Ramadan during the school's morning announcements.

The textbook situation is even worse. A report by the American Textbook Council examined seven textbooks used widely for junior high and high school children. According to Gilbert Sewall, a former professor and head of the Council:

> On significant Islam-related subjects, textbooks omit, flatter, embellish and resort to happy talk, suspending criticism or harsh judgments that would raise provocative or even alarming questions. [93]

Thus, the students on whom these textbooks are inflicted never learn, for example, that freedom of speech and religion are not tolerated in most Islamic countries or that, for millions of Muslims, "jihad," the purpose of which is to bring the entire world under Sharia, or Islamic law, involves armed conquest.[94] The students will also not learn much, if anything, of Muslim involvement in the slave trade, past *or present*, or that most Islamic countries are repressive dictatorships or theocracies.

Why would publishers publish textbooks that whitewash Islam? Fear. Organizations such as the Council on Islamic Education have made it plain that those who do not portray Islam favorably will be called "racists" and "bigots." Moreover, given that textbook adoption for government schools is a political process, the publishers are doubtless on notice that any portrayal of Islam that is unflattering could jeopardize the adoption of their textbooks.[95] Meanwhile, children in American classrooms are being fed false and distorted versions of both Islam and Christianity.

If you remain unconvinced that government schools are increasingly hostile to Christianity, David Limbaugh's *Persecution: How Liberals are Waging War Against Christianity* may convince you otherwise.[96] In the first part of his book, "The War in Our Public Schools," Limbaugh provides over 100 pages of examples that illustrate how Christians, and especially Christian children, are treated abusively in government schools – children being disciplined for praying before meals; Bibles being thrown in the wastebasket while a teacher shrieks, "This is garbage"; students being told that the Ten Commandments are "hate speech." As I said before, the little red schoolhouse isn't what it used to be.

Anti-Christian prejudice is common within government schools, and it is expressed in many ways. Yet, most Christian parents aren't paying attention.

SOW THE WIND, REAP THE WHIRLWIND

Are you still convinced that sending your children to government schools is harmless? Is it plausible to think that giving Wiccans, secular humanists, Gaia worshipers, and sundry purveyors of Eastern religions or Islam the opportunity to proselytize your children through classroom instruction, textbooks, assemblies, field-trips, peer pressure, extracurricular activities, and adult example for at least 35 hours a week makes no difference to their faith?

Evidence that Christians have failed to transmit their faith and values to their children is everywhere. Within two years of graduation from high school, between 70% and 88% of teenagers from evangelical families stop attending church.[97] Over the last forty years, teen suicide has increased by 200%, and since 1970 adult arrests for drug law violations are up over 400%.[98] By 1999, 33% of all children were born out-of-wedlock.[99] This represents an increase in the rate of illegitimacy of over 700% since 1940, with the greatest increase coming after 1960.[100]

Plainly, these results proceed from the values held by individuals. Can anyone really believe that the actions behind these statistics reflect the values of a sincerely held Christian worldview? Do you really believe that attending government schools has no influence on the sort of worldview your child develops?

Fortunately for the doubters, a study conducted by the Nehemiah Institute makes clear how attending government schools shapes the minds of Christian children.[101] In its study the Nehemiah Institute evaluated the worldviews of thousands of children from Christian families attending government schools and private Christian schools in nearly all fifty states.[102] The study was conducted using a test designed to assess how Biblically or non-Biblically students think on culture-shaping issues. Responses to the questions allowed the researchers to categorize the students' worldviews into four categories: 1) "Biblical Theism," 2) "Moderate-Christian," 3) "Secular Humanism," or 4) "Socialism."

The study found significant differences between the worldviews of children who attended government schools and the worldviews of children who attended private Christian schools. For example, only 35.3% of the Christian children in government schools strongly agreed that the foundation of all government is self-government under God, while 67.4% of the children attending private Christian schools strongly agreed.

Even more telling was the response to the following statement: *"Because human nature is constantly changing values and ethics will also change. Therefore each generation should be free to adopt moral standards appropriate to their preferences."* **Only 14.7% of Christian children attending government schools strongly disagreed with this statement, while 74.3% of children attending private Christian schools strongly disagreed.** Overall, the study showed that children from Christian homes who also attended private Christian schools had worldviews that varied from "moderate-Christian" to "Biblical-Theism." On the other hand, the students from Christian homes who attended government schools had worldviews that fell predominantly within the categories of "Secular Humanism" or "Socialism."

The Nehemiah Institute findings demonstrate clearly that when a child is placed under the authority of a government school for 35 to 40 hours a week in which his success or failure depends on conforming to the requirements of the institution and its curriculum, the influence of that institution on the child will be far greater than an hour or two of Sunday school and a few hours, at best, of devotional time during the week with his parents.

Should we be surprised at this? From a practical point of view, a child entering a government school is entrusted to a curriculum that reflects a non-Christian worldview, and he is placed under the authority of administrators and teachers who are charged with propagating that non-Christian worldview. Moreover, the child's academic success in a government school is measured by how well he has mastered the non-Christian curriculum. Thus, not only does the child have the perception from his earliest years that education is something to be provided and controlled by the government, but he also believes that education and knowledge are separate from, perhaps even alien to, Christianity. Yet, Christian parents who send their children to government schools seem to be oblivious to the spiritual and moral risks that their government school habit imposes on their children.

The effects of our government school habit are also showing up in faithlessness and Biblical illiteracy among Christian children. In 2000 the Barna Research Group conducted a nationwide survey of Christian teenagers. While 86% of teenagers claimed to be Christian, only one-third said that they were "absolutely committed" to Christianity.[103] Even more striking were findings that 60% of the teenagers identifying themselves as Christian believe salvation can be earned through good works and that 53% of these teenagers, including 40% of evangelical teenagers, believe that Jesus committed sins while on earth.[104] We are clearly reaping the consequences of our unfaithfulness in the education of our children.

DO YOU THINK YOU WILL NOT BE HELD ACCOUNTABLE?

In whatever we do, we must ask ourselves whether we are being obedient to God (John 14:15). This applies no less to Christian parents in the education of their children. It is obvious, however, that few Christian parents with children in government school have asked this question. Otherwise, how could 85% of Christian children be given into the custody of a pagan seminary every school day – in essence offered as living sacrifices to the gods of rival religions?

Psalm 127:3 tells us that children are a gift from God. As Christian parents, we have a special responsibility to be faithful stewards of that gift. Moreover, we *will* be held accountable for how we have discharged that responsibility. In Matthew 18:6 Jesus says: "But if anyone causes one of these little ones who believe in me to sin, it would be better for him to have a huge millstone hung around his neck and to be drowned in the depth of the sea." Clearly, there are many ways to lead a Christian child into sin, but none is surer than placing a child under false teaching. The question, then, for Christian parents is what does the Bible tell us about the education of our children?

First, as has been pointed out, children are God's gift to parents, not the state. Non-Christians, of course, deny this and have always sought control of education as a means of imposing their worldview. The National Socialists, among others, understood this well:

> When an opponent declares, "I will not come over to your side," I calmly say, "Your child belongs to us already.... What are you? You will pass on. Your descendants, however, now stand in the new camp. In a short time they will know nothing else but this new community." [105]

Similarly, modern humanists clearly view control of a child's education as a means of alienating him from Christianity. Charles F. Potter, a signer of the first *Humanist Manifesto*, wrote in 1930 that:

> [E]ducation is thus a most powerful ally of humanism, and every public school is a school of humanism. What can the theistic Sunday school, meeting for an hour once a week, and teaching only a fraction of the children, do to stem the tide of a five-day program of humanistic teachings? [106]

In fact, Paul Blanchard, a well-known humanist, regarded the destruction of a child's Christian belief as perhaps what government schools do best:

> Our schools may not teach Johnny to read properly, but the fact that Johnny is in school until he is 16 tends to lean toward the elimination of religious superstition. [107]

Can anyone seriously believe that by collaborating in the subversion of our children's faith we are being obedient to God or acting as proper stewards of His gift?

Second, every passage in the Bible that mentions the education of children makes it clear that parents are responsible. In Deuteronomy 6:6-7 the Lord tells parents, "These words I am commanding you today must be kept in mind, and you must teach them to your children and speak of them as you sit in your house, as you walk along the way, as you lie down, and as you get up." In Proverbs 22:6 parents are told: "Train a child in the way that he should go and when he is old he will not turn from it." In Ephesians 6:4 fathers are told to raise their children up in the training and instruction of the Lord.

Reciprocally, children are told to hear the instruction of their parents (Proverbs 1:8-9), not the instruction of a government employee. Nowhere in the Bible does God delegate the education of children to the state or to the disciples of other religions. On the contrary, the Bible requires parents to provide their children nothing less than a Christian education. Indeed, in ancient Israel and among Christians for nearly two millennia the education of children was carried out primarily by families with the assistance of the synagogue or church.

Finally, 2 Corinthians 6:14-18 states that Christians are not to be unequally yoked together with unbelievers. How can we fail to recognize that placing children under the control and instruction of a pagan institution for 35 to 40 hours a week is yoking our children unequally with unbelievers. Indeed, can there be a worse example of unequal yoking than the deliberate yoking of a child with a pagan educational institution?

It now may be fully Constitutional for government schools to bring in turban-wearing yogi-numerologists to teach children the Hindu devotional practice known as "yoga," to have children make images of strange gods, to have children recite the Koran, to sponsor extracurricular activities involving the occult, to have self-proclaimed psychic-telepaths teach children exercises to improve their "concentration," to sponsor meditation programs, to have children make offerings to "Mother Earth," to be initiated into the beliefs of Wicca, and so on. We know that for many parents such practices and more are acceptable. But as Christian parents we will be judged by a different standard than man-made laws or personal preferences. We have to decide whether we are for Him or against Him. Who among us wants to come before the Judgment Seat (Rom. 14:10-12) having sacrificed our children to the Moloch of government education?

DO YOU LIKE YOUR DAUGHTER'S NOSE-RING AND TONGUE STUD?

*All too many churchmen view the undisciplined and amoral
products of statist education as evidences of the failures of these schools.
On the contrary, they are evidences of their success.*

R.J. Rushdoony[1]

Government schools are deforming our children spiritually, but what are they doing to them morally? The news is not good.

Over the last decade many parents have noticed the decadent direction student "fashions" have taken: students with hair dyed colors that are normally only seen on tropical fish; teenage girls who dress like hookers;[2] and, students (particularly girls) with tattoos and body-piercings that suggest they are consorting with the Marquis de Sade. For those in the avant-garde of "body modification" (*i.e.*, body-piercings, tattoos, etc.), the latest "new thing" is tongue-splitting – as in cutting the tongue to make it forked.[3] In addition, the cutting edge of teenage and young adult female fashion is jeans with waists cut so low that a part of the anatomy plumbers sometimes expose by accident is visible.[4] Of course, unlike plumbers, the girls and young women are doing it on purpose.[5]

All right, *your* daughter probably doesn't have a tattoo, nose-ring, or a tongue stud, but many children in your community do. Moreover, these troubling outward signs reflect a far more serious and widespread problem on the inside: the corruption of our children's moral sensibilities. And unfortunately, this affects far more children than just those who choose to advertise their nihilism through their eccentric appearances... perhaps it affects even yours.

Let's begin by noting a fundamental difference in moral outlook between Christian children who attend government schools and Christian children who do not. We will then examine how Christian values have been removed from government schools and what some of the consequences have been to children and society. Finally, we will look at the next "big thing" being promoted by education activists that is beginning to sweep through government schools. So, if you are a Christian with a child in a government school, continue to ask yourself, in light of the evidence, if leaving your child there shows obedience to God's Word and is consistent with your child's spiritual, moral, and physical well-being.

A CULTURAL DIVIDE

There is no greater cultural rift in America than between those who accept the authority of the moral teachings of the Bible and those who believe that moral judgments express only the subjective preferences of individuals. Consequently, it's shocking that, as previously noted, only 14.7% of evangelical Christian children who attend government schools clearly reject the following proposition endorsing moral relativism: "Each generation should be free to adopt moral standards appropriate to their preferences."[6]

Apparently, something leads those students to think that the Ten Commandments are negotiable. Yet, why is it that, in contrast, nearly 75% of evangelical Christian students attending Christian private schools strongly reject the same proposition? In other words, why should the moral thinking of Christian students vary so much depending on whether or not they attend government schools?

There are undoubtedly several factors behind this disparity in moral outlook, but the heart of the matter is that children learn by precept and example. So, just what type of moral teaching have government schools been providing in their curricula and by their institutional example?

DON'T BE SO JUDGMENTAL

Throughout the 19th century and into the 1940s, government schools taught children moral principles that, if not always explicitly Christian, were at least compatible with Christianity. Today, many

Christians wonder how public and private discussions of morality have largely become cliché-ridden gibberish about "not being judgmental," "not moralizing," "not imposing your value judgments on others," and "valuing differences." What this represents, of course, is a massive movement in American society away from the Christian conception of transcendent moral values toward a moral relativism rooted in the conviction that moral values merely reflect subjective preferences.[7] How did this come about?

The main roots of this change, as with so many unwelcome developments in American culture, can be found in the first half of the 20th century. Following the end of World War I the views of European philosophers known as "logical positivists" began to make significant inroads among America's intellectuals.[8] Logical positivists believed, among other things, in a materialistic universe and asserted that everything that is objectively true could be stated in a "physicalistic" language, which they considered to be the language of science. Because statements about values could not be expressed in a language essentially limited to statements concerning logical and mathematical entities and their relationships and spatio-temporal entities and their physical properties, the logical positivists claimed that statements about values were just expressions of feelings and attitudes. Thus, moral discourse was transformed from a discussion concerning the nature and application of transcendent moral truths into self-absorbed chit-chat about the feelings and preferences of individuals.

ANTHROPOLOGICAL MULTICULTURALISM

While the logical positivists in some sense did the necessary "heavy lifting" in intellectual circles that led to the triumph of various versions of moral relativism over competing conceptions of transcendent moral truth, the popular mind was largely won over by the cultural anthropologists who championed cultural relativism – the belief that no culture can rightly be said to be better than another.

In America, at least, this was largely the work of Franz Boas of Columbia University and his students, the best known of whom were

Margaret Mead and Ruth Benedict. A socialist and an atheist, Boas had a fanatic's commitment to the notion that cultures and human behavior are a function of "nurture" rather than nature. In postmodern jargon, Boas could be said to believe that cultures are "socially constructed." Consequently, Boas believed that it would be possible to find healthy, attractive cultures with norms very different from those of Western Civilization because there was no such thing as a "human nature" that would tend to make basic social norms converge. Consequently, the Boasian project was the final overthrow of the Christian view of human nature that was then still dominant in American society; namely, that human nature was sinful and universal.[9]

Boas began with his conclusions and viewed his task as manufacturing the evidence for them, much like English Fabian socialists Sydney and Beatrice Webb, who produced and encouraged much "social research" related to economics around the turn of the 19th century. As the head of Columbia's anthropology department, Boas was well positioned to do just that with a stream of students and assistants generally disposed to please the charismatic "Papa Franz." Not surprisingly, "research" followed over the years that confirmed Boas' views regarding cultural relativism.

The best known of these "scholarly" productions was Margaret Mead's *Coming of Age in Samoa*, which purported to find an idyllic South Seas society whose sexual mores were precisely the reverse of those of Western Civilization. Never mind that the fieldwork that produced *Coming of Age in Samoa* was highly questionable from the start or that Mead's work in Samoa has subsequently been shown to be entirely wrong. The titillating subject matter ensured a wide popular audience.[10] Moreover, because its "findings" suited the prejudices of many academics in the social sciences, *Coming of Age in Samoa* had a long run in college and university courses that, to say the least, was not deserved.

Cultural relativism, of course, leads ineluctably towards moral relativism. If we accept that there is no right or wrong, or better or worse, among cultures, it is difficult to claim that the moral values embedded in different cultures are somehow right or wrong, better or worse. All that could be said is that they are different. If moral values are just different, we can't tell someone else that his moral values are wrong.[11]

This perspective on morality — that our moral judgments are just a reflection of our needs and interests under the circumstances in which we find ourselves – is found in the *Humanist Manifestos* and in the views of humanists generally. Still, through the 1930s and well into the 1940s this relativist view of morality did not penetrate far into the mainstream of American society because a Christian view of morality continued to dominate in government schools.

All of this changed with the Supreme Court's *Everson* decision in 1947. Because the *Everson* Court's new "wall of separation" interpretation of the First Amendment was understood to prohibit the teaching of "religious" values in government schools, *Everson* and the cases that followed it effectively eliminated traditional American teachings concerning moral values from government schools over a period of 15 to 20 years. This, however, created a gap in the government school curriculum — if Christian moral teaching had to be excluded from the classroom, how could values be taught? To fill the gap, government schools turned to the work of humanistic psychologists, the most influential of whom was Carl Rogers.[12]

"Non-Directive" Moral Education and the Dogma of Moral Relativism

Rogers developed a psychotherapeutic technique built around a concept he referred to as the "clarifying response." Using this technique, a psychologist asks questions of his patient to encourage him to express his attitudes and feelings about his problems until the patient spontaneously produces a "clarifying response"; that is, a response that provided insightful understanding concerning his problems.[13] A critical element of this technique is that the psychologist not express any kind of "judgment" concerning the patient's responses that might impair his "self-esteem." Consequently, the psychologist is required to project an unconditional regard and empathy for the patient. In essence, Rogers' view was that patients "will straighten themselves out when they work on their personal problems in the presence of an understanding, accepting and courteous listener."[14] But, as would become evident later, the "nonjudgmental" aspect of Rogers' technique, and its assumption that the only proper reference point for a patient's decisions were his own attitudes and feelings, involved an implicit moral relativism.

In the beginning, Rogers viewed his approach to psychotherapy as helpful to people who were basically sound, but who had encountered some problems in life that were resulting in "neurotic" behavior. Toward the end of his life, however, Rogers repudiated the psychotherapeutic techniques that could be described generically as "Rogerian therapy," as did several of his early collaborators. In a presentation before the 1981 convention of the Association for Humanistic Psychology, Rogers told the audience that the therapy itself was wrong and that "I hope Rogerian therapy goes down the drain."[15] Moreover, he and his colleagues, Abraham Maslow and William R. Coulson, were particular distressed at the damaging effects humanistic psychology was having in schools. Unfortunately for Rogers, his teachings had given rise to an army of "sorcerer's apprentices," and he lacked the power to undo the harm his followers had done or even to dissuade them from continuing in their folly.

SPREADING MORAL RELATIVISM THROUGH SCHOOLS OF EDUCATION

Schools of education, it turned out, proved to be both a vast source of "sorcerer's apprentices" and the channel through which Rogers' humanistic psychology was pushed into government schools. When Rogers began teaching at Ohio State University, his views greatly interested the faculty and the students of the college of education. Louis E. Raths, who was a faculty member in the college of education while Rogers was at Ohio State, and his graduate student, Sidney Simon, ultimately transformed Rogers' concept of the "clarifying response" and his "non-directive" psychotherapeutic techniques into a non-directive curriculum for teaching moral values now known as "values clarification." "Values clarification," along with other non-directive approaches to teaching moral values such as "cognitive-development moral education," and "ethical reasoning for children," in relatively short order became the primary way in which government schools attempted to reintroduce the teaching of values in the aftermath of *Everson* and its progeny.

What is "non-directive" moral education? Non-directive approaches treat moral education as a *process* through which children are supposed to develop their *own* values through participation in games, discussion of moral problems or dilemmas, and use of certain intellectual strategies. In this approach, teachers are not to take moral positions or present their own moral views. Further, proponents of the various forms of non-directive approaches to teaching moral values allegedly had no interest in inculcating any particular values in children. Indeed, proponents of non-directive moral education explicitly rejected the notion of "teaching values" and criticized those who objected to this value-neutral approach as wanting to impose their own "rigid, obsolete value structures" on others through the schools. As a result, *children* were turned loose without any moral guidance on critical, complex issues involving drugs, sex, war, and life and death to arrive at conclusions based upon their limited experience and knowledge and their feelings.

Despite claiming to be value-neutral, non-directive approaches to teaching moral reasoning actually indoctrinate children with the view that all moral values are subjective and relative and that none are objective and universally applicable. While congenial to many elements in society, this view of morality is profoundly anti-Christian.

NON-DIRECTIVE MORAL EDUCATION IN THE CLASSROOM

Values clarification, along with other formats for using Rogers' non-directive style of psychotherapy such as encounter groups, self-esteem training, affective education, and mastery learning, have been taught to teachers and counselors since at least the early 1960s. In addition, programs such as D.A.R.E. (Drug Abuse Resistance Education), Quest, DUSO (Developing Understanding of Self and Others), Pumsey, "dilemma ethics," and other curricula have brought the techniques of non-directive moral education directly into schools at the student level.

Why were government schools so receptive to these types of curricula? As already mentioned, the *Everson* line of judicial decisions had eliminated traditional religion-based character education, and schools needed something secular to fill the vacuum. Non-directive curricula claimed to be secular and purported to be value-neutral, *i.e.*, they claimed to teach children how to think critically about moral decisions without imposing any particular set of values. Why is this a problem?

At a practical level, non-directive moral education turns moral instruction on its head. Efforts by parents, churches, and others to teach children values, let alone the transcendent moral values at the heart of Christianity, are denounced by those trained in values clarification and other non-directive approaches as "moralizing" – the "mistake" of failing to recognize that all moral values are a matter of personal preferences and that, therefore, moral values are always relative, changing, and situational. Thus, "moralizers" are just pushy, intolerant people who are trying to force their values on others. From the perspective of the adepts of non-directive moral education, such people are nothing more than moral imperialists.

Consequently, by using non-directive curricula for teaching moral values, schools are effectively teaching children that their parents' judgments about values and moral issues are necessarily no better than their own. Parents might have the ability to force their children to conform to standards of behavior that their children disagree with, but under the influence of non-directive moral education children now understand this to be arbitrary and illegitimate. As a practical matter, non-directive moral education tells children that they are free to make up any system of values that is "right for them."

Now, consider that non-directive moral education has been mainly applied to AIDS, drug, and sex education programs, and the disastrous consequences to children of bringing these curricula into the classroom begin to become apparent.

AN EXAMPLE: D.A.R.E.

D.A.R.E., which has been used in all 50 states and more than three-quarters of all school districts, illustrates how Rogers' non-directive psychotherapeutic techniques have been applied in the classroom in the form of values clarification.[16]

The D.A.R.E. program is presented by police officers. William R. Coulson, Carl Rogers' former research assistant and colleague, has described the content of the training materials as follows:[17]

> DARE never tells students, "Don't use drugs." Not once in the course of seventeen lessons, does the DARE officer ever say, "Don't use drugs." Instead it works on developing the self-esteem that makes it easier to say "no."

Well, if the officers can't tell the children that using drugs is both wrong and a bad idea, what *is going on* in the classroom?

What happens is this: the children are given a great deal of information about different types of drugs (what kinds of "highs" they produce, what they cost, how they are used, risks, etc.), which is presented in an entirely value-neutral fashion. Then the children are asked to identify reasons *for* (!) and against drug use. The officer's role is to ask the students "non-directive" questions to help them "clarify" their own feelings about whether drug use *is right for them* or not.

In a paper presented in 1997, William Coulson forcefully pointed out the obvious idiocy of using such non-directive techniques with children:[18]

> Imagine a student who proposes to bring a loaded gun to school, which is an example offered in the DARE student workbook. Because DARE is values clarification, the officer is forbidden to issue a warning. He or she is instructed to ask scripted questions instead, designed to promote value clarity. "What bad things could happen?" is one of the questions the officer is to ask, and "What good things could happen?" is another. *What good things could happen!* I said that Rogers had abandoned, then cursed, this approach. Because it is unprecedented to sub-

mit life-and-death matters to "discussion" by fifth- and sixth-graders." [Emphasis added.]

Just so.

Moreover, numerous studies have shown D.A.R.E. to be at best ineffective in discouraging drug use. One writer who had discussed the effectiveness of D.A.R.E. with experts who had done independent evaluations of D.A.R.E. concluded that "DARE should be ranked somewhere between a sham and a mediocrity."[19] A 1994 study commissioned by the federal government concluded that there is no evidence that D.A.R.E. reduces drug use even though $750,000,000 per year was being spent on the program.[20] By now, the ineffectiveness of D.A.R.E. as a drug use prevention program is a notoriously open secret.[21]

In fact, the consequences of using values clarification curricula in drug education are probably worse than simply being "ineffective." At least one important study showed that students in Illinois who took D.A.R.E. had *higher levels* of drug use, violence, and negative attitudes toward police than students who had not.[22] Quest, a values clarification curriculum that has also been widely used in drug education programs in government schools, has shown similar results. One Quest researcher, Liz Reyer, found that the "Quest students showed increases in use and more relaxed attitudes toward use... and, when compared to control group participants, were also less likely to see what was really wrong with using them."[23] The drugs used by the students were "cigarettes, marijuana/hashish, alcohol and crack/cocaine."[24] Another study found that high school students who had been through a Quest program were *more likely* to start using marijuana.[25]

Interestingly, in the early 1990s parental complaints led to efforts to rein in the use of values clarification in drug education programs. It is questionable, however, whether use of such techniques in *drug education* programs was actually reduced, or if they were reduced for more than a brief period. As has been seen with New Age programs, the proponents of ideologically driven curricula often find ways to evade restrictions by changing terminology or other stratagems. DUSO and

Pumsey, for example, are not always "sold" as drug programs.[26]

Moreover, as noted, there are other kinds of curricula that employ values clarification. For instance, one curriculum for 5th graders uses detective fiction as a way of teaching values clarification.[27] In any event, values clarification is just one non-directive approach to moral education, and the principles of non-directive moral education underlie other "decision-making" and values-oriented curricula that *continue* to inculcate the dogma of moral relativism.

Another Example: Academic Honesty

As you might imagine, the moral relativism implicit in non-directive approaches to moral education has created some embarrassing problems for teachers. For example, how can a teacher who has been teaching values clarification, insist that students not cheat in their schoolwork without resorting to the dreaded practice of "moralizing"?

This was a sufficiently troubling issue that the authors of a very influential values clarification textbook felt compelled to provide the following dialogue in an attempt to illustrate to teachers how they can accomplish mission impossible – being faithful to values clarification while simultaneously insisting that students not cheat:[28]

> Ginger: Does that mean that we can decide for ourselves whether we should be honest on tests here?
> Teacher: No, that means that you can decide on the value. I personally value honesty; and though you may choose to be dishonest, I shall insist that we be honest on our tests here....
> Ginger: But then how can we decide for ourselves? Aren't you telling us what to value?
> Teacher: Not exactly. I don't mean to tell you what you should value. That's up to you.... All of you who choose dishonesty as a value may not practice it here. That's all I am saying.

A truly subtle distinction. Ginger can think whatever she wants, but when she is in the teacher's class Ginger will do what she is told. Why? Because the teacher says so. Sounds vaguely parental, doesn't it?

DILEMMA ETHICS

"Dilemma ethics" is another non-directive approach to moral education that has been widely used for many years in "critical thinking" curricula in government schools. As might be expected, one of the selling points of such "critical thinking" curricula is that they allow school districts to say they are doing something about teaching ethics while avoiding inculcating any specific values that might be controversial.

"Critical thinking" and its variants typically involve presenting children with moral dilemmas that have been carefully constructed to be ambiguous. The "lifeboat problem" is a classic example. In the "lifeboat problem" children are told that a ship is sinking and that there is a lifeboat. Unfortunately, the lifeboat will accommodate fewer passengers than are on the ship. Consequently, the children are told they must choose which passengers to put on the lifeboat and which passengers to leave behind to die based upon some limited biographical and other information about the passengers. The teacher then leads the children through a non-directive examination of the problem in which the children are encouraged to discuss their choices and their reasons for making them, which is obviously an exercise in values clarification.[29]

A common variation on the lifeboat problem is the "fallout shelter problem," which presents essentially the same dilemma regarding having to choose who among a group of people will survive because of limited space in a fallout shelter. The lifeboat problem, like the "fallout shelter problem" and other dilemma ethics cases, is designed so that there is no clear right or wrong answer – which, after all, is the very nature of a dilemma. But this gives children a very distorted view of ethics. Most practical moral problems do not present a dilemma at all. By teaching about ethics solely from the perspective of dilemmas contrived so that there are no right answers or wrong answers, however, the child is led, *as a practical matter,* to view all moral decision making as ambiguous and relative.[30]

D.A.R.E., Quest, and dilemma ethics are just *a few examples* of curricula that have made moral relativism pervasive in government schools. What Christian parents need to understand is that government schools are systematically teaching their children an anti-Christian moral code through AIDS awareness, sex education, drug education, "critical thinking," and other programs. Moreover, Christian parents also need to understand how ingrained the culture of moral relativism is.

Because values clarification and similar techniques were widely introduced in the 1960s in both the classroom and the training of educators, many of the teachers using these techniques in government schools now were subject to them when they were students. Indeed, many, if not most, parents of government school children today participated in values clarification or dilemma ethics programs as children. *Thus, for perhaps the majority of the adults connected to the government school enterprise, moral relativism is a familiar, comfortable, and non-controversial way of looking at the world.*

PAYING THE PIPER: SOME CAUTIONARY TALES

The elimination of a Christian moral perspective from government schools has profoundly changed the daily school environment that children must confront. For one seventh grade girl who transferred from a private school to a government school in a small town in Oregon, the experience concerned far more than the drastically lowered academic standards and an annoying focus on building self-esteem. Here is, in part, how she described what it was like:[31]

> Most kids use filthy language at school. The "F" word is the word that is used the most. Students who are heard using bad language are barely disciplined at all. Students also write filthy words in notes and on school property. Some students have pictures of barely-dressed women in their lockers, and one boy has his locker "wallpapered" with condoms. Feminine hygiene products can be found lying around by the locker rooms and on the nature trail.
>
> I experienced sexual harassment every day. Both male and female students behave and speak very suggestively. Not only is

this tolerated, it is expected in order to be "cool." Both male and female students grab each other in inappropriate places on their bodies. Sex is talked about all the time, and in nasty ways, such as "household pets and family members you might have had sex with." If a person has any values or morals at all, they are considered a "geek."

Not surprisingly, the girl was homeschooled the following year.

Speaking of the "F" word, at Chantilly High School in upscale Fairfax County, Virginia, the teacher for a senior English class assigned his students the task of repeating the phrase "F*** you" 10,000 times as homework.[32] Preparation for an Advanced Placement vocabulary test? No. The teacher had assigned J.D. Salinger's *Catcher in the Rye,* in which this phrase and an abundance of other "must know" words and phrases appear, and, according to the teacher, he wanted to "desensitize" his students to the language in the book. Not wanting to miss an opportunity to demonstrate bad judgment, the school district attempted to reassure the parents by letting them know that the teacher just wanted his "students to be aware that this was in the book" and that the teacher was only joking.[33] Apparently the teacher kept his job. Perhaps that's the real joke.

Jesse Ogden, a Michigan high school student, summarizes his experience in another of our "better" government high schools as follows:[34]

> People are right to be cynical of my generation and of public schools. My school is considered to be one of the better ones, and one of the best in Michigan, but I still watch it slip further and further into decadence every year. My school is just an upper-middle class, suburban version of the average public school. We have the teachers pursuing their agendas, collectivist cliques practically enforced by the school, a claustrophobic environment, misinformation passing as education, and too much pandering to non-academics... which contain some of the worst and immoral students. There is really no... real education, everyone is too worried about getting into a good college or making the letter grade, which is usually inflated by teachers....

Slipping into decadence? The kid must be some sort of prude, right? Here are a few examples so you can form your own conclusion.

Our Daughter is Going to Do What in the School Play?!

Even high school theatricals are becoming an extension of the cultural left's sexual politics. Not so long ago, parents and family would dutifully attend high school productions of *Harvey* and *South Pacific* to watch their children display their stagecraft. Today, of course, our ever-improving government schools produce more serious theatrical fare. So, imagine the pride of the parents as they watched their 15-18-year-old daughters perform in Amherst Regional High School's production of Eve Ensler's feminist "classic," *The Vagina Monologues*. Despite the earnest efforts of the Amherst educators to elevate their students' and community's theatrical tastes, however, at least one commentator, columnist Cathy Young, thought the whole business rather odd: "The idea of teenage girls performing Ensler's monologues – complete with graphic sexual descriptions, in-your-face vulgar language, and reenactments of orgasmic moans – in front of an adult audience is rather freaky."[35] Yes, freaky indeed. And, speaking of "freaky," …

Freaking the Night Away

So, now for a little quiz. It's Friday night; you're in a large, dimly lit room filled with very loud, crudely rhythmic, unmelodic sound accompanying a lot of amplified, remarkably vulgar language. In the room several hundred teenagers are doing some rather unusual things. Girls are on the floor with boys on top of them going up and down on them in rhythm with the amplified noise.[36] Other girls have their legs wrapped around boys' waists, and they are grinding their pelvises together.[37] Yet other boys and girls are in pairs in which the head of one is in the other's crotch.[38] Where are you? An audition for a porno film? A Druid fertility rite? Not sure? I guess you haven't been to a high school dance lately.

Freak dancing – often just called "freaking" – is widespread in high schools and middle schools (!) around the country.[39] No one seems to be able to define exactly what this form of "dancing" is, except to say that it consists of simulated sex acts performed to Hip Hop or Rap "music." In fact, freaking is so sexually explicit that it is "freaking out" government school officials – even in places not normally inclined to criticize any sort of sexual behavior, such as Palo Alto, California. According to Sandra Pearson, principal at Palo Alto High School, "Freak dancing, to me, is like pornography… I may not be able to define it, but I sure know it when I see it."[40]

Lately, schools have been busy passing rules to limit freaking. At Palo Alto High, for example, demeaning or sexually explicit dancing is now prohibited.[41] In Puyallup, Washington, the local high school has had to adopt a rule against dancers bending over more than 45 degrees (i.e., no "doggie dancing").[42] A Washington, D.C., high school requires that students pass a quiz on proper dancing, while another is producing an instructional video on "dancing do's and don'ts."[43]

Students, however, have not been responding well to restrictions on freaking. According to one 14-year-old girl, the furor over freaking simply reflects adults' lack of knowledge of history: "It's dancing really close to another person. They've done that for years."[44] A Washington, D.C., high school student is a little more candid in his complaint about the rules: "They're taking all the fun away." Besides, he assures us, "It's just a way of dancing…. You're not really more likely to have sex if you dance this way."[45]

Although rules to tone down freaking may allow adults the illusion that something has been done, enforcement is entirely another matter. As the *Washington Post's* Nurith Aizenman writes "trying to stop freak dancing by breaking up couples is a bit like trying to push back the tide."[46] So far, the only effective antidote for freaking was hit upon by a high school dance disk jockey, who stopped the freakers dead in their tracks by playing the "Barney" theme song (you know, the purple dinosaur who sings "I love you, you love me….").[47] Don't expect government schools to adopt this approach. They really don't care that much – nor do many parents today, I suspect.

DRESSING LIKE (THE OLDEST) PROFESSIONALS

How girls dress at school dances is an additional dimension to the freaking phenomenon. As already mentioned, we are far past the time when, to borrow Cole Porter's phrase, "a glimpse of stocking was looked on as something shocking...." Today, many teenage girls seem quite eager to show as much of their bodies in public as the law allows. As one writer who witnessed the public attire of teenage girls at a carnival in downstate Illinois observed, "with bare-midriff tops, low slung jeans, low-cut haltertops, thongs and see through blouses, there ain't a hell of a lot left to the imagination."[48] Further, many bikinis are now approaching the vanishing point, so much so that it is sometimes hard to tell if girls (and women) at the beach have come to swim or skinny dip.[49]

As with so many other things, however, many parents seem not to notice that something is wrong. In fact, Rita Wilson, vice principal in a California high school, was suspended from her job as a result of parents complaining about her allegedly overzealous effort to make sure that their daughters attending a high school dance weren't wearing thongs (or less) under their skirts.[50]

The problem seems to be that Wilson actually checked for underwear in the case of some provocatively dressed girls, evidently in a location where the inspection could be seen by other students.[51] Now, you are probably thinking that the parents weren't complaining of enforcement of the policy, but that the enforcement was handled badly – no girl should have her underwear checked where other students might see.

The problem with this analysis is obvious. These young lovelies were heading out to the dance floor to engage in a form of dancing which would expose their underwear – and a great deal more. Wilson's defense was that she did what she did precisely to prevent the girls from exposing themselves on the dance floor – which, of course, was exactly why the girls were wearing short skirts, thongs, etc. in the first place.[52] Even assuming that other students might have gotten a glimpse of something during the underwear check, it requires a very unusual sense of modesty to blush if the same flesh is exhibited during an underwear check that the person being inspected intends to expose a few minutes later on the dance floor.

But all of this is far too abstract. A female student interviewed by CNN put the incident in perspective: "[They] were just wearing these little skirts with nothing on under, these tight shorts, shirts showing their cleavage, their [breasts] popping out, everything. They were not dressed like they were going to a high school dance, they were dressed like whores."[53]

Nevertheless, the unhappy parents were outraged at the invasion of their daughters' "privacy."[54] Perhaps Wilson should have just waited until the girls exposed what they weren't wearing on the dance floor and then sent them home. Somehow, though, I think the parents would have just found some other complaint against Wilson.[55]

Did freaking simply spring from the mind of some hormonal adolescent? No, it's the usual transmission mechanism for this sort of social disease: from the open sewer of television and music videos to children's minds to the schools, where the values behind things like freaking multiply like bacteria in a Petri dish.

MORE AND YOUNGER

We have looked at some illustrations of trends in language, dancing, and dress among government school students. Defenders of the status quo are often quick to argue that these external manifestations of character somehow don't really mean anything. Of course, one suspects that the people who do say such things either actually don't see anything wrong with these trends, or that they are strenuously attempting to ignore something profoundly disturbing. No matter. The truth is that these trends are harbingers of exactly what you would expect.

A 2003 report by the National Campaign to Combat Teen Pregnancy found that *one in five children* in the United States have had sex *before they were 15-years old.*[56] So, the odds are that roughly 20% of the children in your local middle school are sexually active. According to the Centers for Disease Control and Prevention almost 10% of children report engaging in sex before the age of 13, a 15% increase since 1997.[57] Other surveys indicate that at least two-thirds of teens engage in sex by the time they graduate from high school.[58]

The reality behind these statistics is tragic. In Houston, a 14-year-old intentionally aborted her second trimester baby at school (I'm sure you will be comforted to know that the abortion was considered legal and that school drug policies were not violated).[59] On a Massachusetts school bus en route to the local junior high and high school, a high school boy and junior high school girl engaged in oral sex to the cheers of other students.[60] In a Michigan middle school two students were suspended for having sex under a table during a science class.[61] Somehow the teacher and class allegedly didn't notice the "science experiment" going on under a lab table in the back of the room.[62] In Houston's Hartman Middle School a special education teacher left her students unattended in her classroom for reasons unknown. Afterward, an adult entered the classroom only to find two students reenacting a scene from the Oval Office during the Clinton administration.[63]

In Kentucky, physicians and government school administrators are concerned over increasing reports of oral sex on middle school campuses and at parties off-campus.[64] One University of Kentucky specialist in adolescent medicine reported that in the first five months of 2002 alone he treated at least 10 middle school students for sexually transmitted diseases contracted through oral sex.[65] What accounts for this epidemic of oral sex among government middle school children? According to Lynette Schmiedeknecht, a middle school counselor: "It's more a part of the culture, more talked about. It seems that in talking with the kids, they don't consider oral sex (to be) sex. They just think its something they do as an adolescent."[66]

Apart from the moral and spiritual consequences of mainstreaming of various forms of sex among younger and younger children, there is also a physical price that is paid. A 2004 report released by the Alan Guttmacher Institute and Advocates for Youth, a nonprofit sex education advocacy group, projects that 50% of all young Americans will contract a sexually transmitted disease by the time they reach the age of 25. Not only would this be unprecedented, but because chlamydia is among the STD's being most widely spread, an epidemic of infertility among girls who have been led to believe that "sex" is just another "choice" is now on the horizon.[67] The solution? According the Guttmacher Institute's Sharon Camp, we just need to provide children with "…realistic sex education that teaches them how to prevent STDs and unwanted pregnancies…."[68] Given what is already happening in the name of sex education in schools, one wonders just how much more realistic it can get or why anyone should listen to organizations like these who have contributed so much to creating this problem.

But if your children are in a government school, they, of course, aren't really affected by any of this. Right?

How can such a moral climate develop in government schools? While some of it reflects the influence of the media and home, the collapse of standards within government schools and their choice of curricula also play a major role.[69] Here are a few examples.

"DIVERSITY" WEEK

During a California high school's "Week of Diversity" a parent who attended a student assembly described the assembly as including "vulgar, inappropriate sex scenes, beginning with a very suggestive dance followed by a scene where a bra, undies, and nylons are thrown from behind a sheet. Another scene, by virtue of sound effects, was suggestive of sexual intercourse taking place behind the sheet."[70] Other presentations during the "Week of Diversity" promoted the increasingly common government school position that homosexuality, bisexuality, and transgendered sexuality are healthy and normal.[71] One presentation portrayed "a person who expresses hatred as a believer in a 'book' (which she reads every day and especially on Sunday) that gives her the right to hate and put others down. While this presenter stated that her book contains the truth, other students shouted 'There is no truth.'"[72] In Chelmsford, Massachusetts, parents discovered that schoolchildren were required to attend an assembly in which the "instructor" used four-letter words to describe oral and anal intercourse, and the children were asked to lick condoms that had been distributed.[73]

FISTGATE

The government of the Commonwealth of Massachusetts has had a bit of a public relations problem as a result of increased awareness of its extraordinary efforts to promote homosexuality within its schools.[74] Since 1992 the state budget has included roughly $1.5 million for the "Governor's Commission for Gay and Lesbian Youth," an organization made up of homosexual activists and their allies. The principal activity of the Commission appears to have been to persuade over 180 Massachusetts schools to establish Gay/Straight Alliance clubs ("GSA's") by offering schools state money and arguing that the clubs will make the schools "safer" for homosexual students.

On March 25, 2000, a statewide conference called "Teach-Out" was held at Tufts University and co-sponsored by the *Massachusetts Department of Education*, the Commission, and the Gay and Lesbian and Straight Education Network, a national homosexual organization active in schools. "Teach-Out" was intended to increase the number of GSA's in Massachusetts and to expand teaching about homosexuality into the lower grades. The attendees included scores of "gay-friendly" teachers and administrators (who got "professional development credits" for attending), homosexual activists from around the country, *and students, some as young as 12-years-old, that had been bused in by government schools from around the state.*

"Teach-Out" offered a smorgasbord of strange and offensive workshops such as "Putting the 'Sex' Back Into Sexual Orientation: Classroom Strategies for Health & Sexuality Educators," "Ask Transsexuals," "Early Childhood Educators: How to Decide Whether to Come Out at Work or Not," and "Struggles & Triumphs of Including Homosexuality in a Middle School Curriculum." But the crowning glory of the entire program was a workshop titled "What They Didn't

Tell You About Queer Sex & Sexuality In Health Class: A Workshop for Youth Only, Ages 14-21" presented by two employees of the Massachusetts Department of Education and an employee of the Massachusetts Department of Public Health. During the workshop the government employees conducted a very explicit discussion regarding homosexual practices such as "carpet munching," "tribadism," "fisting," and other things that psychologically healthy human beings don't really want to know anything about.

Apparently, about 20 teenagers attended this session and were drawn into very explicit discussions of homosexual practices by the government employees. One tape-recorded exchange about "fisting" was described as follows:[75]

> At this point, a child of about 16 asked why someone would want to do that. He stated that if the hand were pulled out quickly, the whole thing didn't sound very appealing to him. Margot Abels [an employee of the Massachusetts Department of Education] was sure to point out that although fisting "often gets a really bad rap," it usually isn't about the pain, "not that we're putting that down." Margot Abels informed him and the class that "fisting" was "an experience of letting somebody into your body that you want to be that close and intimate with." When a child asked the question, "Why would someone do this?" Margot Abels provided a comfortable response to the children in order to "put them into an exploratory mode."

Although once this story broke state officials attempted to distance themselves and the state government from "Teach-Out," this somehow didn't translate into elimination of the program. "Teach-Out II" was held in March 2001 with about 400 students in attendance, again bused in from school districts around the state. While fewer exhibitors were present than at the prior event, the thoughtful people from Planned Parenthood did show up, however, to distribute free fisting kits.[76]

PARENTS DON'T COUNT

Not unexpectedly, many parents become upset when they stumble onto what is being done to their children without their knowledge in many of the more "innovative" government school curricula. In Ohio, a ruckus developed when parents found out what was actually going on in a sex education course based on a curriculum sponsored by the federal government's Centers For Disease Control.

Evidently, students in the course were learning "'practical skills' by using condoms, a penile model, lubricant, spermicide, and paper towels in front of other students."[77] The curriculum also ridiculed abstinent students as "hermits," "so unpleasant that everyone stays clear of you," and unable to "become involved in a romantic relationship."[78] Out of an undoubtedly sincere concern for parents' sensibilities, teachers and students in the course signed a "code of silence" in which everyone agreed that whatever was said or written in class would not be disclosed to anyone, including parents.[79] Despite this interesting precaution, someone "ratted" the school district out, and parents made their displeasure known.

School districts also communicate the message that parents and their values don't count in other ways. Paul and Jodi Hoffman, two Florida parents, were more than a little shocked when they attended a sex education assembly at their children's Broward County School District *middle school* that was attended by 500 students. During the assembly school officials encouraged the children to engage in sex, provided materials encouraging girls to carry condoms, promoted abortion, *and told the children that it is "okay" to lie to their parents.*[80] In settling a lawsuit brought by the parents the school district agreed to stop promoting abortion and to include abstinence education in its curriculum. It is unclear, however, whether the school district also agreed to stop telling children "that it is 'okay' to lie to their parents."

Of course, if you can't keep those pesky parents in the dark, you can always ignore them – even if the law says that you can't. At least, this was the approach of California's Antioch Unified School District in dealing with Pam and Dennis Angelo, parents who wanted to remove their son, Vinnie, from a required class called "Decision Making." "Decision Making" involved instruction in matters such as values clarification, sex, dating, drinking, and stress management.[81] Not surprisingly, the course promoted anti-Christian values. As a result, the Angelos felt that once the class began they virtually had to "deprogram" their son daily and "reinstate" the family's Christian values. When the Angelos finally requested to remove their son from the class, the school district refused, even though the state education code clearly states that school districts should honor written requests by parents to opt their children out of values-oriented classes. This ultimately forced the Angelos to sue the school district so that another of their sons would not have to take the course.

In Florida, Sawgrass Springs Middle School similarly violated various state and local ordinances by forcing children in a *world history* class to watch a presentation on HIV and AIDS that included wildly inaccurate claims such as that the elderly and infants are most at risk for HIV and AIDS.[82] Teachers, of course, didn't tell parents what their children would be getting as a *history* lesson. Although there seems to be some confusion regarding exactly where the presentation originated, a lawyer close to the matter said that the presentation was the work of a homosexual activist group.[83]

In California, homosexual activists have become increasingly aggressive in their efforts to turn government schools there into "sexual re-education camps," and part of the strategy is to keep parents in the dark. The most recent evidence of this was the defeat of AB 950 in the California legislature's Assembly Education Committee. This legislation would have required government schools to give notice to a child's parents if the school was going to bring in outsiders to discuss sexual matters with children. The bill particularly targeted HIV/AIDS prevention programs and required that parents be told the identity of the speakers, the groups the speakers represent, and when the program would occur. Jackie Goldberg, a lesbian activist and the chairwoman of the Assembly Education Committee, fought AB 950 and succeeded in having it killed in her committee.[84]

In Massachusetts, schools are required to notify parents of curricular materials involving sex education or human sexuality issues and exempt any child from such materials at his parents' request.[85] The law notwithstanding, parents are reporting many instances in which government schools have ignored or attempted to circumvent their notification rights. In one case parents were not notified when a transsexual was brought into a first-grade class to describe how sex changes are performed.[86] In another case a Gay/Straight Alliance club hosted a school assembly in which, among other things, a high school student described her first lesbian kiss and other aspects of her sexual "lifestyle." No notification to parents was given, and, when confronted with this breach of the law, the faculty advisor to the club told parents that their desire to exempt their children from the assembly next year would *not* be honored. In yet another case, a school took time out of an algebra class for a four-day seminar on "sexual harassment." This time there was notification. One parent who had reviewed the material and removed his child from the class discovered that the teacher had waited a day and then asked his child to come back, saying, "Your parents don't have to know."

The grand prize for giving parents the "mushroom treatment," however, goes to the officials of Metro High School in St. Louis. Debra Loveless, a mom who had objected to a school-sponsored assembly put on by the Gay, Lesbian and Straight Education Network, was urged by a school board member to go to the assembly.[87] When she attempted to attend, she was not merely told to leave by school officials, but escorted out by an *armed* security guard.[88]

Christian parents, and parents generally, need to understand that these are not isolated phenomena. Government schools are increasingly attempting to avoid scrutiny of their actions and curricula by deception and by ignoring parental rights. This sort of deception is present at the federal level, too. The Centers for Disease Control (CDC), together with organizations such as the Sexuality Information and Education Council of the United States (SIECUS), produced lessons for use in sex education classes around the country known as "Programs That Work."[89] Among the programs that "work" were lessons instructing teachers to send children as young as 9-years-old on "condom hunts" in local supermarkets and to have the children participate in a contest to see who can put a condom on the fastest (presumably only the boys, but with progressive thinkers you can never tell).[90] The lessons for children as young as 13-years-old included role playing exercises in which the children would negotiate "safe" bisexual and homosexual sex.[91] There are other examples, but I think you get the drift. In any event, when the Bush Administration got wind of this, it discontinued the program. But, was that the end of it for the CDC? Well, not exactly, says Robert Rector, a health policy analyst for the Heritage Foundation. According to Rector: "These programs, I can say with confidence, are still being promoted through the CDC – even though they are trying to hide it."[92] Apparently, this bit of civil disobedience by the CDC is motivated by its aversion to "abstinence only" sex education.

School Clinics: Playing Doctor

Laws establishing school-based health clinics have also been used to erode parental rights. In fact, the over 4,500 school clinics funded under the federal government's Title X not only distribute birth control drugs and devices to schoolgirls, they do so without obtaining parental consent and are prohibited by law from notifying the students' parents.[93]

School clinics typically provide a broad range of health care services, including mental health assessment, reproductive services (including birth control and information on sex), and substance abuse treatment. In California, for example, the legislation establishing the clinics leaves it to local "providers" to establish their own parental consent policy. On the other hand, the legislation *mandates* that the child has a right to participate in his own health care decisions and that the clinics shall be "'private', and 'confidential', and should involve parents as is 'age appropriate' for the student AND only with the student's consent."[94] In effect, the school gets to decide whether you are consulted about whether your child is provided birth control, mental health assessments, or drug abuse treatment.

In one of the more bizarre cases of child abuse by school clinics that has come to light, a middle school in Pennsylvania *forced* 59 girls, ages 11 and 12, to undergo a pelvic examination.[95] Many of the girls asked to be excused or to call their parents. The school officials not only denied their requests but also blocked the doors and the windows of the room in which the girls were being held. In the lawsuit that followed, the school was forced to pay damages for violating the girls' civil rights, and it was further discovered that the examinations themselves were conducted in a medically improper way that rendered the exams of no medical value.

In Illinois, a junior high school teacher periodically escorted a thirteen-year-old student that he was molesting to the school clinic so that she could get injections of a contraceptive drug known as "Depo Provera."[96] This apparently went on for 18 months, in part because the girl's parents had no idea about their daughter's clinic visits.

WHOSE CHILDREN ARE THEY?

What is going on? One of the great social struggles through the centuries has been over whether children belong to the state or to their parents. Totalitarian and authoritarian regimes have always claimed that children belong to them and that they have the right to control all aspects of their development, especially the development of their characters. Not surprisingly, "educators" have been central to the efforts of such regimes to wrest the allegiance of children away from their parents and their values. Judith Reisman tells of the role educators in Nazi Germany played in alienating children from their parents' traditional German values:[97]

> Adolph Hitler obtained nearly total cooperation from German librarians and teachers. The German "National Socialist Teachers Association" recruited schoolboys and girls to serve the new media and Nazi party....Maria Trapp gave evidence of such assaults on German traditions in her report of the Trapp Family Singers: "This morning we were told (by the Nazi's) at the (school) assembly that our parents are nice, old-fashioned

people who don't understand the new Party. We should leave them alone and not bother. We are the hope of the nation, the hope of the world. We should never mention at home what we learn at school."

While American government schools are still far from having reached that condition, it is clear that there are more than a few education activists and educators who are intent on seizing the future of America by using government schools as an instrument for inculcating their anti-Christian values in our children. As has been noted, humanists, such as John Dunphy, and New Age gurus, such as Marilyn Ferguson, have said exactly that. The insidious part is that most parents don't have a clue about what is being done.

Increasingly, government schools are taking surveys of children's *attitudes*. In New Hampshire and Vermont, for example, 4th, 5th, and 6th graders were questioned about tobacco and alcohol use by the students themselves and their friends, siblings, and *parents*.[98] In California, *10-year-olds* were surveyed about sexual matters – asking, for example, whether they thought about "touching other people's private parts."[99] Why?

Those in control of government schools now tend to view themselves as having a mandate to remake school children in their own image. One Pennsylvania school district has even floated the idea of giving *parents* report cards grading parents on how they are contributing to their children's education.[100]

The result is a growing number of psychotherapeutic "workshops" and school programs designed to change students' values and personalities. Think of them as mechanisms for enforcing socially liberal conceptions of sexuality, "niceness," and whatever other politically correct attitudes and values are wafting through schools of education.

The *Wall Street Journal* has reported, for example, on government schools around the country earnestly devoting school time to stamping out such things as mean looks and playing alone.[101] In Seattle schools, children participated in something called "Challenge

Day." Apparently, Challenge Day consisted of activities reminiscent of encounter groups and other Rogerian psychotherapeutic flotsam and jetsam from the 1960s and 1970s that one boy described as a "psycho cry fest."[102] The point of Challenge Day, it seems, was to make students more "sensitive" to others' feelings – an exercise in psychological alchemy in which 7th grade boys, for instance, would be therapeutically transformed into warm, caring "Alan Aldas" and junior high school girls would foreswear gossip and mean looks.[103]

Perhaps now the reason for government schools seeking increasing amounts of information about your child's attitudes and values is clearer. If the schools don't know what attitudes and values a child has, *they won't know what to change.* In fact, schools in some places must somehow get this information to implement legally required "thought-reform." California government schoolteachers and counselors, for example, must identify and refer for re-education any child "with the potential to be 'intolerant' of homosexuality."[104] To make it easier to get this kind of information, California has abolished a law requiring schools to obtain parents' prior consent before their children could be included in a sex survey. The sex surveys, by the way, start in kindergarten.[105] Don't delude yourself by thinking that these things only happen in California. Teachers' unions and other activists are undoubtedly pushing for something similar in your state in the name of "Safe Schools," "Diversity Training," "HIV/AIDS Awareness,"or "Anti-Bullying" programs, or by using some other form of rhetorical camouflage.

Now that Christian values have largely disappeared from government school classrooms, here are some of the consequences.

HOLLOWING OUT THE CULTURE – HOLLOWING OUT THE CHILD

Before *Everson,* government schools generally provided children with clear moral guidance. The importance of honesty, sobriety, chastity, hard work, kindness, and many other familiar Christian values was not viewed as a subject for debate by children. As a result, the traits of character that sustained a healthy American society were successfully passed on.

Today, government schools largely function as an instrument for *eradicating* the cultural values that have made America successful. In the process, they have placed a burden on students that children cannot bear. Children are told they must not accept the moral views of their parents or churches and instead must create their own systems of morality. This assumes, of course, that children, lacking in experience and knowledge, and battered by hormones and other stresses of growing up, can carefully evaluate the consequences of accepting or rejecting moral standards and patterns of behavior that have developed over centuries.

Government school curricula have also deliberately set out to alienate children from essential familial sources of guidance that would otherwise help them avoid catastrophic mistakes. This is no small matter. Even under the best of circumstances and with the best advice, we all make mistakes. And we hope that we learn from them and are able to use them to add to the reservoir of knowledge that we pass on. But many mistakes – illegal drug use and illicit sexual activity, for example – are not merely "learning experiences"; they are tragedies that often shunt promising young lives onto a path leading toward severely diminished futures, sickness, and even death.

In the roughly two generations since humanism and other anti-Christian cultural influences took control of government schools, many unfortunate changes have occurred in the behavior of Americans. Here are a few facts to ponder:

- In 1962, 4 million Americans had used an illegal drug. By 1999 that number had increased to an astonishing 87.7 million Americans.[106]
- Marijuana use by teenagers in 1999 was up roughly 300% since 1992. In 1999, 55% of high school seniors reported using an illicit drug, representing almost a 33% increase since 1992. Between 1991 and 1999, illegal drug use among 13- and 14-year-olds increased to 28.3%, which represents a 51% increase over 1991.[107]

- The number of juvenile murderers tripled between 1984 and 1994.[108]
- In the mid-to-late 1950s 8% of girls had sexual intercourse by age 16. By 1999 39% of girls had sexual intercourse by age 16.[109]
- Illegitimate births have increased by over 700% since 1940.[110] By 1997, the illegitimacy rate among teenagers in the District of Columbia reached 96.8%. Between 1960 and today, out-of-wedlock births have increased from 5.3% of all births to 33% of all births.[111] Note that these increases are occurring notwithstanding the widespread availability of abortion, which resulted in an estimated 35 million abortions between 1973 and 1997.[112] Consequently, the increase in the number of out-of-wedlock pregnancies is even higher than the statistics regarding out-of-wedlock births would suggest.
- In 1999 Rutger's University's National Marriage Project reported that the marriage rate was at its lowest point in recorded history.[113]
- According to the Census Bureau, between 1970 and 1998 the number of unmarried couples increased by 800%.[114]
- Between 1970 and 1996 the number of adults who have divorced has more than quadrupled.[115]
- In a 1998 survey of high school students honored for their academic performance by inclusion in Who's Who Among American High School Students, 80% admitted to having cheated, the highest number in the 29 years in which the Who's Who organization has been surveying high school students.[116]
- In 2001 a Rutgers professor published his findings on cheating among high school students: "75 percent had cheated at least once on a test" in 2001, as compared with 50% in 1993 and 25% in 1963.[117] In a 2002 survey, 74% of high school students were found to have cheated on a test within the prior twelve months.[118] Although the research didn't

collect data for determining whether family income levels correlated to cheating, both researchers were convinced that cheating was more common among students in wealthier school districts.[119] In fact, one of the researchers, who runs an ethics institute in Los Angeles, believes that "wealthier school districts generally turn a blind eye to cheating."[120] Why? Because *parents* threaten lawsuits if their children are caught.[121]

These statistical observations reflect just a part of the social and moral decay many of us have witnessed in the course of our lifetimes.

While not all of these changes are entirely attributable to the teaching, curricula, and degradation of the moral environment within government schools over the last fifty years, it would require a special form of obtuseness to believe that what has gone on in government schools to change children's values has not played a significant role in creating the social destruction that these statistics show.

As has already been discussed, there are studies indicating that drug education and "critical thinking" programs in government schools have increased drug use rather than decreased it. Similarly, one of the largest studies ever done investigating the effect of sex education programs on the sexual activity of girls between 15-and 17-years-old found that: (1) 15-year-old girls who had sex education were 40% more likely to begin sexual activity than girls who had not had sex education and, (2) 16-year-old girls who had had sex education were 25% more likely to begin sexual activity than girls who had not had sex education.[122] This is hardly surprising when one considers what passes for sex education in government schools. But, perhaps the best way for parents themselves to assess the culpability of government schools for these outcomes is to become familiar with the curricula used over the years in drug education, sex education, AIDS awareness education, and critical thinking programs.

"Those Kids," or Your Kids?

Some parents doubtless think that even though the data concerning sex and drug and alcohol abuse among secondary school students *in general* is dismaying, the moral rot that permeates government schools doesn't really affect the "responsible" kids – the future-oriented ones who graduate from high school and head off to college. If one is willing to ignore the incredible levels of academic dishonesty among the "best" students, those parents are not entirely wrong. Although they are far too high and unacceptable from a Christian perspective, the levels of sexual activity and alcohol abuse, for example, by these students do appear to be lower than among high school students as a whole.[123] But what happens to these students when they go on to college and parental restraints are reduced or no longer present?

In a 1996 survey of alcohol and other drug use among full- and part-time undergraduate students attending college or university in New York State, the New York State Office of Alcoholism and Substance Abuse Services found the following:[124]

- 36% reported using illegal drugs within the last year
- 14% reported using marijuana at least weekly
- 41% reported "binge drinking" (at least five alcoholic drinks at one sitting) within the prior two weeks ("binge drinking," by the way, is actually a euphemism for getting very drunk, in some cases fatally so)

There is no reason to think that the results of this survey in New York State are atypical for the nation. The Harvard School of Public Health found in 2001, for example, that the national binge-drinking rate among college students (44.4%) is slightly higher than reported in New York State.[125] Interestingly, the "binge drinking rate" for *all* high school seniors, not just those heading off to college, was "just" 30% in 1996.[126]

Perhaps the extent of alcohol and drug abuse on college campuses, while tragic, is no surprise. But perhaps our lack of surprise also reflects how we as Christians have become desensitized to destructive behavior and sin. Drug and alcohol abuse in colleges have been at high levels for years, but this sort of behavior by college students, which many unfortunately now believe is normal, would have been inconceivable at these levels and thoroughly unacceptable before the early 1960s.

HOOKING UP

What have been the fruits of our national experiment with "sex education" for students who reach the relative freedom of a college campus? That it has resulted in much more sexual activity among unmarried students is not what is news today. What *is* news is that sexual morality on college campuses has coarsened to an extent that few parents would believe possible.

A recently published study has brought into national focus the campus phenomenon of "hooking up."[127] As you may suspect, "hooking up" bears no relationship to courtship or dating. "Hook ups" are casual sexual encounters between students who typically do not know each other well *or at all* and who have no expectation of developing the "relationship" further. As a female Rutgers student has described it, "[With a hook-up you'll have his] friends [at a party] coming up and saying, you know, he wants to hook up with you, you're cute, come to his room."[128] Another aspect of hook ups is that they nearly always take place when both students are drinking or drunk.[129] A University of Washington student explains as follows: "[hooking up happens] in the dorms…. That's pretty obvious, because everybody lives together and everybody's drunk all the time."[130]

One journalist offers the following personal vignette from the "hook up" culture:[131]

> The scene: my college dorm's basement bathroom on a Sunday morning early in my freshman year. As hung over girls crowded around the sinks, I caught a friend's eye in the mirror. What happened when she left last night's party with a boy neither of us had ever seen before? "Oh," she said with a knowing look, "we hooked up."

Are "hook ups" rare events that involve only a few students? On the contrary, the study indicates that 40% of female students have been involved in hook ups, and 10% have been involved in "hook ups" six or more times.[132] In fact, "dating" has almost been replaced by "hooking up." According to the study, just half of the women interviewed had been on six on more dates during college, and fully one-third of the college women interviewed had been on no more than two dates.

Because they have lived this sort of social life, "hooking up" will seem normal for much of the next generation of adults. An interesting thought, isn't it?

Do Christian Values Matter?

So, do you think that the elimination of Christian values from government schools has made a moral difference in our children and in our society? We began with the Nehemiah Institute's finding that only 15% of Christian children attending government schools clearly reject moral relativism compared to 75% of the Christian children attending private Christian schools. That's one difference, but it is the key to a great deal more.

Consider this: if a child is convinced that all morality is relative, what is the likely effect of the message given by educators and curricula that the moral instruction of his parents and church should be disregarded? What is the likely impact on such a child when educators and the curricula are giving him extraordinarily explicit information on sex and telling him that there is nothing wrong with pre-marital sex? What is the likely effect on such a child when educators and the curricula are providing highly detailed information on drugs and asking him to produce reasons for and against drug use so that he can do his own informal cost-benefit analysis on drug use? What is the likely effect on such a child when educators tell him directly or indirectly that it is okay to lie to his parents or mislead them? What difference do you think it makes to a Christian child to be in a government school receiving these messages while under the instruction of "educators" who are willing to convey these messages and while under the control of an institution that virtually treats Christianity as a deadly bacillus? Do you think that an elementary school child or a confused adolescent is likely to be influenced to accept some or all of the values of the culture of government schools by peer pressure and by the government school's institutional authority? Do you think that the moral decline that we have witnessed among children, and in society generally, over the last forty years is a cosmic accident? Or do you think that it might in substantial measure be an expression of the values that government school educators and curricula have been programming into children? Do you *really* think that your child's government school is different? Just thought I'd ask.

If none of this concerns you, perhaps learning what is coming *next* to your local government school will.

WHAT'S NEXT: WE'RE HERE, WE'RE QUEER, GET USED TO IT

If you think that government schools can go no further in "defining deviancy down," are you ever going to be surprised to find out what your highly trained education professionals and their homosexual activist friends have planned for your child! Your local government school already has or is about to become a very friendly place for homosexuals so that your children can be re-educated to understand that the "gay lifestyle" is a thing of beauty and, of course, *just fabulous*. And the main national union representing your highly trained education professionals is among those most committed to making it happen.

Over the years the National Education Association has increasingly promoted the homosexual agenda in the nation's schools. At its 2001 national convention, the NEA was poised to adopt a resolution known as "New B." In effect, New B asked schools to promote homosexuality by using pro-homosexual curricula in kindergarten through 12th grade, hiring homosexual teachers, working with homosexual activist organizations in the development and promotion of "gay-friendly" curricula, and encouraging homosexual teachers to bring their sexual identity into classrooms so that they can be "role models" in their schools. Unfortunately for the president of the NEA and the other backers of New B, these proposals generated some embarrassing publicity for the union. So, in a belligerent statement excoriating the opposition to New B, the president of the NEA announced that New B would be tabled. But, said the NEA's president, the sexual orientation issues contained in New B would be examined by a task force. In reality, the NEA leadership saw to it that New B was passed, not in its original form, but piecemeal in a dozen resolutions.[133]

The NEA is probably the nation's most powerful union, and certainly the most powerful force in government schools. While the NEA has supported the homosexual educational agenda for years, the 2001 convention controversy put on display the depth of its leadership's commitment to bringing that agenda into government school classrooms across the nation. What this has done is bring into the open the drive to take into every classroom the curricula and practices that until now have only been implemented in "progressive" enclaves around the country.

The 1972 Gay Rights Platform was adopted by representatives of 85 homosexual organizations at a conference held at a United Methodist church in Chicago and organized by the National Coalition of Gay Organizations. This marked the beginning of a national effort by homosexual activists to, among other things, seek the repeal of all laws governing the age of sexual consent and to obtain state support "for sex education courses, prepared and taught by Gay women and men, presenting homosexuality as a valid, healthy preference and lifestyle as a viable alternative to heterosexuality."[134] Following the adoption of the 1972 Platform, homosexual activists began a low-level campaign to move their agenda into the nation's schools.

The fight in New York City in 1993 over the now largely forgotten "Children of the Rainbow" HIV/AIDS curriculum was perhaps the first nationally visible controversy over bringing homosexual propaganda into the classroom. "Children of the Rainbow" included the now infamous *Heather Has Two Mommies* and *Daddy's Roommate* as books for elementary school children. Ultimately, the curriculum,

Heather, and *Roommate* were sent packing by a coalition of parents led by a New York grandmother, Mary Cummins; the New York City Schools Chancellor, Joseph Fernandez, eventually lost his job.

Following the 1993 dust-up in New York, homosexual curriculum activists again went under the radar and sharpened their marketing techniques for promoting their wares. The teaching of the quaint and colorful folkways of homosexuals has now been carefully repackaged and presented as essential for combating "discrimination" against homosexuals and promoting "safe" schools. As a result, nearly 10 years after *Heather* failed, this approach finally succeeded in getting the New York legislature to enact a bill known as the "Sexual Orientation Nondiscrimination Act," which mandates that all students in New York government schools will be taught that there is nothing wrong with homosexuality – beginning with *five year-olds in kindergarten.*

So, if you object to homosexual curricula today you are opposing "safe" schools and promoting "hate." This is an article of faith, of course, for homosexual activists and their sympathizers within government, media, and education, and it has often proved effective in intimidating and silencing educators and parents who doubt that "fisting," for example, is in the best interest of any child (see "Fistgate," above).

HIJACKING THE LANGUAGE OF "CIVIL RIGHTS"

Before moving on to how the homosexual agenda is being pushed into government schools, consider the message the homosexual activists are using. *Are negative attitudes towards homosexuals the moral equivalent of racial prejudice?*

Unlike true racial prejudice, those who disapprove of homosexuality are criticizing the *behavior* and *beliefs* of the men and women who engage in homosexual practices. From a Christian perspective, homosexual behavior is clearly immoral, but many non-Christians also disapprove of homosexual behavior because it is self-destructive and often predatory. Here are a few findings from a 1994 survey of 2500 homosexual men by a national homosexual magazine:[135]

- 57% reported having more than 30 sex partners in their lifetimes, with 35% reporting more than 100
- 48% had participated in three-way sex within the last five years
- 24% had participated in group sex (four or more) within the last five years
- 20% had participated in "bondage and discipline" sex within the last five years
- 10% had engaged in sadomasochism within the last five years
- 65% had met partners at bars or discos
- 29% had met partners in bathhouses or sex clubs
- 27% had met partners in adult bookstores
- 26% had met partners at parks or restrooms
- 15% had met partners at roadside rest areas

These findings may substantially understate homosexual promiscuity and otherwise understate other common practices of homosexuals. A 1972 study by the U.S. Centers for Disease Control showed that 50% of male homosexuals had had *over 500 sex partners.*[136] A survey of homosexual men and women published in 1991 showed, among other things, that:[137]

- 37% reported engaging in sadomasochism
- 32% reported engaging in "bondage"
- 29% reported urinating on or in their partners
- 42% reported engaging in "fisting"
- 17% reported eating and/or rubbing themselves with the feces of their partners
- 15% reported engaging in sex with animals

In addition to all the rest, anyone who has ever witnessed the nudity and sexual activity at large public gatherings of homosexuals – "Gay Pride" events, for example – knows that homosexuals' public behavior, far from being "normal," displays an astonishing sexual crudity and obsessiveness. In fact, that obsessiveness increasingly is manifesting itself by homosexuals not only having sex in public places, but also insisting that they have a right to engage in this sort of exhibitionism.

WAY OUT OF THE CLOSET

To the chagrin of many families and other bystanders, some homosexuals regard parks, highway rest stops, family theme parks, and public bathrooms as *their* public spaces. For example, families no longer can use Conway Robinson State Forest in Prince William County, Virginia.[138] Why? Homosexuals started using the park for anonymous, outdoors sex and would invite passersby – Cub Scouts, people walking their dogs, etc. – to watch.[139] State troopers have attempted to clean out the park by arresting these sex offenders, but it doesn't seem to have had much effect.[140] Astonishingly, when making arrests some of the troopers were propositioned, and, when they declined, the troopers were physically attacked.[141]

Since 1991 up to 100,000 homosexuals have flocked to Walt Disney World in June for "Gay Days."[142] According to some Disney World visitors chagrined to find themselves there during the "event," the main appeal of Gay Days appears to be the opportunity to engage in public lewdness and recreational drug use in a family-oriented venue. Disney, of course, denies this, claiming that they enforce the theme park's dress code and other rules all the time, including during Gay Days. In 2003, the issue was settled when the Christian Action Network (CAN) videotaped some of the Gay Day festivities. The videotape shows extensive public nudity and other forms of public lewdness, as well as what appears to be illegal drug use. This videotape is available online, so you can decide for yourself whether Disney is enforcing its dress code during Gay Days – just in case you missed the video when it was shown on "The O'Reilly Factor." In any event, why should we be surprised at the behavior CAN videotaped? It is exactly the same sort of public behavior on display at virtually any "Gay Pride" parade or event.

Homosexuals also are becoming more aggressive in insisting that they have a right to have sex in public restrooms, which they refer to as "tearooms." At UC Berkeley, for example, the university-funded Queer Alliance runs an online message board where homosexuals can discuss the "hot" restrooms around campus.[143] Evidently, the campus police are annoyed because the "tearoom" visitors drill holes in the dividers between bathroom stalls to facilitate their activities.[144] According to the *Chronicle of Higher Education*, Boston University campus police have been trying to stop non-students from using BU's public restrooms for sex.[145] Homosexual students have responded, in turn, by claiming that the crack-down discriminates against the participants in what they call "tearoom culture."[146] Meanwhile, in Philadelphia, police have been busy trying to get homosexuals to take their trysts somewhere other than the public restrooms at places such as Strawbridge's and the Mellon Bank Building.[147]

Why is sex in public bathrooms so important to homosexuals? According to William Leap, an anthropology professor at American University: "For some men, their whole connection with gay life stemmed from their experiences in bathrooms.... Tearooms became the basis for social interactions, a way of getting into a friendship network."[148] How weird is that?

Similar homosexual invasions of parks, rest stops, restrooms, and other public places have occurred around the country. As early as 1979, Karla Jay and Allen Young recounted in *The Gay Report* that *51% of homosexuals think they should have the right to engage in public sex at any time.*[149] This phenomenon is not confined to America. In Britain, homosexuals have been indignant about the use of public lewdness laws to arrest homosexuals while "cottaging," *i.e.*, having sex in public restrooms.[150] Plainly, many homosexuals have an unusual sense of entitlement.

Desperately Seeking HIV

Of course, just when homosexual activists are having some success coercing others into pretending that the "gay lifestyle" is normal and otherwise just swell, something slips into the mainstream consciousness that is, well, embarrassing. The latest small eruption of truth occurred early in 2003 when *Rolling Stone* ran an article titled "Bug Chasers."[151]

"Bug Chasers" is an account of a homosexual subculture of "bug chasers" – homosexuals who are HIV negative and are desperately seeking to become HIV positive. Evidently, web sites devoted to "bug chasing" can direct a homosexual who longs to be HIV positive to a "gift giver" – that is, someone who will give him HIV. According to the *Rolling Stone* article, about 25% of new HIV cases every year are the result of "bug chasing" – homosexuals deliberately getting themselves infected.[152] The problem is so severe that public health departments are regularly watching homosexual-oriented web sites for bug chasing and are tracking "conversion parties," parties arranged so that "bug chasers" can be converted to HIV positive by "gift givers."[153]

Lest this seem too bizarre to be true – the source is *Rolling Stone*, after all – Robert De Niro has produced a documentary called "The Gift," which also takes a look at the homosexual "bug chasers."[154] De Niro's lens shows that the chasers seem to be motivated by a combination of anxiety and envy: some want to get HIV so that they can, incredibly, stop worrying about getting it, while others see their HIV negative status as somehow excluding them from the ranks of "authentic" homosexuals.[155]

If actively seeking to contract loathsome diseases is part of being an authentic homosexual, then it may explain why syphilis is on the rise among homosexual men.[156] In fact, as of 2002 San Francisco distinguished itself as being the city with the highest *per capita* syphilis rate – a rate that is almost 20 times the national average.[157] Syphilis, by the way, increases the risk of AIDS transmission by two to five times.[158]

Not content with merely destroying their immune systems through contracting HIV/AIDS, many homosexuals are working to fry their brains though combining their sexual escapades with the use of methamphetamines. *The New York Times* reports that the combination of "crystal meth" and sex is becoming increasingly popular among homosexual white men in Manhattan and that researchers fear this combination will "spread to the wider gay population and beyond."[159] What's the attraction? Meth apparently reduces sexual inhibitions and increases the user's ability to have sex with multiple partners.

Yep, more exposure to the "gay lifestyle." Just the sort of thing that will make your local government school a safer place for your child. If you have any doubts, ask the NEA.

"Intergenerational Intimacy"

Even more disturbing is the predilection among many homosexuals, especially male homosexuals, for sex with children. One obvious indication of this is the longstanding campaign by homosexuals to eliminate laws governing the age of sexual consent. Karla Jay, a lesbian activist and author, has put the pedophile "case" for eliminating such laws crudely, but forthrightly: "[K]ids can take care of themselves, and are sexual beings way earlier than we'd like to admit... nice bodies and young bodies are attributes, they're groovy."[160]

Arguing that pedophilia should be acceptable because children have "nice bodies" is not likely to win over the public, so more recently homosexual pedophiles and their friends have tried to "intellectualize" pedophilia, *arguing for the decriminalization of pedophilia on the ground that distinctions between generations are arbitrary and politically motivated.* Harris Mirkin, a pedophile apologist (but not himself a pedophile) and professor at the University of Missouri, claims in the *Journal of Homosexuality* that pedophiles have been "disadvantaged" by the political power of the "sexually privileged" just as whites "disadvantaged" blacks prior to the civil rights movement.[161] In an interview in *Paidika*, the leading pedophile academic journal, Gilbert Herdt, a homosexual and professor at San Francisco State University, expresses the view that "the category 'child' is just a rhetorical device for inflaming what is really an irrational set of attitudes" against sex with children.[162] *Paidika*'s editorial board, by the way, is dominated by homosexuals.[163]

In essence, homosexuals and heterosexuals who intellectualize their pedophilia argue that child molestation is just a "culture bound social construct."[164] You see, "breeders" (that's homosexual-speak for "heterosexuals") who object to pedophilia are just bigots who are prejudiced against "intergenerational intimacy."[165]

The American Psychological Association recently lent pedophiles a helping hand by publishing an article in *Psychological Bulletin* in which the authors claimed that child-molestation really isn't all that harmful to children, or as the authors delicately put it, "the negative effects [of sexual abuse] were neither pervasive nor typically intense."[166] Because, as the article's authors claimed, child-molestation isn't really all that bad, child sexual abuse shouldn't be referred to as "abuse" in scientific inquiry. Instead, child molestation should be "re-conceptualized" and described using value-neutral terminology.

Some suspect that publication of the article was a trial balloon by elements within the APA to see what the response would be to an effort to begin "normalizing" pedophilia, just as homosexuality was "normalized" some years ago. Whatever the APA's motive in publishing the article might have been, the APA has distanced itself from the article and its conclusions as a result of the torrent of criticism that followed the article's publication. Undeterred by the controversy created in the APA by the suggestion that child molestation should "reconceptualized," the American Psychiatric Association sponsored a symposium at its May 2003 annual convention in San Francisco at which the subject of removing pedophilia from the psychiatric manual of mental disorders was debated.[167]

More generally, those concerned about child abuse have been noticing a boomlet in academic articles and books attempting to de-stigmatize the pedophile.[168] A relatively recent book published by the University of Minnesota Press, *Not Harmful to Minors: The Perils of Protecting Kids from Sex,* argues that pedophilia isn't really so bad for children, citing, for example, "research" regarding "happy consensual sex among kids under 12."[169] The author, Judith Levine, a feminist, claims that she isn't defending child abuse, but instead wants us to understand that having sex with an adult can be a *really* positive experience for a child, which she claims "research" validates.[170] Once we have understood this, then we benighted Americans will be happy to lower the age of consent to 12 years of age, just like the more humane, unrepressed Dutch. Or something like that.

Not wanting to be left out of anything strange and utterly destructive, the United Nations did its part by funding a book through UNICEF that demonstrated a breath-taking commitment to "diversity." Obscurely titled *Theoretic Elements for Working with Mothers and Teens*, and produced in collaboration with the government of Mexico,[171] this learned tome made the following suggestions to Latin American mothers and their teenage daughters:[172]

> Situations in which you can obtain sexual pleasure: 1. Masturbation. 2. Sexual relations with a partner – whether heterosexual, homosexual, or bisexual. 3. A sexual response that is directed toward inanimate objects, animals, minors, non-consenting persons.

Obviously, this advanced bit of thinking was the work of a "big tent" committee, and it was allegedly intended to be used as a training manual for those seeking to discourage teen pregnancy. In fairness, it certainly appears that many of the recommendations for sexual activity recommended by the book would preclude getting pregnant. Unfortunately, the recommendations were a bit too "inclusive" for many of the less advanced thinkers who found out about them, and the book has been pulled from circulation.[173] I'm not sure whether it was the sex with minors, animals, or non-consenting persons that ultimately proved to be a bit over the edge for the U.N.

On a more mundane level, The North American Man-Boy Love Association (NAMBLA), a well known organization that vocally advocates sexual relationships between men and boys, is further evidence that pedophilia is fairly mainstream among homosexuals. NAMBLA typically participates in "Gay Pride" events and generally seems to be viewed, at worst, as only a bit indiscrete by homosexual activists.[174] NAMBLA, however, does not merely advocate lowering the age of consent; it has posted on its website techniques showing pedophiles how to attract boys for sex and what pedophiles should do if they are caught. Deroy Murdock, a nationally syndicated columnist, recently reported that NAMBLA also publishes a manual titled "The Survival Manual: The Man's Guide to Staying Alive in Man-Boy Sexual Relationships," which is also sometimes referred to by critics as "The Rape and Escape Manual."[175] Like the website, NAMBLA's manual tells pedophiles how to develop relationships with children, how to allay the suspicions of their parents, where to take children for sex, and when to leave America if they get caught.[176] NAMBLA, by the way, is currently being sued in connection with two pedophiles' murder of a 10-year-old Cambridge, Massachusetts, boy. One of the murderers, Charles Jaynes, had written in his diary that "…he had reservations about sex with children until he discovered NAMBLA."[177] Jaynes also apparently made use of some of NAMBLA's techniques, but obviously didn't study with adequate care "The Rape and Escape Manual's" chapter on when to head for Paris or Copenhagen.

For pedophiles who would rather not take their chances in the United States, "Gay" travel guides provide information about where to find boys in foreign countries and about foreign countries' laws concerning sex with boys.[178] Travel to countries with high levels of boy prostitution is also heavily advertised in homosexual publications.[179] In Britain, homosexuals have recently succeeded in reducing in the age of consent for boys to age 16,[180] and in the U.S. and elsewhere there is a movement developing to legalize homosexual relations between adult homosexual males and 10- to 16-year-old boys.[181]

WE'RE DOING IT FOR THE CHILDREN

Homosexual pedophiles undoubtedly feel misunderstood. Their hearts are in the right place, they argue, even if, perhaps, some of their other body parts aren't. An article in the homosexual magazine *Guide* explains that the homosexual pedophile's interest in children proceeds from the purest of motives:[182]

> We can be proud that the Gay movement has been home to the few voices who have had the courage to say out loud that

children are naturally sexual... [and] deserve the right to sexual expression with whoever [sic] they choose.... [I]nstead of fearing being labeled pedophiles, we must proudly proclaim that sex is good, including children's sexuality... we must do it for the children's sake.

Consequently, they say, moms and dads shouldn't view pedophiles with revulsion. Instead, as suggested in an article appearing in *The Journal of Homosexuality*, they need to see their son's pedophile lover "not as a rival or competitor, not as a theft of their property, but as a partner in the boy's upbringing, someone to be welcomed into their home."[183]

To better connect with children, homosexuals have even come up with their own "Joe Camel" – the "Pride Bear" mascot. Pride Bear shows up at homosexual events to entertain children and pose with them for photographs.[184] Of course, one wonders what children are doing at these "events" in the first place.

Homosexuality: A Risk Factor for Pedophilia

In a 1979 survey, fifty to seventy-three percent of homosexual men reported having sex with boys under 19-years old.[185] In a study comparing sex ads in a major homosexual magazine with those in a magazine with similar demographics other than sexual orientation, researchers Judith Reisman and Charles Johnson found that homosexual men were soliciting sex with boys at a rate over *thirty times higher* than heterosexual men were soliciting sex with girls (15% of ads versus less than one-half of one percent of ads).[186] Reisman also reports that homosexual magazines provide explicit advice to pedophiles on obtaining access to children. In 1976, *Palaver*, a magazine for pederasts, advised its readers how to obtain access to children while avoiding arrest:[187]

[L]ook for employment.... If you want to spend all of your time with children you must have a legitimate reason for doing so; *as a teacher helping children learn...* as a *social work-*

er helping children in difficulties; as a *play or youth leader* helping children to enjoy their leisure time.... (Emphasis in original.)

Crime statistics tell an even sadder story.

In a recent study by the Department of Justice, boys were fully 64% of reported forcible sodomy victims between the ages of 0 and 11-years of age.[188] In one study of child sexual abuse, the investigator found that the average male homosexual offender molested 150 boys, while the average male heterosexual offender molested 20 girls.[189]

Another researcher points out that using accepted estimates of sexual child abuse, between 6 to 8 million boys and approximately 8 million girls are sexually abused by age 18.[190] The difference is that the vast majority of sexual abusers of boys are homosexual men, who only constitute 1 to 2 million[191] out of the total population (using 1991 population estimates). In fact, a 2001 study by the University of Pennsylvania estimated that homosexuals account for 95% of the instances of sexual molestation of boys.[192] In contrast, while the vast majority of sexual abusers of girls are heterosexual men, heterosexual men constitute 86 to 88 million out of the total population (again, using 1991 population estimates).[193] In a 1987 study by Dr. Stephen Rubin of child sexual molestation by public school teachers, one-third of the cases involved adult male homosexuals sexually molesting boys, again confirming that 1-2% of the population is responsible for a very disproportionate share of all child sexual abuse.[194]

According to Peter Wood, associate professor of anthropology at Boston University, anthropological studies also confirm that in societies where male homosexuality has been normalized, a social pattern almost always results involving sexual use of young boys by adult male homosexuals, along with other patterns involving "initiation into secrets, male exclusivity, and a low status for women."[195] While there are some variations in the cultural patterns shown in the research, Wood points out: "The general results, however, are predictable on the basis of ethnography: heterosexual marriage will be weakened; the birth rate will decline; the status of women as mothers will further erode; *and young boys will be a much greater target of erotic attention by older males.*"[196] (Emphasis added.) Wood acknowledges that many homosexual men are primarily interested in other homosexual men and that most child molestation is committed by heterosexual males. Nevertheless, Wood observes that "we are also left with the stubborn empirical fact that societies that have indeed institutionalized something akin to 'gay marriage' have done so in the form of older men taking adolescent boys as their partners. To imagine that we could have gay marriage in the United States without also giving strong encouragement to this form of eroticism is, in the light of the ethnographic evidence, wishful thinking."[197]

Plainly, *not every homosexual male is a pedophile or endorses pedophilia*, and it is certainly the case that many homosexuals are appalled by homosexual advocates of child molestation. Nevertheless, it is undeniable that homosexual males as a group engage in pedophilia at a far higher rate than heterosexual males and, as a group, homosexuals have expended considerable energy in attempting to normalize pedophilia. By mainstreaming homosexuality, government schools will eventually be responsible for child molestation on a scale that will dwarf the pedophile priest tragedy. This is good news only for tort lawyers.

In light of all of this, is it any wonder that homosexuality is not viewed favorably by most people, let alone Christians? Moreover, we might ask how homosexuals "suffer" because of the disapproval of their behavior. The average homosexual household has an average income equal to 170% of the national average. Homosexuals are over three times more likely to be college graduates or to hold a professional or a management jobs than the national average.[198] The political influence of homosexuals greatly outstrips their numbers. There is probably no better evidence of this than the extraordinarily disproportionate funding of AIDS research. For example, in 1994 AIDS research received roughly 7.5 times more per patient afflicted with AIDS than cancer research received per patient – and cancer research receives between three and ten times more money per patient for research than heart disease, diabetes, and Alzheimer's disease.[199]

SAFE SCHOOLS — WINK, WINK, NUDGE, NUDGE

What about the other part of the argument by homosexuals for bringing homosexual activists and curricula into schools? By teaching that homosexuality is "a valid, healthy preference and lifestyle" are children being made safer?[200] *Are you kidding*? Suppose someone were to propose changes in the personnel, curricula, and operation of schools that would make it more likely that children would become involved in behavior that would:[201]

- Reduce their (boys') life expectancy at age twenty from between 8 to 20 years
- Increase by 500% their (boys') risk of contracting HIV/ AIDS (the average AIDS patient dies at about age 40)
- Increase by 860% their (boys') risk of contracting a sexually transmitted disease
- Increase by 4,000% their (boys') risk of contracting anal cancer (the increase in risk is 8,000% for those who are HIV positive)
- Significantly increase their (boys') risk of contracting hepatitis and gastrointestinal infections
- Significantly increase their (girls') risk of bacterial vaginosis, breast cancer, and ovarian cancer
- Significantly increase their (boys' and girls') likelihood of abusing drugs, alcohol, and tobacco
- Increase significantly their risk (boys – probably girls too) of being victims of domestic violence

What would you call such a person? Psychotic? Deranged? What would you call someone who acquiesces in such a proposal? What would you call parents who send their children to a place where such changes have been made?

The fact is that everything about the homosexual activists' claim that schools must become more gay-friendly in order to end "discrimination" against homosexuals and promote "safe" schools is a lie. Disapproving of homosexual behavior and beliefs is nothing at all morally like disapproving of someone for no other reason than his skin color. Moreover, bringing homosexual activists and their curricula into schools only make the schools a far more deadly and dangerous place for children. The point of the lie, of course, is simply to silence parents and others while the programs of the homosexual activists are implemented.

Beneath the mesmerizing and intimidating rhetoric of "human rights" lies something appalling. "Fistgate" is one example, but a program in Vermont provides a further glimpse into what the homosexual activists are really after. As in Massachusetts, Vermont homosexual activists have been permitted, and even subsidized by the state, to bring the homosexual agenda into schools.[202]

The Vermont Department of Health provided a $121,575 three-year grant to a homosexual organization called "Outright Vermont" that allegedly provides "safe schools" training for *middle schools and high schools*. An investigation of Outright Vermont's activities initiated by a state legislator showed, however, that Outright Vermont's mission seemed to involve far more sex than safety. It was found, for example, that Outright Vermont was spending money on recruiting children for "youth retreats" that featured, among other things, "demonstrations, guided practice & skill evaluation" in the use of prophylactics and education in how to engage in homosexual sex acts. Outright Vermont also sponsored social events for "lesbian, gay, and transgendered youth." One such social event was called the "Emerald City Ball," at which Outright Vermont handed out prophylactics and lubricants "at the door and in the bathroom." The event, by the way, was attended by 60 teenagers *and 80 adults*. Do you think that the 80 adults were there as chaperones?[203]

Bringing the "Love"-that-won't-Shut-Up to a School Near You

Actually, it is already there, and more is on the way. The sex education industry, and particularly the homosexual activists within it, have been working for years to "sexualize" children at ever younger ages, especially under the rubric of "HIV/AIDS education."[204] Occasionally this sort of thing gets some press play. One particularly over-the-top incident was reported involving elementary school children:[205]

> On January 21, 1992, CNN headline news had a short feature on the latest breakthroughs in the public classroom. Elementary school children were nervously trying to elude the camera. They looked ashamed. They had just seen a movie that would easily qualify as pornography. The teacher proudly barked her disclaimers into the camera. "No, this is not sex-ed, the kids are having their AIDS awareness heightened." These young children had just seen a film of full-on genitalia with a condom being donned. What was illegal in the 1950s porno houses was now sanctioned in public elementary schools.

Just another example of your tax dollars at work.

Of course, the effort to indoctrinate children with the notion that homosexuality is normal and healthy generally has been more subtle, with most of it consisting of the familiar propaganda that, apart from a few unusual things that they do in private, homosexuals are exactly like everyone else. This message has been relentlessly promoted through government schools and the media at least since the 1980s, and has borne fruit among children.

A study conducted in 2001 by Hamilton College and Zogby International involving a random poll of 1,003 high school seniors found that 85% of the students surveyed thought that homosexual men should be accepted by society, and 79% supported laws banning job discrimination against homosexuals. *Roughly two-thirds thought that homosexual marriages should be legal* (about double the support found in the general adult population), *and believed that homosexual couples should be allowed to adopt children.*[206] Government schools, aided and abetted by the media, seem to have been quite successful teaching our children that it is just fine for Heather to have two "mommies." This, however, is just the beginning phase of the program. More is coming that will transform the government schoolhouse into something almost unrecognizable.

The NEA's resolution "New B" reflects the vision that a coalition of homosexual activist groups and their cultural allies such as the NEA and the National Parent Teacher Association are pursuing. Of the homosexual activist groups working to bring their "lifestyle" into schools,[207] the Gay, Lesbian and Straight Education Network ("GLSEN") is the most prominent player. Established in 1994 to pursue the homosexual educational agenda nationwide, GLSEN has grown rapidly and has perhaps 100 chapters nationally. Apart from lobbying policy makers and pursuing public relations efforts, GLSEN appears to devote most of its energy to forming and supporting the activities of student organizations known as "Gay-Straight Alliances" ("GSA's"). According to GLSEN's website, GSA's are:

> … school-based, student-led, non-curricular clubs organized to end anti-gay bias and homophobia in schools and create positive change by making schools welcoming, supportive and safe places for all students, regardless of sexual orientation or gender identity.[208]

The number of GSA's is growing rapidly, and there are currently well over 2,000 across the country.[209]

One of the more effective tactics for forcing GSA's into recalcitrant school districts has been the threat of lawsuits under a 1984 federal statute known as the "Equal Access Act." This legislation was intended to prevent government schools from prohibiting Bible clubs from meeting on campus. Unfortunately, homosexual activists have turned the Equal Access Act into their primary legal tool for attacking school districts that decline the honor of having GSA's – homosexual clubs – in their middle schools and high schools.

The GSA/Equal Access Act drama is a four act play: first, homosexual activists locate a student who is willing to be a plaintiff in a lawsuit; second, a demand is made that the school district allow a GSA to operate in one or more of its schools; third, if the school district resists, the ACLU, or some other legal organization willing to do the bidding of homosexual activists, files a lawsuit and issues press releases claiming that the school district is rife with "homophobia"; and fourth, the school district capitulates. Shazaam! Your school district is now "gay friendly"!

While the school districts portray themselves as victims in these sorts of affairs, that's not entirely true – they typically collaborate in scripting the GSA drama's "happy ending." A targeted school district could, for example, avoid having GSA's forced into its schools by eliminating "non-curricular clubs." What this means is that any club or extracurricular activity that is directly related to curricular offerings – for instance, foreign language clubs, debate clubs, bands and orchestras, or computer clubs – could continue. Non-curricular clubs, which might include such things as ski clubs, scuba clubs, or hiking clubs – would have to be discontinued.

Of course, school districts are generally not taking this course. After all, it is better to *appear* to be forced into accommodating homosexual clubs than to become the target of the wrath of parents who will blame you, a highly trained education professional, for *deciding* to discontinue the ski club, or some such other "essential" school activity. No, it's better just to let the GSA's in and let people think you had no choice. Another defense against GSA's would be to decline the roughly 8% of the district's budget that comes from federal money… wait a minute. Reduce spending for the safety and welfare of students? Silly of me to mention it. Never mind.

The palpable cowardice and hypocrisy of our highly trained education professionals in failing to resist the demands of homosexual activists is almost comical. How do you think they would respond to proposals for Smoker/Non-smoker Alliance clubs (SNA's) purporting "to end anti-smoking bias in schools and create positive change by making schools welcoming, supportive and safe places for all students, regardless of tobacco orientation or tobacco preference"? The tobacco activists could claim, just as the homosexual activists do, that the SNA's wouldn't be advocating tobacco use – they would just promote understanding and tolerance between tobacco users and non-tobacco users. School officials would rightly dismiss this drivel and argue that the net result from allowing SNA's would be greater acceptance of tobacco use among impressionable children, and that this would increase the likelihood of students eventually contracting emphysema, cancer, and other diseases. In fact, they would probably indignantly point out that, as reported by the *New England Journal of Medicine*, men who smoke on average cut 7.3 years off of their lives.[210] Yet, when confronted by the demands of homosexual activists, school districts tend to surrender faster than the Iraqi army, even though the health risks, including the average reduction in life expectancy (8-20 years), are far greater from homosexuality than from smoking.[211]

THE BRAVE NEW SCHOOLS

So, how are the NEA, GLSEN, and their allies planning to remake your neighborhood school and your child's school experience? It will look something like this:[212]

- Sex education and its variants (*e.g.*, "AIDS awareness," "family studies," etc.) will begin in kindergarten and continue through 12th grade. This curriculum will explicitly affirm homosexuality (along with bisexuality and transgenderism) as a healthy, normal alternative sexual orientation. Elementary school children will regularly be shown films such as the PTA's "That's a Family!" and GLSEN's "It's Elementary" that teach homosexuality is normal.
- From kindergarten through 12th grade all textbooks and classroom materials will portray homosexuals positively and discuss the contributions of homosexuals in all subject areas. Teachers will, for example, be asked to draw pink triangles (a homosexual symbol) when teaching children about shapes. History teachers will be required to cover topics such as "Gays and Immigration" and "Gays in American History."
- School libraries will be required to provide a selection of books and other materials on the "gay lifestyle."
- October will be designated as "Gay History Month."

- School districts will be required to have affirmative action plans for hiring homosexuals and will have on staff homosexual counselors and advisors.
- Homosexual teachers will be encouraged to "come out" to the children in their classrooms by discussing their own sexual orientations.
- Virtually every school will have a GSA. The GSA will coordinate with the schools on sponsoring "gay" proms and other social events. The GSA's will also work with the schools in sponsoring special workshops for educators and students on the finer points of the homosexual lifestyle (like, for example, "Fistgate").
- Schools will have speech codes mandating the immediate suspension of any child who makes a derogatory comment about someone's sexual orientation.
- Schools will have separate restroom and locker-room facilities for "transgendered" children.

While this portrait may strike you as a future that is purely dark speculation, you should know that most of it (including the special restroom facilities) has already been recommended by the California Department of Education or the NEA. Other parts are GLSEN proposals, and bear in mind that GLSEN works closely on these issues with the NEA and state and local governments.[213] California, by the way, has already revised its government school "anti-discrimination policies" to require that each child be allowed to "choose" his or her own "gender."[214] So, in California schools, being a boy or a girl is a matter of personal taste. Implementing the revised guidelines will indeed be interesting. Will unisex restrooms be required? What will school administrators do about boys who perceive themselves to be "girls" and want to hang out in the girls' lockerrooms? The possibilities are endless.

Beyond these measures for "homosexualizing" government schools, government school textbook publishers also appear to be aiding and abetting homosexual activists. For example, Houghton

Mifflin, a major government school textbook publisher, publishes a textbook titled *A History of Western Society* that is used in some high school AP history courses. This textbook presents the following absurd revisionist account of early Christian attitudes and practices regarding homosexuality:[215]

> Early Christians, too, considered homosexuality a conventional expression of physical desire and were no more susceptible to anti-homosexual prejudices than pagans were. Some prominent Christians experienced loving same-gender relationships that probably had a sexual element.

Now, you may recognize this as ridiculous, but I can assure you that the teenagers and teachers who are fed this sort of material will come to see it as authoritative. In fact, they will regard the truth as suspect precisely because it conflicts with what is being taught in their government school textbooks. So, if you intend to continue sending your children to government schools, you can look forward to many meaningful conversations attempting to persuade your teenage sons and daughters that what they are learning about homosexuality and Christianity in school is false. Good luck.

MOVING INTO THE HEARTLAND AND THE BIBLE-BELT

Homosexual activists have been working aggressively to establish their vision of education in California, Connecticut, Massachusetts, Minnesota, Utah (!), and Wisconsin government schools. In 2000, however, GLSEN began training a cadre of activists to carry its program into Florida, Georgia, Louisiana, North Carolina, Tennessee, and Texas. According to Brenda Barron, GLSEN's Assistant Director for Southern Organizing, this was necessary to "create strong chapters with a strategic and highly-localized approach... [and to increase] the ability of chapter leaders to organize effectively in hometown schools and communities."[216] Southern schools, says GLSEN, score well below the "national failure rate" in "protecting and serving" homosexual, bisexual, and transgendered students.[217] So, all you Cajuns, Tarheels, Volunteers, Longhorns, and the rest should expect to be getting a whole lot more "education reform" so that your government schools can better serve the alleged interests of homosexual, bisexual, and transgendered students.

In addition to working to organize local educators and homosexual activists, GLSEN and similar groups have worked hard to influence state legislative and regulatory processes. Much of the success GLSEN has had in Massachusetts is the result of a law requiring equal education for all, "regardless of sexual orientation." Similar legislation is popping up in Virginia and elsewhere.[218] "Hate crime" legislation is another favorite of homosexual education activists because such legislation often includes a requirement that "diversity" curricula be developed to deter "hate crimes" based on a variety of factors including "sexual orientation." Texas is a recent example where this strategy has worked. California has enacted similar legislation that mandates, among other things, that a new "diversity" curriculum be implemented in California government schools by 2008.[219] These types of curricular "reforms" are in the process of bringing homosexual activism and advocacy into government school classrooms across the country.

How is this happening? Rabbi David Eidensohn, an opponent of New York's Sexual Orientation Nondiscrimination Act, puts it succinctly:[220]

> The biblical and traditional family community is hiding its head in the sand. Surely, people think, this can't be for real. Nobody is going to demonize or criminalize the traditional family and the Bible. But this is exactly what gay rights bills are doing, and nobody notices, or nobody cares. The gay lobby thrives… on the ignorance of the masses of Americans, who, like the hapless masses of Russia and Germany were too busy to confront a nasty and determined element determined to seize power and destroy its enemies.

Indifference born of ignorance. Sounds about right.

A Full Court Press

Even though homosexual activists have advanced their agenda within government schools at an astonishing rate, the pace of that change has been vastly accelerated by the Supreme Court's decision striking down a Texas homosexual sodomy statute in *Lawrence v. Texas*. Why? Because the majority opinion by Justice Kennedy in this 6-3 decision was not narrowly aimed at homosexual sodomy statutes. Instead, the rationale for striking down the Texas statute that made homosexual sodomy a misdemeanor is in large part that it *stigmatizes* homosexual conduct and is "an invitation to subject homosexual persons to discrimination in both the public and private spheres." The *Lawrence* majority, then, doesn't merely disapprove of public "discrimination" against homosexuals, but private "discrimination" as well. Evidently, in the eyes of the Court, anything that indicates disapproval of homosexuality is suspect.

Justice Scalia's dissent correctly observes that *Lawrence* will entail "a massive disruption of the current social order." More important for discerning the direction that courts will be taking on this issue, however, is Scalia's comment about the prospects for future judicial activism advancing the homosexual agenda:

> It is clear… that the Court has taken sides in the culture war, departing from its role of assuring, as neutral observer, that the democratic rules of engagement are observed. Many Americans do not want persons who openly engage in homosexual conduct as partners in their business, as scoutmasters for their children, *as teachers in their children's schools*, or as boarders in their homes. They view this as protecting their families from a lifestyle that they believe to be immoral and destructive. *The Court views it as "discrimination" which it is the function of our judgments to deter.* [emphasis added]

Christians need to reflect on this. Justice Scalia is telling us that expressions of the values of our Judeo-Christian culture are something that our unelected judicial mandarins intend to deter. Now go back and look at the homosexuals' wish list for "homosexualizing" your local government school, and consider how much less resistance there will be to such measures from our highly trained education professionals as a result of *Lawrence*.[221]

Justice Scalia is not alone in his assessment of the importance of this decision. Homosexual activists also view *Lawrence* as a major tool for advancing their program for remaking our society. As the executive director of an Arizona homosexual activist group, Greg Polzin, put it following the announcement of the decision in *Lawrence*: "It gives us the momentum to pursue our agenda."[222] Exactly. Less than six months after *Lawrence*, an emboldened Massachusetts Supreme Court "found" in *Goodridge vs. Department of Health* a right to homosexual marriage in the provisions of the Massachusetts Constitution. Never mind that the Massachusetts Constitution is the oldest state constitution, the primary draftsman of which was John Adams. Conveniently for the Massachusetts Supreme Court, however, the descendants of the Massachusetts Bay Colony Puritans and Plymouth Colony Pilgrims who ratified the Massachusetts Constitution are no longer around to point out the obvious — that the constitution they ratified had nothing to do with creating a right to something virtually every one of them would have regarded as an abomination.[223]

In any event, *Goodridge* has already spawned "curriculum guides" produced by homosexual activist organizations that are being used in government school classrooms across the country to structure "debate" about homosexual marriage. As Brian Camenker, president of the Massachusetts-based Parent's Rights Coalition, describes the situation in Massachusetts: "They have started the campaign in a big way.... These guys are in Massachusetts high schools as we speak, and they are proselytizing the kids in a huge way."[224] With more than 2,000 Gay/Straight Alliance Clubs in middle schools and high schools across the country, the odds are good that these same friendly folks are in your schools too – or soon will be – touting homosexual marriage.

So, if you persist in thinking that *your* government schools are "different," we can at least agree on one thing – they certainly are going to be.

WHAT COMMUNION HATH LIGHT WITH DARKNESS?

There is a Roman adage to the effect that "What a society does to its children, its children will do to society." We now stand just past the close of the 20th century as Christians looking into the future. Widespread cheating among the best students, rampant alcohol and illegal drug use, high levels of violence, and an utter collapse of sexual morals all indicate that government schools are producing morally hollow children who are becoming morally hollow young adults. The future consequences of this to society and to the church are dreadful to contemplate. Yet Christian parents overwhelmingly continue to deliver their children over to that morally corrosive environment. If you are one of those parents, you now know just a part of what your children are being subjected to and what is being planned for them. The questions you must face are fundamental. Why are you placing your child under false teaching? Whom are you serving? Do your children belong to the state and those who are able to best manipulate its institutions, or do your children belong to God and you?

CHAPTER THREE

MY CHILD IS ON THE HONOR ROLL

"A false balance is abomination to the Lord: but a just weight is his delight."
Proverbs 11:1

"In the long run, the greatest weapon of mass destruction is stupidity. In an age of artificial intelligence, too many of our schools are producing artificial stupidity...."
Thomas Sowell[1]

Not all the news about government schools *seems* to be bad. In 2001, the Horatio Alger Association conducted a "State of Our Nation's Youth" survey of students and parents that, it says, offers positive news about our government schools.[2] According to the survey, 61% of teenagers reported that they had gotten nothing less than a B on their last report card, 26% reported that they had B's and C's, 7% reported that they had mostly C's, and just 6% got grades mostly below a C.

Not surprisingly, students and parents are quite pleased with a system of education in which only 13% of students perform at an average level or below. The same survey shows that 68% of students and 65% of parents gave their local government schools a grade of A or B, while only 27% of students and 25% of parents gave their local government schools a grade of C. Teachers and administrators were even more enthusiastic about the effectiveness of their schools: 82% said that their schools do an A or B job.

Even higher levels of teacher and parental satisfaction were reported in 2003 by Public Agenda, a New York-based non-profit polling organization. According to Public Agenda, 73% of parents and an incredible 93% of teachers rate public schools as excellent or good.[3] Moreover, other surveys have shown that American students have remarkable levels of academic self-esteem. Plainly, students, parents, and educators are generally happy with the educational performance of government schools.

THINGS AREN'T ALWAYS WHAT THEY SEEM

Unfortunately, perception and reality are not always the same. The Public Agenda report already mentioned points out that employers and college professors have a somewhat less exalted view of how government schools are performing than students, parents, and teachers. In fact, 59% of professors and 57% of employers say government schools are doing a "fair" or "poor" job. Moreover, 73% of employers and 75% of professors rate government school graduates as having "fair" or "poor" writing skills; 73% of employers and 74% of professors rate government school graduates as having "fair" or "poor" skills in grammar and spelling; and 63% of employers and 65% of professors regard government school graduates as having "fair" or "poor" math skills.

As for students' grade point averages, selective colleges and universities are increasingly discounting or recalculating GPAs in their admissions processes. Grade inflation, inconsistent grading and curricular standards, and politically correct forms of assessing student achievement all have contributed to the decline in the usefulness of this nearly ubiquitous measure of student achievement.[4] Consequently, as pointed out in an article appropriately titled "Why Colleges Scoff at Your Child's GPA," GPAs "have in some cases become almost meaningless...."[5]

Minority students also seem to be voting against government schools with their feet. The national "non-graduation" rate for black students, for example, is roughly 45%.[6] Moreover, it doesn't appear that this high rate of attrition is limited to any particular part of the country.[7] In fact, the reported non-graduation rate for all students stands at 31% – an astonishing state of affairs that indicates polling students and their parents, rather than all school-age children and their parents, probably produces a very distorted picture of satisfaction with government schools.[8]

What is the truth? Are students today, as is often repeated in the media, the best educated ever? Are there heroic levels of educational achievement in government schools to justify reporting to parents that only 13% of students perform at an average level or below? To answer these questions *we need to compare perceptions with facts.* You may not like the answers.

OUR SEMI-LITERATE PRESENT AND ILLITERATE FUTURE

Would it shake your confidence in the academic performance of government schools if you knew that 68% of American 4th grade children cannot read proficiently and that 47% of urban 4th graders can't read at even a basic level? Would you be surprised if nearly 40% of students at a large state university with high school grade point averages above 3.0 had to be enrolled in college remedial English and math courses?[9] Would you be surprised that a 2001 Roper poll of *college seniors attending the 55 most prestigious colleges and universities in America* found, for example, that 50% could not identify the Constitution as the source of the doctrine of separation of powers, only 22% knew that the phrase "government of the people, by the people, and for the people" comes from the Gettysburg Address, and only 34% knew that George Washington was the American commanding general at Yorktown (37% thought it was Ulysses S. Grant)?[10] Not so very long ago the average 8th grader knew these basic facts of American history.

If this doesn't bother you, perhaps you might be more concerned if you knew that the CEO of Intel, Craig R. Barrett, has repeatedly sounded the alarm that the poor academic quality of government schools, especially in math and science, threatens our economic future.[11] Without dramatic improvements in primary and secondary education, Barrett argues, we will lose our ability to compete in areas such as information technology. But, instead of preparing our children for a very competitive future, we behave as if "We somehow think that we have a God-given right to be the world's No. 1 economy forever."[12] Others, the British, for example, once harbored such thoughts, much to their regret. Barrett, by the way, has stated publicly that he would never send his grandchildren to their neighborhood public schools.[13]

IT WASN'T ALWAYS THIS BAD

As with almost any area of government school performance, the truth about what passes for education in government schools is almost too painful to bear. But before telling that story, perhaps it would be better to say a few words about where we began so we can better understand how far we have fallen.

Until the appearance of the emotional revivalism of the Second Great Awakening in 19th century America,[14] American Christianity had traditionally had a strong intellectual emphasis. That emphasis on the importance of the intellect and its development was a reflection of Reformation theology. If, as Reformation Protestants believed, man had an obligation to work out his salvation and develop a personal relationship with God, then it was incumbent upon all Christians to learn to read the Bible.

Although the primary reason Reformation Protestants insisted on literacy was to enable Christians to understand God's special revelation contained in the Bible, literacy and other intellectual skills were also understood to be important for enabling Christians to grasp God's general revelation in nature. As a result, literacy soared in the Protestant parts of Europe following the Reformation, even in countries such as Scotland that before the Reformation had been desperately poor, illiterate, and superstition-ridden.

The colonists who settled America brought this Christian tradition of learning with them. Moreover, the vast majority of the institutions of higher learning founded in early America were Christian institutions, including Harvard, Yale, Brown, William and Mary, and Princeton. In his 1765 *Dissertation on the Canon and Feudal Law,* John Adams remarked on the spread of knowledge in Europe following the Reformation and on the commitment to education in America from the earliest times:

> From the time of the Reformation to the first settlement of America, knowledge gradually spread in Europe, but especially in England; and in proportion as that increased and spread among the people, ecclesiastical and civil tyranny... seem to

have lost their strength and weight…. The leading men among them [Puritans], both of the clergy and the laity, were men of sense and learning…. Their civil and religious principles, therefore, conspired to prompt them to use every measure and take every precaution in their power to propagate and perpetuate knowledge. For this purpose they laid very early the foundations of colleges…. They made an early provision by law, that every town consisting of so many families, should always be furnished with a grammar school…. The consequences of these establishments we see and feel every day. *A native of America who cannot read and write is as rare an appearance… as a comet or an earthquake.*[15] [Emphasis added.]

Although Adams' observations on literacy were undoubtedly colored by his experiences in New England and its neighboring states, it is important to remember that the culture of learning was characteristic of those who embraced Reformed theology. And, as will be pointed out in Chapter 6, even at the time of the War for Independence a significant majority of Americans were associated with a Reformed confession.

Because the Protestantism that shaped early America also encouraged women to read, high levels of literacy were not restricted to men. Professor Page Smith notes, for example, that in the colonial era, "The relationship between Protestant fathers and their daughters…was an especially close one…. Most Puritan fathers were directly concerned with the education of their daughters." [16] So, it is not surprising that in 1820 Daniel Webster observed: "A Youth of fifteen, *of either sex*, who cannot read and write, is very seldom to be found."[17] [Emphasis added.]

The breadth and depth of literacy was so pronounced in early America that, as John Taylor Gatto points out in his book, *The Underground History of American Education*, visiting Europeans found it noteworthy:

By 1812, Pierre DuPont was claiming that barely four in a thousand Americans couldn't read well and that the young had disciplined skill in argumentation thanks to daily debates at the common breakfast table.... In 1835, Richard Cobden announced there was six times as much newspaper reading in the United States as in England.... In 1853, Per Siljestromm, a Swedish visitor, wrote, "In no country in the world is the taste for reading so diffuse as among the common people in America." [18]

DuPont's claims, by the way, reflected in part the findings of a treatise on American education, which DuPont wrote at the request of Thomas Jefferson in 1800.[19]

The well-known American historian, Henry Steele Commager, confirms not only the remarkable literacy present in colonial America and the America of the early republic, but also the essential relationship between that widespread literacy and the American republic's original political institutions:

How interesting that almost everyone, in Europe and America alike, agreed that the American people were the most generally enlightened on the globe, that here in these little American settlements a larger proportion of the people were educated, read their Bible, almanacs, and newspapers, than anywhere else on the globe. How remarkable that this uprooted and transplanted people, scattered along a far-flung frontier, should have created nine colleges before independence.... How extraordinary that Jefferson's principle that self-government depended on an educated electorate should have been vindicated with such unprecedented promptness: the constituency was enlightened, and self-government worked. How impressive the level of public discussion of great political questions such as independence, or the state and federal constitutions, in town meetings, state conventions, the Constitutional Convention, and the press. Imagine publishing *The Federalist Papers* in our newspapers today. [20]

Commager wrote these words in 1964. Today we might ask how many Americans *could read The Federalist Papers*, let alone have the moral and intellectual seriousness necessary to *want to read* them, or anything of similar depth and importance.

If all of this seems too anecdotal, in a study of colonial adult male literacy Professor Lawrence Cremin found that literacy among free adult males in the colonies was between 70% and 100%.[21] Education analyst and writer Andrew J. Coulson has noted that in the census of 1850 only ten percent of the people identified themselves as illiterate.[22] Gatto also reports on more systematic data:

> Looking back, abundant data exists from states like Connecticut and Massachusetts to show that by 1840 the incidence of complex literacy in the United States was between 93 and 100 percent wherever such a thing mattered. Everyone was literate, rich and poor alike. In Connecticut only one citizen out of 579 was illiterate and you probably don't want to know, not really, what people in those days considered literate; it's too embarrassing.[23]

The "complex literacy" to which Gatto refers, as with so many other things in early America, proceeded from American's religious traditions. As Page Smith has observed: "[A] constant reflection on subtle points of [Christian] doctrine produced even in the simplest farmer a precocious skill in dialectic that was as readily applied to political as well as theological questions."[24]

Remember, these levels of literacy were achieved in an America that by today's standards would be considered utterly impoverished. It was a society that lacked electricity, central water systems, modern plumbing, modern heating and cooling systems, and all but the most rudimentary means of transportation and communication. Doctors then still did more harm than good, and infant mortality and fatal diseases were commonplace. Oh, and by the way, there was no ubiquitous system of government schools, nor were there compulsory education laws, not even in Massachusetts. Children were typically taught at home, and often also received a few years of formal education in community schools largely organized, paid for, and controlled by the students' parents. But that was a sporadic affair at best. George

Washington, for example, had no more than five years of schooling, and perhaps as few as two. Benjamin Franklin left school after two years at age 10. Abraham Lincoln had in the aggregate about 50 weeks of "schooling" in his entire lifetime. Frederick Douglass and many other well-known figures had less or even none.[25] Yet, no one then would have thought it strange. It was simply the way education oc-curred in the days when America's Christian educational tradition was still dominant. It was also a time when no one confused obtaining an education with government schooling.

While it is always possible to criticize America's original educa-tional traditions from some utopian perspective, they were effective and adapted well to changing circumstances. Moreover, as is discussed in Chapter 6, the Common School movement that over time replaced those traditions and that gave birth to our current system of govern-ment schools was the product of *social and political motivations*, not a response to educational failure.

JACK SPRAT'S WIFE

How American education reached its current state is an interest-ing story, but it won't be told here.[26] Instead, what Christian parents *must* understand is what the government schools are doing to our children academically now. What that means for their future is for you to decide.

Perhaps the best place to begin is with the sheer vastness of the government education leviathan. In 2001, roughly 43 million children[27] in 1st through 12th grades attended approximately 91,000 government elementary or secondary schools.[28] Resources in govern-ment schools are not scarce.[29]

- From 1970 to 2000, per pupil expenditures in government schools practically doubled in constant dollars from $3,883 to $7,086. For the school year ending in June 2001, aver-age per pupil government school spending had risen to over $8,800.[30] In 2004 we spent close to $500 billion on elementary and secondary education. To put this in perspective, the State of New York now spends about $200,000 to "educate" a child through high school.

- Class sizes in 1970 were 24 students per teacher in elementary schools and 20 students per teacher in secondary schools. By 1999 average class sizes were down to 18 students in elementary schools and 14 students in secondary schools.
- The average salary of government schoolteachers in 1998-1999 was $42,459 *plus* benefits (in 2001 dollars).
- 98% of schools have Internet access.
- Schools have a computer for roughly every five students.
- 52% of schools operate below capacity; 26% operate at capacity; and, 22% are overcrowded.

If that doesn't convince you that government schools are not being starved for resources, consider that no country at any time has ever spent more in the aggregate on elementary and secondary education than we are currently spending. Moreover, according to a study by the Thomas B. Fordham Foundation of twenty-two economically advanced nations, the United States spends 75% more than those nations' average per pupil expenditure on primary education and 54% more than their average per pupil expenditure on secondary education.[31]

Remember, in comparison to today, America spent almost nothing on education in the early 19th century when what John Taylor Gatto refers to as "complex literacy" was relatively widespread. Whatever the source of the academic failure of government schools may be, it is *not* a lack of money.

DUMB AND DUMBER

At the beginning of the 20th century, pupils in Kansas who wanted to graduate from the 8th grade had to pass a test requiring them to be able to spell words such as "elucidation" and "animosity," define words such as "zenith" and "panegyric," diagram sentences, and solve problems in arithmetic such as finding the interest earned on a $900 note, at 8%, after two years, two months, and six days. They were also expected to be able to answer equally challenging questions in geography and history.[32]

Of course, those young scholars *were prepared* to succeed. Reading instruction in those days was phonetic and still largely in the hands of "America's Schoolmaster," William H. McGuffey, whose *McGuffey's Eclectic Readers* sold over 120 million copies from their first publication in 1836 to 1920.[33] Joseph Ray's arithmetic textbooks were then as common as *McGuffey's* books and also as demanding.[34] Grammar instruction may well have been provided to the young scholars by *Harvey's Grammars*, another mainstay of American schools into the early part of the 20th century. So, those turn-of-the-century eighth graders, many of whom attended one-room rural schoolhouses, were ready. Those who passed could undoubtedly give today's average college freshman a run for his money academically. Do you think I am exaggerating?

Dr. Donald Hayes, a Cornell University professor emeritus, developed a computerized system called LEX to analyze the difficulty of textbooks.[35] A typical newspaper would have a LEX score of 1. A higher LEX score would indicate a greater level of difficulty. Thus, the *New England Journal of Medicine* has a LEX score of 26, while *Time* magazine scores 1.6. When the LEX analysis was applied to *high school* textbooks the results were startling. The average high school science textbook had a LEX score of -.05, a lower score than a newspaper. Literature textbooks scored an amazing *negative* 22.3. In a Cornell study of textbooks used in elementary schools, middle schools, and high schools between 1919 and 1991, the researchers found that textbooks in grades four through eight were less difficult than at any time in American history. Further, literature textbooks used in the 12th grade today are written in language that is simpler than the language in 7th or 8th grade readers before World War II.[36] If you doubt this, go take a look at *McGuffey's* third, fourth, fifth, and sixth readers (any edition).

Still not convinced? Many years, and trillions of education dollars, after those young Kansan scholars sat for their eighth grade graduation test, the Educational Testing Service conducted a National Adult Literacy Survey of 26,000 adults over age sixteen and with an average of 12.4 years of schooling. Based on that 1993 survey, the Educational Testing Service concluded that forty-two million adults in the United States cannot read, and another fifty million can read at a fourth or fifth grade level, but cannot write a simple message.

Another fifty-five to sixty million are only able to read at a sixth, seventh, or eighth grade level and, incredibly, most of them could not figure out the per ounce price of a 20 ounce $1.99 jar of peanut butter even if they were allowed to round the answer to a whole number. Thirty million more can read at a 9th or 10th grade level, but cannot understand a written description of how attorneys and judges select juries.

Only 3.5% of the sample group had the literacy skills to do traditional college level work. In contrast, 30% of all high school students achieved that level of literacy in 1940, and it is achieved today by 30% of secondary school students in other developed countries.[37] This is why even the most "rigorous" of government school 12th-grade exit exams test students for competency at what today passes for an 8th or 9th-grade level.[38] In fact, a 2004 study by Achieve, Inc., a non-profit organization, found that the high school graduation exams for the six states that volunteered for the study covered material that would be "considered middle school content in most other countries."[39] This is also why half the students who go on to four-year colleges have to take remedial work and a study by the Manhattan Institute found that only 32% of recent high school graduates were prepared to attend a four-year college.[40]

The literacy story isn't getting any better. The National Assessment of Educational Progress (NAEP) found in 2000 that 68% of all American fourth graders cannot read at a proficient level, and 63% of African-Americans, 58% of Hispanic Americans, 60% of children living in poverty, and 47% of children in urban schools cannot read even at a basic level. This should horrify us. Fourth graders who cannot read at a basic level, in essence, *cannot read.*

Even worse, researchers recognize that 4th grade is a critical benchmark for reading. A child who cannot read, or who only has marginal reading skills, by 4th grade is likely to become an illiterate or functionally illiterate adult. Consequently, 68% of all children are heading towards the margins of literacy, and a majority of African-American and Hispanic children may well turn out to be functionally illiterate.[41] To compound this travesty, the achievement gap between white and African-American children is enormous.[42]

Young adults are not doing any better. A 2001 study by the Organization for Economic Cooperation and Development found that 60% of Americans between the ages of 16 and 25 are functionally illiterate.[43]

DON'T KNOW MUCH ABOUT HISTORY (OR ANYTHING ELSE, FOR THAT MATTER)

One of the staples of modern journalism is the story reporting how American high school students have trouble answering questions that a 5th grade schoolchild should be able to answer. A spate of stories in this genre appeared after the results of a survey done by the Colonial Williamsburg Foundation were published in the summer of 2001. According to the survey, almost a quarter of the teenagers had no idea that American states fought each other in the Civil War; more than a fifth of the teenagers questioned did not know that the original thirteen colonies declared their independence from England; 17% were unaware that the United States was formed from thirteen original colonies; 15% did not know what significant event in American history happened on July 4, 1776; and, 10% could not identify the first President of the United States.[44]

This is not a recent phenomenon. The same grasp, or breathtaking lack of a grasp, of basic historical facts and basic mathematics and writing skills was demonstrated by 17-year-olds in an administration of the NAEP in the 1990s. For example:[45]

- One-third didn't know whom the U.S. fought in World War II.
- One-third didn't know who Abraham Lincoln was.
- One-third had no idea that the Mississippi flows down to the Gulf of Mexico.
- One-third thought Columbus sailed to the Americas after 1750.
- Nearly two-thirds didn't know when the Civil War occurred.
- 50% did not know how to find the area of a rectangle.
- Just 20% were able to compose a one-page job-application letter to a local supermarket manager.

At about the same time as many of America's 17-year-olds were demonstrating that they had roughly the same grasp of American history as they did of, say, particle physics, the National Geographic Society surveyed eighteen- to twenty-year olds on their knowledge of geography. Not surprisingly, their geographical knowledge was astonishingly poor: given a map, just 45% could find New York State; one-third could locate Michigan; one-quarter knew where Massachusetts was, and slightly more than one-third was able to find England.[46] A 2002 National Geographic survey, by the way, found that young Americans are continuing in their state of blissful geographical ignorance. Only 17% of young Americans, for example, could find Afganistan on a map, and only 13% could find Iraq.[47]

Results from the 2001 NAEP examination on American history underscore the depth of the problem. Based on a national sample of 23,000 students in 1,100 government and private schools, only 17% of government school 4th graders, 15% of government school 8th graders, and 11% of government school 12th graders had a proficient or advanced understanding of American history, while 35% of government school 4th graders, 38% of government school 8th graders, and 58% of government school 12th graders *lacked even a basic understanding* of American history appropriate to their grade.[48]

As bad as these results are, they mask the utter failure of government schools to educate Black, Hispanic, and American Indian children in even the basics of American history. By 12th grade 80% of Black children, 74% of Hispanic children, and 66% of American Indian children lacked a basic understanding of American history appropriate to their grade.[49] Note, too, that the 2001 NAEP results show an unmistakable trend toward greater historical ignorance (relative to their age) the longer students are in government schools.[50]

Children consigned to government schools, it seems, contract a form of historical Alzheimer's that becomes increasingly severe until the average government school 12th grader is only able to distinguish between being in the United States and, say, Bulgaria, by the differences in the languages spoken and the relative quality of the shopping malls. This is not entirely a laughing matter. In his 2003 testimony before a committee of the United States Senate, David McCullough, a distinguished historian, testified *that the ignorance of American history among students and teachers in American high schools and colleges is now so profound that it represents a threat to the nation's security.*[51]

According to McCullogh, it is not merely that students and teachers are historically illiterate; it's that the illiteracy has assumed such proportions that they don't understand the values undergirding our free society or our constitutional framework: "We can't function as a society if we don't know who we are and where we came from."[52] Is McCullough engaging in a bit of academic hyperbole? Consider this from his testimony: "We need to know the Constitution, and we don't. When you have students at our Ivy League colleges saying they thought Germany and Japan were our allies in World War II, you know we have a very serious problem."[53] Germany and Japan were our allies? According to the 2001 NAEP American history assessment, over 50% of 12th-graders think that at least one of Italy, Germany, and Japan were our World War II allies. Remember this next time someone starts bloviating about how our children are the best educated ever.[54]

THE ZOGBY "COLLEGE BOWL":
TODAY'S COLLEGE SENIORS VERSUS 50S HIGH SCHOOL GRADUATES

In 2002 Zogby International surveyed a random sample of college seniors using questions testing general knowledge.[55] The questions were virtually identical to those used by the Gallup Organization in a survey of high school graduates in 1955. Zogby found that the high school graduates in 1955 actually did a little better than today's college seniors.

Were the questions especially difficult? Here are a few examples: "Which planet is nearest the sun?", "What great scientist do you associate with the Theory of Relativity?", and "What is the capital city of Spain?" I trust you got them right.

THE MATH AND SCIENCE DEBACLE

Well, perhaps the problems with literacy skills, historical knowledge, and general knowledge are just an aberration. What about science and mathematics? Surely with all the money, computers, and Internet connections that have been poured into American schools, aren't American children doing well in those areas? Unfortunately, the story regarding science and mathematics may be even worse.

A few years ago the Third International Mathematics and Science Study (TIMSS) was completed. This international survey of mathematics and science skills involved 500,000 students in 41 countries and measured the relative performance in mathematics and science of each country's fourth, eighth, and twelfth graders. In mathematics, American fourth graders placed twelfth out of the fourth graders tested from 26 countries. Our eighth graders came in 28th in mathematics out of the eighth graders tested from 41 countries. By twelfth grade, American students' mathematics scores placed them at 19th out of the twelfth graders from twenty-one countries reporting (American twelfth graders only did better than the twelfth graders from Cypress and South Africa). In science, the results were not dramatically different. American fourth graders were third out of the fourth graders from twenty-six countries reporting; American eighth graders were 17th out of eighth graders from twenty-six countries reporting; and American twelfth graders were 16th out of the twelfth graders from twenty-one countries reporting.[56]

The TIMSS reveals two interesting facts about American elementary and secondary education. The first is obvious. Overall, the performance of American students in relation to their peers in other countries is dismal. It is dismal not merely because (with the exception of the fourth graders) the scores are horrible; it is especially dismal in light of the hundreds of billions of dollars given to the government education bureaucracy. By twelfth grade even the students from relatively impoverished countries such as Slovenia and the Russian Federation do better than American twelfth graders in mathematics and science. The second fact is astonishing. The TIMSS clearly shows that *the longer American students are in government schools the more ignorant they become in relation to their international peers.* In fact, the data suggest that perhaps what we have created with our annual expenditures of hundreds of billions of dollars on government schools is not a system of education, but an institutionalized method of degrading the intellect of children.

THE WORLD'S LEAST PRODUCTIVE SCHOOLS

In 1998 the Thomas B. Fordham Foundation studied the education data published by the Organization for Economic Cooperation and Development (OECD) to evaluate the performance of American schools against the performance of schools in other economically developed countries.[57] Unlike the TIMSS, this study was conducted to examine the "value added" by schools in different countries by evaluating student progress.

The study found that expenditures per pupil by the United States on primary and secondary education were third highest among more than 20 advanced countries. Unfortunately, between ages 9 and 14 the average American's student's reading progress was only 78% of the international average, which placed American students dead last in reading progress among the OECD countries. This is particularly shocking because the American 9-year-olds scored second only to Finnish children in reading skills. In mathematics, out of students from 24 countries, American students also made the least progress between grades seven and eight. In sum, this study of the "valued added" by our government schools also indicates that the longer children stay in government schools the worse they do internationally. It also led the author, Herbert J. Walberg, to conclude that American schools "can be fairly termed the *least productive* among those in economically advanced countries."[58] (Emphasis added.)

ADVANCED PLACEMENT: "BODICE RIPPERS" AND "FILMS"

Don't suppose that the reading progress statistics would be significantly better if that assessment were made with respect to American high school students. Apart from plummeting textbook LEX scores, the reading skills demanded in high schools are in decline. In fact, even the summer reading lists for schools attended by the children of upper-income parents are showing definite signs of intellectual and cultural rot. Students attending New Jersey's Watchung Hills High School, for example, were given *Palomino*, a Danielle Steele "romance," as a part of their summer reading.[59] Other toney schools across the country have included such fare as Stephen King and John Grisham novels.[60] No wonder that yet another government study recently found that 12th grade reading scores declined between 1998 and 2002.[61]

While the decline in the quality of what high school students are expected to read is one reason for a deterioration in literacy skills, another significant factor is that, under the guidance of our highly trained education professionals, high schools are increasingly promoting concepts such as "media" literacy and are substituting "films" for reading. For the uninitiated, "film" is simply a pretentious way of referring to a movie, as in "art films." Doubtless, those pursuing "film" degrees at schools like NYU regard themselves as aspiring "artistes," but the reality in high schools is that less serious literature is being read because the students are too busy going to the movies in class.

For example, in the Seattle area's solidly middle-class Federal Way School District, the highly trained education professionals rose in indignation over a school district policy that would restrict the showing of *R-rated movies* in class and set some guidelines for the showing of movies rated G through PG-13.

When this dispute moved into the pages of the Seattle area press, the beleaguered president of the school board, Earl A. VanDorien, Jr., explained that there had been "many occurrences of teachers showing inappropriate films in classes, substitute teachers using films instead of continuing with the scheduled teaching plan, and films taking nearly a third of the time in some classes. There were times when PG-13 and R-rated movies were shown with no permission slips sent to the parents, a clear violation of previous procedure."[62] One highly trained education professional evidently felt that showing "Toy Story" would enhance students' knowledge of geometry.[63]

VanDorien went on to lament that he had been deluged with *teacher complaints* about the new policy restricting their ability to show any R-rated film they wanted during class time, although non-teachers who contacted him about the policy were supportive and wondered "why we never had such common sense in the first place."[64] Interestingly, VanDorien also pointed out that for all the energy being expended against the R-rated film policy, not much was being made of the fact that only 36 percent of district high school students and 27 percent of district junior school students were meeting the state math standards and that only 65 percent of district high school students and 41 percent of district junior high school students were meeting the state reading standards.[65]

The counterpoint to VanDorien was expressed by a high school Advanced Placement English and journalism teacher, Keith Swanson. According to Swanson:

> [I]t is not our job to sugarcoat history and literature. Rather we are called upon to prepare our students for success as citizens of this country. That means giving them skills and knowledge,

which is where movies can help. Since many students are visual learners who have been raised in a video age, films *can* be excellent tools when teachers use them to supplement their curriculum.... As for the argument that teachers use films for "entertainment" instead of teaching reading, *I would offer that films can help students become better readers.*[66] [Emphasis added.]

As a former professor of mine once said, "I get it all except the 'therefore.'"

I suppose that under some rare alignment of the stars and planets it is possible that almost anything *can* help something else. As for whether spending class time watching movies is *actually* a better way for students to acquire "skills and knowledge" or become "better readers" than traditional academic methods, the school district's math and reading scores would seem, as a practical matter, to settle the issue rather decisively.

This sort of thing is not limited to the Federal Way School District, of course. There are many teachers in government schools (and I fear elsewhere) who don't seem to understand that Hollywood writers, producers, and directors do not have historical accuracy, for example, as their first, or even second or third, concern. They want to make money, continue to be invited to the right parties, win awards from their colleagues, indulge fantasies, and so on. Oliver Stone, Quentin Tarantino, Michael Moore, and Steven Spielberg are simply not in the business of producing scholarship.

Moreover, contrary to Swanson's claims, films are not supplementing the reading and analysis of serious literature – they are supplanting it. Swanson himself, it appears, uses class time to show and discuss movies. Every classroom minute that is spent watching and talking about "Catch 22" is a minute that has been taken from serious discussion of serious literature.

In truth, one rather suspects that many of the indignant e-mails that board president VanDorien received were from highly trained education professionals who rather like being able to substitute films for work, and whose taste in films runs to the R-rated variety rather than those rated "G". In any event, if these trends continue, perhaps there can be a discussion of reducing property taxes by giving children a season pass to the local cineplex and closing the government schools.

YES, BUT "OUR" GOVERNMENT SCHOOLS ARE DIFFERENT

Some parents delude themselves by thinking that the bad news brought by the TIMSS and other measures of student and school performance don't apply to their children. After all, their children are "top" students in "good" government schools, and everyone knows that while the "riff raff" may not be up to snuff, our best students can compete with anybody. Really?

I forgot to mention that the TIMSS also included tests of advanced mathematics and science that were given to twelfth graders. In advanced mathematics the students from the United States came in 15th out of the students from sixteen countries reporting. In advanced science the students from the United States were dead last out of the students from sixteen countries reporting. It would have been even worse, but several countries (mainly Asian countries) whose students had consistently turned in superior performances did not participate. Even so, it is bad enough that our best students were beaten by students from relatively poor countries such as Cyprus.

By the way, the 2000 results for the NAEP science assessment show that 12th graders did even worse in 2000 than they did in 1996.[67] Because these results included the scores of children attending private schools, who performed significantly better than their government school counterparts, the reported 2000 NAEP results actually mask the extent of the worsening of the government schools' performance.[68] So, don't expect the international standing of American students in science to improve anytime soon.

NOT MEASURING UP? JUST CHANGE THE YARDSTICK!

As embarrassing as the TIMSS results have been to the government school establishment, it is the marked decline in performance by students since the early 1960s on the S.A.T. that over the years has gotten the most public attention. The S.A.T. was developed as a test of scholastic aptitude to help predict a student's success in college. Essentially, what the S.A.T. traditionally has measured is a student's reading comprehension, vocabulary, verbal reasoning skills, and ability to do mathematics through geometry and algebra. Not surprisingly, despite dramatic increases in expenditures for government schooling over the last forty years or so, the academic preparedness of American high school students for college as measured by the S.A.T. has arguably dropped significantly.

It would be hard to understand the S.A.T. and the controversy engulfing it today without understanding its origins. The S.A.T. was first administered to just over 8,000 students in 1926 – just 21 years after Alfred Binet had invented the IQ test. Before Binet's development of the IQ test, intelligence was viewed as in some sense generally inheritable, although the extent to which this was true remained strictly conjecture. The significance of Binet's work, which Stanford's Lewis Terman developed further, was that it moved these general, unsystematic observations about intelligence into the realm of science, or so it seemed. In essence, Binet was believed to have made "intelligence" reliably measurable. The development of the IQ test also coincided with a period of national anxiety over immigration, and many among the American elite were concerned that mass immigration of certain groups from Southern Europe and elsewhere would dilute America's "superior" racial stock. Consequently, the histories of IQ testing and the eugenics movement in America are intertwined through the first decades of the 20th century, but that is another story.

While IQ testing was initially done individually, psychologists interested in gathering IQ data successfully lobbied the government to implement mass IQ testing of all army recruits during World War I. One of the psychologists who had worked on the IQ test used by the army, known as the "Army Alpha," was Carl Brigham, a Princeton faculty member. Brigham, in turn, created the S.A.T. by adapting the Army Alpha for use in college admissions. Originally, Brigham marketed the S.A.T. to the military academies and a few Ivy League schools. Harvard adopted it in the early 1930s, and by the late 1930s the rest of the Ivies were also using the S.A.T. Thus, prior to World War II the S.A.T. was used for admissions at very few colleges and was taken by only a few thousand applicants each year. Following the end of the second World War, however, the S.A.T. began to grow into a widely used admissions tool. Today, the S.A.T. is taken by approximately 1.4 million students every year. Not surprisingly, the S.A.T. also generates tens of millions of dollars in revenue annually for the Educational Testing Service (ETS), which administers the S.A.T. This, by the way, is an important fact for understanding the current politics of the S.A.T.

How did the S.A.T. become a routine element of the admissions process? Its advocates were interested in having a tool that would allow colleges and universities to identify intellectually able students from unknown schools or schools *known* to be academically weak. The driving impulse was to make colleges and universities, and especially prestigious colleges and universities, more open to intellectual talent and to decrease reliance in admissions decisions on family connections and attendance at elite prep schools. Without the S.A.T., or something like it, this aspiration could never have been implemented in an enormous country with no national curriculum and dramatic variations in quality and academic orientation among thousands of local school districts.

So, what kind of psychometric tool is the S.A.T.? At least as it existed into the early 1990s when the antonym portion of the verbal test was eliminated, the verbal portion of the S.A.T. incorporated most of the basic tools of IQ testing. The math portion of the S.A.T. was a more straightforward test of a rather basic level of mathematical competence.

From the 1950s until the mid 1990s the basic design of the S.A.T. remained fundamentally unchanged, which made it useful for intergenerational comparisons of college preparedness. This feature of the S.A.T., as it turns out, also proved embarrassing to the K-12 education industry. Average S.A.T. scores peaked in 1963 and 1964 at 478 on the verbal section of the test and 502 on the mathematics section of the test.[69] After 1964, scores dropped steadily until 1980 when the average scores were 424 on the verbal section and 466 on the mathematics section. Until the mid 1990s verbal scores stayed near their 1980 lows and the mathematics scores crept up a bit to an average of 482.[70]

When confronted with these declining test scores, apologists for the education establishment typically claimed that the S.A.T. results had declined over the years because our schools had become more "democratic" and more students, particularly, minority students, were taking the S.A.T. Consequently, they suggested, the decline in scores did not indicate that schools were doing a worse job. Rather, the decline simply indicated that the pool of students taking the test had become more "inclusive."[71] In other words, the education establishment sought to prevent the public from seeing declining S.A.T. scores as evidence of educational deterioration in government schools by blaming blacks and Hispanics.

One problem with this excuse is that a more careful look at the data – data available to the government school apologists, I might add – indicates clearly that the overall decline in S.A.T. performance by college bound students *is* evidence of a profound deterioration in the educational performance of government schools. In 1972 over 116,000 students scored above 600 on the verbal portion of the S.A.T.[72] Ten years later fewer than 71,000 scored above 600.[73] In 1972, 2,817 students had verbal scores above 750, but only 1,438 did in 1994.[74] If the overall decline in S.A.T. scores from the 1960s into the early 1990s were just a matter of a larger pool of test takers pulling down the average rather than progressive educational failure by government schools, you would not have a startling decline in *absolute* terms in the scores of our most able students. In fact, the staggering magnitude of the collapse in performance by our most able students during this period suggests that they were the group most victimized by the decline in academic standards in government schools. In addition, the S.A.T. verbal scores of non-Hispanic white students didn't rise above 450 (on the pre 1995 test score reporting scale) from the late 1970s into the early 1990s.[75] Moreover, the modest improvement in S.A.T. mathematics scores before the S.A.T. was "re-normed" in 1995 appears to correlate with higher enrollments in algebra and geometry courses.[76] None of this supports the view that the greater "diversity" of test-takers explains the fall in S.A.T. scores.[77] Yes, who takes the S.A.T. can affect the average score. But the decimation of the ranks of the high scorers on the S.A.T. and the overall performance of non-minority test-takers indicates that demographic factors were a very small part of the story of the decline in S.A.T. results.

HIDING THE BALL

In 2003, news stories trumpeted that S.A.T. math scores had reached a 36-year high of 519 and that S.A.T. verbal scores had reached a 19-year high of 507.[78] Does this dramatic improvement in S.A.T. scores, compared to scores in the 1980s and early 1990s, demonstrate that our college bound students are now truly the best prepared ever? Hardly.

In 1995, ETS "re-normed" the scoring of the S.A.T. As a result, a performance that would have earned a verbal score of 428 before the "re-norming" was reported as a 505 after the "re-norming."[79] Overall, the change in testing standards caused roughly a 100-point upward shift in combined S.A.T. verbal and mathematics scores. With respect to the 2003 results, the news stories dutifully reported ETS' claim that the news about the year's "high" S.A.T. scores *did* take into account the 1995 re-norming.

What wasn't reported so widely, however, was that the 2003 S.A.T. was a very different exam from the test ETS administered in the 1960s, 1970s, 1980s, and early 1990s. How so? Since 1994, students have been able to use calculators on the mathematics test, and, in the same year, an antonym test, considered one of the harder sections of the verbal test, was dropped in favor of an easier "vocabulary in context" test.[80] And, just to make sure that no child is left behind, students claiming certain learning disabilities now get extra time on the test.

GOING INTO "OVERTIME"

Of the changes made to the S.A.T. since the mid 1990s, providing extra time to the "disabled" could eventually prove to be one of the most significant factors in rendering invalid comparisons of current and future S.A.T. scores with scores from earlier decades. Prior to September 2003, about 2% of students taking the S.A.T. had taken the test under what ETS refers to as "nonstandard conditions," and those scores were reported to colleges and universities with an asterisk to indicate that the student had received a special accommodation while taking the test.[81] "Nonstandard conditions" can refer to a number of deviations from normal testing protocols. Blind students may take the test in Braille, or have someone read the questions, and get extra time; students without hands taking the test on a computer using a trackball and a pressure pad may get extra time; and so on. Today those entitled to accommodations are not restricted, however, to students with serious physical disabilities. Students with "learning disabilities" also qualify for accommodation. There's the rub.

Under pressure from activists for the disabled, ETS decided in July 2002 to eliminate the asterisk, beginning September 2003.[82] Consequently, those who obtain a suitable "learning disability" diagnosis can get up to 200% of the normal time on the S.A.T., *and college admissions officers will be none the wiser.*[83] Predictably, this has resulted in "diagnosis shopping" by parents who understand that more time can produce a higher S.A.T. score and who can also afford to "buy" a diagnosis. In fact, in the run-up to the first asterisk-free testing season, diagnosis shopping became so flagrant that it was the subject of a September 2002 front-page story in *The New York Times.*[84] The *Times*, however, seems to have missed a major part of the story. ETS' own website makes it clear that part of determining eligibility for "testing accommodations" is whether a student's high school gives him accommodations such as extra-time for his "disability." Given the importance of high SAT scores for sustaining a school district's public support and maintaining the district's property values, school districts – along with doctors, psychologists, and psychiatrists – are going to become the willing allies of parents looking to give Biff and Buffy an extra edge on the S.A.T.

One mildly amusing indication of how well some parents understand the importance of getting extra time on the S.A.T. is that even *before* ETS removed the asterisk from S.A.T. scores, it was discovered that 10% of the students at 20 elite New England preparatory schools were designated in 2000 as "learning disabled" for purposes of taking the S.A.T.[85] As time passes, the ranks of the blind and deaf receiving accommodations will almost certainly be dwarfed, if they aren't already, by students receiving accommodations because of their AD/HD, dyslexia, and whatever other diagnoses will provide some extra time on the S.A.T.

ETS: PLAYING DEFENSE

What is this S.A.T. score manipulation all about?[86] From the perspective of ETS, it seemed to be a matter of preserving its influence and cashflow through the politics of appeasement. Appeasing whom? The K-12 education industry, which wants ETS' help in burying its mistakes, and university leftists, who see the S.A.T. as a barrier to achieving their vision of institutional "diversity" through affirmative action. Consequently, ETS' changes to the S.A.T. have reflected a consistent strategy of deflecting criticism: re-norming helped eliminate the embarrassing optics of low S.A.T. scores; introducing calculators helped mask the destructive effects of ill-conceived K-12 math curricula; eliminating the antonym test helped hide the egregiously poor education government schools are providing blacks and Hispanics; and removing the infamous asterisk both mollified disability activists and had the added benefit of allowing upper-middle class parents and school districts to game the system to provide some additional upward pressure on math and verbal scores.

These changes, however, have also accomplished the *intended result* of rendering meaningless the use of S.A.T. scores for intergenerational comparisons of college preparedness. The post-mid 1990s S.A.T. is simply a different test from the one taken by generations of students in the 60s, 70s, 80s, and early 90s. As a result, the headlines announcing the results of the 2003 S.A.T. should have read: "**No Statistically Significant Changes in 2003 S.A.T. Scores – Effect of Diagnosis Shopping on Averages Not Known.**"

KILLING THE MESSENGER

Of course, the simplest way to dispense with angst over S.A.T. scores is to dispense with the test. That, not surprisingly, is exactly what some of the noblest minds among our highly trained education professionals are proposing. Not satisfied with the last dumbing-down of the S.A.T., academic leftists led by the President of the University of California, Richard Atkinson, Harvard Law School professor Lani Gunier, and Texas Law School professor Gerald Torres have been agitating to eliminate the use of the S.A.T. altogether by deploying the familiar and banal canards that the test is "unfair" and "biased against minorities." [87]

Why must the S.A.T. die? As already noted, the underlying issue for the university left is affirmative action. With affirmative action having been weakened by court decisions, university mandarins, especially at more selective colleges and universities, recognize the S.A.T. as an obstacle to the admission of minorities in accordance with their institutions' *de facto* quotas.[88]

Not wanting to lose its largest customer, the University of California, or, worse, run the risk of losing the substantial revenues that the S.A.T. generates, ETS has announced a "redesign" of the test that will take effect in 2005. As redesigned, questions on verbal analogies will be eliminated from the S.A.T. verbal test, reducing it to a test of reading comprehension.[89] A written essay will also be included as part of the redesign.

Not surprisingly, the "redesign" will move the S.A.T. even further away from being a measure of general academic aptitude toward becoming a simple achievement test that is more "aligned with curricula."[90] This means that the S.A.T., if it survives at all, will no longer serve its original purpose of helping college admissions officers identify bright students who otherwise might be overlooked because they attended unknown or weak schools.[91] Instead, a student's S.A.T. results will tend to reflect the strength of his teachers and the curricula of the schools he attended. Ironically, this may make it easier for the opponents of standardized testing eventually to eliminate the redesigned S.A.T. because disparities in S.A.T. results may then, in fact, more closely reflect disparities in educational resources.

Interestingly, the inclusion of an essay component in the redesigned S.A.T. carries with it the risk of further politicization of the test, school curricula, and college admissions. The essay portion of the test will require students to take a position on an issue and defend it. Obviously, if the topic requires arguing the merits of tonal versus atonal music or discussing the influence of the ancient Greeks on the Romans, the potential for political mischief is slight.

Consider, however, that every college to which a student applies will be given a copy of the student's essay and that students could be asked to write about topics such as abortion, the "environment," affirmative action, capitalism, feminism, or the United Nations. It then becomes clear that this seemingly innocuous requirement could be used to enforce the social and political views of those who grade the test and use the results. Obviously, it is no secret to students applying to competitive colleges and universities, or to their teachers, that those who make admissions decisions have political views far to the left of the mainstream. This is also likely true of those who will grade the essays for ETS. How do you think this would influence the way that social and political subjects are taught in schools and how students would feel they need to respond to the essays? I thought so.

In addition to the redesign, it also appears that the 2003 S.A.T. math scores may reflect efforts behind the scenes at ETS to produce inflated scores that could be considered "good news." How so? The results from the ACT, the second most used college entrance exam in the country and released a week before the S.A.T. results, show *no change at all* in college-bound students' proficiency in math and science over the previous year.[92] In fact, the administrators of the ACT stated that the results show only 26% of college-bound students are prepared for college-level science and that only 40% are prepared for college-level math.[93]

This less than glowing report from the ACT is corroborated by studies examining the number of college students enrolled in remedial math and science courses. According the Michael Kirst, a Stanford University education professor, the ACT results are consistent with his research, which indicates that increases in achievement scores do not reflect generally higher levels of student preparedness for math and science.[94] Speaking of the disparity in the 2003 S.A.T. and ACT math results, an ACT vice president, Cyndie Schemer, put it this way: "I think what we have here is a real issue supported by remedial course work that supports our data."[95] So, do we believe the stories coming out of ETS with headlines like "Math Scores at 35-year High!," or do we believe the data from our colleges and universities concerning the number of students taking "bonehead" math and science? I'll let you decide.

LIARS CAN FIGURE AND THE LAKE WOBEGON EFFECT

The education establishment knows that if the public loses confidence in the government school system the flow of hundreds of billions of dollars a year to government school constituencies may be jeopardized. So, if you are a highly trained education professional, what do you do when there is mounting evidence of educational failure and the public is demanding additional tests of performance to ensure accountability? Cook the numbers!

No doubt you're thinking that this surely cannot be true, but it is. In fact it has been openly discussed for years in the obscure professional journals devoted to the arcana of educational testing. The problem of the manipulation of test results by educators was first forcefully raised by John Cannell, a West Virginia physician. Cannell noticed some statistical anomalies in the reported data for some widely used standardized tests implemented in the 1980s as "accountability systems" in response to public pressure. Cannell found that *no state* reported being below average at the primary level on any of the six major nationally normed commercial tests; 90% of the school districts were reporting that their students were scoring above the national norms (averages) for those tests; and 70% of students tested nationwide were told they were performing above the national average.[96]

This palpably preposterous statistical state of affairs came to be referred to satirically as "the Lake Wobegon Effect" after Garrison Keillor's mythical small town in Minnesota, where "all the women are strong, all the men are good-looking, and *all the children are above average.*" But the practical effect, Cannell concluded, was that "standardized, nationally normed achievement tests give children, parents, schools systems, legislatures, and the press inflated and misleading reports on achievement levels." Do you think that it is an accident that the test scores were inflated?

EVADING ACCOUNTABILITY: TESTING AS A SHELL GAME

The real issue Cannell's findings raised was: how was this happening? Among the reasons suggested were the use of old norms, the repeated use of the same test *form* year after year, excluding children not likely to do well on the test at a higher rate than in the norming studies, and "teaching to the test." While researchers examining this question have politely declined to "pin the tail on the donkey" by flatly saying that most, if not all, the systematic inflation of standardized test scores results from dishonesty within the education establishment, research following Cannell's finding strongly points in that direction.[97]

A 1989 study commissioned by the U.S. Department of Education concluded that "with respect to national averages, districts and states are presenting inflated results and misleading the public."[98] In two studies done in the early 1990s researchers established that when a standardized test that had been in use for several years was replaced by a test designed to test the same content, there was a sharp drop in student scores in the first year followed by gains in subsequent years that eventually returned performance roughly to prior levels.

These results confirmed that the states and school districts were using standardized tests to inflate impressions of student achievement. But what the test scores also strongly suggested was deliberate manipulation of results. Clearly, if the tests are designed to cover the same material and the students know the material at the levels reported, then switching test forms should not result in appreciable changes in test scores. The fact that test results dropped sharply and then rebounded over the next few years strongly suggests that the students "knew" the tests rather than the material *and* that those in charge of the testing at the state and district levels were doing whatever was necessary to bring the test scores back up to acceptable levels.[99]

This sort of manipulation can be facilitated by using the same tests for years. For example, in 1989 Maryland schools were still using the same version of the California Achievement Test that had been used in 1977.[100] After 12 years, it is a virtual certainty that the teachers knew exactly what questions were on the tests and were teaching the questions rather than the skills and knowledge that the test was supposed to measure.

Researchers have also found evidence of score inflation in the administration of the Title I Evaluation and Reporting System (TIERS), which was established by Congress in 1965 to hold accountable the recipients of funds under Title I of the Elementary and Secondary Education Act.[101] More recently, evidence involving at least 14 states has surfaced that NAEP scores are being inflated. The NAEP is often referred to as the "nation's report card" and is used to evaluate the reading, mathematics, and other academic skills of 4th graders, 8th graders, and 12th graders.[102] It is tremendously influential in the world of government K-12 education and was President Clinton's choice for his proposed national assessment.[103]

How are our highly trained education professionals inflating state NAEP scores? The main tactic has been to increase the number of "learning disabled" students excused from taking the test.[104] Obviously, the more students likely to make low scores you can eliminate from the pool of test takers the better the test results will appear. In 1992, the difference between the lowest rate of exclusion of learning disabled students and the highest rate of exclusion was 6%, and no state excluded more than 8% of its students from the NAEP. In 1998, the difference between the highest and lowest rates of exclusion of learning disabled students was 10%, with Louisiana leading the pack by excluding fully 13% of its students from the NAEP.

Kentucky is a good illustration of how this particular educational scam works. Of the states participating in the NAEP in both 1994 and 1998, Kentucky's gains in reading scores were among the highest. Interestingly, in 1998 Kentucky also excluded 2½ times more students from taking the NAEP than it did in 1994 on the basis that they were "learning disabled."[105]

More recently, the press dutifully reported on small gains by 4th graders and 8th graders over their 1996 NAEP results on the 2000 NAEP mathematics test. What wasn't reported was the rate of increase for exclusions, which one expert described as "noticeably larger than on the 1998 NAEP reading tests."[106] Thus, North Carolina, for example, showed gains in the NAEP results, but nearly 10% of the children in North Carolina who *could have taken the test in 1996* were excluded as learning disabled in 2000.[107] Notwithstanding the increase in the rate of exclusions, the scores of 12th graders on the 2000 NAEP mathematics test were actually lower than they were in 1996.[108]

The results from the NAEP 2002 reading test followed the same familiar pattern: 4th graders showing no or minimal improvement (depending on which prior NAEP test results are used as a benchmark); 8th graders showing no improvement; and 12th graders getting worse.[109] Also familiar, though typically not reported to the public, was the wide variation in "exclusion rates" among the states. Moreover, some states had enormous increases in their exclusion rates – Delaware, for example, increased its exclusion rate by 800%.[110] Nevertheless, the board that governs the NAEP has decided not to flag the scores of states whose exclusion rates changed by at least three percentage points from the prior test claiming that they "could not establish any precise point at which changes in exclusion rates would have a significant impact on average test scores."[111] Such evasions about precision aside, it is known that increases in exclusion rates generally correlate with increased state NAEP reading scores, which is hardly surprising, because the excluded students are excluded precisely because our highly trained education professionals know that they will do poorly on the test and drag the average score down.[112]

Perhaps the most hilariously audacious testing swindles based on excluding students from standardized testing occurred in Oklahoma in 1991. Oklahoma law places schools on probation if average student scores on the Iowa Tests of Basic Skills rank in the bottom quarter of schools statewide. In 1991, 121 schools got off probation, but a subsequent investigation found that a number of them had managed to do it by excluding very large numbers of students from the test as "special education" students. In fact, in 20 schools *two-thirds* of the students were exempted from taking the test.[113]

It appears that the "exclusion" gambit is not going to work much longer to cover-up poor performance on the NAEP. This could be why elements of the education industry have begun pushing to change the NAEP so that it will "measure" teamwork and sociability along with knowledge of academic subjects.[114] Presumably, our highly trained education professionals think that parents will be mollified if their children are given "world class" scores in "sociability" even though they can't read or do arithmetic. The one thing that you can be certain our highly trained education professionals won't suggest, however, is the honest administration of nationally-normed, standardized achievement tests to *all children* in government schools.[115] They know how ugly the results would be.

"CREATIVE ACCOUNTING" AND THE TEXAS TAAS "MIRACLE"

States have also proven quite willing to move the goalposts to avoid having to report embarrassing standardized test results. In 2001, for example, the Texas Education Agency announced that Texas students had passed the Texas Assessment of Academic Skills (TAAS) at the highest rate ever. Education bureaucrats, superintendents, principals, and teachers promptly began providing the press with statements such as "Texas students are on a roll," which were obligingly repeated in print and broadcast media, undoubtedly to the delight of credulous parents.[116]

Similar stories regarding TAAS results appeared in 2002, giving parents even more reason to be pleased. Probably few parents realized, however, that the standard for passing the TAAS had been shifting downward. For example, 4th grade students needed to answer correctly eight fewer math questions out of 50 in 2002 than they did in 2000; 6th grade students had to get the right answers on ten fewer math questions out of 56 than they did in 1997; and 8th grade students had to give seven fewer right answers out of 60 math problems than they did in 2000.[117] Moreover, during the period in which TAAS pass rates were reported as rocketing upward SAT and ACT scores actually declined.[118] Fortunately for Texas' highly trained education professionals, no one noticed this anomaly until the TAAS had been "retired."

Unfortunately, even the lowered passing scores on the TAAS were deemed insufficiently helpful by some administrators in the Fort Bend School District. To improve one high school's prospects for obtaining the coveted "Exemplary" rating from the Texas Education Agency, some students who were not likely to score well were prevented from taking the test, and the scores of some low scorers were voided.[119]

Having gotten about as much mileage as possible from the strategy of lowering passing scores on the TAAS to increase passing rates, the Texas subsidiary of the nation's government school industry abandoned the TAAS for something new and really improved: the Texas Assessment of Knowledge and Skills, or "TAKS." Does the TAKS herald a new era of educational accountability in Texas? Not quite.

TEXAS AND TAKS: A PREEMPTIVE SURRENDER

Having been warned by school officials before the test was to be administered for the first time that tens of thousands of their expensively government schooled students would fail the TAKS, the Texas educational establishment *preemptively lowered the passing standards* for the TAKS for all grades.[120] Consequently, under the TAKS, a student can pass the high school exit exam, for example, by answering correctly only 25 of 56 math questions, 23 of 50 social studies questions, 41 of 73 reading and English questions, and 27 of 55 science questions.[121]

Even these low standards for the TAKS resulted in protests and expressions of "concern" from educrats. For example, Mike Moses, the superintendent of Dallas Independent School District and a former Texas Education Commissioner, proposed in early 2003 that the passing scores be "re-examined" (read "lowered") after the spring test results were in.[122] In fact, a report on TAKS by his school district argued that TAKS is too "difficult."[123] But what "difficult" really appears to mean to Moses and his colleagues is that, unless the passing scores are lowered even more, TAKS will further expose what a bad job Texas government schools are doing in educating minority children.[124]

Perhaps Texas needs a 12-step program for "test result manipulation recidivists." In any event, be on the watch for future newspaper headlines and television news stories breathlessly reporting how Texas children are passing the TAKS at the "highest rates ever!"

LOW TEST SCORES? NEVER MIND

Another strategy for burying inconveniently low test scores is to blame the test and throw the test results out. This is exactly what North Carolina's Board of Education did with the 2002 results for a statewide writing test for 4th graders and 7th graders.[125] The students, it appears, were asked to "write about a time you had a great day in school." 53% of the 4th graders and 37% of the 7th graders failed the exam, and, as a result, the Board of Education declared that the dismal scores were the result of *the exam not being written clearly enough and an increase in time for writing*. Of course, this last excuse makes no sense, because there is nothing particularly unclear about the topic and increased writing time was given to improve scores in the first place. Apparently no excuse for abject educational failure is too shameless for North Carolina's Board of Education.

New York followed the same path as North Carolina when it threw out the results of the June 2003 Regents' math exam. Historically, high school graduates in New York State have received either a Regents' diploma, which is viewed as a college prep degree, or a local diploma. To earn a Regents' diploma students must score 65 or above on the Regents' exams, which are state-wide standardized tests. A score of 55 or better is typically required to get a local diploma.

When roughly 63% of the students taking the June 2003 Math A Regents' exam failed, howls of execration could be heard across the state.[126] An "independent panel" of experts was promptly convened to investigate. Subsequently, the state Education Commissioner declared that there were "anomalies" in the 2003 exam and ordered the scores revised so that students scoring as low as 39 would be deemed to have achieved a score of 55.[127] But apparently this was not enough to bring the pass rates up to a politically acceptable level. As a result, schools were allowed to substitute coursework grades for Regents' exam scores.[128] Yet, even this retreat from attempting to enforce accountability proved insufficient to calm the political waters. As a result, New York State's education commissioner finally set aside the Math A exam results and declared that he would reduce the failure rate on the Regents' physics exam.[129] In addition, it appears that school districts will be allowed to use 55 as a passing score for the next two years.[130]

Anomalies? Well, according to the panel, the exam's lack of trigonometry questions was unfair to students who knew trigonometry *and* the fact that there were three questions involving the Pythagorean Theorem was unfair to students who didn't understand the Pythagorean Theorem.[131] How adding trigonometry questions would help juniors and seniors unconversant with the Pythagorean Theorem was left unexplained, as well as why it was unfair to expect high school graduates to be able to apply a simple and absolutely fundamental mathematical formula. But, of course, the "expert panel" and its findings were simply providing cover for what was really going on. The truth about the decision to jettison the Regents Math A Results was, perhaps inadvertently, uttered by Education Department spokesman Jonathan Burman in an interview:[132] "It was changed, really, in response to the calls we had gotten.... We just wanted to respond in the fairest way to the students."

These incidents from New York and North Carolina illustrate the real moral of the story: explanations don't need to make much sense as long as the evidence of educational failure is buried.

AND NOW, THE REST OF THE TESTING STORY

Now that we know that our highly trained education professionals are cooking the numbers, what does it look like from the perspective of the classroom? This matters because millions of children are entrusted daily to government schools for instruction. Part of what they learn is through classroom teaching, but they also learn from the example of teachers and administrators. If teachers and administrators are dishonest in how they handle standardized testing, there is a substantial risk that the children know it and are being lead to believe that dishonesty is just another way of getting by. So, how visible is the institutional dishonesty of government schools to schoolchildren? When we send them to government schools are they seeing or, worse, being made accomplices in a fraud? Unfortunately, the news isn't good.

On December 8, 1999, *The New York Times* broke a story reporting an epidemic of cheating on standardized reading and math tests in New York City schools. The cheating took place in 32 schools over a five-year period. It also involved misconduct by more teachers, students, and schools than any other reported cheating scandal in recent history.[133] As reported by the *Times*, teachers would give students the correct answers prior to taking the test, allowed students to correct answers in test booklets after telling them which answers were wrong, and, in some cases, changed wrong answers themselves. In one school, this resulted in reading test scores improving by 22%. Why were teachers and other school employees doing this? According to an investigator for the New York City schools, the test results were important to careers and reputations, and the teachers wanted to make it appear "that they were doing a good job." The investigator also alleged that the school board's Office of Investigative Services had failed "to expose or punish the cheating."

On February 25, 2000, *The New York Times* ran a story on a similar scandal in Massachusetts.[134] According to the *Times*, at least 19 Massachusetts schools had become embroiled in cheating on statewide exams. For example, "educators" apparently were telling students to change their answers and were giving students two days to complete required essays when they were supposed to have only one. One teacher even e-mailed copies of the test questions to teachers in other schools with a note acknowledging that passing the questions along was "probably illegal." Moreover, this involved some prestigious schools, not just low-performing schools or troubled urban schools. In the finest bureaucratic tradition, however, state officials did not describe what had happened as "cheating." Instead, the schools were charged with "administration of the test under possible nonstandard conditions."

In Memphis, a highly regarded principal retired in 2003. Why? She was thought to have turned her elementary school in a tough neighborhood into a success story, at least as measured by the Tennessee Comprehensive Assessment Program.[135] It turned out, however, that her school's remarkable success was based on some familiar short cuts – falsifying answer sheets and making sure that weak students didn't take the test.[136] Her pursuit of "excellence" even extended to locking classroom doors and refusing to let inspectors into the school while the students were being tested.[137] Meanwhile, Memphis school officials assured everyone that this is just an isolated incident. In fact, they are so confident that it is an isolated incident that, according to the Memphis schools' spokesman, the school system will not be investigating test-taking procedures at other schools.[138]

In Silver Springs, Maryland, five teachers were caught in 2001 violating "testing protocols" for a mandated standardized math test. Apparently, the teachers didn't realize that there was something wrong with photocopying and distributing the test so that it could be used to "prepare" their classes, including using questions from the test in class and in homework assignments.[139] When the teachers went to the school district headquarters to explain themselves, they were cheered by a group of *students and parents* when they went in.[140] Undoubtedly, the students and parents wanted the teachers to know that they, unlike the narrow-minded sorts who were insisting on honest testing, understood that the teachers were simply trying to bolster their students' self-esteem.

Similar testing misconduct has been reported in suburban Potomac, Maryland, and in Columbus, Ohio.[141] Incredibly, the Austin, Texas, school district managed to get itself indicted for criminal tampering with standardized testing in order to inflate test scores.[142] The school district avoided a criminal trial by accepting a deal that resulted in "deferred prosecution." Presumably, the curriculum in Austin has now expanded beyond reading, writing, and arithmetic to include plea-bargaining.

THE CHICAGO WAY

In 2002, Chicago teachers and principals were caught cheating in the administration of the Iowa Tests of Basic Skills.[143] It appears that these highly trained education professionals were giving students tips during the test, erasing incorrect answers, filling in answers, and pointing out the right answers.[144] As the director of DePaul University's Center for Urban Education, Barbara Radner, observed after the cheating was reported: "This is blatant. It's amazing.... Pointing out answers to kids – its teaching the kids a really bad lesson."[145] Precisely.

What is really interesting about this instance of academic larceny is that it was uncovered, in part, as a result of the application of statistical methods developed by a University of Chicago economics professor, Steven Levitt. Overall, Professor Levitt's statistical methods indicate that there was cheating on the Iowa tests in roughly 2000 Chicago government school classrooms per year between 1993 and 2000.[146] As you might suspect, education officials around the country have not been stampeding to Dr. Levitt's office to request a statistical audit to confirm the integrity of the accountability tests in their districts and states.[147]

While these are just some of the recently reported cases of blatant cheating by teachers and administrators, this is scarcely a new phenomenon. In 1992 *U.S. News & World Report* published an investigative report on widespread cheating in the administration of standardized tests. In that report the authors revealed: [148]

- In Illinois the principal of a school touted as "one of the nation's outstanding elementary schools" was found to have told teachers to "doctor" standardized test scores to improve the school's image.
- In Greenville, South Carolina, a teacher was fired for inflating test scores by giving her students answers to a standardized test.
- In Trenton, New Jersey, a 1989 administration of the California Achievement Test showed that 12 of 17 elementary schools met New Jersey's minimum performance standards for 3rd graders. The following year the test was given under state supervision because of charges of "test tampering," and only 3 elementary schools satisfied the state's standards.
- In 1989 widespread cheating in the administration of the California Achievement Test was revealed by a survey of 3,000 teachers in Memphis, Tennessee. One teacher had even posted the correct test answers on the walls of her classroom.
- In 1990 a teacher in Winston-Salem, North Carolina, was suspended for giving the students in her English classes a list of spelling words that just happened to be on the California Achievement Test that they subsequently took.
- Between 1986 and 1990 the principal of a Staten Island elementary school changed his students' incorrect answers on standardized reading tests so that his school had the highest reading scores in the borough. The principal's cheating came to light when a local paper reported that, a few years prior to the discovery of the fraud, a child with learning disabilities had scored in the 90th percentile on a reading test. The child's mother twice raised questions about the inflated test score *with the school board*, but was ignored.

An unspeakably ugly classroom reality underlies the abuses documented in these studies and reports. For the education industry, however, it is just a matter of doing what they know is necessary to maintain and increase their funding and keep their jobs. Everything else is secondary.

If you think that these are isolated incidents, invest a little time searching the internet for stories on cheating by teachers. You will be surprised.

TAKE JOHNNY, JUST LEAVE HIS TEST SCORES

In the never-ending quest to avoid educational accountability, Ohio, Missouri, Iowa, and perhaps some other states allow neighborhood schools to use test scores of children *who don't attend those schools* to inflate the neighborhood schools' performance reports under the No Child Left Behind Act.[149] Why? Would it surprise you that it is to *protect* academically gifted students from their neighborhood schools? The story is actually rather simple.

Many districts have programs for academically gifted students that allow those students to attend special schools with curricula designed to provide them with more challenging work. Not surprisingly, these students have appreciably higher test scores than average. The No Child Left Behind Act sets performance benchmarks for schools, and if the benchmarks are not met, parents are given the option of transferring their children to schools that do meet the benchmarks. Not surprisingly, failure to meet these minimal standards can also adversely affect the careers of administrators and teachers.

To make their schools look better, administrators and teachers in neighborhood schools began, in some cases, to refuse to nominate talented children for programs for the academically gifted. In other cases, the administrators and teachers actively discouraged parents from putting their children in those programs. In fact, the problem was so severe at the local level that some advocates of special programs for gifted children went along with the test score deception because, according to Maria Cougras Pappas, a former supervisor of programs for gifted children, they believed that, if the plan for inflating neighborhood schools' test scores was not adopted, "local administrators and boards of education would begin to dismantle programs for gifted education..."[150] Consequently, *to prevent neighborhood schools from "sabotaging" the education of academically gifted children*, states such as Ohio implemented a rule that allowed neighborhood schools to count in their performance reports *the test scores of children they were not educating.*[151]

The problem with this, of course, is that the No Child Left Behind Act's performance reporting is supposed to let parents know how well schools teach the children that actually attend them. Including the scores of children who are educated elsewhere is simply a form of fraud on parents. It may be illegal under federal law as well. When informed of this interesting exercise in test score manipulation, Eugene Hickok, an acting deputy secretary in the Education Department, remarked that the practice may violate the No Child Left Behind Act. More to the point, however, Deputy Secretary Hickok observed that, "'It sounds as if the folks who want to keep gifted kids in the neighborhood schools 'are putting the system ahead of the kids.'"[152] Just so.

THE GOVERNMENT SCHOOLS' "ENRON": THE "CORRUPTION OF INDICATORS"

While parents and other members of the public have attempted to require accountability from the government education leviathan through testing, our highly trained education professionals have been aggressively devising ways of concealing their failure. As Robert L. Linn, a researcher in the field of educational assessment, has euphemistically put it, "Corruption of indicators is a continuing problem where tests are used for accountability or other high stakes purposes."[153] In a 1999 article discussing the widespread problem of school employees' and students' intentional and unintentional violations of standardized testing protocols, a Rand Corporation senior research analyst, Stephen P. Klein, addressed the situation more

MY CHILD IS ON THE HONOR ROLL 161

bluntly: "There's no testing program I know of that is immune to the problem....We spend a lot of money on these tests, and it's like throwing money away because you can't ensure the validity of the test scores....When tests are given under controlled circumstances, and you have security, you get radically different results."[154] Well, of course, but those are precisely the kinds of results your highly trained education professionals don't want known.

Unfortunately, this is no mere technical problem with testing in government schools; the purpose of this "corruption of indicators" is simply to deceive. But far worse than "corrupting the indicators" is the fact that our highly trained education professionals are corrupting the children entrusted to them with their dishonest examples and by encouraging them to participate in defrauding their parents and the public.

We began our discussion of the dishonesty of the education industry by looking at what has been done with the S.A.T., the Lake Wobegon Effect, and research on how scores are being deceptively inflated in both the TIERS tests and the NAEP. We then looked at two concrete examples at the state level showing how Texas and North Carolina educrats have gone about deceiving parents and the public concerning how government schools are doing. Finally, we have tried to put a face on the statistics by providing some examples of what the practices reflected in the systematic data look like "on the ground" – that is, in schools and the classroom.

To some, it may be hard to believe the lengths to which the education industry will go to evade being held accountable for its performance. As will be pointed out in Chapter Five, however, the motivation for evading accountability becomes clearer once you understand that in reality the prime concerns of the education industry are who gets how much of the roughly $500 billion spent on K-12 education each year and what ideological agendas government schools will serve.

As is also obvious, spending $500 billion or so annually cultivates a lot of friends. That is why local, state, and national media, government agencies, colleges and universities, and other institutions for the most part simply find it expedient to ignore the proverbial elephant-in-the-living-room of the education industry's corruption of educational indicators and children – a scandal that dwarfs the business accounting scandals of recent years. Doubtless, Enron's executives and accountants would have been profoundly grateful if their corruption of public accounting indicators had enjoyed a similar lack of sustained scrutiny and real accountability.

A MODEST PROPOSAL

Because of the technical nature of the testing controversy and of the high stakes the education industry faces when standardized testing seeks to hold it accountable, the education industry never lacks for excuses, apologists, and explanations for why evidence of failure is really evidence of success. To cut through smog, here's a modest proposal for settling how government school students are doing academically: (1) for the next two administrations of the S.A.T. give college-bound seniors versions of the tests used in the 1960s under precisely the same rules relating to administration of the test and accommodations used then and under strict security provided by third party administrators, and (2) require every standardized achievement test given in grades K-12 to be strictly administered by third parties (rather than teachers and school administrators, as is currently the case) and under strict rules designed by third parties limiting exclusions.[155] Rest assured, there won't be any takers. They don't want you to know.

SELF-ESTEEM AND MR. ROGERS' CLASSROOM

What the government education industry lacks in academic effectiveness it seems to try to make up with "innovation." Over fifty years ago the phonetic approach to reading gave way to "whole language." More recently "invented spelling" – making up your own way of spelling words – has been making headway in schools of education and some government schools opposed to traditional spelling (you know, the kind of spelling in which you are expected to get it right).

The consequences of these sorts of innovations are all too apparent in the collapse of American literacy. They also account to a very large extent for the high level of dissatisfaction among employers and professors with the writing, grammar, and spelling skills of today's high school graduates.

In the sixties regular mathematics gave way to the "new math," and in recent years something variously called "constructivist," "whole," "Chicago," "fuzzy," or "connected" math has become the latest fad pushed by our highly trained education professionals.[156] "Constructivist math" rejects traditional methods of teaching mathematics in favor of having children discover their own ways of solving mathematical problems while working individually or in groups.

This ultimately involves the preposterous assumption that a child is capable of reinventing 2,400 years of mathematics on his own. This is one of the reasons the use of calculators has proliferated in the lower grades – children actually don't know how to do simple arithmetic. Perhaps the most insidious part of constructivist math, however, is that it teaches children that correct solutions to mathematics problems are not important.

A variation on constructivist math is known as "rainforest math" because it has more to do with indoctrinating children with politically correct beliefs than with teaching mathematics. An infamous rainforest math algebra textbook is full of irrelevant material – diatribes on environmental matters, pictures of former President Clinton, and poetry by Maya Angelou, to name a few. One mother whose daughter was taking rainforest algebra discovered that her daughter, who had received an "A" in beginning algebra, didn't understand "that what you do to one side of an equation you must do to the other."[157]

The effect on students of rainforest, whole math, and similar innovations in math curricula is entirely predictable. In 1998, for example, the Texas Education agency reported poor statewide algebra scores after the adoption of a rainforest algebra text that gave information about jalapeno recipes, Vietnam War protests, and environmentalism priority over mathematical principles.[158] Similarly, math test scores fell markedly in Palo Alto, California, after the adoption of a whole math text in 1995.[159] Evidently incapable of learning from the experience of others, New York mayor Michael Bloomberg and his school's chief, Joel Klein, have forced this sort of failed math curriculum (as well as a reading program that is not phonics-based) on almost all New York City schools.[160] It is heart-breaking to think of the damage this is going to do to the futures of many tens of thousands of inner-city students.

Endless articles and books have been written about the harm done to American education by the hothouse pedagogical theories produced by schools of education. Yet, no more profound change has occurred in government schools than the transformation of the government school from being primarily a place of academic learning to an institution whose primary mission appears to be the delivery of psychotherapy.

THE DOCTOR IS IN

While behavioral psychologists such as Watson, Thorndike, and Skinner and, to a lesser degree, psychologists influenced by Freud's psychoanalytic theories have all left their marks on government schools, today the "third force" humanistic psychology birthed by Carl Rogers, Rollo May, and Abraham Maslow permeates government schools. The "third force" humanistic psychology that developed out of the work of Carl Rogers, Rollo May, and Abraham Maslow dominate government schools. Rogers' nondirective therapy and values clarification methods, for example, are reflected in the teaching methods used in many behavioral programs in government schools.[161] Similarly, Maslow's "hierarchy of needs" and "self-actualization" theories are often incorporated in government school curricula.[162]

Humanistic psychology views man's nature as inherently good and as containing within it virtually limitless potential. In the sixties the demand for "relevance" that swept the educational establishment was a direct outgrowth of Rogers' view that students should not have to learn, and schools shouldn't attempt to teach, things the student doesn't see as relevant. This, of course, introduced a radical subjectivity into the educational enterprise: if something doesn't seem important to a student, then he shouldn't be asked to learn it. Moreover, because relevance is relative to an individual's interests and knowledge, the Rogerian focus on "relevance" subverted the very notion of a common curriculum. It also tended to limit learning to the things that a child with his necessarily limited levels of knowledge and experience could understand are relevant to his future. This point of view survives today in American education in many subtle ways, but the most overt mark of Rogers' influence in the American classroom today is the odd obsession educators have with students' self-esteem.[163]

Among the more influential beliefs of humanistic psychologists is that teachers need to "humanize" the classroom and help students build their self-esteem. This view has gained widespread acceptance in schools with some attention-getting results. A University of Michigan psychologist studied the self-confidence of American, Japanese, Taiwanese, and Chinese students in their mathematics abilities. Not surprisingly, he found that the American students ranked far ahead of the others in self-confidence, but the American students' actual performance in mathematics was far behind.[164]

In his book, *Inside American Education*, Thomas Sowell examines how American students suffer from an excess of self-esteem. Sowell first takes up the results of an international study in which the mathematics skills of 13-year-olds were compared.[165] Korean students came in first and, not surprisingly, the American students came in last. Ironically, a survey done in connection with the study found that 23% of the Korean students, and an astonishing 68% of the American students, responded that they thought they were good at mathematics. Later in his examination of the inflated self-esteem of American students, Sowell recounts the following exchange between a reporter and a graduating senior at a Los Angeles high school, described as "the smartest student in his class," about what the student had learned in school concerning the Vietnam War:

> I learned that in the Vietnam War, North and South Korea fought against each other, and then there was a truce at the 38th parallel, and that Eisenhower had something to do with it.

The reporter asked:

Would it bother you to know that the things you learned were wrong?

The answer was:

Not really. Because *what we really learned* from Miss Silver was that we were worth listening to, that we could express ourselves and that an adult would listen, even if we were wrong. That's why Miss Silver will always be our favorite teacher. She made us feel like we mattered, like we were important. [166] [Emphasis added.]

This exchange reflects how humanistic psychology leads to the triumph of "unconditional academic love" over "academic tough love." No judgments; no accountability to facts; just acceptance. Oh, and of course, no learning.

Another of the ways that the self-esteem fad has been legitimized in schools is through the work of academic psychologists such as Harvard University's Howard Gardner. In his influential book *Frames of Mind*, Gardner argued we have "multiple intelligences" and that academic tests only measure two of them, linguistic intelligence and logical-mathematical intelligence. Musical, spatial, bodily kinesthenic, intrapersonal, and interpersonal intelligences, the advocates claim, are ignored. Thus, some educators argue that schools make invidious distinctions among children and damage their self-esteem because the tests and curricula don't equally value all intelligences. Moreover, Gardner's theory has been used to argue that deteriorating performance on tests is not the fault of students or teachers, but rather a reflection of a flawed system of measurement.

Curricula that have been revised to reflect Gardner's theories attempt to devote equal time to all of the intelligences. So, what does a teacher do in a curriculum revised to reflect Gardner's theory? One suggested activity is to have children stand in a circle and toss a ball to each other while paying each other compliments. After this strenuous exercise the children would write songs about the experience, play charades, and talk.[167] Meanwhile, children in Japan are learning algebra, and Chinese high school students are earning 800s on the Graduate Record Exam.[168]

Still, one might ask whether self-esteem programs somehow work, their palpable absurdity notwithstanding. The answer to this question was available, even to the public, as early as 1990. An article published in the April 1, 1990 *U.S. News & World Report* noted that there is virtually no research indicating that self-esteem programs work.[169] With respect to academic learning, *U.S. News & World Report's* research led it to conclude that self-esteem programs actually undermine education:

> When the self-esteem movement takes over a school, teachers are under pressure to accept every child as is. To keep children feeling good about themselves, you must avoid all criticism and almost any challenge that could conceivably end in failure. In practice, this means that every child is treated like a fragile therapy consumer in constant need of an ego boost. Difficult work is out of the question, and standards get lowered in school after school. Even tests become problematic because someone might fail them. [170]

In an article published two years later, *Newsweek* similarly noted the firm hold that the self-esteem industry had in schools and the problems it was causing. Moreover, *Newsweek* noted that there had been roughly 10,000 scientific studies of self-esteem and that, nonetheless, "there isn't even agreement on what it is."[171]

More recently, a study commissioned by the Joseph Rowntree Foundation, Britain's largest independent social research and development charity, has turned the "self-esteem" debate on its head. The conventional line regarding low self-esteem is that it's a risk factor for all sorts of social pathologies ranging from alcohol abuse to violence. It turns out, however, that *it is people with high self-esteem, rather than those with low self-esteem,* who are more likely to drink too much, drive too fast, and otherwise pose a higher risk of injury to others. According to the author of the study, the belief that raising self-esteem will reduce social problems is "threatening to become the psychotherapeutic equivalent of snake oil."[172]

The final irony of the strange tale of the influence of humanistic psychology on government schools is that both Rogers and Maslow came to have reservations concerning the moral consequences to *adults* resulting from the application of their theories.[173] Moreover, they both eventually *repudiated* the use of their theories with children. In fact, Maslow explicitly criticized schools for providing children with what he termed "unearned applause."[174] Nevertheless, the second thoughts and reservations of the high priests of "self-esteem" have done little to restrain their acolytes.

The Synthesis of Self-Esteem and Political Correctness

Once they become a part of the mainstream education industry, foolish educational theories never seem to die. Instead, they are repackaged or mutate into new forms. While programs reflecting "self-esteem" and other concepts of humanistic psychology are still present in government schools, theories asserting the importance of self-esteem have found a vigorous new life among multicultural education theorists.

One example is the 1994 controversy over proposed national standards for teaching history in 5th through 12th grades. The proposed history standards were produced with over $2 million from the National Endowment for the Humanities and the Department of Education by a committee of 28 scholars, teachers, and advocates of history education and was overseen by Gary Nash, a professor of history at U.C.L.A.[175] This project began in 1988 and resulted in a set of proposed national teaching standards that were made public in 1994.

Because radical leftists dominate American colleges and universities, much of what has passed for historical scholarship over the last two or three decades has been largely a neo-Marxist multicultural rant about race, class, and gender. It is hardly surprising, then, that the committee's standards were controversial. The standards themselves actually consisted of general learning goals and examples of teaching activities for achieving the standards. While the general learning goals (*e.g.*, differentiating between historical facts and interpretations, considering multiple perspectives, evaluating debates among historians, etc.) were for the most part unobjectionable, the teaching examples, which as a practical matter would determine how the history standards would actually be taught in classrooms, were another story. As Lynne Cheney, a leading critic of the proposed standards, put it:

> Imagine an outline for the teaching of American history in which George Washington makes only a fleeting appearance and is never described as our first president. Or in which the founding of the Sierra Club and the National Organization of Women are considered noteworthy events, but the first gathering of the U.S. Congress is not. [176]

The standards also had a number of other peculiarities.[177] For example, while the Ku Klux Klan was mentioned 22 times, the Constitution was mentioned only once. Harriet Tubman was mentioned 6 times, while Ulysses S. Grant was mentioned only once and Robert E. Lee wasn't mentioned at all. Also missing were Alexander Graham Bell, Thomas Edison, Albert Einstein, Jonas Salk, and the Wright brothers. Mansa Musa, a 14th-century West African king, did make the cut, as did a recommendation that children study the architecture, skills, labor systems, and agriculture of the Aztecs (but not, of course, their cannibalism and practice of human sacrifice). Similarly, as an activity for studying the early period of American history it was suggested that students understand the elements of Native American's religions, but no similar suggestion was made concerning the Europeans' religions. These and many more aspects of the history standards created such a controversy that the United States Senate passed a resolution disapproving the standards by a vote of 99-1.

This ultimately forced a revision that reduced, but did not eliminate, the history standards' leftward slant. Further, the National Council for Social Studies, the national organization for teachers of history, political science, and other social sciences that was involved in creating the history standards, has continued its war against any meaningful history instruction in schools.[178] In fact, the NCSS has been so successful in eliminating American history in colleges and universities that the few states that still have rigorous K-12 history standards are having trouble finding teachers who can implement them because, as Kay Hymowitz, a senior fellow at the Manhattan Institute, has put it: "Many young people entering teaching today went to schools where, thanks in part to the influence of the NCSS, their experience with American history was largely limited to reports on Sojourner Truth, dioramas of Navajo villages, and 'reasoned judgments about specific cultural responses to persistent human issues.'"[179]

While the history standards may simply seem like another example of eccentricity by a group of educators, the standards are a manifestation of the multiculturalist orthodoxy reigning in our educational institutions. A key tenet of the multiculturalist faith is that all cultures are of equal value and that one of the sins of American society (and the West generally) is that its history and cultural norms have "privileged" whites, particularly white males, thereby damaging the self-esteem of minorities.

Thus, the proposed history standards, through the recommended teaching activities and examples, were in part a therapeutic effort intended to deflate what the multicultural left considers to be the excessive self-esteem of some groups while raising the self-esteem of others.

"Afrocentric curricula" present another egregious example of how the emphasis on raising the "self-esteem" of students has led to the falsification of history in the classroom.[180] Beginning in the 1980s government schools in urban areas such as Atlanta, Cleveland, Detroit, Kansas City, Milwaukee, Oakland, Washington, and Portland, Oregon, began adopting history curricula intended to boost the self-esteem of black students and thereby keep them in school. These curricula claim, for example, that Socrates was black, Aristotle got his philosophy from studying at the library at Alexandria, Egypt (impossible because Aristotle died twenty-five years before the library was built), ancient Egyptians used gliders for "expeditions and recreation," and the Dogon tribe of Mali discovered the white dwarf star Sirius B 700 years ago (only if they had also invented telescopes 700 years ago, because Sirius B is only visible under good conditions with a five inch telescope).[181]

These and other claims made by the Afrocentrists range from the unsupported to the absurd. Nevertheless, in many school districts Afrocentric curricula are well entrenched and aggressively defended. In Milwaukee, for example, Leon Todd, a black member of the school board, sought to prohibit the use of Afrocentric curricular materials in the district's African-American-immersion schools which taught, among other things, the beliefs of African religious cults and that ancient Egyptians (whom the Afrocentrists claim were black) used to *levitate* around the Pyramids.[182] He also objected to the school district's practice of hiring teachers primarily because of their commitment to African culture. According to Mr. Todd, teaching fiction as history "leads to the miseducation of children of color."[183] Unfortunately, Mr. Todd's concerns were not well received. His resolutions were not passed by the board; angry parents threatened him with a recall; and, just in case the point hadn't been fully made, his home was firebombed.[184]

In Texas, an alleged fear of alienating Mexican and Mexican-American students has led government school bureaucrats to attempt to push the story of the Texas revolution to the back of textbooks, if not to virtually eliminate it.[185] Apparently, the battle cry for many of Texas' highly trained education professionals is "Forget the Alamo."

Of course, the use of self-esteem to justify the adoption or modification of curricula in government schools is not limited to multicultural historians and Afrocentrists. Feminists and homosexual activists have successfully deployed similar "self-esteem" based arguments in the pursuit of their curricular agendas.

Others with leftist agendas, environmentalists for example, are hijacking classroom time.[186] Even "hip hop" music is beginning to show up in classrooms. Doubtless, many California parents and taxpayers would be surprised to find that some high school students are spending time studying Tupac Shakur's "Shorty Wanna Be a Thug" and pondering the rich poetic meaning of such lyrics as "Blaze up, gettin' with hos through my pager."[187]

More insidious is the wholesale elimination of words from textbooks and other materials to reflect the ideological enthusiasms of the politically correct left. Thus, words and phrases such as "Founding Fathers," "snowman," "lumberjack," "senior citizen," "dialect," "senile," "hut," and "fraternize," (to name but a few), are being systematically taken out of educational materials.[188] In New York, a recent examination of ten Regent's English tests revealed that 19 of 30 passages by prominent authors used in the tests had been subjected to politically correct censorship. An excerpt from a work by Nobel Prize winner Isaac Bashevis Singer, for example, was edited to remove all references to Judaism, even though Mr. Singer's fiction is about Jews and Jewish culture.[189] The works of other authors were also edited in ways to remove any reference to race, religion, ethnicity, and other topics somehow deemed sensitive by the political commissars in charge of the test.

This rampant political manipulation of textbooks and tests has been thoroughly examined by Diane Ravitch, a well-known education scholar, in *The Language Police: How Pressure Groups Restrict What Students Learn*. In 2003, Ravitch wrote in *The Wall Street Journal* of some additional examples that have come to her attention:

> A freelance writer sent me the "bias guidelines" for a major publisher of texts and tests.... All lessons, test questions, and illustrations must reflect the following ratios: 50-50 male-female; 45% Caucasian; 25% African American; 22% Hispanic American; 5% Asian American; and 3% "persons with disabilities." These figures do not total 100%, nor do they represent actual census numbers, but the principle of representation is well understood by writers and editors.... The specifications for photographs I have learned, are exquisitely detailed. Men and boys must not be larger than women and girls. Asians must not appear shorter than non-Asians... nor should anyone be depicted eating with the left hand. Things to avoid: holiday

decorations and scenes in which a church or a bar appears in the background. [190]

While some of this is simply silly, the net result academically is continuing deterioration of curricular standards. Moreover, it is further evidence of the Orwellian lengths to which those in the education establishment will go to impose their ideological neuroses on our children and our culture.[191]

A Generation of Hewers of Wood and Drawers of Water?

The majority of parents, Christian and otherwise, with children in government schools seem to be largely unaware of what is being done to their children academically. While they may have some doubts about *other* schools, most believe that *their* schools are doing a good job. After all, the schools are telling them so and handing out bumper stickers and yard signs trumpeting what, on inspection, are likely to be meretricious achievements. Their children, on the whole, are happy academically because nothing much is asked of them and failure is seldom encountered. The prospects for their future, however, are unsettling. They will inherit a society whose continuance, both economically and politically, will demand levels of skills and knowledge and traits of character that they are unlikely to have. While it is hard to know exactly what the consequences will be if nothing is done, it is a virtual certainty that there will not be much of a market in 2020 for graduates with majors in self-esteem from Mr. Rogers' classroom. We would also do well to remember Jefferson's admonition that "If a nation expects to be ignorant and free, in a state of civilization, it expects what never was and never will be."[192]

FOUR

A BLACKBOARD JUNGLE

"The way of the wicked is as darkness...."
Proverbs 4:19

Do you avoid places at work because you are afraid of being beaten-up? Does your employer want to drug you to improve your performance and make you easier to manage? Will your employer suspend you from your job if he discovers you have Midol in your purse? You are probably thinking that these questions are absurd, and that you wouldn't tolerate working at such a place. Good. But if these conditions are unacceptable to adults, why would the overwhelming majority of Christian parents force their children to spend the equivalent of a work day five days a week in a place where they are subjected to these problems – and worse? Let's take a brief look at government schools from a child's point of view.

What does having to attend a government school look like from the perspective of the Christian child, or any child for that matter? For those who care to remember, school dominates a child's daily life like no other institution. In the course of twelve years, the average child is likely to spend well over 15,000 hours in school, traveling to and from school, doing homework, and participating in school activities before and after school. Moreover, every child knows that teachers and administrators have an enormous influence over his future through grades, recommendations, and other information that they accumulate and pass on. Small wonder that reformers of all stripes have recognized that schools provide the Archimedean point for transforming a society through the extraordinary influence they exert over the minds and characters of children.

Today, government schools, like prisons, seek comprehensive control over their charges, in part to suppress violence and disorder, and in part because those who control government schools see themselves as agents of social change. In a very real sense, children are at the bottom of the government school food chain; they are not the actors, but the acted-upon. They are compelled to be there, and they have nearly nothing to say over the terms or conditions of their institutionalization.

A child's concerns about attending a government school today are likely to be mundane and personal: "Am I safe?" "Does the school treat me fairly?" "Is it a hostile place?" Many children in government schools live with these worries every day. After taking a look at some of the conditions they confront daily in government schools, ask yourself whether these burdens are properly borne by our children.

THE NEW WILD WEST

While school shootings at Columbine High School (Littleton, Colorado), Springfield High School (Springfield, Oregon), Westside Middle School (Jonesboro, Arkansas), and elsewhere symbolize school violence in the minds of many parents, these incidents are only part of the much larger problem of crime within government schools. In a sense, these high profile mass-shootings in government schools may even be a distraction from the deeper problem: a government school culture of chronic violence, crime, and disorder.

As with so many aspects of government school dysfunction, the levels of crime and other forms of destructive behavior we see today have risen over the last fifty years or so. How much have things changed? Consider what *U.S. News & World Report* tells us teachers reported as the top school disciplinary problems in 1940 versus 1990:[1]

1940	1990
Talking-out-of-turn	Assault
Chewing gum	Robbery
Making Noise	Drug Abuse
Running in the halls	Alcohol Abuse
Cutting in line	Pregnancy
Dress-code violations	Suicide

To adults these changes are startling, but somewhat remote. For children, however, this is what they live with daily. So how bad is it?

AND NOW FOR A LITTLE QUIZ

Here's the question: Persons institutionalized in a large North American institution suffered serious violent crimes (*e.g.*, rape, sexual assault, aggravated assault) at a rate of approximately 12 per 1000.[2] Was the institution the U.S. federal prison system for the year ending June 30, 1990, the Canadian prison system for the year ending December 31, 1990, or urban American government middle schools and high schools in 1997? If you answered "urban American government middle schools and high schools," you're right.

Why drag the U.S. federal and the Canadian prison systems into this? For the year ending June 30, 1990, "assaults on inmates" in U.S. federal prisons occurred at a rate of 7.4 per 1000.[3] From 1990 to 1991 the rate of "major assaults" in Canadian prisons was not quite 4 per 1,000 inmates.[4] While the data aren't directly comparable, it appears that inmates in U.S. federal and Canadian prisons may arguably be as safe or safer from serious assaults than students in urban American middle schools and high schools.[5] Lest parents with children attending suburban government middle schools and high schools think that their schools are different, the rate of serious violent crimes reported for middle schools and high schools in the suburbs in 1997 was 8 per 1,000.[6] Bear in mind, too, that these rates of serious violent crimes are reported for boys and girls combined. The rates of serious violent crime are higher for boys.[7]

Yes, this comparison may be a little tendentious, but do you think that anyone in 1940 would have regarded a discussion of whether a 14-year-old would be safer in a prison or a government school as even remotely plausible?

SCHOOL CRIME: YES, IT REALLY IS "THAT" BAD.

Indicators of School Crime and Safety is a frequently cited compilation of information on crime in schools produced periodically through a joint effort of the Bureau of Justice Statistics and the National Center for Education Statistics. Here are a few interesting findings from the 1999 edition of that publication:[8]

- In 1995, 4% of government school students ages 12 through 19 reported being the victim of a violent crime at school.
- In 1995, 12% of government school students ages 12 through 19 reported that they were victims of a crime against their property at school.
- In 1997, about 7% of students in grades 9 through 12 reported being threatened or injured with a weapon such as a gun, knife, or club on school property.[9]
- In 1995, 9% of students ages 12 through 19 avoided one or more places at school for fear of their own safety, 9% reported fearing being attacked or harmed at school, and 7% reported fearing being attacked or harmed on the way to or from school.[10]
- In 1995, 31% of students in government schools reported street gangs were present at their schools, while only 7% of private school students reported the presence of street gangs.
- During the 1993-94 school year, 12% of all elementary and secondary school teachers in government schools were threatened with injury by a student, and 4% were physically assaulted by a student.[11]

To the extent that the data included in the 1999 *Indicators of School Crime and Safety* is broken down between public and private schools, there is, not surprisingly, more crime in public schools than private schools. With respect to reported property crimes the difference is not large, but both students and teachers in public schools were 100% more likely to be victims of violent crimes than students and teachers in private schools.[12]

The 2003 *Indicators of School Crime and Safety* reports little or no change in rates of suicide, alcohol use, marijuana use, drug distribution, violent crime against teachers (with public school teachers continuing to be twice as likely to be victims of a violent crime), and threats or injuries to students involving weapons such as guns, knives, or clubs compared to prior years.[13] On the other hand, however, the 2003 report claims that fewer students reported being victims of property and violent crimes at school (although public school students continue to be more likely victims of both violent and property crimes).[14] This purported decline in such reported crimes is rather oddly coupled, however, with unchanged levels of violence against teachers, threats and injuries involving guns, knives, and clubs (7% to 9% of students in each survey year), and levels of drug distribution (24% to 32% of students reporting having been offered drugs at school in each survey year).[15]

YOUNG STUDENTS, VIOLENCE, AND THE SHAPE OF THINGS TO COME?

Certainly, the most disconcerting recent development is an apparent trend toward increased violence among elementary school children. According to some state and local statistics and reports of school safety consultants, the youngest of students are more violent than ever.[16] In California, for example, "crimes against persons" by elementary school students almost doubled from 1995 to 2001. In Massachusetts, between 1995 and 2000, suspensions more than doubled for students in third grade and below.[17] The 2003 National Association of School Resource Officers (NASRO) survey of school-based police officers confirms these trends. Over 70% of the officers reported increases in aggressive behavior by elementary school children in their districts during the last five years.[18] What accounts for this is unclear, but two recent studies by the University of Minnesota and the National Institute of Child Health and Human Development link aggressive and disobedient behavior with increased time spent in day-care.[19] If these studies are correct, the tide of violence in government schools may be set to increase significantly now that nearly two-thirds of mothers with children under six-years-old are working outside the home.

In any event, it is easy to be diverted into discussions about fluctuations over the last ten years or so in rates of government school crime, but that would miss the larger point. Unlike teachers of their grandparents' generation, today's teachers have to worry about being assaulted rather than things like gum chewing, and many students now must view parts of their schools as "off-limits" out of fear for their own safety.

TOTAL SURVEILLANCE: THE BRAVE NEW WORLD OF SCHOOLS

Lest the government school crime problem seem too abstract, consider some of the measures that are being implemented to combat school crime. Like prisons, some government schools are trying to stem the flood of crime by installing webcams to provide surveillance of every student, hallway, gym, and classroom every minute of every day.[20] Professor Walter Williams describes the elaborate security staffing and measures in a Queens, New York, high school:

> Jamaica High School, with a student body of 2,500, has eight deans…. Student discipline occupies much of their time. The school has an assistant principal for security, and two secretaries and a school aide assigned to the dean's office. There are 10 school security agents assigned by the New York Police Department to patrol Jamaica High School's halls; there're more when there is random scanning of students for weapons. At least $1 million is budgeted for school safety, and that excludes the cost of the 10 security agents paid by the police department. [21]

To combat what has been termed "New England's heroin epidemic," the federal government's "Drug Czar" has recommended that the New England states implement random drug testing in their schools.[22] If the recommendation is adopted, any student may be required on any given day to provide a urine sample. The proliferation of these sorts of security measures in government schools marks an odd sort of convergence between the institutional climates of schools and prisons.

How did government schools become this way?

WE'RE FROM THE GOVERNMENT, AND WE'RE HERE TO HELP YOU

Would you be surprised if this epidemic of violence and criminality within government schools is in large part the result of federal court orders that have subverted school discipline? In their never-ending quest to be "helpful," the federal courts decided in the late 1960s and early 1970s that government schools would be vastly improved if the courts involved themselves in disciplinary matters. The capstones of this effort were the Supreme Court's 1969 decision in *Tinker v. Des Moines School District* and its 1975 decision in *Goss v. Lopez*.

Tinker was a Vietnam war-era protest case concerning whether a government school had the right to prohibit students from wearing armbands protesting the Vietnam War while in school. The Supreme Court found that the school district had no such right, but the most significant aspect of the Court's opinion was its assertion that school-children have a *Constitutional right* to freedom of speech or expression *even in school*. Having opened the Pandora's box of "Constitutional rights," the question then became what other "Constitutional rights" do schoolchildren have? Six years later, the Supreme Court found in *Goss* that students had a Constitutional right to "due process" *before* they could be suspended for misbehavior.[23]

Before the federal courts invited themselves into your school district, discipline in government schools was treated as a local matter for schools and school boards. As a result of *Tinker*, *Goss*, and other decisions by lower federal courts, however, the federal government became the ultimate authority on discipline in primary and secondary schools for the first time in American history. In effect, federal judges have become the ultimate vice principals in charge of discipline in every government school.

John Taylor Gatto, an education writer and an award-winning former teacher in the New York City schools, describes the destructive effect of federal intervention in school discipline:

> [There was] a tremendous rise in school violence and general school chaos which followed a policy declaration... that the disciplining of children must henceforth mimic the "due pro-

cess" practice of the court system. Teachers and administrators were suddenly stripped of any effective ability to keep order in schools since the due process apparatus, of necessity a slow, deliberate matter, is completely inadequate to the continual outbreaks of childish mischief all schools experience.... [W]ithout the time-honored *ad hoc* armory of disciplinary tactics to fall back on, disorder spiraled out of control, passing from the realm of annoyance into more dangerous terrain entirely as word surged through student bodies that teacher hands were tied.... Who had ever seen kids behave this way?[24]

The tying of teachers' hands went well beyond forcing schools to adopt the cumbersome machinery of "due process" in connection with disciplinary matters. The courts' declaration that students could assert Constitutional rights against teachers, administrators, and school districts in matters of school discipline also made educators and school districts vulnerable to litigation over real and perceived violations of those "rights." Not surprisingly, fear of litigation also contributed to the near disappearance of effective discipline in government schools.

BEHIND THE NUMBERS

Statistics are bloodless abstractions; children are not. We should not forget that there is something indecent and inhumane behind the numbers reporting school-related crime. Unfortunately, the problem is so widespread that only some of the most egregious cases are deemed news-worthy. Here are a few examples as reminders:

- According to the *Los Angeles Times*, order broke down so completely at Washington Prep High in Los Angeles that the teachers had resorted to filing a complaint with their union stating that the school was "out of control."[25] How so? Students at Washington Prep were regularly beaten and robbed, and students also reported avoiding parts of the school, such as the upper floor corridors, because of the sex and drug use that commonly occurred there. In addition to these concerns, teachers were also seeking increased security to prevent "students roaming in packs and wreaking havoc."[26] Why did the teachers go to the union? The administrators simply had ignored the teachers' requests for discipline – evidently they had trouble recognizing sex in the hallways and must have been unfamiliar with the odor of marijuana that permeated parts of the school.[27]

- Sheepshead Bay High School in Brooklyn has sent graduates to Ivy League schools, won a football title, and has had winning debate and law teams.[28] These are the sorts of things that lull some parents into thinking that their child's school really is "different" from the grossly dysfunctional schools they read about. Yet, Robert Kornhiser, an English teacher at the school, describes the daily reality there in a way that few parents would expect: "…the atmosphere is sapping and debilitating, if not downright poisonous…False fire alarms daily. Fights daily. Chaos in and around the cafeterias. Students banging on doors during class. Wanton vandalism…No one makes this up. And my school is not considered a failing school."[29] Moreover, by mid December of 2003 six teachers, a school aide, and a security officer had been assaulted, and a student nearly lost an eye in an incident in which another student punched him with brass knuckles.[30]

- In Denver's Hill Middle School a thirteen-year-old girl who had lost a leg to cancer was forced to leave school. Why? Taunts and pranks by a group of girls escalated to physical threats against the young amputee. Finally the harassment and bullying reached the point where she and her parents feared for her physical safety.[31]

- In an incident recorded by a bus video camera, a Jacksonville, Florida, 12-year-old boy was beaten savagely on the school bus on the way home.[32] No one tried to help him, not even the driver, who, instead of stopping the bus and the beating, just finished her route as if nothing had happened. After viewing the video, the boy's mother, Sashemia Small, remarked: "At one point you couldn't even see my child. There are so many individuals on him you couldn't even see him."[33] As for the boy, his mother made it clear he won't be returning to his school: "You want me to send my child back there?…What will the next call be; for me to view my son's body sending him back there?"[34]

- In Austin, a group of students roamed their high school campus looking for someone to beat, finally settling on a mentally retarded special education student who was standing about fifty feet off the school grounds waiting for a bus.[35] After circling their victim for several minutes and taunting and laughing at him, the group of students knocked him to the ground and beat him with fists and feet. An investigation of the incident determined that up to eight other students knew the attackers' plans and watched the attack. Even though it turns out that the assault was videotaped, the parents of one of the assailants claimed that their son was an "exemplary student who was about to begin interviews for college scholarships."[36]

- A videotaped savage beating of junior girls by senior girls at Glenbrook North High School, a school located in a wealthy suburb outside of Chicago, became news in Spring of 2003. Apparently expecting to go through a mild hazing connected with "powderpuff football," the victims soon found that they were being kicked, punched, and beaten with baseball bats, as well as being pelted with human feces and pig intestines.[37] One of the victims was knocked unconscious and afterwards suffered memory loss and headaches.[38] According to *Newsweek's* account, this spectacle was cheered by "a crowd of beer swilling students." What was the school administration's response? According to a *Chicago Sun-Times* story, the principal has stated that any punishments will be "possible actions on students through extracurricular activities."[39] In other words, if you beat someone senseless with a baseball bat at toney Glenbrook North High School, you can expect that you may not be able to participate in the French Club or field hockey.

- The NBC affiliate in Philadelphia reported in February 2004 that gang activity is making girls at Turner Middle School afraid to come to school.[40] The Crips? The Bloods? No, a lesbian gang called "DTO," which stands for "Dykes Taking Over." According the NBC affiliate, "The straight students say lesbians are bullying, groping and harassing them in gym and in the girls bathrooms."[41] The mothers of one of the girls being harassed described the situation a little less abstractly: "She [her daughter] called me last week screaming and hollering and crying because they had her in the gym cornered off, telling her what they were going to make her do."[42] A student being harassed put it this way: "Don't nobody wanna be gay. Don't nobody wanna be harassed. Don't nobody wanna be scared to come to school."[43] That sums it up pretty well.

Remember, these are just seven examples. Similar stories are behind each of the "data points" that go into the government school crime statistics. Moreover, despite the apparent cultural and sociological differences, a close analysis would probably show that Washington Prep and Glenbrook North, for example, have much more in common below the surface than outward appearances might suggest. But, of course, *your government schools are different.*

As time passes, the tides of violence and other crimes in government schools will ebb and flow. One thing, however, is certain: government schools *cannot* recover the "*ad hoc* armory of disciplinary tactics" that made talking-out-of-turn and chewing gum head the list of disciplinary problems in the 1940s. Even if the wisdom and the will to restore a reasonable level of order existed at the local and state levels, *Tinker, Goss,* and other federal court decisions, laws, and regulations have effectively frozen government schools into the disciplinary *status quo* for as far as the eye can see. Moreover, the coarsening of society that has occurred over the last forty years means that many students in government schools come from homes that would *resist* a restoration of effective school discipline. Public relations gimmicks may allow government schools to persuade parents from time to time that the problems of school violence and crime are under control, but at best it would likely only mean that these problems have been temporarily stabilized at levels considered unconscionable before 1960. Is that good enough for your child?

A CHILD'S BURDEN?

Let's bring this into sharper focus. How many of us work where between 5% and 10% of the employees avoid one or more places *at work* for fear for their own safety? How many of us work where 7% to 9% of the employees have been injured or threatened with a gun, knife, or club *at work* in the last year? How many of us work where as many as 32% of the employees have been offered illegal drugs at *work* in the last year? Yet, this is the "workplace" of the government schools into which 80% to 85% of Christian children are sent.

HIDING THE BAD NEWS ABOUT SCHOOL VIOLENCE

As bad as these statistics are, there is reason to believe that, as with other kinds of negative information about government schools, the bad news is significantly underreported. Georgia, for example, requires that school districts provide detailed discipline reports to the state annually. The Gwinnet County School District recently had to file an amended report after an investigation found that in the 2001-2002 school year the district had underreported "discipline incidents" by 85%.[44]

As revealed by the *Atlanta Journal-Constitution*, the Gwinnet schools' original report omitted "some 24,568 *serious infractions*, including violations of state and federal weapons laws, drugs and sex offenses."[45] (Emphasis added.) In the amended report the district reported 48,501 discipline incidents rather than the 4,258 previously reported.[46] How could there be such a disparity between the original and amended reports? Evidently, the investigation helped the school district officials discover what the meaning of "is" is: In the *amended* report: "All knives are reported as knives; court referrals are included; lewd exposure is considered a sex offense; bullying and oral, written or physical threats are reported as acts of intimidation."[47] There is, we are assured, no evidence that the district originally underreported disciplinary incidents on purpose. Gwinnet's highly trained education professionals simply didn't understand, for example, that "'lewd sexual exposure' fit the state's 'sex offense' category."[48] On the other hand, cynics might be excused for thinking that Gwinnet's gross underreporting of crime, violence, and disciplinary problems proceeded from other motives and is, *perhaps,* not an isolated phenomenon. Just perhaps.

UNDERREPORTING SCHOOL VIOLENCE IN CALIFORNIA, PENNSYLVANIA, FLORIDA, TEXAS, AND VIRGINIA

Well, actually, we know that the answer is more than just "perhaps." Underreporting of crime in schools has been exposed recently in Sacramento, California; Philadelphia; Palm Beach County, Florida; Texas; and Virginia.[49] For instance, reported crimes jumped from 84 in 2000-2001 to almost 7,500 in 2001-2002 in Roanoke, Virginia, after underreporting was exposed. In November 2003, *The New York Times* broke a story on the gross underreporting of crime by Houston Independent School District (HISD). HISD, for example, reported only 761 assaults to the state over the last four school years, even though HISD's own police force had logged 3,061 assaults in the database that they share with the Houston police.[50] Were these minor or borderline offenses? Not exactly. Here are just three examples of the unreported assaults: the stomping and beating of a middle school student (who was left injured on the floor of the school cafeteria); the stabbing of a high school student in the chest by another student;

and the rape of a wheelchair bound high school student in a boys' lavatory.[51] Even though you may not be a highly trained education professional, would you have trouble identifying these incidents as assaults? I didn't think so.

After the *Times* story, HISD provided the standard ritual denial of wrongdoing. [52] You see, in the case of the rape, for example, HISD claims it really did comply with the state's reporting requirements. How? Well, if you don't take disciplinary action against a student you don't have to report the incident to the state. Because the school authorities never took any disciplinary action against the student rapist, there was nothing to report.[53] For a bureaucrat, this is apparently a satisfactory explanation. But why would they do this? I suppose one explanation is "compassion": the rapist was likely to be jailed eventually (he was), so taking immediate disciplinary action against him might have damaged his self-esteem excessively in the eyes of HISD's compassionate highly trained education professionals. On the other hand, some might think that failing to take disciplinary action, and thereby having a technical defense to a charge of failing to report, just reflected an unwritten policy of keeping as much bad news as possible out of the reporting system.

Are you having trouble making your mind up between the alternative explanations for HISD's reluctance to discipline a rapist? If so, it might help if you also knew that two years before the *New York Times* ran its story the senior director for safe schools at the Texas Education Agency (TEA) found that even though HISD had transferred 2,000 students to alternative schools because they had committed serious crimes in school, only 200 were reported to the TEA.[54] This time HISD blamed the underreporting on "computer problems."[55]

OK, if you are still having trouble figuring this out, here's the final hint. Houston Federation of Teachers President, Gayle Fallon, has told the press that "district administrators consistently refuse to honestly report on-campus violence."[56] Fallon points out that violence on HISD campuses (and, presumably, all Texas government school campuses) is at its worst before October 30. Why? Because this is the "snapshot day" on which Texas determines the number of students at each school, and that number determines how much money the school gets in per capita financing.[57] Consequently, according to Fallon, "A student would damn near have to kill somebody…to be expelled before that snapshot date."[58] Fallon has also stated publicly that teachers are reporting to her that students who have assaulted or threatened them have been allowed to remain in school in violation of state law.[59]

NO, IT'S NOT AN "ISOLATED PHENOMENON": 87% PERCENT OF SCHOOL POLICE OFFICERS SAY SCHOOL CRIME IS UNDERREPORTED IN THEIR DISTRICTS

These instances of schools getting caught underreporting crime and disciplinary infractions notwithstanding, state departments of education generally have not been enforcing their reporting requirements. Ken Trump, director of a Cleveland-based consulting firm that provides advice and training regarding school security and crisis-preparedness, puts it this way: "It's a policy of don't ask, don't tell.…State departments of education are, for their own political expediency, not wanting to enforce it."[60] So, perhaps we can excuse the cynics for thinking that the falsification of crime and discipline reports perhaps fits the pattern of government schools' fraudulent reporting of test results and underreporting of dropout rates to manage school news, all for the purpose of maintaining and increasing government school funding.

Apart from the press coverage of specific incidents in which government schools have been caught making false reports, there is additional strong, statistical evidence that government schools are attempting to conceal their true levels of crime and disorder. As reported in NASRO's 2003 survey, 87% of school police officers say that school crime is underreported in their districts (in NASRO's 2002 survey 89% stated that school crime is underreported).[61] The 2003 NASRO survey also showed that over 61% of the respondents believe schools will underreport crime to avoid being labeled "persistently dangerous."[62]

The motivation for underreporting is just what you would expect. Being thought of as a dangerous school is "the scarlet letter in education today" – something to be avoided by any means necessary.[63] Parents, after all, might get upset and take their children out of government schools if they knew the truth. The intensity of the education industry's desire to avoid meaningful reporting on school crime and disorder was put on full frontal display in connection with the first reporting period for identifying "persistently dangerous schools" under the No Child Left Behind Act.

The 2001 No Child Left Behind Act mandates that states announce whether they had any schools that are "persistently dangerous." Under the *Act*, if a school is found to be persistently dangerous students must be allowed to transfer to any safer school within the same district. Care to guess how many "persistently dangerous schools" were reported by California, Massachusetts, Florida, or the District of Columbia in 2003 (which was the first reporting period under the *Act*)? If your answer is greater than zero, you are wrong. In fact, 40 additional states also reported that they didn't have even one persistently dangerous school. As Chester E. Finn, Jr., president of the Thomas B. Fordham Foundation and former Assistant Secretary of Education, remarked: "It does not pass the laugh test, or maybe I should say in this case, the cry test....Everybody knows better."[64] More to the point, Ken Trump notes: "States are sending a message that creates a false sense of security among parents."

PERSISTENTLY DANGEROUS SCHOOLS? UH, NO, WE DON'T HAVE ANY OF THOSE HERE

How could this happen? Easily – let your highly trained education professionals and their friends in the states define what "persistently dangerous" means. Not surprisingly, California's state school board helped set the trend by defining "persistently dangerous" so that even Washington Prep High School in Los Angeles did not qualify. Commenting on the reaction to the definition adopted by California, an education consultant and former Assistant Secretary of Education in the Bush, Sr. administration, Christopher Cross, re-marked: "The reaction, I think, among most of the people I've talked to is incredulity that the [state] board could adopt a definition that includes no schools….People felt it was an insult to parents."[65] Of course, California's ever resourceful board of education has also been a leader in devising ways to evade the No Child Left Behind Act's other modest attempts to make our highly trained education professionals more accountable, as is pointed out in Chapter 5's discussion of the California "Miracle of the Highly Qualified Teachers."

Much of the reaction in the handful of states that did designate a few schools as "persistently dangerous" has been indignant stam-mering about the unfairness of being stigmatized for playing by the rules when other states obviously have acted in bad faith.[66] At least one of these states, however, didn't sit still for being played like a rube at a county fair shell game. Texas education officials, who had designated six schools as "persistently dangerous," simply decided to give themselves a "do over." Once they were on to how the game should be played, Texas officials declared that they didn't have "persis-tently dangerous schools," they were just the victims of "flawed data" and of a "data collection system that was confusing, overly broad and frequently changed."[67] In essence, Texas took itself off the list of states with "persistently dangerous schools" by declaring: "We aren't danger-ous, we're just inept." Any port in a storm, I guess.

Showing that even some of our elected representatives can even-tually learn to recognize a game of Three Card Monte, a freshman Congresswoman from Colorado, Marilyn Musgrave, reacted to the "persistently dangerous schools" reporting fiasco with remarkable restraint: "I think they're trying to convince parents that their en-vironment is good for children…and sometimes it's not."[68] Well, of course. But the real point is that now that school crime data is in play as an accountability factor, you can bet grandma's heirloom silver that our highly trained education professionals will be as aggressive in corrupting this data as they have been with respect to standardized test scores and drop-out rates.[69] So now, if you thought my little quiz regarding violence levels in government schools and in prison systems was a bit "over-the-top," let me ask you – are you still certain that your child wouldn't be safer in a prison than a government school? If your answer is still "yes," be sure to continue reading.

SO YOU THINK PEDOPHILE PRIESTS WERE A PROBLEM? THE EMERGING SCANDAL OF SEX ABUSE OF CHILDREN BY PUBLIC SCHOOL EMPLOYEES

By now, virtually every parent has heard the painful story of the Catholic Church's problem with pedophile priests. Many know, too, that a study by the U.S. Conference of Catholic Bishops reported that nearly 11,000 minors were sexually abused by priests over the fifty-two year period spanning 1950 to 2002.

What few parents know, however, is that the No Child Left Behind Act required a study of the incidence of sex abuse of students by public school employees. The draft report – titled "Educator Sexual Misconduct: A Synthesis of Existing Literature" – has now been submitted to the U.S. Department of Education. As an article in *Education Week* points out, the report indicates a sex abuse problem in government schools that dwarfs the scandal of the pedophile priests.[70] And, as might be expected, the NEA is in full denial mode.[71]

The author, Charol Shakeshaft, a professor specializing in educational research at Hofstra University, first surveyed all research sources "…that discussed educator sexual misconduct in some format."[72] She discovered that among those were only 14 empirical studies that were on point, and some of those were from Canada or the United Kingdom.[73] After winnowing the available data, professor Shakeshaft concluded that a 2001 study by the Association of American University Women regarding the incidence of bullying, teasing, and sexual harassment provided the best source of data for estimating the incidence of sexual misconduct toward children by public school employees.[74]

After reanalyzing the AAUW study's data, professor Shakeshaft found that 6.7% of students in 8th through 11th grades reported sexual harassment by school employees *involving physical contact*, with 8.7% of students reporting "non-contact" harassment (sexual remarks, etc.).[75] Overall, 9.6% of students had been subject to one or the other form of harassment or both.

According to professor Shakeshaft's report, if the AAUW's data "…accurately represent the experiences of all K-12 students, more than 4.5 million students are sexually harassed or abused by an employee of a school sometime between kindergarten and 12th grade."[76] As professor Shakeshaft puts this in perspective, "So we think the Catholic Church has a problem?…the physical sexual abuse of students in schools is likely more than 100 times the abuse by priests."[77] I know, I know, *but your government school is different.*

Professor Shakeshaft acknowledges, "Educator sexual misconduct is woefully understudied" and that more data is needed.[78] Nevertheless, the incomplete data available suggest a horrifying problem that demands immediate scrutiny. When professor Shakeshaft accepted the task of making her study, she understood that the purpose of her work was to lay the foundation for a comprehensive national study.[79] Now Department of Education officials are saying there are no plans for any further work on the subject.[80] The obvious question is "Why?" That is the $500 billion question… or maybe $500 billion is the answer.

In addition to scholarly studies, newspaper journalists have dug into the problem. The best work of this sort so far has been done by writers at the *Pittsburgh Post-Gazette,* which has published a series of articles on sexual abuse of students by teachers and other school employees. In an examination of a sample of 727 sex abuse cases across the country, the *Post-Gazette's* journalists found, for example, that those who were caught had been molesting students for years, and that after someone is caught, administrators sometimes help the offender find a new teaching job – a practice known among educators as "passing the trash."[81]

Another *Post-Gazette* article reports on Dr. Sherry Bithnell's book, *Educator Sexual Abuse,* which estimates that 5% of teachers have engaged in sexual abuse of students, and research by Dr. Dan Wishnictsky, a professor at Winston-Salem State University, whose studies of North Carolina students have shown extraordinary levels of sexual harassment or abuse of students by school employees (*e.g.*, roughly 12.5% of girls reported having had sexual intercourse with a teacher).[82]

While current trends and other aspects of the violent crime and sex abuse data for government schools can be discussed and quibbled about endlessly, it is absolutely clear that in the span of a few generations government schools, even the so called "good ones," have indeed become persistently dangerous compared to what they once were, that private schools are much less dangerous to both children and teachers, and that the education industry has and will continue to expend considerable effort to prevent parents and others from discovering just how persistently dangerous government schools are. *These facts have been hiding in plain sight.* And, no, your child's government school is *not* different. Yet, parents, Christian and non-Christian alike, continue to entrust their children to violent and disorderly government schools day after day and year after year. Can you imagine the risks that children attending government schools are subjected to as a normal part of their daily lives? And if the child is a boy, it is worse. Read on.

THE "FEMINAZIS" HATE YOUR LITTLE BOY

By nature, most boys are daredevils, and want to spend their time in active pursuits and having "adventures." So not surprisingly, many boys have a problem with the relatively passive routine of schooling. Frankly, as most parents know, sitting quietly just doesn't come as easily to most boys as it does to girls. Today, however, a radical feminist ideology pervades government schools that is damaging boys in unprecedented ways. As one family therapist and author has noted, "If Huck Finn and Tom Sawyer were living today, they would have been sent to a psychiatrist, given Ritalin, [and] diagnosed with Attention Deficit Disorder and a conduct disorder...."[83]

Tragically, very few parents have any idea about what is being done to their sons in the name of propagandistic phrases such as "gender equity." As with most pathologies in government schools, this travesty begins with rank falsehoods and is propagated through curricula, attitudes of educators, and various institutional arrangements. The net result is that government schools are now a particularly hostile environment for boys and are getting worse.

HYSTERIA AND ITS USES

The story of how virulent strains of feminism have increasingly found their way into government schools begins a little over a decade ago with a *New York Times Magazine* article.[84] The article reported that a Harvard University School of Education professor of "gender studies" had discovered that adolescent American girls were undergoing a "crisis" in which they were allegedly being pushed into the background by society. This, in turn, was causing them to lose their self-confidence. Alarmed by this finding, the American Association of University Women (AAUW) proceeded to hire a polling firm to investigate. The poll reported that "Most girls emerge from adolescence with a poor self-image."[85] Having confirmed its belief that girls were being "shortchanged in the classroom," and having received a lot of publicity for its poll results, the AAUW had a second study produced, *How Schools Shortchange Girls*. This study claimed to find that girls had a second-class status in the classroom and that this was diminishing their self-esteem. In addition to investing $100,000 in the study, the AAUW spent an additional $150,000 on a public relations campaign for its "findings." The public relations effort resulted in over 1,400 news reports and other media coverage trumpeting the study's finding that adolescent girls' self-esteem was being harmed by discrimination in the classroom. In the study's wake also came a flood of books portraying adolescent girls as victims of schoolhouse discrimination that was causing their "self-esteem" to implode.

THE GENDER EQUITY FRAUD

As a result of the hysteria whipped up by academics, the AAUW, and the media over the "crisis" adolescent girls were suffering, Congress enacted the Women's Educational Equity Act in 1994. The Act's legislative findings alleged, among other things, that girls were being "shortchanged" by teaching practices in schools and that "Federal assistance for gender equity must be tied to systemic reform, involve collaborative efforts to implement effective gender practices at the local level, and encourage parental participation...."[86] This legislation authorized the Secretary of Education to make grants to individuals and organizations for a range of "gender-equity" purposes, including developing model gender-equity programs and funding the implementation of equity programs in schools across the nation.[87] Thus, the Congress' imprimatur was placed on the image of the delicate, victimized girl propagated into the mainstream through the media. More important, the federal floodgates were opened unleashing a torrent of "gender-equity" dollars.

Not surprisingly, those gender-equity dollars are funding an army of professional gender-equity activists who create curricula, workshops, and other resources for conforming schools to their preconceptions. What are those preconceptions? Well, one tenet shared by many of these feminists seems to be that there are no essential gender differences between males and females.[88] Thus, gender identities are socially constructed; that is, a male child can as easily be raised to have the "gender identity" of a "girl" as that of a "boy." All that is required is an iron-willed resolve to make certain that male children are not exposed to or permitted to exhibit those evil "boy" gender traits.

Another tenet is that Western Civilization is hopelessly "patriarchal" (that's not good, in case you were wondering) and is suffused with violence and discrimination against women. All this bad stuff is largely the result of Western Civilization's defectively constructed "gender identities," particularly those of men. So, the heroic mission of these self-appointed paladins of "gender justice" is to "deconstruct" existing gender identities and replace them with new improved versions that they have concocted. Because the gender-equity movement obsesses about male violence and other alleged forms of male oppression, this really means "deconstructing" and "reconstructing" males. Stripped of the pretentious language, the gender-equity movement aims at using schools to force boys to act and think like girls.

FEMINIST STATISTICS: COOKING THE NUMBERS

A further tenet of the gender-equity movement, although it may not be part of the official catechism, is that facts and statistics are like ghost stories: they are something you make up in order to frighten people. One of the beneficiaries of the federal dollars flowing toward the gender-equity feminists, Katherine Hanson, illustrates the anti-male prejudices of these (mostly) women and their casual attitude toward the truth. According to Hanson, male violence against women in the United States is at genocidal levels.

In her book, *The War Against Boys*, Christina Hoff Sommers summarizes Hanson's claims about violence against women as follows:[89]

- Every year nearly four million women are beaten to death
- Violence is the leading cause of death among women
- The leading cause of injury among women is being beaten by a man at home
- There was a 59% increase in rapes between 1990 and 1991

Not only are these claims wrong, but they are evidence that gender-equity feminists actually occupy some sort of parallel universe.

How far have Hanson and her ilk departed from reality? Farther than anyone is likely to imagine. As Sommers reports:

In fact, the total number of annual female deaths in the entire country *from all causes combined* is approximately *one* million. Only a miniscule fraction of these deaths is caused by violence, and an even tinier fraction is caused by battery. According to the FBI, the total number of women who died by murder in 1996 was 3,631. But according to... Hanson, 11,000 American women are beaten to death *every day*.... Male violence is also far down the list of cause of injury to women. Two studies of emergency room admissions, one by the U.S. Bureau of Justice Statistics and one by the Centers for Disease Control and Prevention, suggest that approximately 1 percent of women's injuries is caused by male partners. Hanson's other factoids are no more reliable: between 1990 and 1991 rapes increased by 4 percent, not 59 percent, and the number has gone down steadily since.[90] [Emphasis in original.]

Plainly, the gross statistical fictions served up by feminists such as Hanson are not the result of inadvertent errors. What purpose do wildly false statistical assertions serve within the gender equity movement? Sommers explains:

> Hanson… and other "gender-fair" activists regularly whip themselves into an anti-male frenzy with their false statistics. They use their lurid "facts" to devise and justify programs and curricula spreading the gospel of gender "equity."[91]

And they're doing it with your tax dollars.

Are Hanson's preposterous assertions the claims of just any gender-equity feminist? Not quite. Hanson runs the Women's Educational Equity Act Equity Resource Center, which is a national distributor and publisher of "gender-fair" materials, and claims to have played a key role in the success of the Women's Educational Equity Act.[92] According to Sommers, Hanson's organization is:

> [T]he "primary vehicle" by which the U.S. Department of Education promotes gender equity. As director, Hanson works with schools and community organizations to "infuse equity" into all education policies, practices, and materials.[93]

This is far from harmless.

HARASSING BOYS

As you might suspect, the feminists in the gender-equity movement don't much like men. And while they profess a concern for boys, Sommers points out that their attitude towards boys is in fact quite hostile:

> Leaders in the equity movement take a very dim view of errant boys, speaking with straight faces about schoolyard harassers as tomorrow's batterers, rapists, and murderers.[94]

Because it is too late to re-socialize men, and because they tend to view boys as rapists and murderers in training, the gender-equity crowd is very focused on getting their materials and programs into schools where they believe they can properly socialize boys. Bear in mind, they aim at making sure that your sons are socialized their way, not yours.

ENFORCING A FEMINIST GRADE SCHOOL REICH

A North Carolina elementary school, for example, suspended a six-year-old for sexual harassment. His crime? He kissed a girl on the cheek "partly because he liked her and partly, he said, because she asked him to."[99] School officials initially justified their action on the grounds that this boy (who was obviously a sexual predator in training) had violated the school's written rules against sexual harassment. Later they claimed that he had only broken a "general school rule prohibiting unwarranted and unwelcome touching of one student by another."[100]

John Leo tells of another incident that, from the gender equity viewpoint, illustrates the horrors of playing tag:

My favorite is… the third-grade boy accused of touching a girl on the breasts, though it is perhaps fairer to say that during a game of tag, he tagged her on the very spot where her breasts would presumably appear in three or four years. This is like being accused of robbing a bank that hasn't been built yet.[101]

Not every incident of out-of-control gender equity enthusiasm has an element of humor. Christina Hoff Sommers writes of a Virginia nine-year-old charged with aggravated sexual battery:

When he was accused of deliberately rubbing up against a girl in the cafeteria, school officials notified police. The boy was charged with aggravated sexual battery, and was handcuffed and fingerprinted. The family's lawyer… said "This is really a case of political correctness run amuck. A 9-year-old bumps into a girl in the lunch line while reaching for an apple and all of a sudden you've got World War III declared against a fourth grader." Eventually the charges were dropped.[102]

In case you're thinking that these sorts of incidents represent a local misinterpretation of the sort of school environment the gender-equity movement is trying to create, don't.

When California passed a law preventing schools from *expelling* students for sexual harassment *unless they were in the fourth or a higher grade*, Sue Sattel was displeased. Sattel is an employee of the Minnesota Department of Education and a co-author of a curriculum that instructs first graders that teasing boys who want to jump rope is "homophobic."[103] According to Sattel, "California is sending a message that it is OK for very little kids to sexually harass each other."[104]

What are feminists like Sattel really trying to accomplish? Linda Chavez sums up well the intentions of the gender-equity movement:

> If the feds and their feminist allies have their way, every little boy and girl in the nation will be taught that flirting is a crime, and even an admiring look, much less a kiss, can land you in court.[105]

Apparently not content with just getting money and "curricular shelf space" for gender-equity, the gender-equity movement also has insinuated itself into drug education.[106] The Department of Health and Human Services (HHS) currently funds an anti-drug program called "Girl Power," which is based on the improbable premise that girls who are taught to reject traditional notions of femininity are less likely to smoke, drink, and use drugs. HHS is also considering creating an analogous anti-drug program for boys called "Boy Talk," which, not surprisingly, proceeds from the premise that if boys would give up traditional notions of masculinity they will be less likely to get involved with smoking, alcohol, and drugs. So, there you have it. If boys and girls just quit being boys and girls, the drug problem will be solved.

SOWING THE SEEDS OF DISTRUST

Splendid. Boys now increasingly have to endure being systematically vilified and demeaned in government schools for no other reason than that they are boys, while girls are being indoctrinated with a delusional view of the world and of boys and men. It's reminiscent of a practical joke that goes like this: Pick two persons at a large social gathering, and tell each one separately that you would like to introduce him to the other. Be sure, however, to confide in each of them that the person that he is about to meet is hard of hearing and sensitive about it, so it will be necessary to speak very loudly and enunciate distinctly to the other person. Make the introduction and a strange spectacle will unfold.

A more malicious variation on this "practical joke" is to find a subtle way of telling each individual that the other has been saying negative things about him. This is what the gender-equity movement is actually doing, and it can sow permanent seeds of distrust between people who otherwise would be disposed to like each other. That this is being done systematically to boys and girls in government (and some secular private) school classrooms is profoundly damaging, not merely to their present well-being but to their futures as well. After being subjected to this institutionalized form of child abuse, can many boys help but be suspicious and resentful toward girls and women? Can many girls help but be suspicious and resentful toward boys and men? As they mature can this have anything other than a negative effect on their ability to form the bonds of trust, respect, and affection that lead to and sustain successful marriages and families? As Christian parents, this is something that should concern us deeply.[107]

IT'S THERE — EVEN IF YOU DON'T KNOW IT

Don't think that your local government school is somehow immune to all of this. The gender-equity ideology is now inscribed in legislation, Supreme Court decisions, and Department of Education regulations. If a particularly virulent form of the gender-equity movement hasn't yet made it to your school district, don't worry. It soon will. In any event, rest assured that it is there now in some form or other. Moreover, don't count on school personnel to shield your child from this rubbish. Our highly trained education professionals like having jobs, and they don't like lawsuits. Any school district that fails to fall in line runs a serious risk of being sued. If a school official has to choose between putting his career in jeopardy and calling the police because your son accidentally bumped a girl in the cafeteria line reaching for an apple, what do you think he is going to do? In case you have any doubts, consider how one of the high priestesses of the gender-equity movement has described the response of school administrators to the current regime of sexual harassment laws and regulations: "I'd say they are in a panic.... There have been so many lawsuits with so many monetary damages.... They are panicked."[108] And don't think that she isn't quite pleased about it.

THE REAL "GENDER" PROBLEM IN SCHOOLS

Would it surprise you that the "findings" of the Harvard professor of "gender studies," the AAUW, and the others who so breathlessly reported on the psychological crisis among adolescent girls were, to put it politely, not true? While the esteemed Harvard professor was promoting the notion that adolescent girls were immersed in misery because of a catastrophic assault on their confidence in the classroom, the University of Michigan and the Department of Health and Human Services were conducting a study of a scientific sample of three thousand high school seniors to determine how satisfied they were with their lives. Almost 86% of the girls and 88% of the boys reported that they were "pretty happy" or "very happy."[109]

Similarly, while the AAUW public relations machine was generating lots of press coverage for its sensational "findings," leading adolescent psychologists were questioning the validity of the AAUW's poll.[110] Their doubts, however, somehow didn't make it into the reporting about the poll. The truth of the entire matter was summarized years later by Diane Ravitch, a former Assistant Secretary of

Education for Educational Research and Improvement and New York University professor, in a 1998 *New York Times* article:

> The AAUW report was just completely wrong. What was so bizarre is that it came out right at the time that girls had just overtaken boys in almost every area. It might have been the right story 20 years earlier, but coming out when it did it was like calling a wedding a funeral…. There were all these special programs put in place for girls, and no one paid any attention to boys.[111]

Of course, by the time that the "girl crisis" was exposed as a fraud, it wasn't considered news. Besides, it didn't matter. The gender equity movement had already obtained the laws, regulations, and federal and state money it needed to institutionalize itself within America's schools.

Ironically, as the AAUW and others were manufacturing the myth of the "short-changed girl," the AAUW *knew* that students, both boys and girls, were reporting *precisely* the opposite – that teachers were consistently favoring girls in the classroom. In data from the AAUW's 1990 Self-Esteem Survey that *the AAUW did not publish*, both boys and girls reported that classroom teachers were paying more attention to girls than boys, preferred being around girls rather than boys, complimented girls more often than boys, called on girls more often than boys, and thought that girls are smarter than boys.[112] Moreover, these perceptions were held by significant majorities of both boys and girls. For example, 57% of girls and 64% of boys reported that teachers pay more attention to girls than boys while only 33% of girls and 29% of boys thought that teachers paid more attention to boys. Fully 80% of girls and 73% of boys reported that teachers preferred to be around girls while only 12% of girls and 21% of boys reported that teachers preferred to be around boys. Similarly, 89% of girls and 81% of boys reported that teachers complimented girls more often, while only 7% of girls and 15% of boys reported that the reverse was true. Note that children were reporting these results in *1990*. As a consequence of the gender-equity movement becoming firmly entrenched in government

204 THE HARSH TRUTH ABOUT PUBLIC SCHOOLS

schools in the mid to late 1990s, the classroom environment for boys can only have become more hostile since then.

One moral of this story is that the gender-equity movement has prospered through intimidation and by "constructing" a gender "narrative" that bears little relationship to the facts. The more important point, however, is that the gender-equity movement has succeeded in institutionalizing a form of psychological child abuse against boys in government schools. And this has not been without consequences.

ALIENATING BOYS

Thanks to the efforts of the gender-equity activists, boys are increasingly less likely to attend college than their female classmates. One psychology professor describes the role that boys' experiences in primary and secondary schools play in producing the college enrollment gap:[113]

> Males are... more apt than females to believe that the school climate is hostile to them, that teachers do not expect as much from them and give them less encouragement to do their best.

Girls also get better grades in school and are significantly more likely than boys to participate in non-athletic extracurricular activities such as student government, newspaper or yearbook, and honorary societies.[114] Thus, it is hardly surprising that a 1999 Horatio Alger Foundation survey reported that the most optimistic and successful students were disproportionately girls (63% girls versus 37% boys).[115]

Boys are becoming alienated from the educational enterprise. In 1978 the number of undergraduate women in 2- and 4-year degree institutions exceeded the number of men.[116] By 2007 the Department of Education projects that the imbalance of total enrollment in 2- and 4-year degree institutions will be roughly 57% women to 43% men.[117] If only full-time enrollment is considered, in 1997 men constituted just 45% of full-time college students.[118]

"FEMINIZED" SCHOOLS YIELD THE SAME HARMFUL RESULTS IN CANADA AND THE UK

This phenomenon is not limited to the United States. In Canada, where feminism has probably had even more influence, boys and men are opting out of the educational system at least as fast as in the U.S. In 2002, only 43% of the graduates of Canadian universities were male.[119] At the University of Calgary only 39% of graduates were male in 2002.[120] In Britain it is reported that the feminized school environment is increasingly leading to a culture among boys in which it is "cool not to learn."[121] This problem is especially acute for "white working-class boys," who are falling behind so rapidly that they may well become the "the worst educated group of children."[122]

What accounts for this in Britain? According to David Miliband, the government's Schools Minister, boys are known to thrive in schools with a "culture of achievement," limited homework, and strong discipline.[123] These are not characteristics of the feminized schools in Britain, and Miliband believes that British schools need to change so that "boys get as much out of schools as girls."[124] Don't expect any such frank admission concerning the source of the problem or its solution in the United States. The feminists and their enablers like things just as they are.

The truth is that boys are increasingly being treated abusively by the "gender-equity" interventions in government schools. Their masculinity is demeaned, they are being systematically slandered as psychologically disturbed for no other reason than that they are boys, and their interests and learning styles are being ignored. As a result, the futures of a vast number of boys are being profoundly diminished. Yet, as bad as this is, the emergence of government schools as the nation's preeminent drug-pusher may do even worse violence to boys.

RITALIN: RUNNING FOR THE SHELTER OF TEACHER'S LITTLE HELPER

In 1966 the Rolling Stones recorded "Mother's Little Helper," a song about adults hypocritically using drugs to escape the unpleasantness of their lives.[125] In case you're wondering, the "mother's little helper" was, of course, a little yellow pill that helped "mother" through her "busy day." It seems that in the last ten to twenty years government school educators have discovered that psychotropic drugs can help them get through the unpleasantness of their "busy days." In this case, however, the drugs are being given to children, and especially to little boys.

Ritalin, Adderall, Prozac, Zoloft, Paxil, and other psychotropic drugs,[126] but mostly Ritalin and Adderall, are being used to drug schoolchildren at rates that are difficult to comprehend.[127] According to a 2000 ABC News story, Ritalin is prescribed to an estimated 4 million schoolchildren each year.[128] Roughly 75% of those children are boys.[129] The Drug Enforcement Administration has estimated that 8 million children and adults were on Ritalin in 2000.[130] Prescriptions for Ritalin increased by 700% from 1990 to 2001.[131]

In testimony before a panel of the United States House of Representatives in May 2003, medical experts testified that psychotropic drugs such as Ritalin and Adderall are being over-prescribed to children for the purpose of calming them down.[132] In fact, according to the testimony of the director of Behavioral Pediatrics at Children's Hospital of Philadelphia, Dr. William B. Carey, psychotropic drugs such as Ritalin are being prescribed to up to 17 percent of school-aged children.[133] What is Ritalin, and what is it being used for?

THE POOR MAN'S COCAINE

"Ritalin" is a tradename for a psychotropic compound called "methylphenidate" that was approved by the Food and Drug Administration in 1955 and that was often prescribed in the 1960s for behavioral control.[134] By 1999 the Drug Enforcement Administration was reporting that more than 90% of the world's Ritalin is bought and consumed in the United States.[135] Methylphenidate is pharmacologically classified with amphetamines.[136] In fact, the textbook *Treatments of Psychiatric Disorders* notes that cocaine, amphetamines, and methylphenidate are neuropharmacologically alike and that their clinical effects cannot be distinguished in laboratory tests.[137] Moreover, both the World Health Organization and the Food and Drug Administration place methylphenidate in the same high addiction category (Schedule II) in which they place amphetamines, morphine, opium, and barbiturates.[138]

So, it should come as no surprise that Ritalin is being abused as a street drug, sometimes being referred to as "Vitamin R" or "Poor Man's Cocaine." Perhaps it may be more surprising that a 1999 survey of 6,000 Massachusetts teenagers attending government high schools found that *13% reported using Ritalin recreationally.*[139] The main source of the drug is, of course, the schools themselves. In a *New York Times* article, Janet Douglass, a director of the School Health Institute at the University of Massachusetts at Lowell commented on the prevalence of psychotropic drugs after visiting a nearby *elementary* school:

> I think they give out more psychotropic medication than a psych hospital did when I did psych... .Not just Ritalin, but heavy duty psychiatric medications.[140]

According to a study conducted in Wisconsin and Minnesota, 34% of government school students ages 11 to 18 taking medication for ADHD reported being approached to sell or trade their drugs.[141] In addition, according to the DEA, Ritalin is one of the ten most stolen pharmaceuticals.[142]

The problem of the recreational use of Ritalin has become so pronounced that federal officials had to begin investigating government schools over the theft, illegal sale, and abuse of Ritalin and similar drugs.[143] Moreover, this problem involves principals, school nurses, and other school employees, not merely students.[144] Indeed, in 2000 the chairman of the House Committee on Education and the Workforce, William Goodling, characterized Ritalin as perhaps "the greatest drug problem we have in this country."[145] Researchers at the University of California have found that Ritalin is also a "gateway" drug to other drugs, especially cocaine.[146] According to the lead researcher for the study: "[Ritalin] makes the brain more susceptible to the addictive power of cocaine and doubles the risk of abuse."[147] Government schools are awash in this stuff. So why is it there?

ADHD AND DRUGGING SCHOOLCHILDREN

The most diagnosed "mental illness" among American children is Attention Deficit/Hyperactivity Disorder (ADHD),[148] and it is the ADHD diagnosis that has led to the mass drugging of America's schoolchildren. ADHD's status as a mental illness was established in 1987 by a vote of a committee of psychiatrists belonging to the American Psychiatric Association (APA).[149] According to the APA's *Diagnostic and Statistical Manual of Mental Disorders* (*DSM-IV*), there are two types of ADHD, one characterized by inattention and the other by hyperactivity-impulsivity.

Each of these types of ADHD has nine symptoms, and a child is diagnosed with ADHD if: (1) he exhibits six or more of the symptoms from either category and they persist for more than six months to a degree that is maladaptive and inconsistent with developmental level, (2) there is clinically significant impairment in social, academic, or occupational functioning, (3) the impairment is evident in at least two settings (*e.g.*, home and school), and (4) there must be the onset of symptoms causing impairment by age seven.[150]

ADHD: A DIAGNOSIS IN SEARCH OF A DISEASE

What are these symptoms? Here are the nine symptoms for the "inattention" form of ADHD:[151]

- Often fails to give close attention to details or makes careless mistakes in schoolwork, work, or other activities
- Often has difficulty sustaining attention in tasks or play activities
- Often does not seem to listen when spoken to directly
- Often does not follow through on instructions and fails to finish schoolwork, chores, or duties in the workplace

(not due to oppositional behavior or failure to understand instructions)

- Often has difficulty organizing tasks and activities
- Often avoids, dislikes, or is reluctant to engage in tasks that require sustained mental effort (*e.g.*, schoolwork or homework)
- Often loses things necessary for tasks or activities
- Is often easily distracted by extraneous stimuli
- Is often forgetful in daily activities

The symptoms for the hyperactivity-impulsivity form of ADHD are:[152]

- Often fidgets with hands or feet or squirms in seat
- Often leaves seat in classroom or in other situations in which remaining seated is expected
- Often runs about or climbs excessively in situations in which it is inappropriate (in adolescents or adults, may be limited to feelings of restlessness)
- Often has difficulty playing or engaging in leisure activities quietly
- Is often "on the go" or often acts as if "driven by a motor"
- Often talks excessively
- Often blurts out answers before questions have been completed
- Often has difficulty awaiting turn
- Often interrupts or intrudes on others (*e.g.*, butts into conversations or games)

Plainly, many, if not most, children "often" display six or more of these "symptoms," and they certainly do so both before and after reaching age seven. Moreover, even a cursory examination discloses the utterly subjective nature of the DSM-IV diagnostic standards (notice, for example, how the diagnostic criteria rely on the term "often"). For those who believe, however, that ADHD is a specific mental illness or brain-disease, these symptoms tend to be seen as identifying a mental disorder with a genetic and biochemical cause.[153] This is generally the view of the ADHD industry.

In 1996, an article in *Scientific American* repeated the Ritalin advocates' view; namely, that by pointing to the rapid rise of ADHD diagnoses as evidence of overdiagnosis, the critics had things backward.[154] According to the experts quoted, the rise in diagnoses just reflected the fact that ADHD had previously been under diagnosed.[155] While the article admitted that diagnosing ADHD is subjective, the article cited several studies that had been done which, while they *did not establish any physiological basis* for ADHD, were characterized as beginning to bring the biology of ADHD into focus.[156]

In essence, those who advocate the use of Ritalin to mitigate the behavior diagnosed as ADHD have generally argued: (a) ADHD has a physiological basis in some abnormal brain structure or brain chemistry, (b) ADHD seriously impairs 5% to 10% of schoolchildren, (c) Ritalin is a relatively mild, safe drug, and (d) those who reject the claim that ADHD is a mental illness properly treated by psychotropic drugs are mired in outmoded, unscientific views of disorders and, instead, are wrongly blaming ADHD on parents and schools.[157]

In 2002 and 2003, a spate of stories supportive of the ADHD diagnosis appeared in the popular press with headlines such as "Ritalin is Safe – and it Works" (*Detroit Daily News*) and "Attention-Deficit Gene is Located" (*Wall Street Journal*).[158] These stories, and others like them, report that there is now substantial evidence to indicate that ADHD is a neurological problem. Case closed. Or is it?

QUESTIONING THE ADHD ORTHODOXY

This view of ADHD and Ritalin has been sharply questioned.[159] In 1999, Dr. Richard Bromfield, a member of the faculty at Harvard Medical School, expressed his concern over the use of Ritalin:

> Ritalin is being dispensed with a speed and nonchalance compatible with our drive-through culture, yet entirely at odds with

good medicine and common sense. The drug does help some people pay attention and function better…. But too many children, and more and more adults, are being given Ritalin inappropriately… the five-fold jump in Ritalin production in the past five years clearly suggests that… Ritalin is being *vastly over prescribed*.[160] [Emphasis added.]

One of the oddities of the ADHD epidemic is that it has been essentially an American and Canadian phenomenon.[161] For example, into the mid-1990s ADHD was rarely diagnosed in European countries such as Denmark, Norway, and Sweden.[162] As of 2000, it was reported that fewer than 6,000 children in France were being prescribed stimulants.[163] In 1997, the British Psychological Society published a major report in which British physicians and psychologists were warned *not* to apply the ADHD label to the wide variety of behaviors to which it is applied in the United States and Canada.[164] Indeed, the report questioned whether ADHD was a mental illness at all: "The idea that children who don't attend or sit still in school have a mental disorder is not entertained by most British clinicians."[165] In particular, the report expressed concern that the widespread practice of prescribing Ritalin and similar drugs for children diagnosed with ADHD in the United States *not be replicated* in Britain.[166] Further, the International Classification of Diseases published by the World Health Organization, which is the diagnostic manual used by most European health professionals, does not include as a mental illness any broad, ill-defined disorder comparable to ADHD as it is defined in *DSM-IV*.

THE ADHD DIAGNOSIS: DISSENT EMERGES

In the late 1990s even those who had been prescribing Ritalin began to question vigorously what was being done in the name of ADHD. One example is Dr. Lawrence Diller, whose 1998 book, *Running On Ritalin*, points out that *schools are pressuring* parents to put their children on Ritalin, and that the result is widespread use of the drug when it isn't necessary. Interestingly, this came from a doctor who prescribes Ritalin and believes that there are circumstances when its use is appropriate. As a result of the publicly expressed doubts of health practitioners such as Dr. Diller, however, a more fundamental critique of the ADHD/Ritalin phenomenon began to receive more attention.

Recall that ADHD is alleged by its partisans within the American Psychiatric Association to be a specific "mental illness," not just a way of describing how children can misbehave. Resorting to Ritalin (and similar drugs) has been justified, in turn, on the ground that a child with ADHD has a genetic and/or biochemical problem that drugs are needed to overcome.[167] In light of this, one might reasonably ask whether there is clear evidence that the broadly defined forms of common childhood misbehavior set forth in the *DSM-IV* as symptoms of ADHD are the result of brain malfunction. This is the question that began to get more serious public attention after the publication of Dr. Diller's book.

One of the leading voices against ADHD as a diagnosis is Dr. Fred Baughman, a pediatric neurologist. Like a number of other critics, Dr. Baughman points to the lack of scientific data to show any link between brain malfunction and the "symptoms" of ADHD:

> This is a contrived epidemic, where all 5 million to 6 million children on these drugs are normal. The country's been led to believe that all painful emotions are a mental illness and the leadership of the APA knows very well that they are representing it [ADHD] as a disease when there is no scientific data to confirm any mental illness.[168]

Dr. Peter Breggin, psychiatrist and author of several books, including *Talking Back to Prozac*, has similarly argued that not only does ADHD not exist, "there is a great deal of scientific evidence that stimulants cause brain damage with long-term use...."[169] So, is there substantial evidence to support the claim that ADHD is a mental illness, or is it, as many have suggested, an example of normal childhood behavior being voted into an "illness" by a professional organization?[170]

PUTTING "THERAPY" BEFORE SCIENCE?

Because of the controversy surrounding ADHD and skyrocketing levels of administration of psychotropic drugs to schoolchildren, the National Institutes of Health convened a Consensus Development Conference on the Diagnosis and Treatment of Attention Deficit Hyperactivity Disorder in 1998. Thirty-one scientific presentations concerning ADHD and its treatment were made to the panel, which concluded:

> We *don't* have an independent valid test for ADHD; there are *no* data to indicate that ADHD is due to a brain malfunction; existing studies come to conflicting conclusions as to whether the use of psychostimulants increases or decreases the risk of abuse, and finally after years of clinical research and experience with ADHD, our knowledge about the cause or causes of ADHD remains *speculative*.[171] [Emphasis added.]

Apparently stung by their failure to get the NIH Conference to declare that ADHD is a real brain malfunction, ADHD partisans eventually drafted their own "International Consensus" letter in which they graciously compare those who question the validity of the ADHD diagnosis to "flat-earthers."[172] This letter has proved a useful public relations tool with those who are not familiar with the conclusions of the NIH conference. All in all, the debate among psychiatrists on the validity of the ADHD diagnosis often seems to resemble politics more than science.

ADHD: HOW GOOD IS THE EVIDENCE?

What about the studies that *Scientific American* reported were beginning to point the way toward the biological basis of ADHD? Upon scrutiny, they were less than they appeared to be. For example, the statistical significance of the findings of one study that claimed to find increased brain metabolism among adults with a history of childhood ADHD evaporated when it was found that a disproportionate number of women were included in the controls.[173] In another instance, it appears that rather than establishing a biological basis for ADHD, the study confirmed earlier work indicating that long-term use of stimulant therapy causes brain atrophy.[174]

Well, what about more recent articles in the popular press reporting that the ADHD diagnosis has been vindicated? These also fail to bear up under scrutiny. For example, the 2002 *Detroit Daily News* story trumpeting that Ritalin works and is safe was based on a 2002 brain imaging study published in the *Journal of the American Medical Association*.[175] That study was described as establishing that ADHD children have brains 3% to 4% smaller than "normal" children and that when treated with Ritalin the ADHD children enjoyed enhanced brain growth. Consequently, the article reassures, parents can relax. ADHD is now shown to have an organic basis, and Ritalin, when properly used, is not merely harmless, but beneficial. In other words, the worries about ADHD and Ritalin are simply based on now discredited myths.

Unfortunately, for the journalists responsible for the story, the study doesn't end any "myths" about Ritalin or ADHD. The lead researcher, Dr. F. Xavier Castellanos himself has only claimed that the study raised the *possibility* that medication *might* enhance the maturation of the brain in children with ADHD.[176] But on examination, the study itself is deeply flawed. It turns out that the claim that children with ADHD have 3% to 4% smaller brains was based on comparing a control group of "normal" children (*i.e.*, children who had not been diagnosed with ADHD) with unmedicated children that had been diagnosed with ADHD *who were also both two years younger and shorter and lighter than the control group*. As a recent scholarly analysis of the Castellanos study points out, however, "most research on brain size has found brain size to be correlated with body weight.... In fact, given all these other variables [height, weight, and age] it would be noteworthy *if they* [the unmedicated children diagnosed with ADHD] *did not have smaller brains*."[177] [Emphasis in the original.]

As already noted, the Castellanos study was based on brain-imaging, and the use of various brain imaging technologies has been one of two major approaches for trying to discover a brain pathology that underlies the ADHD diagnosis. In a 2003 article published in *The Journal of Mind and Behavior*, Dr. Jonathan Leo and Dr. David Cohen carefully examine the 35 brain-imaging studies that have been produced over the last 25 years in an effort to tie the ADHD diagnosis to an underlying brain pathology.[178] The goal of the researchers has been, of course, to identify a brain pathology that would distinguish children diagnosed with ADHD from "normal" children. The analysis by Leo and Cohen shows that virtually all of the studies have been unsound because of a failure to control for medication history and alcoholism. Castellanos' study, which did attempt to control for medication history, was fatally flawed for failing to control for age, height, and weight.

So, what is to be made of the brain imaging studies? Leo and Cohen describe the current state of play as follows:

> [T]here is virtual unanimity that this [using brain imaging technology to identify a brain pathology with the ADHD diagnosis] cannot be accomplished at present. Experiments with highly selective patient and control groups are, at best, only preliminary studies, and we have shown – in complement to the critical analysis by Baumeister and Hawkins (2001) – that the findings of these studies must be called into question. In response to persistent pressure from critics such as Baughman (1998) and Breggin (1991), it seems that neuroimaging researchers now acknowledge the importance of medication history. The publication of the Castellanos *et al.* (2002) article, using non-medicated children, essentially trivializes any further studies that use medicated children. Yet, after twenty-five years, and thirty-five studies, there is not a single straightforward experiment comparing typical unmedicated children with an ADHD diagnosis to typical controls. We are perplexed.[179]

In other words, no brain imaging study establishes that a biological pathology gives rise to the ADHD diagnosis. Parents should also be "perplexed," as Leo and Cohen put it, that in twenty-five years no one has done the straightforward research project that Leo and Cohen describe.[180]

ADHD: A GENETIC PROBLEM?

Another major approach to legitimizing the ADHD diagnosis is to attempt to associate it with a genetic source. The previously mentioned 2002 *Wall Street Journal* article reports on a study published in the *American Journal of Human Genetics* that was produced by a research team lead by Dr. Susan L. Smalley of the UCLA Neuropsychiatric Institute. As is typically the case in the popular press, the headline is way out in front of the science. The "Attention-Deficit Gene Is Located" headline notwithstanding, Dr. Smalley's own claims are substantially more modest:

> Dr. Smalley said the work would need to be replicated, and that years of effort would still be required to find actual genes that contribute to ADHD. "Finding a gene is like finding a contact lens at Disneyland," she said, and the current research is equivalent to finding that the contact lens "probably is in Space Mountain."[181]

In fact, the Smalley study's claims are even more circumscribed – the researchers think that they have found a gene that *could* account for as much 30% of the genetic cause of ADHD, which they also believe is influenced by environment. Consequently, the results of the Smalley study at best indicate a direction for future research.

The tentative nature of the Smalley study is nothing new. A critical review published in 2000 by Dr. Jay Joseph of the studies investigating connections between the ADHD diagnosis and possible genetic causes provides reason to believe that claims that ADHD has a genetic cause are at present far from well supported.[182] More to the point, however, there is no genetic test that identifies whether someone has ADHD or is somehow predisposed toward ADHD. None.

This should not be surprising given that the entire field of genetics is in its infancy. Moreover, it appears that the workings of the human genome are far more complicated than supposed even a relatively short time ago. For example, it has long been thought that the sequence of a person's genes determines such physical characteristics as hair color. Now it appears that environmental factors such as a mother's diet during pregnancy can activate or silence the expression of genes so that identical gene sequences for hair color can produce different hair colors in offspring.[183] Scientists hope that this may point toward a research program that will explain, for instance, why identical twins do not always have the same genetic diseases.

Since our knowledge of the human genome and how it works is at best rudimentary, why is there so much talk about genetics in connection with ADHD, especially when the genetic studies are far from establishing that ADHD has an organic basis? As one proponent of the ADHD diagnosis has written:

> Another influence of genetic findings is in the area of education and medication compliance. Many parents are reluctant for their children to take psychotropic medication and others find it difficult to maintain the prescribed regimen. These problems are mitigated by discussing the genetic etiology of ADHD....[184]

Get it? If a parent is reluctant to drug his child, it helps to invoke an unproven hypothesis about the "genetic etiology" of ADHD to get the parent to "comply."[185] As should be apparent, the practice of administering psychotropic drugs to children for ADHD is an ethical and medical minefield.[186]

ADHD: A DISEASE THAT DISAPPEARS DURING SUMMER VACATION?

This lack of any identifiable brain, biochemical, or genetic abnormality and its absurdly broad and subjective diagnostic criteria are not the only strange things about ADHD as a disease. Dr. Peter Breggin points out that the *DSM-IV* states that a child may manifest "symptoms" of ADHD when in settings "that lack intrinsic appeal or novelty" and tend to disappear when "the person is under very strict control, is in a novel setting, is engaged in especially interesting activities, is in a one-to-one situation."[187] Breggin also notes that most supporters of ADHD as a diagnosis admit that it tends *to disappear during summer vacation!*[188] Could it be that the fidgeting, lack of attention, and many of the other "symptoms" of ADHD do not reflect a mental illness but that children, and especially boys, are bored with, frustrated by, and alienated from the schools in whose custody they are placed? Could it also reflect a lack of parental attention and effective discipline at home and at school? Of course, this is just speculative, but, then, it seems so is the validity of the ADHD diagnosis.

RITALIN: A DRUG THAT CAN GIVE ANYONE A "BUZZ"

Some have attempted to claim that the existence of ADHD is confirmed by the fact that children diagnosed with ADHD tend to become more focused and obedient after taking Ritalin. The truth is, however, that giving Ritalin to normal children also has the same effect.[189] In fact, almost everyone's attention is improved by stimulants such as Ritalin, amphetamines, caffeine, and nicotine.[190] Consequently, seeing an improvement in someone's attention span after taking Ritalin doesn't establish that he has some disorder known as "ADHD." If it did, then we would have to conclude that virtually everyone in the world has ADHD.

A recent study gives further reason to question just what is being diagnosed when a child is labeled as having ADHD.[191] According to the study, which was led by researchers from the Boston University School of Medicine, children with sleep disorders manifest symptoms of ADHD at a higher rate than other children. In fact, snoring or other sleep-disordered breathing problems were found to be associated with a two-fold increase in the symptoms of ADHD. These sleep disorders affect an estimated 2% to 3% of children. But if sleep-disordered breathing problems are associated with an increase in the symptoms of ADHD, could it be that other factors causing children to get insufficient sleep are also associated with an increase in the symptoms of ADHD? Could we be drugging many children for ADHD, when the real problem is a lack of sleep because of over-scheduling, too many late hours in front of television or playing computer games, and a failure by parents to enforce reasonable bedtimes?

Don't Worry, It's Perfectly Safe

But if the very existence of ADHD is questionable, what about the benign public perception of Ritalin as a mild stimulant and the safest psychotropic drug available?[192] This appears not to be quite true either. Sweden banned Ritalin in 1968 because of abuse.[193] The International Narcotics Control Board has reported that Ritalin's pharmacological effects are essentially the same as those of amphetamines and methamphetamines (*i.e.*, "speed").[194]

In 1995 the Drug Enforcement Administration reported that Ritalin is similar to cocaine: "It is clear that Ritalin substitutes for cocaine and d-amphetamine in a number of behavioral paradigms."[195] In 1996 the Drug Enforcement Administration held a conference on the use of stimulants in treating ADHD. In a report about the meeting, Gene Haislip, deputy assistant administrator of the Drug Enforcement Agency's Office of Diversion Control, pointedly warned parents about a *lack of candor* in how Ritalin has been promoted, especially as a drug for schoolchildren:

> Regrettably, much of the literature and promotion of the drug in recent years has ignored or understated the potency and abuse potential of methylphenidate and Ritalin.... This appears to have misled many physicians into prescribing the drug as a quick fix for problems of school and behavior.[196]

In fact, even the official version of the risks of taking Ritalin indicates that the dangers are far from trivial.

Well, Now That You Ask, There Are a Few Side-Effects

Here are some of the side effects for Ritalin listed by the *Physician's Desk Reference*: inability to fall asleep and stay asleep, nervousness, loss of appetite, abdominal pain, weight loss, abnormally fast heartbeat, chest pain, dizziness, headache, hives, jerking, pulse changes, skin rash,

Tourette's syndrome, and severe and multiple twitching and writhing movements. Users are also warned that "suppression of growth has been reported with the long term use of stimulants," long-term abuse can lead to tolerance and mental dependence with varying degrees of abnormal behavior, and *"Long term effects of Ritalin in children have not been well established."*

Critics of Ritalin are less circumspect about the risks so blandly described by the *Physician's Drug Reference*. Dr. Peter Breggin, for example, notes the following:[197]

- Ritalin can cause inattention, hyperactivity, and aggression – in other words, the symptoms of ADHD!
- Ritalin can suppress a child's growth (height and weight), but there are no studies of how this growth suppression might affect the child's brain development. Moreover, there are studies that indicate that long-term use of Ritalin can result in shrinkage of parts of the brain.
- Ritalin can cause permanent, disfiguring tics and muscle spasms.
- Ritalin can often make children anxious, sometimes causing them to act in ways that seem "crazy."
- Ritalin can cause withdrawal symptoms when one or more doses are missed.

A 2001 study by researchers at the University of Buffalo reports that Ritalin may cause long-term changes in the brain similar to those produced by amphetamines and cocaine.[198] More specifically, Ritalin was found to activate certain genes linked to addiction known as "c-fos genes." Moreover, these genes were activated "in a pattern similar to that seen among those who use cocaine and amphetamines,"[199] which may provide the biological basis for the University of California study's finding that Ritalin is a "gateway" drug.

THE LONG-TERM EFFECT ON YOUNG CHILDREN? WHO KNOWS?

Dr. Jerry Rushton of the University of Michigan emphasizes

how little is really known about how Ritalin and other psychotropic drugs affect young children:

> I think the safety of these medications – in the young child especially – is not known, and when you take them in combination it's a whole new level of safety concern.... It's something that needs to be studied further.[200]

Well, as it turns out, it has been studied further. In 2003 the results of a study conducted at the Brookhaven National Laboratory comparing the effects of cocaine and Ritalin on the brain were published in the *Journal of Neuroscience*. The associate laboratory director for life sciences at Brookhaven National Laboratory, Nora Volkow, described the data from the study as clearly showing "that the notion that Ritalin is a weak stimulant is *completely incorrect*."[201] [Emphasis added.] As reported in the Brookhaven study, Ritalin has a stronger effect on the dopamine system than cocaine.[202]

This is significant because the dopamine system, according to doctors, is an area of the brain in which drugs such as cocaine and Ritalin have the most effect.[203] Apparently influenced by the benign image of Ritalin that has been cultivated within the medical profession, Volkow, a psychiatrist, described herself as "shocked as hell" that Ritalin had such a profound effect on the dopamine system.[204]

An article that appeared in 2003 in the *American Journal of Psychiatry* gives more reason for concern regarding the use of Ritalin and other psychotropic drugs with children and adolescents. The study concluded that adolescents may be more susceptible to drug addiction than adults because of the stage of the development of their brain structure.[205] Moreover, the lead author of the study, who is also a psychiatrist on the faculty of Yale, R. Andrew Chambers, believes that far more research should be done specifically on the impact of psychiatric medicines on adolescents and their susceptibility to drug addiction.[206] Like the researchers in the Brookhaven study, Chambers also notes that addictive drugs and psychiatric medicines act on the same brain systems.[207]

HERE'S YOUR BRAIN ON RITALIN (AND SOME OTHER DRUGS)

Yet another cause for concern over "Ritalinizing" children was raised by a study of rats conducted by a research team led by Dr. William A. Carlezon, Jr., an associate professor at Harvard Medical School and the director of the behavioral genetics laboratory at McClean Hospital, published in the December 15, issue of *Biological Psychiatry*.[208] In the study, juvenile rats were divided into a control group that received a placebo and another group that was given Ritalin. The behavior of the rats as adults was then compared. The brains of the rats who had been given Ritalin as juveniles appeared to have been permanently altered. According to Dr. Carlezon: "Rats exposed to Ritalin as juveniles showed large increases in learned-helplessness behavior [determined by testing how quickly a rat under stress gave up on behavioral tasks] during adulthood, suggesting a tendency toward depression."[209] The researchers do not believe that the effects they observed are specific to Ritalin, but are rather a general reflection of how stimulant drugs affect developing brains – "early studies indicate that juvenile exposure to cocaine instead of Ritalin produces the same pattern of results."[210] While the results of rat studies are obviously not conclusive with respect to humans, the research by Dr. Carlezon's team makes it clear that very little is known about the long-term neurobiological consequences of exposing children to psychotropic drugs.[211] Nevertheless, the possibility that the promiscuous drugging of school children may lead to millions of adults who are depressed and who have little problem-solving ability is a disquieting prospect.

In 2003, the very real dangers of using insufficiently researched psychotropic drugs came into clearer focus when the British Medicines Control Agency (an agency similar to our FDA) ruled that the psychotropic drug Paxil should not be given to anyone under 18 years-old. Why? Because evidence indicates that Paxil (marketed as Seroxat in Britain) increases a child's risk of suicide. Shortly after the action taken in Britain, the FDA recommended against pediatric use of Paxil.[212] The maker of Paxil, Glaxo SmithKline, is also being sued by over 800 Paxil-addicted adult users in Britain because of inadequate warnings regarding the risk of addiction posed by Paxil.

What a difference a day makes. Before these warnings came out, many parents were being assured by their medical professionals that Paxil was perfectly safe to use on their children, just like Ritalin, Adderall, and the rest of the pharmacopia of psychotropic drugs.

How many parents of the at least four million children being drugged with Ritalin and other psychotropic drugs do you think have been candidly informed about all these risks? *How many of these parents do you believe are told candidly about how little is known about the long-term effects of Ritalin and other psychotropic drugs on infants, children and adolescents?*

THE ADHD INDUSTRY: TELLING THE TRUTH, THE WHOLE TRUTH, AND NOTHING BUT THE TRUTH?

Of course, the threshold issue concerns the diagnosis of ADHD itself. To paraphrase Gertrude Stein's comment about Oakland, do you think that parents have been told there may not be a "there" there? How many parents do you think have been told that in reality Ritalin is a cure for a "mental illness":

- established by a vote of psychiatrists in the American Psychiatric Association[213] – the very same American Psychiatric Association that in the 1970s declared by vote that homosexuality was no longer a mental disorder and that is now debating whether pedophilia and sadomasochism should continue to be considered mental disorders[214]
- defined by highly subjective criteria that include common forms of childhood behavior
- that historically has been largely confined to the United States and Canada and that mental health professionals in countries such as Britain have resisted recognizing
- for which there is no valid test, for which there are little or no data to support the claim that it is due to a brain malfunction or neurochemical imbalance, and for which knowledge of the cause or causes is purely speculative?

In sum, American society is currently drugging its *schoolchildren* at an almost inconceivable rate based on an alleged mental illness that cannot be shown to have any organic basis and that appears to be diagnosed on the basis of little more than persistent unruly behavior.

GOVERNMENT SCHOOLS: "JUST SAY 'YES'"

In 1999 the Drug Enforcement Agency reported that 10% of schoolchildren had been diagnosed with ADHD,[215] and, as previously noted, the chairman of a congressional committee believes that Ritalin may be the biggest drug problem we have in this country. How is this happening? Are millions of parents spontaneously dragging Junior to see a psychiatrist or psychologist? Not quite. Unfortunately, not only have government schools become major distributors of psychotropic drugs, but they have also been instrumental in promoting the ADHD diagnosis and the drugging of children.

While school personnel cannot prescribe Ritalin or other psychotropic drugs, they do "evaluate" children for ADHD. These "evaluations" are typically performed through school officials filling out what is known as the "pencil/paper diagnostic exam," which is a form based on the highly subjective *DSM-IV* ADHD symptoms.[216] Based on these evaluations, school officials make recommendations that parents seek a "medical evaluation" for ADHD for their child. As pediatrician Dr. Lawrence H. Diller describes it, this is "teacher-speak for 'Get your kid on Ritalin.'"[217]

PROMISCUOUSLY DIAGNOSING ADHD

Worse, the school officials' evaluations are typically used by doctors in making their diagnoses of ADHD.[218] The economics of our health care system compound the problem posed by doctors' use of these school prepared subjective evaluations. As the head of the National Institute of Mental Health, Dr. Richard K. Nakamura, has put it:

We are concerned about improper diagnoses of ADHD. There's a possibility that physicians are told, "You have X amount of time to diagnose XYZ" by their managed-care organization. I believe physicians are being given too little time and money to properly diagnose.[219]

Some New York parents have reported, for example, that doctors have spent only 45 minutes with their children before prescribing Ritalin. This contrasts with Dr. Nakamura's description of a proper diagnostic procedure, which would involve "extensive tests to determine whether a child-behavior or learning disability may be attributed to other problems...."[220] Consequently, it is no surprise that these evaluations and recommendations by school officials have lead to the promiscuous prescription of Ritalin.

Dr. Gretchen LeFever, a pediatric psychologist, performed a study of 30,000 students in two Virginia school districts as a result of the number of ADHD referrals she was receiving.[221] Her concern was that ADHD was being over diagnosed. As a result of her study, Dr. LeFever found:[222]

- 8% to 10% of children in elementary grades routinely received ADHD medication in school. This sharply contrasts with National Institutes of Health estimates that ADHD only affects 3% to 5% of schoolchildren nationally, although it is consistent with the Drug Enforcement Administration 1999 estimates that 10% of schoolchildren have been diagnosed with ADHD.
- Three times as many boys as girls were being medicated for ADHD, and twice as many whites as African American children were being medicated for ADHD.
- By fifth grade 18% to 20% of white boys were being given medication for ADHD.
- Criteria for diagnosing ADHD vary widely across the United States.

Until Dr. LeFever's study, reports that Ritalin use in schools was heavier than had been estimated were unconfirmed. Now, according to Dr. LeFever, "we have reason to believe that there are other regions that probably look more like we do than the national estimates."[223] Evidently, government school educators are getting really proficient in filling out the "pencil/paper diagnostic exam."

In the face of clear evidence that ADHD may not exist, that ADHD is being diagnosed at levels that are obviously unreasonable, that Ritalin poses substantial risk of harm to children, and that, as a result of its prevalence in schools, Ritalin is being widely abused as a recreational drug, what are our highly trained education professionals doing? *Threatening parents* who don't want to drug their children. Are you surprised?

DRUG HIM OR LOSE HIM

As incredible as it may seem, school districts are beginning to threaten parents with the *loss* of their children if they don't want to medicate them. Here are just two examples:[224]

- A 7 year-old boy's parents were concerned about the side-effects he was suffering from Ritalin. After the parents spoke to the school administrators about their decision to take their son off the drug, the school administrators called Child Protective Services alleging child abuse. As a result, the parents were placed on a state-wide list of alleged child abusers and ensnared in a court battle to clear their names and keep their child.
- In another case, a mother decided to take her 9 year-old son off of a drug cocktail that included Ritalin, Paxil, and Dexadrine because they caused him to hallucinate. This led to the school district officials calling the police and Child Protective Services in an effort to enforce their preference that the boy be drugged.

According to observers, government schools "are increasingly using accusations of child abuse and neglect" if parents resist drugging their children.[225] David Lansner, a New York City lawyer who has seen cases similar to those described, reports, "The schools are now using child protective services to enforce their own desires and their own policies."[226] Similarly, Dr. Lawrence H. Diller has noted: "It is no longer simply an issue of which school or class a child will attend. Instead, some parents are being threatened with the possibility of losing custody of their children if they refuse to comply with suggested treatment for an alleged medical condition [ADHD]."[227]

One of the shocking aspects of these developments is that the government has traditionally respected parental decisions regarding medical treatment for their children unless the life of the child was in danger. In these cases, nothing of the sort is at stake. The government school officials in these instances simply believe that drugging the child is a better medical decision, and they obviously mean to have their way.

Trying to Rein in Schools' Promotion of Psychotropic Drugs

Evidence of government schools pressuring school nurses and parents to put children on Ritalin also surfaced in a congressional hearing. In her testimony before a House Committee, Ohio Representative Deborah Pryce told the Committee that Ohio State Board of Pharmacy officials had reported to her that they were "concerned about the use of Ritalin among school-age children in Ohio and the pressure placed on school nurses and parents to put children on this drug."[228] This sort of promotion of psychotropic drugs by government schools led the Colorado Board of Education to vote to discourage school employees from suggesting the use of drugs like Ritalin and to encourage them to rely on discipline and instruction to reduce unruly classroom behavior.[229]

The aggressive efforts by schools and others to force parents to drug their children with psychotropic drugs finally led to a legislative response. In May 2003 the United States House of Representatives voted 425 to 1 in favor of a measure prohibiting schools from requiring any child to take any psychotropic drug in order to attend school or get school services. This bill has been introduced in the United

States Senate by Nevada Senator John Ensign and Tennessee Senator and former Secretary of Education Lamar Alexander.[230] Connecticut, Minnesota, Virginia, Illinois, and Colorado have already enacted similar legislation.

CHANGE HIS DIAPER, THEN GIVE HIM A "HIT" OF RITALIN

School age children and adults are not the only ones enriching the psychotropic drug industry.[231] Research done at the University of Maryland shows that the number of children ages 2-4 taking psychotropic drugs such as Ritalin, Prozac, Zoloft, and Paxil increased by 50% between 1991 and 1995.[232] Moreover, it is reported that over a quarter of a million pediatricians are prescribing Ritalin to children *under* age 6.[233] Apparently, a lot of two, three, four, and five year-olds are showing unmistakable signs of ADHD. You know, stuff like not wanting to sit still, often not listening when spoken to, and having a short attention span. Do the pediatricians and psychiatrists have the vaguest idea what they are doing to these children? Of course not. In a February 23, 2000, article in the *New York Times*, Dr. Joseph Coyle, the chairman of psychiatry at Harvard Medical School, commented on the drugging of these very young children:[234] "These interventions are occurring at a critical time in brain development, *and we don't know what the consequences are.*"[235] [Emphasis added.]

Evidently, elements of the medical research community wanted to remedy their lack of knowledge about how these drugs affect toddlers. This appears to explain a federally funded 72-week study on the effects of Ritalin on very young children begun in late 2001 in New York City by six medical institutions.[236] Most of the children were under 5 years old, with some of them being as young as age 3.[237] According to reports, the children were started on small doses of Ritalin, and then the doses were increased to see how much they could tolerate.[238] After the children reached the maximum dosage they were able to tolerate, they were placed in a simulated classroom with one-way mirrors so that the researchers could study their behavior while being weaned off Ritalin.

If this sounds a bit like the kind of medical research performed in Eastern Europe by certain German medical professionals who "relocated" to South America in the mid to late 1940s, don't worry. An official at one of the participating institutions (who, understandably, wanted to remain anonymous) avers that the study will enable doctors to "make intelligent decisions."[239] I guess we are supposed to feel better knowing that, after already drugging millions of toddlers and children, the psychiatric profession is now trying to figure out what it has been doing.

Where does the idea that toddlers suffer from ADHD and need to be drugged come from? Dr. Julie Magno Zito, the author of the University of Maryland study, cites as a factor the increased reliance on daycare and the consequent need to have children "conform in their behavior."[240] This observation is confirmed by the New York City study in which some of the "research subjects" (a.k.a. "children") have been referred by schools.

Just in case you continue to be skeptical that our trusted professionals could really be doing this to children, consider that in 1994 over 3000 prescriptions for Prozac were written for *children under 12 months old.*[241] And just exactly how does a psychiatrist or a doctor determine that a 10 month-old baby, for example, is depressed and is in need of Prozac? Do you think that there is a sound body of research indicating that its just okey-dokey to give Prozac to infants? Do you think that anyone has the slightest idea what the long-term effects of giving Prozac to infants and preschoolers are?

PSYCHOTROPIC DRUGS AND CHILDREN: "READY, FIRE, AIM!"

When we get beyond the surface, it's clear that something very wrong is going on. Advocates of the ADHD diagnosis are still searching for a biological justification. That means that millions of children are being drugged to treat something that has not yet been shown to be a real disease, as distinguished from unruly or bad behavior. Worse, no one really knows what the true short-term or long-term effects of administering these drugs to children are. It is shocking that the drugging of millions of schoolchildren has been allowed to proceed without proof that there is a disease and, *especially*, without sufficient testing of the effects of these powerful psychotropic drugs on children. In fact, it is hard to think of a more egregious example of medical malpractice than to prescribe drugs to infants, preadolescents, and adolescents when the consequences to them in those particular stages of development are largely unknown.

When the legitimacy of the ADHD diagnosis is challenged, more than a few of its defenders resort to deriding the skeptics as "flat-earthers," "Scientologists," or "prejudiced." Some of the skeptics claim, on the other hand, that this ad hominen defense of the ADHD diagnosis reflects venality and professional arrogance. Perhaps, but I don't doubt that the name-calling may also reflect in some cases a passionately held view that ADHD diagnosis is valid and that prescribing psychotropic drugs to, by some estimates, as many as twenty percent of our schoolchildren is somehow medically justified.[242] Still, those of us who are not psychiatrists might be excused if the votes, consensus letters, public relations efforts, and naming-calling that appear to be integral to establishing a psychiatric diagnosis strike us as resembling politics rather than science.

It is *possible* that among the children swept up in the very broad and subjective ADHD diagnostic criteria that there may be some children that do have an organic problem that psychotropic drugs relieve (whether they do it safely is another matter). Nor is it impossible for Ritalin and other psychotropic drugs to have some legitimate applications.[243] But no one now really knows whether that is the case with ADHD and children. Instead, schools and parents are medicating rather than disciplining, medicating rather than providing a stimulating environment, medicating instead of having recess, and medicating instead of correcting the institutionalized abuse of boys in government schools. The price of allowing schools to rely on "mother's little helper" to maintain order is likely eventually to carry a price tag that we can't even begin to comprehend now.

"As Jazzed as Any Speed Freak"

There is ample scientific evidence to indicate that Ritalin is a very powerful drug with serious side effects. But what is it really like to be medicated with Ritalin? What is it like on the "inside"? Children, unfortunately are not articulate or experienced enough to give us much insight into this question. But Walter Kirn, a professional writer, describes eloquently his experience with Ritalin after he had been diagnosed with adult "ADD." According to Kirn, the "Ritalinized" state of mind is far from benign – no matter how calm or in control the Ritalin user may *seem* to outside observers:

> I felt guilty each time I renewed my prescription, but like Ritalin's other effects, it didn't show. I felt guilty because the drug was so damned powerful – easily as euphoria inducing as any illegal substance I'd ever tried. In fact, its effects were better. Cleaner. Tighter. Plus, compared to street drugs, the stuff was cheap. For the same amount cokeheads pay for one night's high, I could soar for a month, without fear of the police. Not that I didn't feel paranoid anyhow. During the eighteen months I took the drug, I rehearsed countless times a scene in which a cop pulled me over for a traffic infraction, looked deep into my dilated pupils, then spotted the pill bottle on the seat beside me. "It's a prescription, officer," I'd say. And what could he do about it? Not a thing. There I am, as jazzed as any speed freak who's just put his girl-friend in the hospital after an all-night quarrel in a motel room, and yet I'm untouchable, innocent, free to go.[244]

Are you still wondering why Ritalin is being abused as a street drug or why it is being widely used as a recreational drug by teen-agers? Kirn's experience with Ritalin also showed him how Ritalin could be prescribed to so many children: "It's no wonder, I thought, that parents and teachers love the stuff.... Forget how the little white pills make Johnny feel… they make the adults looking after him feel great."[245] Kirn ultimately took himself off of Ritalin. Children don't have that option, even if they, like Kirn, could understand what is being done to them.

WHAT IS GOING ON?

There is more to this controversy than mere institutional stupidity and professional cupidity, although they are present in good measure, too. *Schools do have serious discipline problems*, and the reasons are many. Effective discipline of students, particularly the highly effective corporal variety, has been virtually eliminated from schools because of court rulings and biases against traditional discipline in schools of education and among some elements of society. For some of the same reasons, discipline is often largely absent in the home. This problem is particularly acute when fathers are absent from the home or uninvolved with their children. Many boys undoubtedly resent being treated as "disturbed" for no reason other than the fact that they are boys and are frustrated by the schools' failure to teach them how to read properly. Boys and girls alike are also doubtlessly bored by the thin intellectual gruel that government schools ladle out today. The increasingly politically-correct curricula inflicted on children – often by marginally competent or incompetent teachers – also invite rebellion. Values clarification and other non-academic curricula subtly undermine the authority of the teacher and school as well as that of parents, and the values of street gangs are present in schools as never before. For these and other reasons, government schools *are* difficult places to teach and to manage.

Viewed from this institutional perspective, ADHD and psychotropic drugs such as Ritalin are godsends. Faced with a severe breakdown of discipline, many teachers and administrators undoubtedly believe that Ritalin and similar drugs are perhaps the only effective classroom management tools left to them. And what is even better, government schools can get *extra money* from the federal government for children diagnosed with ADHD, courtesy of the Individuals with Disabilities Act. Further, because the Elementary and Secondary Education Act of 1965 brought an army of psychologists, psychiatrists, social workers, and psychiatric programs into government schools, in some sense it is probably natural now for many educators to see behavioral problems as medical problems. This may give you some insight into why Dr. Fred Baughman, a pediatric neurologist who is one of the more outspoken critics of the ADHD epidemic and Ritalin, believes:

> *Every child who goes to public school is at risk.* Psychology and psychiatry await. Teachers teach no more. They have become "diagnosticians."[246] [emphasis added]

But how does all of this look to schoolchildren?

Surely schoolchildren must view the situation as deeply ironic. They are told that they shouldn't use drugs (unless, of course, they have reached the opposite conclusion as a result of participation in a program that taught them "critical thinking" or "values clarification"), and yet their schools have been turned into virtual pharmacies of psychotropic drugs that school officials are *urging* them to take. The ubiquitous presence of Ritalin and other psychotropic drugs, in turn, has created massive recreational abuse of these drugs in schools. Students may well be asking themselves why using drugs is bad if they use them to escape their problems for a while, but it's just fine if the school nurse gives them drugs so that teachers can escape from their ADHD, oppositional defiance disorder, or some other psychiatric mumbo jumbo diagnosis? Perhaps they are concluding that it is just a matter of whose problems count.

By the way, if you think that it sounds as if the Cali drug cartel has infiltrated government schools, our highly trained education professionals recommend that *you* seek a "medical evaluation."

THE ZERO TOLERANCE GULAG

Here is another little quiz: What do you do if an eight year-old boy in a school cafeteria picks up one of his chicken fingers, points it at a teacher, and says "Pow!"? Do you tell him not to play with his food, or do you suspend him from school for making terroristic threats? If you answered that the boy should be told not to play with his food you probably aren't cut out for a career in a government

234 THE HARSH TRUTH ABOUT PUBLIC SCHOOLS

school. This incident, and others like it, really happened.[247] Welcome to the "zero tolerance" gulag.

WHAT'S IN A NAME?

While many of the serious problems in the government schools take place out of the public eye, by the 1990s the public began to notice increases in school disorder and crime, and public confidence in government schools started to erode. In an effort to restore confidence, government schools began announcing in the early 1990s that they were adopting "zero tolerance" policies regarding such matters as guns, drugs, and sexual harassment. This trend gathered momentum in 1994 when Congress jumped on the bandwagon by passing the Gun Free Schools Act. That legislation imposed a national "zero tolerance" policy regarding weapons that required states to expel for at least one year any student who brings a weapon to school or risk the loss of federal funds.

What is "zero tolerance"? It refers to school disciplinary policies that establish broad rules regarding such matters as drugs, weapons, and sexual harassment that are strictly and severely enforced. Typically, if a student breaches a "zero tolerance" rule, the student is automatically suspended from school or worse. Unfortunately, the creators and enforcers of "zero tolerance" policies have proved strangely incapable of distinguishing between nail clippers and a switchblade, a Midol tablet and a syringe filled with heroin, or a hug by a five-year-old and rape.

Don't be tempted to think that this is simply evidence of rank stupidity on the part of government school educators. That isn't really the story. "Zero tolerance" is best understood as a public relations slogan that has readily lent itself to the institutionalized abuse of schoolchildren by agenda-driven zealots.

CRIMINALIZING MIDOL

Of course, guns, illegal drugs, and sexual assault were against school rules even before government educators discovered "zero tolerance." But with the public becoming restive over school crime and the general lack of discipline within schools, government schools needed to show they were "doing something." At the margins, "zero tolerance" policies may have made punishment more certain for serious rule infractions, but it is not clear that even that is true. Nothing in the crime data indicates that "zero tolerance" policies have stemmed the tide of *illegal* drug use and trafficking on school campuses or reduced overall school crime. What "zero tolerance" clearly seems to have done, however, is allow elements within government schools who *are fixated on* issues such as gender, violence, and drugs to satisfy their obsessions by creating and enforcing ill-defined, irrational rules to the detriment of children. Here are a few examples, and remember, as Dave Barry might say, I am not making these up:

- Two New Jersey second graders "were charged with making 'terroristic threats' after playing cops-and-robbers with paper guns."[248]
- A New Jersey boy, whose father is in the military, was suspended for five days for drawing a stick figure of a Marine shooting a member of the Taliban.[249] School officials claimed the drawing was "not the work of a normal mind." Perhaps the same could be said of the school officials' judgment.
- A Florida sixth grader was arrested, handcuffed, and taken to jail in a squad car for the "crime" of stomping in a puddle and splashing classmates and a school employee.[250]
- In Oregon a thirteen-year-old was suspended for combating his halitosis with Scope mouthwash while at school. Why? Because Scope contains alcohol.[251]
- A six-year-old boy in Ohio "was suspended from school for sexual harassment after he jumped from the tub in which he was bathing at home to wave out the window at the school bus that was picking up his sister."[252]
- A thirteen-year-old Texas girl was suspended after a drug-sniffing dog detected drugs in her backpack.[253] She had a bottle of Advil.

- A six-year-old was disciplined for carrying a weapon to school in his lunch sack. The "weapon," it turns out, was a plastic knife that his grandmother had put inside so he could spread his peanut butter.[254]
- After being commended by school officials for taking a knife from a student who was threatening suicide, a Virginia middle schooler was suspended because the school board decided that he had not given the knife to an adult quickly enough.[255]
- A Colorado Springs six-year-old was suspended from school for drug possession. Was it heroin? Hashish? Cocaine? No, lemon drops. His mother was told that "a child who brings candy to school is comparable to a teen who takes a gun to school."[256]
- A 10-year-old Colorado girl was suspended for sexual harassment. Apparently she was part of a group of girls, and she committed the unpardonable sin of "sexual harassment" by repeatedly asking a boy on the playground if he liked them.[257]
- A boy who offered a friend a Certs breath mint was suspended for distributing drugs.[258]
- A third grade boy was suspended from his Mobile, Alabama, school for five days. His "crime" was taking a vitamin with his lunch in violation of the school's "zero-tolerance policy for substance abuse."[259]
- A sixth grade South Carolina honors student was hauled off in a police car after school officials discovered that she had a weapon. She was guilty of packing "a paring knife in her lunch box to cut up a piece of left-over chicken."[260]

LAWRENCE MIDDLE SCHOOL: "GOING TO THE BATHROOM IS A PRIVILEGE, NOT A RIGHT"

In a display of true zeal for discipline that might be considered a variation on the "zero tolerance" theme, the Associated Press reports that Lawrence Middle School in Lawrence, New Jersey, *prohibits* 7th and 8th-graders from leaving class to go to the bathroom more than 15 times *a month*.[261] The result has been children decreasing their consumption of liquids and, in some cases, trying to "hold it" until they get home. This, however, can lead to infections, incontinence, and constipation, according to urologists. A pediatric urologist interviewed for the story by the Associated Press, Dr. Christopher S. Cooper, stated that the policy obviously doesn't make sense: "When children need to go, they should be allowed to go. It isn't good to hold it in or drink less fluids. It could have long-terms effects on a child's health."[262] One parent called the school to complain about the policy and was told by a highly trained education professional that "...*going to the bathroom is a privilege, not a right*...."[263]

Far from being isolated instances, there are so many examples of "zero tolerance" abuses that it is difficult to decide which are the most egregious or absurd. Even the American Bar Association (ABA) has recognized that those in charge of school discipline have become strangers to commonsense. Noting that "zero tolerance" policies apply theories of punishment to first graders that were previously directed to adult criminals and have led to "*thousands* of unnecessary expulsions and suspensions," the leadership of the ABA has voted that "zero tolerance" policies be abolished.[264]

In light of what they are doing to children in the name of "zero-tolerance," rather than drugging children with Ritalin, perhaps our highly trained education professionals ought to be evaluated for Prozac.

BURIED ALIVE

Government schools have increasingly become seething cauldrons of behavioral and institutional pathologies. The Norman Rockwell image of the local government school is at least two generations out of date. Modern government schools are places of chronic violence, disorder, and rampant drug abuse. They are also places where children must learn to live with being the subject of "educators'" ideological enthusiasms, bullying, and hostilities. Worse, they are in danger of being coerced into the largest uncontrolled pharmacological experiment in the history of the world.

Children attending government schools today bear a daily burden of anxiety, frustration, and alienation that few adults would be willing to tolerate. For Christian children it is worse. The very nature of government school curricula, practices, and standards today oppose and denigrate the Christian schoolchild's young faith. This, in turn, forces on the Christian child a conflict between his faith and finding peace and acceptance within the government school that looms as a colossus in his life. And because they are children, they have no choice except to bear it.

Can it be a surprise, then, that over time these pressures tend to lead Christian children to double-mindedness and a falling away from their faith? We know that roughly 70% of Christian children in government schools stop attending church within two years after graduation from high school. We know that children attending government schools are in greater danger of being seduced by the world than are those who attend sound Christian private schools or who are homeschooled. And while there are always exceptions, you can probably confirm the truth of these propositions in your own church.

If *you* have placed your children, God's gift to you, under the authority of pagans and the godless during their most vulnerable and impressionable years, do you truly expect to be told at the end of your race, "Well done, good and faithful servant"?

SCHOOL REFORM: A POPULAR DELUSION

*"But be ye doers of the word, and not hearers only,
deceiving your own selves."*
James 1:22

"[T]he willingness to endure four years in a typical school of education
often constitutes an effective negative intelligence test."
John Silber, former president of Boston University[1]

If you are still thinking that government schools can be reformed, you haven't been paying attention. First, a government school by its very nature cannot provide an education appropriate for Christian children. Indeed, the very fact that Christians are suffering from government schooling is the direct result of many 19th century Protestants wrongly believing that government schools *could* be created and maintained as Protestant schools. Second, Christians must understand that even conventional reforms aimed merely at restoring traditional academic and moral standards to government schools are, as a practical matter, impossible. Let's first take a look at the reasons why the education industry has frustrated, and will continue to frustrate, conventional reforms. Then we will examine in the next chapter why Christians must not attempt to make government schools Christian schools, even if such a thing were possible.

CAN'T WE ALL JUST GET ALONG?

"School reform" has been a staple of American social and political debate since at least the 1830s. Of course, school reform has also always meant different things to different people. For social and political reformers, school reform is typically a subterfuge for getting control of government schools to promote their version of social and political change; for those associated with the education industry, "school reform" always means pouring more money into government schools; and, for parents and the man-on-the-street, "school reform" generally means trying to improve academic and moral standards within government schools. Of course, this last kind of school reform is precisely the type of reform that is least likely to succeed.

Unfortunately, most Americans, and especially parents, charitably assume that everyone advocating reform is also primarily concerned with having schools do a better job of teaching children to read and write, do mathematics, and develop sound traditional moral standards. Those with other social, political, or economic agendas understand this, and they are all too willing to claim disingenuously that they share these as their primary goals. Worse, they have managed to convince the public that the way to make these improvements in government schools is by "investing" more money in them. This has become such an article of faith that the political debate on funding for education is typically nothing more than an argument over how much more tax money should be given to the education industry.

As you know by now, America spends more per pupil on education than almost any other country and, among developed countries, has the world's least productive schools. Nationally, the average teacher's wages exceed the average worker's wages by 34.9%, and the average teacher also receives benefits equal to 26.6% of his salary.[2] Nevertheless, S.A.T. scores since the 1960s have declined, and NAEP scores *at best* have remained more or less flat,[3] despite the fact that since 1960 spending on education has increased by between 200% to 300% per pupil after adjusting for inflation. Further, an extensive academic study of the effect of spending on student achievement has shown that there is no strong or consistent relationship between spending and student performance.[4]

Lavish funding and dismal results notwithstanding, the education lobby continues to clamor for more money. Recently, even Secretary of Education Rod Paige felt constrained to speak out against the education establishment's ritual bleatings that education is underfunded. In fact, Secretary Paige points out that from 2001 to 2003 K-12 education spending increased 40% at the federal level, and that nationally roughly $500 billion is now spent on K-12 education.[5] That is more than we spend on national defense. Still, Americans remain amazingly oblivious to the truth and all too willingly accept the claim that more money is a key part of what is needed to fix education.[6] Because the systematic data showing there is no correlation between ever higher spending and improved education doesn't seem to make much of an impression, let's use one last example to drive the point home.[7] Then we will be in a position to consider why more money will not reform government schools and why any meaningful reform of government schools won't happen anytime soon.

EVERYTHING'S UP TO DATE IN KANSAS CITY

Whenever government schools fail to improve after there has been a reform-driven increase in spending, the excuse is always that enough money wasn't spent. Most Americans still buy this argument. After all, it is at least *theoretically* possible that yet more money could do the trick. Suppose, however, that we were able to take a large, troubled school district and undertake a comprehensive program of reform in which money is no object. Suppose, also, that the reforms were overseen by an independent party committed to making use of all of the very best government school reform strategies. If we could make such an experiment, don't you think that it would finally settle the issue? Well, there was such an experiment, and people still seem to lose control of their critical faculties when reformers appeal for more spending on government schools.

In 1985 federal district court judge Russell G. Clark seized control of the Kansas City School District to implement a school desegregation plan. As part of Judge Clark's reign, he invited educators to think big and come up with a wish list of everything that they thought would improve student achievement in Kansas City schools. To implement the dreams of Kansas City's highly trained education professionals, Judge Clark ordered over $2 billion spent to create the perfect school system. To finance all of this spending, the judge by fiat almost doubled the Kansas City property tax rate, imposed a 1.5%

income tax surcharge, and forced the State of Missouri to provide all additional funds needed to implement his plan.

Kansas City schools *did* change dramatically as a result of the spending mandated by Judge Clark. Here are *some* of the things that $2 billion bought:[8]

- Per pupil spending rose to $11,700, the highest in the nation on a cost-of-living adjusted basis for any major school district in the nation.
- The student teacher ratio fell to 13 to 1, the lowest for any major school district in the nation.
- Teachers' pay was increased 40% across the board and their workloads were cut.
- Students were given field trips to Mexico and Senegal.
- A model United Nations facility was built that included simultaneous translation capabilities.
- 15 new schools were built. Amenities included an Olympic-sized swimming pool with underwater viewing room, a zoo, a twenty-five acre wildlife sanctuary, television and animation studios, and a robotics studio.
- Teachers from Belgium, Cameroon, Puerto Rico, Argentina, and Germany were recruited to provide foreign language immersion programs for students in kindergarten through 5th grade.
- Computer magnet elementary schools were equipped with one personal computer for every two students.

So, $2 billion bought a lot of perks, salaries, and stuff. But what did it do for the school district's performance? Are you embarrassed because you find yourself cynically thinking the answer is "nothing"? If so, relax. You are in fact a wild-eyed optimist. The results are worse than that. Here they are:

- The dropout rate went up.
- The Missouri Board of Education stripped the school district of its accreditation in May 2000 for failure to meet even one of eleven performance goals.

- The school district hemorrhaged students to charter schools, leaving the school district in a financial crisis with overstaffed programs and half-empty buildings.
- The educational performance of black students did not improve, and the three grade-level achievement gap between black and white students didn't improve.
- Kansas City Superintendent, Bernard Taylor, Jr., was so desperate to raise standardized test scores that he proposed *paying* students to improve their test scores.[9]

Maybe they just needed more money.[10]

GOVERNMENT SCHOOLS CAN'T REFORM THEMSELVES BECAUSE THEY ARE A SUCCESS FOR THE CONSTITUENCIES THAT COUNT

Kansas City is only a failure if you insist on looking at it from the point of view of the hapless man-in-the-street, who naively thinks that the waves of "reform" that periodically sweep over government schools are primarily intended to improve the intellect, morals, and safety of students. On the other hand, if you are among those with a social, political, or economic agenda, Kansas City was a fabulous success. "Educators" got vastly better salaries, less work, and much improved working conditions. Those concerned with social and political issues got all the money they could want for implementing programs (the model United Nations must have been fun). General contractors, engineers, and architects got a lot of construction business. Lawyers, accountants, and investment bankers made a lot of money from helping issue school bonds. Vendors of textbooks, computers, desks, carpet, and electronic gear of all kinds got their share of the $2 billion. Even the travel industry got in on the feeding frenzy (remember the boondoggles to Senegal and Mexico?). This far from exhausts the list of the beneficiaries of the Kansas City reform.

In truth, Kansas City reveals in microcosm the interests that American education really serves. The government school system functions first and foremost as a way of obtaining and distributing almost $500 billion to various special interest groups, and as a means of gaining influence over children. Teachers, administrators, textbook publishers, contractors, architects, engineers, lawyers, maintenance workers, food service workers, providers of security services, psychologists, nurses, bus drivers, curriculum developers, educational consultants, vendors of all kinds of equipment, services, and food, and issue advocates of all kinds have a vital interest in the concept of "reform" as more money. Not surprisingly, they have relatively little interest in proposals that might threaten their share of the hundreds of billions of dollars that the government school system makes available annually to the education industry.[11]

This is not to say that most government school teachers and administrators are indifferent to whether children learn traditional academic subjects and are kept safe. Doubtless, they would be pleased if that were to occur and, in many cases, they are genuinely puzzled over why their schools can't manage, for example, to teach reading or reduce the presence of drugs and violence. It is to say, however, that *institutionally* these sorts of things are no longer really the primary concerns of the government schools. As a result, efforts to restore a focus on traditional educational and moral values cannot succeed because the necessary changes would threaten too many powerful constituencies. Moreover, any change that would imperil the flow of dollars to schools and their spending constituencies will meet determined opposition.

The 2003 session of the Texas legislature provided a particularly astonishing illustration of how the education industry worships at the shrine of Mammon. By now, virtually everyone is aware that obesity and obesity related diseases such as diabetes are increasing at an alarming rate among school-age children. One important reason is that government schools have become part of the distribution chain for fast food and vending machine companies. According to a 2000 study by the Centers for Disease Control, 20% of schools sell branded fast food in competition with the schools' regular lunch program.[12] In addition, the Centers for Disease Control found that virtually all high schools, three-quarters of middle schools, and nearly half of grade schools have vending machines.[13] Why? Schools make no money, and sometimes lose money, on their traditional federally subsidized school lunch programs. Fast food and vending machine items such as potato chips, however, can offer the schools profit margins of 50% or more.[14]

Over the last decade or two, fast food and vending machine sales have become a significant source of revenue for school districts. Houston Independent School District, for example, reports that it grosses about $2 million per year from vending machine sales alone. Consequently, when Texas State Senator Eddie Lucio, Jr., sponsored a bill in the 2003 session of the Texas legislature that would have merely restricted the availability of some vending machine food and drinks during school meal times, the schools and the junk-food industry responded with a lobbying blitz that blocked the bill in committee.[15] Instead, Lucio's bill was converted into a measure creating a committee to "study" the problem.[16]

After the legislative dust had settled, Lucio observed: "I realize revenues from vending machines and other competitive foods are important, but what is the price of the health of our children?"[17] Well, the price tag placed on children's health by school districts is not really that hard to figure out. If we assume, for example, a 50% profit margin on vending machine snacks, for the Houston Independent School District it would seem that the price tag for its students' health is about $1 million per year.

In time, embarrassing criticism from groups such as the American Academy of Pediatrics may well force government schools in Texas and elsewhere to give up their addiction to junk-food money.[18] If they do, however, it will only be the result of having been shamed by disclosure of how schools have placed financial gain ahead of children's health.

THE JOY OF MONOPOLY SCHOOLS

The government school system is a textbook case of a monopoly. It has roughly an 85% to 90% market share, and as well confirmed economic theory predicts, the government monopoly school system delivers a shoddy product at a high price. But the government school system is not just any garden-variety monopoly. It is one whose services government requires every American to purchase whether he uses it or not. If, for example, you were the monopoly provider of passenger airline service, consumers would still have the option of not using your services by staying home, taking a bus, driving, traveling by ship, and so on without having to pay airfare for a service they don't use. If your passenger airline service monopoly had the same rights as the government school system, however, not only would those not using your service be compelled to pay you the cost of airfare anyway, they would be compelled to do a certain amount of traveling. So, the government school system isn't just a monopoly; it's a monopoly on steroids – let's call it a "hyper-monopoly." Obviously, having control of a monopoly like that would be very valuable. In case you are wondering, the recipients of the nearly $500 billion in government school spending have already figured this out, and no one has figured it out better than the teachers' unions.

WE'RE FROM THE UNION, BUT WE'RE NOT HERE TO HELP YOU

The teachers' unions, the National Education Association (NEA) and the American Federation of Teachers (AFT), are by far America's most powerful unions. Together they have about 3.7 million members, with roughly 2.7 million of those belonging to the NEA. Of the combined membership, about 2.4 million are teachers, who represent roughly 70%-80% of the teachers in America.[19] The AFT, which was founded in 1916 and from whom John Dewey received membership card #1, was originally conceived of as a traditional labor union and is an affiliate of the AFL-CIO. Until the 1960s, the older and larger NEA, unlike the then more radical AFT, thought of itself as a professional association. In the 1960s the NEA was radicalized and reshaped as a union. Today, the radicalization of the NEA has gone so far that it makes the AFT seem almost staid in comparison. Nevertheless, both unions share the same economic concerns and far-left political orientation. In keeping with the broad range of constituencies on the payroll in government schools, these unions are not just collective bargaining agents for teachers; they actively recruit as members anyone who works in a school (including colleges and universities).

The strength of the NEA and the AFT is both organizational and financial. The NEA, for example, has an affiliate in every state and in over 13,000 communities. Moreover, the NEA itself has at least one representative in every congressional district, and generally more. Although the official duty of these NEA employees is to assist the affiliates in collective bargaining, they also constitute a larger group of paid political organizers and lobbyists than the Republican National Committee and Democratic National Committee *combined* are able to muster.[20] And that is just the NEA. The teachers' unions are financial Goliaths, having dues-based income alone of over a billion dollars a year.[21]

With these resources the NEA, the AFT, and their local affiliates can marshal truly impressive forces at the local level. In Washington State, for example, the NEA affiliate (WEA) alone collects roughly $51.5 million dollars annually from over 75,000 members.[22] Where does this money go? According to Bob Williams of the Evergreen Freedom Foundation:

> Based on our investigations, no more than 20 percent of that amount [annual WEA dues] is actually being used for traditional, chargeable union functions, such as collective bargaining [or] maintenance of the contract and grievances. The rest, $41,196,375 is used for other, mainly political purposes. This means that one union in one state has more than $80 million to spend per two year election cycle. That is six to eight times the amount spent from voluntary sources by Republicans and Democrats in Washington State.[23]

These resources allow the WEA pay for, among other things, a dozen political operatives, 22 full-time regional directors, and more than 300 local union representatives who are entitled to be released from their teaching obligations to carry out WEA activities. Thus, in a relatively small state the NEA's affiliate has a force of nearly 350 paid operatives that it can use for lobbying and political work.[24] Bear in mind that this doesn't even count the local paid representatives of the NEA itself. Resources of this magnitude make the NEA's state affiliates almost untouchable politically and legally.[25]

For example, it is illegal for teachers to strike, but they strike anyway, and the law is seldom enforced against them. In fact, the 2001 teachers' strike in Middleton, New Jersey, became national news precisely because a judge was enforcing the law against the striking teachers, something the union representatives said hadn't happened since 1978![26]

Anti-striking laws are not the only laws teachers' unions flout. It is illegal under Title VII of the Civil Rights Act of 1964, for example, for a union to force an employee to support the union financially if doing so violates the employee's sincerely held religious beliefs. When there is a conflict between the employee's religious beliefs and union activities, the employee is supposed to be allowed to donate his dues to a charity of his choice. The NEA and its affiliates have so flagrantly obstructed employees' exercise of these rights that in May 2002 the Equal Opportunity Employment Commission was finally forced to issue an order demanding that the NEA and its affiliates stop violating the religious rights of their members who conscientiously object to the organizations' political activities.[27] As legal counsel for the conscientious objectors put it: "The NEA union's illegal scheme is intended to force teachers of faith to shut up and pay up.... The EEOC's action further underscores that the nation's largest teacher union is systematically persecuting people of faith."[28]

It also appears that, like Leona Helmsley, the NEA believes that "taxes are for the little people." In September 2003 Landmark Legal Foundation requested that the IRS and the Criminal and Tax Divisions of the U.S. Department of Justice investigate the NEA for flagrantly violating federal reporting and tax requirements.[29] According to Landmark, its exhaustive study of the NEA's internal strategic planning and budgetary documents, tax returns and other materials clearly demonstrate that the NEA illegally and routinely uses enormous amounts of tax-exempt dues for political activities – expenditures for which the NEA is legally required to pay taxes.[30] As a result, the IRS has commenced an audit of the NEA.[31]

Unless the Justice Department and IRS lose their nerve, the hubris of the NEA may prove its undoing as a result of an investigation of its alleged use of tax-exempt dues for political activities: since 1994 the NEA has reported to the federal government that it has spent *not a single dollar* on political activities on which it would be required to pay taxes.[32] Landmark claims that a review of NEA internal documents will make it clear that in fact the NEA has been spending tens of millions of dollars to fund political activities for which the NEA should have paid taxes.[33] While there may be a reasonable question regarding the exact amount, it is very hard to believe that the NEA hasn't spent significant sums on political activities since 1994.[34]

Washington State provides another example of the power of the teachers' unions' affiliates. In 1992, 72% of Washington voters passed a campaign reform initiative banning employers from deducting money from employee's paychecks without obtaining written permission annually.[35] This enraged the WEA, and it promptly obtained the assistance of elected officials in devising regulations intended to frustrate the purposes of the initiative. When vouchers and charter schools were put on the ballot in 1996, the WEA deliberately violated even the watered down provisions of the campaign reform initiative by putting together a $1.5 million campaign against the initiatives even though it only had political income of $12,000 per month.

Once this lawbreaking was uncovered, a complaisant attorney general preempted lawsuits against the WEA by secretly negotiating a settlement involving a small fine and little else.[36] Why were *elected* state officials so eager to assist the WEA in circumventing the campaign reform initiative and to ensure that the WEA's intentional lawbreaking carried no serious consequences? Go back and take a look at the political resources that the WEA can put into the field. Imagine the power NEA affiliates wield in large states such as New York, California, Pennsylvania, and Michigan.

Teachers' Union Bargaining: Negotiating With Yourself and Winning Big

The vast majority of education dollars are spent at the school district level. How those dollars get spent is influenced by *elected* local school boards. Further, school boards also exercise some control over how much there is to spend through their ability to affect bond elections and tax rates. Consequently, if you are on the receiving end of those dollars wouldn't it be nice to have influence with the school board too? The NEA and the AFT figured this out a long time ago, and that is a major reason why nothing much about the government school system really changes for the better – that is, from the *consumers'* point of view.

How do the unions typically manage to make sure that school boards are "friendly"? It's not hard, really. Consider the following: serving on a school board is generally an unpaid position, school board elections are non-partisan, and they are held at odd times that virtually ensure a low voter turnout.[37] The only groups that have a large, direct interest in the outcome of school board elections are the teachers' unions and all the other allied interests who make a good living at least in part from the school district's spending.

The average voter, on the other hand, has little information on what is really at stake in these elections and little incentive even to show up at the polls. As a result, the teachers' unions and their friends can pretty much ensure that most of the time school boards won't resist their demands and projects too strenuously. If you doubt this, let me ask you a question: Can you name all the members of the school board in your school district? I guarantee that the local representatives of the NEA and AFT affiliates in your district can. Moreover, what proves difficult to obtain at the local level the teachers' unions and related interests are often able to obtain through mandates imposed at the state and federal levels. In fact, local control of schools is increasingly becoming just a memory. State, and especially federal, legislation have removed a great deal of decision-making power from school boards. This, in turn, makes the possibility of reforming government schools at the local level even more remote.

No, It's Not Going to Change

Still, you may be thinking that even if this is true, why isn't it possible to reform government schools so that we are just overpaying for good schools? Well, one answer is that that is not how monopolies work. While the monopolist is always interested in increasing the resources flowing to him, he has no particular incentive to improve his product because he has no competition. This is all the more true when the monopolist has a "hyper-monopoly." But rather than discuss these theoretical issues, let's take a look at a few of the factors that make the government school monopoly unreformable from within.

The vast amount of money spent through or in connection with government schools is the cement that binds together a broad informal coalition of interests that effectively controls government schools. In fact, a vested interest in the nearly $500 billion spent by government schools is probably the only significant common interest shared by the teachers' unions, architects, engineers, vendors of food to lunch programs, and all the others involved in the education industry. If government school spending were stagnant or declining, this coalition would be splintered by rivalries for the available funds. Of course, those involved know this, and that is why all of the interested parties can generally be relied upon to support strongly bond elections, school tax increases, increased state and federal funding, and the election of the "right" candidates to school boards.

The dramatic increase in government school funding over the last forty years, despite the increasing failure of government schools to educate, testifies to the effectiveness of the informal network of interests that benefits from government school spending. All of the groups interested in increased spending are not, however, equal. Because of their huge membership, geographical reach, wealth, and vast political influence, the teachers' unions are clearly the senior partners among the multitude of interested parties. This makes a tremendous difference regarding the extent to which change can occur within government schools.

UNIONS AS POLITICAL PARTIES

There are two key reasons why the teachers' unions will never willingly accept any meaningful reform of government schools. The first is that as organizations the teachers' unions, and especially the NEA, have morphed into a hybrid of a political party and a traditional union. Not only have they increased their explicit political activism over the last thirty to forty years, but teachers' unions have also sought to gain additional political allies. The NEA, for example, has followed a clear strategy of aligning itself with a wide variety of activist groups on the far left in order to expand its political base.

One motivation for this is financial.[38] While the unions have been very successful at obtaining ever-greater amounts of money through local taxes, they recognize that risk of taxpayer backlash limits how much money can be extracted at the local level. Consequently, state and federal funding increases are essential to keep the financial pie growing.

By working in concert with homosexual activists, abortion groups, left-wing feminists, environmentalist radicals, and others on the radical left, the teachers' unions have greatly expanded their influence over state and federal government. In fact, the NEA claims that its members alone have been the single largest bloc of delegates to the Democratic National Convention since 1976. At the 1992 Democratic National Convention, the NEA accounted for nearly one delegate in eight, an extraordinary level of participation that the NEA was able to maintain at both the 1996 and 2000 Democratic National Conventions. And remember, these numbers do not include the delegates belonging to the AFT. Moreover, the teachers' unions put their money where their mouths are: Democrat candidates got 95% of the teachers' unions' political contributions in the years 1996 to 2000.[39]

This doesn't take into account the value of the unions' staff work that is often indistinguishable from the activities of the Democratic National Committee and other Democrat organizations. As Jami Lund of the Evergreen Freedom Foundation points out: "Everything that you can imagine a political party does, these unions do. But because it is all in the area of staff activity, it doesn't show up on the radar screen."[40]

As if this weren't enough, students are now being drafted as foot-soldiers for promoting the economic and political agenda of the teachers' unions. How? Through manipulation of school district requirements mandating "community service" or "service learning" credits for graduation. Montgomery County Maryland's highly trained education professionals, for example, were able to boost attendance at an Annapolis political demonstration in favor of a bill authorizing $1.3 billion in education spending by offering students "service credits" for attending.[41] No wonder many now view the teachers' unions as the "heart and soul" of the Democratic Party.

All of this has paid off handsomely for the teachers' unions, beginning with the creation of the Department of Education during the Carter administration and continuing to the present with increased education spending and enhanced influence over legislation at both the state and the federal levels. This has also enabled the NEA to move ever further leftward. As left-wing activists have helped the teachers' unions with their legislative agendas, the teachers' unions have increasingly adopted the political, social, and curricular agendas of the activists. This is why, for example, the resolutions at the NEA's annual conventions have come to resemble the planks in a political party's platform, departing far from traditional education concerns to stake out positions on foreign policy, the environment, abortion, homosexual rights, health care, and a host of other social issues.

At the local level, all of these activist groups are interested in seeing their policies and curricular proposals adopted in the schools. This results in some dissension and negotiation among factions within the teachers' unions because there is a fixed amount of curricular and policy "shelf space." What is clear, however, is that the teachers' unions don't have well-organized, powerful internal constituencies demanding that the unions pressure school districts to adopt programs that will foster, for example, complex literacy and traditional morality. Internally, the debate is about how to accommodate the competing curricular and policy demands of environmentalist radicals, homosexual activists, feminists, and all the rest. Because the teachers' unions have virtually become political parties of the left, there is no prospect that real school reform – that is, "school reform" as it is understood by, say, the average parent – will become the focus of the teachers' unions' efforts in the foreseeable future.

TEACHERS' UNIONS AS TERRORIST ORGANIZATIONS?

Well, maybe not literally, but this was how the Secretary of Education, Rod Paige, characterized the NEA at a private meeting with governors in February 2004.[42] Secretary Paige later amended his remarks to say that "terrorist organization" might have been a poor choice of words, but he made it clear that he believed that the union uses "obstructionist scare tactics" to thwart any meaningful reform of education and that "the NEA's high-priced Washington lobbyists have made no secret that they will fight against bringing real, rock-solid improvements in the way we educate our children regardless of skin color, accent or where they live."[43] Predictably, the NEA demanded that President Bush fire Secretary Paige.[44]

Perhaps because of his roots in urban schools, Rod Paige has championed serious school reform more aggressively than any of his predecessors. His somewhat hyperbolic remarks about the NEA are certainly a measure of the frustration of a man who knows as well as anyone the urgent need for change in American education, and who also sees the strength of the entrenched special interests that pursue their interests at the expense of America's children.

But Secretary Paige is not the only major political figure to erupt in frustration over elements of the K-12 education industry. In January 2004 Illinois Governor, Ray Blagojevich, took on the Illinois State Board of Education in his annual "State of the State" address. In his speech, Governor Blagojevich referred to the State Board of Education as, among other unpleasant things, "...a bureaucratic nightmare of biblical proportions," an "old, Soviet style bureaucracy," an organization that "isn't accountable to anyone for anything," and "an organization that exists more for the benefit of its own administrators than for the benefit of the children of this state."[45] On the whole, perhaps the Illinois Board of Education would have preferred to have been referred to simply as a "terrorist" organization.

As if all of this were not enough to suggest that there is a great deal of turmoil behind the respectable brick façade of the government school system, in spring 2004 a judge in Kansas *ordered all Kansas schools closed* because of funding inequities.[46]

You can expect to see many more stories like these in the future. Whether one looks at the academic and moral collapse of the schools, their voracious appetite for tax dollars and precarious financial condition, or the ways in which they attempt to evade being held accountable, it is clear government schools are in crisis and the media are beginning to notice.

Union Officials: Livin' La Vida Loca

Peter Brimelow, a veteran education reporter, and others have chronicled the lavish salaries and perks enjoyed by teachers' union officials and how teachers' union officials attempt to conceal this from the rank-and-file.[47] While this may not be entirely surprising, what is also being discovered is that some very well compensated teachers' union officials representing very large school districts have been stealing from the rank-and-file teachers.

In Washington, D.C., a grand jury investigated a former president of the local American Federation of Teachers affiliate, Barbara Bullock, her aide, and a former treasurer of the union local for their involvement in an embezzlement scheme that apparently involved the misappropriation of at least $5 million in teachers' union dues.[48] Evidently these officials were unable to live large enough on their salaries to satisfy their egos, so they turned the union rank-and-file teachers' dues into a supplemental source of income. The money, it was alleged, was used for such life-style necessities as a fleet of Cadillacs, mink coats, a 288-piece set of Tiffany sterling silverware, custom-made clothing, wigs, art, jewelry, Caribbean vacations, outings to nightclubs and restaurants, furniture, gifts, and spending money.[49] Bullock eventually pled guilty to mail fraud and conspiracy charges. As a result, she will be taking a nine to ten year sabbatical at Club Fed.[50]

Even though AFT policy requires that locals conduct audits every two years, the Washington organization had not had an audit since 1995.[51] It seems that no one in the national headquarters of the AFT cared, or noticed, that one of its largest affiliates was ignoring a critical safeguard for protecting members' dues. Instead, the looting of the union treasury came to light because a union member saw in the summer of 2002 that $160 in dues had been taken from his paycheck when the deduction should have been $16.[52] The rank-and-file member complained to the AFT's national organization, which finally audited the local and found the financial irregularities that became the subject of the grand jury investigation.[53] As a result, Bullock and her cronies were forced out, and Bullock promptly took a job as – surprise, surprise – executive director of the Washington, D.C., Democratic Committee.[54]

It's not that the looting of the local wasn't rather obvious. Indeed, the U.S. District Court judge presiding over this matter criticized the AFT national headquarters for dereliction in its oversight of its Washington, D.C., local: "It's a sad commentary.... It seems everyone in a responsible position fell asleep at the switch. The only ones who were vigilant were the thieves who took everything that wasn't nailed down."[55] Perhaps no one really wanted to notice.

An isolated incident? Perhaps, but in late April 2003, the FBI and Miami-Dade's Public Corruption Task Force served a search warrant on the local NEA affiliate, United Teachers of Dade, which is the sole bargaining agent for almost 28,000 teachers.[56] Sources familiar with this criminal investigation say that the union local's president, Pat Tornillo, had been suspected of embezzling money for personal expenditures such as homes, hotel bills, and other perks, as well as other misuses of members' dues.[57] It doesn't appear that Tornillo went to much trouble over the years to conceal what was going on. As one critic of the local union, Damaris Daughtery, has observed: "The mismanagement and lavish lifestyle and all of the perks at the members' expense have been pretty obvious."[58] Like Bullock, Tornillo finally copped a plea and will also be spending some quality time in a federal facility.[59]

In Massachusetts, the former finance director of the Massachusetts Teachers Association, Richard Anzivino, was convicted in 2003 for stealing $802, 000 from the union local. Evidently, most of the money was gambled away. Even though Anzivino may have been unlucky in the casinos, he hit a hot streak with the courts: he was only sentenced to one year in prison and doesn't have to pay any of the money back.[60]

What is particularly striking about these incidents is that they occurred in large, highly visible locales, not in the backwaters of the teachers' unions' empire. There had to have been many people associated with these large local unions who knew what was going on or who suspected that something improper was occurring. Yet it appears that the corrupt local officials were able to perpetrate their frauds for years without being questioned. Over the next few years we may learn that the lawlessness that characterizes union activity in the political realm – including their unlawful use of dues for political purposes and their refusal to abide by the Supreme Court's *Beck* decision – has broadly infected their internal operations, further victimizing the rank-and-file.

And just what is the NEA doing to make sure that its affiliates protect their members' union dues? Insisting on careful reporting and disclosure by the affiliates? No, suing the Department of Labor to *prevent* NEA affiliates from having to disclose their income and expenditures (including the salaries and perks of officers) in annual reports under the Landrum-Griffin Act.[61]

JOB SECURITY FOR THE PEDAGOGICALLY CHALLENGED

The second reason the teachers' unions will never willingly accept any meaningful reform of government schools has to do with the nature of unionism itself. From an economic point of view, one of the key things a union does is sell job security in exchange for dues. No union has a better record of protecting members from layoffs or dismissal than the teachers' unions. Firing a teacher for incompetence is virtually impossible.[62] In fact, probably only unionized civil servants have job security comparable to tenured teachers. This level of job security is fatal to the prospects for genuine school reform because real reform would require, among other things, wholesale changes in school personnel. Why? Because testing has confirmed anecdotal evidence that a large number of those to whom the education of children in government schools is entrusted are incapable of doing their jobs.

Prior to 1980 in most, if not all, states you could become a teacher simply by taking a prescribed course of study in a school or department of education. As a result of the increasingly poor performance of government schools over the last three decades or so, the public began demanding that the education industry demonstrate the competence of those drawing salaries as teachers. Competency testing of government school teachers was implemented in Texas in the mid 1980s as a result of school reform measures pushed through the Texas legislature by a select committee headed by Ross Perot. The teachers' unions in Texas fiercely resisted testing, and the test ultimately used was shrouded in secrecy to conceal from the public how low the standards had been set.

The low standards notwithstanding, many Texas teachers initially failed the exam. The failing teachers got a second chance, however, and after some "adjustment" of the test and intensive coaching almost all of those who failed were able to pass. Over the objections of the teachers' unions, competency testing has become more widespread in the last decade and half. They are not, however, typically required of incumbent teachers. Instead, some form of competency testing is now almost universally tied to certification of those wanting to become teachers. Still, teacher competency testing is a charade because of low standards, and because many states allow candidates to become teachers even if they fail the competency exams. At the same time, the test results are shocking because of the number of prospective teachers who cannot pass tests that demand almost nothing. Not unexpectedly the teachers' unions continue to fight any sort of competency testing, let alone meaningful testing.

Forty-one states and the District of Columbia require some form of teacher-certification test. Here are just a few examples of what testing has revealed:

- California required teacher candidates to take a simple literacy test for the first time in 1995. Twenty percent of the 65,000 test takers failed.[63]

- In 1998 Massachusetts implemented a teacher certification examination for new teachers. Even though the test was rated at about the 8th grade level by the chairman of the State Board of Education, 59% of the prospective teachers failed.[64] One illustration of the depth of the failure on the test was the dictation portion of the test included to evaluate knowledge of spelling and punctuation. The test takers were read a portion of the *Federalist Papers* and asked to write down what was being read to them. Many of these supposedly educated teacher candidates could not accurately copy what they heard. The result was broken sentences and "innovative" spellings such as "bodyes," "relif," and "bouth" (for "both").[65] This was in a state where the average teacher in the 1998-99 school year received over $45,000 per year plus benefits (about 27% of salary) for roughly 185 days of work that year.

- Over 50% of the teachers hired in Hawaii for the 1997-98 school year had not completed or passed teacher-certification tests.[66]

- In 2001 only 60% of Virginia's education students were able to pass a test of basic reading, writing, and mathematics skills (Praxis I), which is required for initial teacher licensure. What was the Board of Education's response? Lower the standards. It will be now be sufficient if a teacher candidate can pass the test in two of the three skill areas. Not to be outdone by the Board of Education, both 2001 gubernatorial candidates demonstrated their concern for quality education by promising more money for teacher salaries (current average salary is about $40,000 plus benefits, which are about 25% of salary).[67]

- In 2000 more than half the students from five Georgia teacher training programs failed the Praxis II test of subject matter knowledge.[68]

Apologists for government school educators would respond to these and other examples by saying that in many states between 80% and 96% of teachers are passing competency exams. These statistics, however, are highly misleading.

TEACHING: SOON TO BE THE BEST PAID SEMI-SKILLED, PART-TIME JOB IN THE WORLD

To understand how the public is mislead by pass rates on teacher competency examinations, let's briefly look at the Educational Testing Service's Praxis I, one of the most widely used teacher competency tests. The Praxis I is a licensure test of basic skills for aspiring teachers. It allegedly tests at the 10th grade level, and at least twenty-five states use it.[69] Here are two questions from a version of the Praxis I:[70]

1. Which of the following is equal to a quarter of a million?
   a. 40,000
   b. 250,000
   c. 2,500,000
   d. 1/4,000,000, or
   e. 4/1,000,000
2. Martin Luther King, Jr. (insert the correct choice) for the poor of all races.
   a. spoke out passionately
   b. spoke out passionate
   c. did spoke out passionately
   d. has spoke out passionately, or
   e. had spoken out passionate

As you are contemplating the depth of learning required to answer these questions, you should also be aware that there are *no national standards for passing* the Praxis I or any other teacher competency examination. Thus, in some states a teacher can score *less than 50%* on the Praxis I or similar tests and pass.[71] Obviously, to say that 96% percent of the teachers in some state passed the Praxis I, for example, means nearly nothing. Further, an education professor who took the Praxis I reported that the test is largely based on "progressive" educational theories. As a result, part of what qualifies a prospective teacher for the classroom, for example, is his knowledge of the whole language theory of reading instruction rather than his knowledge of phonics and spelling.[72]

In many instances, passing a certification test such as the Praxis I is not even a requirement for being in a government school classroom. For example, in a September 6, 2001, story the *Chicago Sun-Times* reported that in Illinois various "loopholes" allowed nearly 900 teachers into classrooms without having passed the basic skills test.[73] In fact, according to the *Chicago Sun-Times*, one teacher who had *flunked* 11 of 12 basic skills tests and all 12 tests on teaching learning-disabled children was *assigned to teach learning-disabled children.* In connection with its story, the *Chicago Sun-Times* gave the basic skills test used by Illinois to ten high school students (freshmen through juniors). The students took between 11 and 23 minutes to finish the test. All but two passed the mathematics and grammar portions, and about half passed the reading comprehension portion.

Low Standards and High Barriers to Entry

A 2002 report by Rod Paige, Secretary of Education, puts all of this in context.[74] Of the 29 states that use the Praxis I to assess prospective teachers' basic skills in math, reading, and writing only Virginia requires that prospective teachers demonstrate that they can read at the national average level.[75] The 28 other states accept as teachers those who score below the national average.[76] In fact, in the District of Columbia, Florida, Texas, and twelve other states you can qualify to be a teacher if your reading ability is below the 25th percentile.[77] California – not wanting to be outdone by the District of Columbia, Florida, or Texas – requires that prospective teachers be able to pass the California Basic Educational Skills Test, a test that is set at about the 10th grade level.[78] Secretary Paige himself has observed that state teacher hiring rules manage to "maintain low standards and high barriers [to entry] at the same time."[79]

A former Arizona state superintendent of education and chief executive officer of the Education Leaders Council, Lisa Graham Keegan, minces no words in describing the fraud of teacher competency testing:

> The tests that teachers are being asked to take are not just basic, they're painfully basic… it is only what we expect the children to know at the end of their journey with us. On top of that the state sets its own cutoff score, usually way below the 80 percent limit. The fact that teachers are not passing these basic tests is outrageous…. The NEA is appalling on this matter. They say it is demeaning to give teachers these examinations; that it suggests they aren't professional. Well, it's only demeaning when they fail them, proving they aren't professionals….The victims are the students they're hired to teach.[80]

Given that teachers *today* only need to demonstrate that they can *sort of* read, write, and do math, we could probably relieve the teacher shortage, improve instruction, and save money by putting smart high school students in classrooms part-time and letting those who are in the lower reaches of the teacher applicant pool replace the high school kids at the local Burger King.[81]

SCHOOLS OF EDUCATION: DISABLING THE ABLE

It's no secret that teachers as a group score lower on standardized tests, such as the Scholastic Aptitude Test and the Graduate Record Examination, than just about any other group in college or graduate school.[82] So, many critics have concluded that attracting more intellectually capable teacher candidates is the key to fixing the problem. While that in itself would not be a bad thing, it still would not discernibly improve government schools. The pervasive and baleful influence of schools and departments of education and other institutional factors are too strong for mere intellect to overcome.

Simply put, it is a mistake to claim that the undistinguished intellectual talents of the average government schoolteacher and administrator are a major factor in the failure of government schools. The average teacher doesn't need to be able to write a novel, compose a symphony, do advanced mathematics, or understand quantum mechanics to do a good job of teaching children such things as reading, writing, music, history, and mathematics. What a good primary or secondary school teacher does need, however, is a thorough grounding in what is to be taught and personal qualities such as diligence, enthusiasm, and patience. None of this is beyond the reach of people of normal intelligence. In fact, all things being equal, traits such as patience are undoubtedly far more important for teaching a six year-old arithmetic than an above average I.Q. So, if the inherent intellectual ability of most of those who become teachers is not the reason many government school teachers and administrators are not up to their jobs, what is the problem? The problem is those peculiar institutions known as "schools of education."

A SCHOOL OF THEIR OWN

From the beginning of the public school movement, creating special schools for training teachers was integral to the plan for creating a system of government schools in America.[83] Early on these institutions were referred to as "teachers' seminaries." Later they were called "normal schools" or "teachers' colleges," but today they are commonly known as "schools of education."

Within academia, schools of education have long been notorious for low standards and susceptibility to spurious theories. In 1933, for example, the president of Harvard University made his contempt for Harvard's Graduate School of Education clear by telling Harvard's board of overseers that the Graduate School of Education was a "kitten that ought to be drowned."[84] More recently, Dean Edwin J. Delattre of the Boston University School of Education has explained the situation as follows:

> Schools of education are cash cows to universities.... They admit and graduate students who have low levels of intellectual accomplishment, and these people are in turn visited upon schoolchildren. They are well-intentioned, decent, nice people who by and large don't know what they are doing.[85]

In general, schools of education have the reputation of being the "intellectual slums" of the university.[86] How did this come about?

As they currently exist, schools and departments of education are the creation of proponents of "progressive" theories of education. In fact, most of what these institutions are today can be traced to the influence of John Dewey, Ellwood Cubberly, and other educational progressives in the first half of the 20th century.

In the progressive's vision of education, schools and departments of education were to serve as the channels of distribution for their educational theories. To ensure that their theories were in fact inculcated in aspiring teachers, progressive educational "reformers" made these institutions gatekeepers for the teaching profession through teacher certification and licensure laws.

Since at least the 1930s those who pursue a teaching career have generally been required to pass through a school or department of education. In Tennessee, for example, a student who wants to become a teacher is required to complete a teacher preparation program through an accredited college or university. The teacher preparation program must include, among other things, certain professional education courses. This is typical of how schools and departments of education function by law and regulation as gatekeepers in the government school hyper-monopoly. While some alternative certification programs now exist, they account for relatively few teachers and are vocally opposed by the teachers' unions.

The progressives' vision of using schools and departments of education to control what happens in America's classrooms has probably succeeded far beyond their expectations. Schools and departments of education have relentlessly de-emphasized the development of traditional academic skills and the teaching of content. Instead, students' class time is increasingly devoted to indoctrination in politically correct social and political attitudes and the teaching of alleged skills such as "how to think." These attitudes have resulted in a wild proliferation of psychotherapeutic and other non-academic programs in government schools. They have also created strange beliefs among educators such as: "if children know how multiplication is used, they don't need to know multiplication facts" (because calculators are presumably always available), or "children really don't have to learn particular historical facts" (because they can always look up the facts). [87]

Here's a report of a conversation one author had with a high school principal demonstrating the ingrained bias our highly trained education professionals have against actually teaching children anything in particular:

> The high school principal in Colorado insisted… that students did not have to learn any specific facts of history or be able to define either World War II, The Holocaust, or the Great Depression. It was, the principal was convinced, "arbitrary" to single out one event in history as being more important than any other. Likewise, students didn't have to know the location of Florida as long as they mastered "geographical thinking," whatever that is.[88]

Believing that you can teach "geographical thinking" or "historical thinking" without teaching facts of geography or history is like thinking you can have a Cheshire cat's grin without the cat. It may sound good in books, but don't expect that it will happen in reality.

It should be clear by now that the very existence of schools and departments of education is intimately bound up with the odd belief that prospective teachers really only need to be taught the mysteries of the "discipline" of education rather than learn actual subject content. After all, if it were acknowledged, for example, that the most important thing for a mathematics teacher to know is the mathematics he is going to teach, why would you need degree-granting schools of education and their faculties? Prospective teachers would then just major in real subjects such as history, English, biology, chemistry, and mathematics rather than in "education." Moreover, they could do that in the traditional departments of colleges and universities devoted to those subjects.

Unfortunately, a great many students are being taught by teachers with little or no training in the subjects they teach. A 1993-94 study by the National Center for Education Statistics found that nearly 28% of teachers nationwide are teaching academic subjects in which they neither majored nor minored – ranging from 13% of foreign language teachers to 40% of science teachers.[89] More recently, the U.S. Department of Education reported that 41% of 8th grade mathematics teachers did not major in mathematics, and 20% of English teachers neither majored nor minored in English literature, communications, or journalism. The fact that there are teachers in government schools teaching history, mathematics, or biology who may never have taken a college level course in those subjects is just one result of the belief that there is a discipline called "education," the mastery of which qualifies someone to teach. In fact, the teachers' unions' are enormously hostile to prospective teachers from outside the usual teacher's certification/school of education channels, and they regularly oppose programs making it easier for uncertified college graduates *with degrees in the fields in which they would teach* to enter the teaching profession.[90] As a result, it is easier for someone with a teaching certificate and a slender grasp of mathematics to get a job teaching algebra than it is for someone who majored in mathematics.

Beyond these concerns, schools and departments of education today have become highly politicized. This is primarily a reflection of the social and political views of their faculties. For example, a study of Colorado's schools of education by the Colorado Council of Higher Education found that that the program in the University of Colorado's school of education (the flagship program at Boulder, Colorado) was "systematically shaped by progressive theories of social justice" and that most of the courses involved "excessive proselytizing" and "strident indoctrination of students."[91] According to the syllabus for one beginning education course, the students "will be examining general curriculum issues, questions about teacher professionalism, academic success and race, class, ethnicity, gender, sexual orientation and power."[92]

A study by David M. Steiner of Boston University of more than 200 course outlines from 16 schools of education, including 14 ranked in the top 30 by *U.S. News & World Report*, reached similar conclusions. Not only did Professor Steiner report that prospective teachers are being given a preparation that "is at best uneven and at worst intellectually thin and ineffectual," their professors "are too often trying to teach an ideology to teachers."[93] What ideology? The usual "multiculti" stuff – "traditional knowledge is repressive," "meaningful knowledge must bubble up from each individual and ethnic group," and "teachers should first and foremost respond to the diversity before them."[94] Also interesting was Steiner's finding that 28 of 61 outlines for reading instruction courses indicated the use of a "balanced approach" – in other words, an approach to teaching reading that includes a small amount of phonics as camouflage for what is, in substance, a "whole language" curriculum.[95] Think of it as whole language in drag. An additional ten reading course outlines showed that the courses were unabashedly based on the discredited "whole language" approach, while only three courses appeared to prepare reading teachers to use a traditional phonics-based approach.[96]

As you may expect, defenders of the education establishment have been eagerly attacking Professor Steiner's results and methodology. What you should know, however, is that Steiner's work is simply the latest research confirming the results of the survey presented by E.D. Hirsch in his 1996 book, *The Schools We Need*.[97] In that work, Hirsch describes how schools of education continue to promote faulty theories of learning, even in the face of well confirmed research showing the theories to be wrong.[98] As Hirsch observes, "the education community, operating behind a web of slogans and brooking no internal dissent, resists scrutiny and the rough-and-tumble of scientific criticism that characterizes subject matter disciplines."[99] This explains how toxic theories such as whole language and constructive math continue to thrive, even in prestigious schools of education.

In a similar vein, John Leo wrote a few years ago of the course offerings in the school of education at the University of Massachusetts-Amherst in his *U.S. News & World Report* column. There, education students were being nurtured on such fare as: Leadership in Changing Times, Social Diversity in Education, Embracing Diversity, Diversity and Change, Oppression and Education, Introduction to Multicultural Education, Black Identity, Classism, Racism, Jewish Oppression, Lesbian/Gay/Bisexual Oppression, and Erroneous Beliefs.[100] This may give you some idea why schools of education, to paraphrase Thomas Sowell, don't merely fail to attract the best students, they repel them.[101]

ENFORCING IDEOLOGICAL CONFORMITY: NCATE'S CATECHISM FOR EDUCATORS

The use of schools of education as political re-education camps is not uncommon. In fact, the National Council for Accreditation of Teacher Education (NCATE), which is the national accrediting organization for schools of education, requires adherence to such politically correct shibboleths as "multiculturalism" and "diversity" in hiring and curriculum as a condition of accreditation.[102] Think of NCATE as the enforcer of the ideology embraced by the educator elites.[103]

At its 2001 Las Vegas convention, NCATE's agenda moved farther into the open. During a presentation just prior to the opening of the convention, NCATE's senior vice president, Donna Gollnick, told an audience of 1,000 highly trained education professionals from around the country that "diversity" is the most important standard by which NCATE will evaluate those who train teachers.[104]

And just what is "diversity"? According to NCATE's glossary for its "Professional Standards," "diversity" means "differences among groups of people and individuals based on ethnicity, race, socioeconomic status, gender, exceptionalities, language, religion, sexual orientation, and geographical area."[105] Why is this important? Because now NCATE wants to require that teachers *demonstrate* that they are *showing correct "dispositions"* regarding diversity and that they are teaching "multicultural and global perspectives."[106]

It turns out that "global perspective" and "multicultural perspective", like "diversity", also have detailed, ideologically driven definitions buried in NCATE's glossary. "Global perspective" is defined as:

> The viewpoint that accepts the interdependency of nations and peoples and the interlinkage of political, economic, ecological and social issues in a transnational and global character.[107]

A "multicultural perspective" is:

> (1) The social, political, economic, academic, and historical realities experienced by individuals and groups in complex human encounters; (2) the representation and incorporation of issues related to culture, demographics, ethnicity, race, gender, sexual orientation, religion, socioeconomic status, and exceptionalities in the education process; and (3) the inclusion of a cohesive, inclusive curriculum representing the contributions of diverse populations.[108]

Despite the definitions' rather smoggy prose, you probably already recognize NCATE's real project: imposing a mandatory ideology of cultural Marxism on those who would be part of the teaching profession, whether they want to teach in schools of education or in K-12 schools.

As you might also have already surmised, NCATE's view of the correct "disposition" with respect to, say, "sexual orientation" is that homosexual marriage and "Heather having two mommies" is just fine. I imagine you can figure out what the correct "dispositions" are regarding global warming, the United Nations, affirmative action, Christianity, abortion, and any number of other social and political issues. If you want to be a member of the education industry in good-standing, NCATE wants you to toe an ideological line in how and what you teach – theirs.

Not surprisingly, NCATE is a coalition of thirty-three specialty professional associations, *including the teachers' unions*. Because schools of education generally have faculties that are quite politically left, it is a measure of NCATE's political heavy-handedness that only about half of the nation's 1,200 schools of education are willing to be accredited by NCATE.[109] Still, that amounts to considerable influence, and in some states prospective teachers *must* have attended an accredited school if they want to become licensed.[110] Moreover, if the National Commission on Teaching and America's Future (NCTAF) has its way (NCTAF is an organization funded by the Carnegie Foundation and located at Columbia University's Teachers College), *no one will be allowed to teach if he hasn't graduated from or been certified by an NCATE accredited school of education.*

What does this mean for parents? First, you need to realize that the cultural Marxism NCATE promotes is the dominant worldview of schools of education, and they have been catechizing their students in the creeds of globalism, multiculturalism, social justice, and diversity for years. Because, as previously pointed out, education majors tend to be drawn from the ranks of the students least able to resist indoctrination through critical thought, they leave their schools of education having absorbed much of this worldview. Not satisfied, however, with merely immersing education students in their worldview and hoping it shows up in the classroom, NCATE is aiming at making sure that their teaching reflects it. That is the point of NCATE's blather about showing correct "dispositions." So, NCATE now wants to make sure that the schools it accredits, and all students graduated or certified by those schools, demonstrate allegiance to NCATE's ideology in their professional activities. Moreover, if NCATE is successful, there will be no path to teaching except through an NCATE accredited school.

Now, just how is it that *your* government schools are different?

Making the Sighted Blind

Every year large numbers of 18-year-olds and others enter colleges and universities with a desire to become teachers. Some are intellectually very capable, but most are of ordinary intellect. Because the vast majority attended government schools from kindergarten through 12th grade, most of them have significant gaps in their academic skills and knowledge and have little capacity for critical thinking. Nevertheless, for the majority of these students, a demanding, well-conceived undergraduate program could certainly overcome their academic deficiencies and enable them to do a good job in their chosen profession.

Instead, these students are forced into an intellectual wasteland in which they are bludgeoned with political indoctrination, and must endure a diet of courses promoting absurd educational theories, frequently taught by professors who have the same intellectual weaknesses that the students have. This, in turn, leads many of the more intellectually able and well prepared to seek other career paths. The more credulous students, the students who feel irresistibly called to teach, and the students who don't believe that they have attractive career prospects outside of teaching reconcile themselves to, or embrace, their professors' politics. In effect, they must accustom themselves to having to believe, like Lewis Carroll's White Queen, "six impossible things before breakfast." Moreover, it is from these remaining students that much of the next generation of professors of education will be drawn.

Thus, schools of education engender a kind of adverse self-selection, perpetuating themselves as a strange inbred institution within an institution. This is one important reason why real education has been declining for decades in government schools.[111]

Government schools are *necessarily* staffed by large numbers of people whose academic growth has been stunted by schools of education and who have absorbed the false and harmful views that pass for thought in those institutions. Moreover, today's climate in government schools certainly encourages talented teachers to leave. This is a key reason why more money will never fix government schools, and it is *the reason* why real school reform would require something that the teachers' unions would never permit – wholesale changes in school personnel.

DRIVING AWAY MISS DAISY

Unfortunately, the pathological phenomenon of adverse selection continues beyond graduation from schools of education.

For the hardy souls who are both competent and able to endure fulfilling the inane requirements for a degree or certificate in education, further trials await. Public Agenda, a nonprofit organization based in New York, recently published "Where We Are Now: 12 Things You Need to Know About Public Opinion and Public Schools," a report covering the results of its surveys regarding education in government schools. According to Public Agenda, 43% of teachers say that they spend more time trying to keep order in their classrooms than teaching, and 86% of teachers said that better student behavior and parental support were more important to them than more money.[112] According to superintendents, the overwhelming reason *talented teachers leave teaching* is politics and bureaucracy, not low pay and prestige (81% versus 5%).[113] Violence against teachers, however, is another reason many leave. In many urban schools, teachers evidently now joke that in their schools "corporal punishment is a thing of the past, except when students beat them up."[114]

How bad is the problem of teacher attrition? According to Tom Carroll, executive director of the National Commission on Teaching And America's Future: "We have a bucket with huge holes in it. They're leaving as fast as we pour them in."[115] In Texas, for example, 40% of new teachers leave within their first three years of teaching, which has been estimated to cost the state as much as $2.1 billion in termination, recruiting, and training expenses.[116] Nationally, half of all new teachers leave before their fifth year.[117]

While it isn't possible to say precisely how many competent teachers are leaving teaching in government schools, it is a certainty that every year many of the capable teachers in government schools are moving on because they are spending too much time on discipline, politics, and bureaucracy. And, of course, it is precisely these government school teachers who have the skills to pursue other careers.

IF GOVERNMENT SCHOOLS CAN'T REFORM THEMSELVES, CAN THEY BE REFORMED FROM THE OUTSIDE?

Today government school reformers generally pin their hopes on competition from charter schools, outside management, and vouchers to force improvement on government schools. All of these efforts to use external pressures to force reform are meeting with massive resistance from the education industry, especially the teachers' unions.

CHARTER SCHOOLS: NICE TRY, NO CIGAR

Charter schools are government schools that operate under special legislation that allows individuals, non-profit organizations, and for-profit organizations to operate a school under contract with a school district. The first charter school was established in Minnesota in 1991, and by the late 1990s there were roughly 150,000 students attending about 1,000 charter schools in twenty-nine states and the District of Columbia.[118] By the end of 2002, roughly 2,700 charter schools in 39 states were educating between 600,000 and 700,000 students.[119]

In theory, charter schools are supposed to provide an alternative to traditional government schools because they operate outside of the constraints of the traditional government school and can be more innovative. They were conceived of broadly as secular, government funded quasi-private schools. Precisely because charter schools have the potential for creating a large system of schools in competition with conventional government schools, teachers' unions have worked hard to cripple the charter school movement. How? In part, through using their political influence to have so many regulations imposed on charter schools that they really can't be all that different from traditional government schools.[120] In particular, the teachers' unions have been adamant about requiring charter schools to hire only certified teachers. One sign of the political success that the teachers' unions have had against charter schools is that charter schools are typically only funded with 90% of the operating dollars that traditional government schools get, and they receive no funding at all for capital costs such as buildings.[121]

Even where charter schools have been successful (and some have not been), teachers' unions and their allies have been able to frustrate both parents and the charter school movement. In San Francisco, for example, the lowest performing elementary school in the city became a charter school run by Edison Schools, Inc., a for-profit company. The new operator of the school improved discipline and raised the students' reading and math scores dramatically. Under the new management children were happy and parents were delighted. So what happened? Feeling threatened by the success of Edison, the teachers' unions got a group of candidates elected to the local school board who were willing to revoke the charter school's contract with the school district over the loud protests of parents.[122]

New York State legislators and teachers' unions have concocted perhaps the most breathtakingly absurd argument deployed against expanding charter schools. In order to stop the opening of a dozen charter schools already approved for operation, the usual suspects floated the argument that opening more charter schools should be postponed because of budget constraints resulting from the 9/11 attack on the World Trade Center.[123] No one seemed to have a good explanation of how charter schools that only get roughly 70% of the government school operating budget per pupil would strain New York's general budget. As Alnando Learpel, a New York parent with a child in a charter school, accurately assessed the situation: "The schools have become consumed with politics and controlled by special interests who don't put the kids first."[124] This is a parent who "gets it."

Though few in number, charter schools have introduced a small element of competition. According to research by Caroline Hoxby, an economics professor at Harvard, charter schools are more likely than conventional public schools to have teachers from selective colleges and with better than average academic records. Teachers in charter schools are also more likely to devote more time to academics than their conventional public school counterparts.[125] But the competition isn't limited to what goes on in the classroom. According to Kathy Christie, a policy analyst for the Education Commission of the States, charter schools, unlike their conventional public school counterparts, need to keep parents happy as "clients."[126] So, it isn't surprising that according to one estimate, the children on waiting lists for existing charter schools could fill another 900 charter schools.[127]

Let's see – smarter, better educated teachers, more emphasis on academics, and a parent-friendly attitude. Teachers' unions and the rest of the government school education establishment have got to hate it – and they do. Feeling threatened by even a handful of charter schools, the usual suspects have marshaled their overwhelming resources to strangle the charter school baby in its crib.

For example, school districts in Oklahoma and Massachusetts have sought moratoria on the creation of any new charter schools.[128] In Illinois, Michigan, and North Carolina legislation to raise caps on the number of charter schools and their enrollment has been defeated.[129]

In Texas, the K-12 virtual charter school lead by William Bennett had its charter denied at the last minute after having received repeated assurances that it would be granted. Roughly two years after Bennett's K-12 was sandbagged by Texas bureaucrats, Texas teachers' unions intimidated the University of North Texas into withdrawing its proposal to create an online public (charter) school.[130]

In Ohio, a teachers' union is both litigating the constitutionality of charter schools and spending money on advertising to convince the public that charter schools are a menace to education.[131] Jeanne Allen, president of the Center for Educational Reform, a charter school advocacy group, summarized the overall situation: "We have had obstacles and nuisances all along, but there hasn't been a concerted effort like the one we have seen recently."[132]

The government school establishment's strategy for thwarting the charter school movement is simple. First, use funding limitations and caps on the number of charter schools and on charter school enrollment to restrict the growth of charter schools. Second, where charter schools already exist or cannot be prevented, dilute their quality by gradually imposing a regulatory regime that makes them almost indistinguishable from conventional government schools.

The truth is that teachers' unions and their allies have the money, manpower, and political influence to prevent charter schools from becoming a source of significant and embarrassing competition any time soon, if ever.

VOUCHERS AND TRENCH WARFARE

Education vouchers are another strategy that reformers have pursued as an end-run around the government school hyper-monopoly. Vouchers, of course, have been bitterly opposed by teachers' unions. Peter Brimelow, for example, recounts in his book, *The Worm in the Apple*, how the NEA's California affiliate attempted to prevent a voucher initiative from getting on the ballot in 1992. To get the voucher measure on the ballot, California law required its proponents to obtain a large number of signatures on a petition. The union's tactics against the voucher measure included "blocking [physically] would-be signers access to the petition in shopping malls, allegedly sabotaging the petition with fake names, and offering a signature-collecting firm $400,000 to decline the account."[133]

How could a teachers' union justify this sort of behavior? According to the president of the NEA's California affiliate, D.A. Weber, "There are some proposals that are so evil that they should never be presented to the voters."[134] Evidently, teachers' unions are for democracy only if it doesn't threaten their economic and ideological interests.

An *Atlantic Monthly* interview with Bob Chase, a former president of the NEA, further demonstrates the unions' implacable opposition to any voucher measure that might allow students to escape the failing government school system. In that interview, writer Matthew Miller asked Chase whether the union might relent in its opposition to vouchers for inner-city students if vouchers were coupled with more money for government schools:[135]

Miller: Is there any circumstance under which that would be something that....

Chase: No.
Miller:...you guys could live with? Why?
Chase: No.
Miller: Double school spending....
Chase: No.
Miller:...in inner cities?
Chase: No.
Miller: Triple it.
Chase: No.

In case you missed it, the answer is "No." Get it?

Union opposition notwithstanding, in 2002 the Supreme Court held in *Zelman v. Simmons-Harris* that Cleveland's voucher program, which allows vouchers to be used at any secular or religious private school, does not violate the Establishment Clause of the First Amendment. But don't think that *Zelman* is the harbinger of the rapid spread of voucher programs. Vouchers are, in fact, still a long way from becoming a significant feature of the educational landscape. Immediately following the *Zelman* decision the NEA issued a press release in which it "pledges to continue to fight... divisive and counterproductive proposals to divert energy, attention, and resources to private school tuition vouchers...."[136] This means that the NEA and its allies are going to continue waging the very effective campaign against vouchers at the state and local levels that they have been conducting for years. In particular, the teachers' unions will be looking for help from the state courts to block vouchers.

State court litigation is an increasingly important component of the NEA's strategy for delaying or stopping voucher programs. Having lost in their effort to have the United States Supreme Court declare vouchers unconstitutional if they can be used in religious schools, the teachers' unions and their allies are fighting vigorously in state courts claiming that voucher programs violate state constitutions.[137]

Unknown to the general public, the state constitutional provisions on which the teachers' unions are relying are known as "Blaine Amendments," after their inspiration, James G. Blaine, a 19th century U.S. Senator from Maine. In 1875 Blaine proposed an amendment to the United States Constitution that would have prohibited the states from directly or *indirectly* aiding with tax dollars any church or religious denomination *or institution.* Blaine's motive was well known. Blaine aspired to the presidency at a time when anti-Catholicism was widespread. Although not apparent from the legislative language, the whole fight was about schools. As will be discussed later, "public schools" at the time were largely Protestant schools, though unofficially so. As a result, Catholics wanted to establish their own schools, and Blaine and his nativist, anti-Catholic allies were determined to see as many Catholic children as possible forced by economic necessity into government schools so that they could be "Protestantized." This was the sort of legislation that even the Klan could, love. Fortunately, the federal Blaine Amendment was not ratified. Unfortunately, every state except Louisiana, Maine, and North Carolina eventually incorporated in their constitutions "Blaine Amendment" language or something similar.[138]

As a result of *Zelman*, teachers' unions have become the chief enforcers of state "Blaine Amendments," and their efforts have produced fruit. In the summer of 2002, for example, a Florida state court struck down a 1999 voucher law designed to help mostly poor and minority students in failing schools on the ground that it violated a provision in the Florida constitution prohibiting state assistance to religious organizations – in other words, a state "Blaine Amendment."[139] A successful appeal followed, but for a time Florida's modest voucher plan and the students who benefited from it were put on hold. Moreover, Florida's voucher plan continues to be subject to legal and political uncertainty. Challenges to vouchers have not been based only on Blaine Amendments, however.

In 2004, the Colorado Supreme Court killed the state's voucher law before it could go into effect. According to the judge, the law was unconstitutional because it strips local school boards of control over education.[140]

This process of litigating existing and future voucher programs will play itself out across the country for years. Moreover, even if the courts eventually clear the way for vouchers, there will remain many political battles to be fought at all levels of government. In Florida, for example, the government school industry is now trying to pass legislation that would regulate Florida's pilot voucher program to death.[141] Voucher proponents scored one visible victory when Congress finally enacted a small voucher program for execrable Washington D.C. school system in 2004. Under the program, a maximum of 2,000 of the school district's 68,000 students would be able to participate. Shortly afterward, Senator Kennedy and others announced that they will work to repeal the program.[142]

The legislative and legal battles over vouchers will generate headlines for years to come. The fact remains, however, that there are tens of millions of children in government schools, while in 2004 vouchers were available, at best, to roughly 40,000 students.[143] As with any controversial political program with a narrow base, the demise of any voucher program is always just one election away.[144]

How effective has the government school hyper-monopoly's war against vouchers been with the public? For some years teachers' unions' have deployed their considerable resources to wage an effective political and public relations campaign against vouchers. Vouchers, in fact, have had even less success than charter schools. Such voucher programs as exist have been largely limited to minority children in failing schools and involve far fewer children than charter schools. Even more ominous for the prospects of voucher programs is that voters have been turning down ballot initiatives to provide parents with vouchers as a way of opening government schools to competition. For example, a 2000 California initiative that would have provided parents with a voucher worth $4,000 lost overwhelmingly even though the "for" campaign enjoyed substantial financial support from a California venture capitalist. A similar voucher measure went down to defeat in 2000 in Michigan. Teachers' unions have played no small part in shaping the perceptions that led to those outcomes.[145]

As should be clear, voucher proponents' victory at the United States Supreme Court in *Zelman* was not the final battle of the voucher wars. It was, instead, the first battle of what will prove to be a long, long war of attrition. Unfortunately, no significant change is likely to be forced upon government schools in the foreseeable future as a result from competition created by vouchers.[146]

But even if a nationwide voucher system were put in place tomorrow, would the government schools be transformed? Of course not. How could they be? Government schools would still be drawing faculty and administrators primarily from the same dismal pool of school of education graduates; the multiculturalists, feminists, environmental fanatics, and other liberal special interest groups would still have a hammerlock on the curriculum; and the administrators would still be hamstrung by all the court decisions and regulations that make effective discipline within the schools an impossibility.

But, of course, a universal voucher system *will not* be put in place tomorrow. So, at best, vouchers *might* in the great by-and-by partially depopulate government schools. But even if one has a favorable view of vouchers, and not all opponents of the government school hypermonopoly do, *it is very unlikely that vouchers will provide dramatic improvements in educational opportunity in time to help this generation of schoolchildren.*[147] **If you are waiting for vouchers to rescue your children from government schools, you have effectively decided to abandon your children to the pathologies of government schools.**

THE EDUCATIONAL HYPER-MONOPOLY: COMMITTED TO WINNING BY FAIR MEANS AND FOUL

Two recent events on opposite sides of the country put the exclamation point on the teachers' unions' refusal to allow any change that might challenge the government school hyper-monopoly. In November of 2001 a ballot initiative was defeated that would have allowed the government schools in the Los Angeles community of Carson to secede from the Los Angeles Unified School District and form its own school district.[148] Advocates of the initiative believed that by seceding local residents would be able to substantially improve education in the local schools. The teachers' unions and other public employee unions, on the other hand, opposed the measure fearing that a trend toward creating smaller school districts and smaller cities would erode their power base. As a result, the teachers' unions and their allies outspent the advocates of secession by a factor of twenty-five to one, scores of teachers were mobilized to walk precincts and work telephone banks, and the secession initiative was defeated by a margin of nearly three to one.

In Philadelphia, the teachers' unions and their Democratic Party allies have shown how brazenly they will oppose change even in the face of abject failure by government schools. Philadelphia has 210,000 students in its government schools. Nearly 60% of those students fail state-mandated mathematics and reading tests, 176 of 264 schools are on a list of failing schools, and there is a 50% dropout rate.[149] Of the students who stay in school long enough to become high school juniors, only 13% can read a newspaper with basic comprehension.[150] Because of this massive government school failure the state government announced that it would take over Philadelphia's schools, fire the school district's top 55 administrators and replace them with managers hired from Edison, and turn over the district's 60 worst performing schools to Edison or other private firms to operate in partnership with clergy, universities, business owners, and local politicians.

Needless to say, this didn't sit well with the local teachers' unions and their political friends. To make their displeasure known, the opponents arranged to have several hundred students walk out of class in protest, a crowd of unionized school district employees march to city hall to disrupt a Christmas tree-lighting ceremony, and the NAACP and a group of black ministers block an intersection during rush hour on a Friday afternoon.[151] Of course, the part of the plan that is drawing the most fire from the teachers' unions is the role to be played by Edison and other private companies in the reorganized school system.

Just prior to Pennsylvania's takeover of the Philadelphia government schools on December 22, 2001,[152] a secret memorandum surfaced that had been circulating within the office of Philadelphia's Democrat mayor, John Street.[153] The 67-page memorandum included headings such as "Making the Takeover Difficult" and outlined ways to help "accelerate Edison's anticipated failure" through acts of sabotage against Philadelphia's school system such as refusing to collect taxes and stripping the school system of key personnel.[154] What this means, of course, is that the Democrat machine in Philadelphia and its teachers' union allies are quite willing to destroy Philadelphia's government schools to prevent reform. This obviously strips away the pretence that the welfare of schoolchildren is of any real significance to the unions and politicians who have controlled Philadelphia's schools.

But it appears that Street's plan for sabotaging the schools wasn't really necessary. By the middle of April 2002, the Philadelphia School Reform Commission, which was given broad legal power to implement reform, had limited privatization to only 42 of 176 failing Philadelphia schools and had substantially diminished the role that Edison would play in the central administration of the Philadelphia School District.[155] What is especially striking about the situation in Philadelphia is that the Commission was given all the power it needed to do the necessary job, but it lacked the heart for the fight.

As the state plan goes forward, Philadelphia's teachers' unions and their political allies will keep up the fight. If history is a guide, they have good prospects for prevailing eventually. School districts in Hartford and Minneapolis adopted private management of their schools over the objections of teachers' unions, but were eventually forced to abandon private management. More recently, after a seven year battle, the Massachusetts teachers' unions finally managed to oust Edison from Boston Renaissance Charter School by first getting the school board to take away Edison's freedom to hire teachers and make other instructional decisions, and then, like Captain Louie Renault in the film "Casablanca," expressing "shock" that the school's test scores were lagging.[156]

It is quite clear that teachers' unions subscribe to their own version of the Lombardi principle – "Winning isn't everything; it's the only thing." In fairness to Vince Lombardi, however, I should point out that he was not advocating winning by breaking the rules of football. He was just emphasizing that you play to win. The teachers' unions' version is rather more like Saul Alinsky's Marxist dictum, "The only rule is that there are no rules."

THE EVER-HELPFUL UNCLE SAM

If charter schools and vouchers can't do the reform job, what about the *ubermenschen* in Washington, D.C.? In 2002 the federal government passed the No Child Left Behind Act. Like most education legislation, it really should have been titled the "No Dollar Left Behind Act." Nevertheless, this piece of Washington ingenuity does seem to be rapidly and overtly achieving something that "school reform" legislation normally only accomplishes slowly and imperceptibly – lowering academic standards. Funding under the legislation is tied to the performance of subgroups of students that are defined by racial, ethnic, limited English proficiency, economic, and "special needs" criteria. States will be penalized in their federal funding unless approximately 75% of the students in each subgroup pass reading and math tests. Faced with this politically correct system of "accountability," what is a busy education bureaucrat to do? Lower the standards for passing. In fact, not long after the passage of the No Child Left Behind Act, the Connecticut Board of Education took up a proposal to lower Connecticut's proficiency standards to avoid losing federal funds when the Act's "accountability" standards went into effect.[157] Other states, including Texas, Michigan, and Colorado have followed Connecticut's lead, prompting long-time education reformer and former assistant secretary of education, Chester E. Finn, Jr., to remark: "Some states are lowering the passing scores, they're redefining schools in need of improvement and they're deferring the hard task of achievement-boosting into the distant future.... That's a really cynical approach."[158]

CALIFORNIA'S MIRACLE OF THE HIGHLY QUALIFIED TEACHERS

If you still aren't grasping that "school reform" is really about *who gets how much money* rather than improving education, consider California's recent beatification of 40,000 teachers as "highly qualified."[159] As a requirement of getting federal Title I money under the No Child Left Behind Act, schools serving poor children must be staffed by "highly qualified" teachers within four years. Unfortunately, the genius Washington politicians responsible for this latest fantasy in school reform "forgot" to define what a "highly qualified" teacher is, thus leaving it up to the states. Naturally not wanting to leave any federal dollar behind, and recognizing that coming up with enough truly "highly qualified" teachers would require real work, California's highly trained education bureaucrats simply redefined what counts as a "highly qualified" teacher. So, in California you now can be a "highly qualified" teacher without ever having been in a classroom or having received a California teaching certificate.[160] The main requirement under the new definition is, I think, being able to breathe.

This bit of credentialing alchemy proved a bit cheeky even for California Congressman George Miller, a leftist stalwart, who, along with Senator Ted Kennedy, helped usher the No Child Left Behind Act through Congress. Apparently astonished that, like past school reform efforts, this "reform" was going to prove to be no reform, Congressman Miller sputtered in a telephone interview, "They're getting jillions of federal dollars, and still trying to do it the old way. They want to fund the status quo.... They keep gaming the system."[161] In a subsequent letter to the members of the state board of education, Miller continued to excoriate their action, complaining that it was an "audacious and truth-defying step" and that, "By declaring every teacher 'highly qualified,' the state has essentially abandoned any effort at reform."[162] Of course, the state officials simply felt that they were doing what was necessary to get more money. As one state official helpfully pointed out in response to Miller's comments, without the new definition California would lose some federal funding.[163]

Just in case people who think that receiving vast amounts of public money requires some accountability didn't fully grasp the point, less than a year after the miracle of the highly qualified teachers California's Board of Education scuttled another much heralded "reform." This time it cancelled the California High School Exit Exam. Passing the exam was to be a requirement for graduation for the Class of 2004 and subsequent classes.[164] Unfortunately, it seems that only 48% of the victims of California's government schools in the Class of 2004 had been able to pass the test by the summer of 2003 – even after the passing score had been lowered to just above 50%.[165] Consequently, not wanting to harm the students' self-esteem, or to draw more attention to the utter failure of California's government schools, the requirement was delayed for 2 years. The Board promises that it really will make passing the test a requirement for the Class of 2006. Scout's honor – unless, of course, the results would be embarrassing.

MEETING THE CHALLENGE OF PROVIDING "HIGHLY QUALIFIED TEACHERS"

California, of course, is not alone in having to meet the No Child Left Behind Act's requirement that virtually 100% of teachers be "highly qualified" by the 2005-2006 school year.[166] As of 2003, however, the U.S. Department of Education reported that only about half of teachers currently qualify. Some may think it's obviously impossible for 50% of teachers to become "highly qualified" by 2005-2006, but is it?[167]

Pessimism about achieving the 100% goal may simply reflect an outmoded "inside the box" traditionalist mentality. California has bravely pointed to one solution, but there are others in prospect. In 2003 *The Wall Street Journal* ran a front-page story on how many of our highly trained education professionals have been obtaining their much-coveted master's degrees.[168]

As you probably know, teachers who have master's degrees are typically paid significantly more than those who do not. In many states, getting a master's degree is a condition for continued employment after the first few years of teaching. Although the demands imposed by traditional schools of education master's degree programs are notoriously slender, the *Journal* discovered that they are nevertheless deemed too demanding by many of the highly trained education professionals to whom we entrust our children.[169] As the *Journal* found, increasing numbers of government school teachers are obtaining their "master's degrees" from schools that are not much more than diploma mills – none of these graduate schools require entrance examinations, and some don't even require a minimum grade point for admission.[170]

At one of these schools, Cambridge College, the typical student completes one-half of the master's degree course work in five weeks (one course is completed each week).[171] How can you cram what normally takes at least a semester into five weeks? According to one instructor, James Jenkins, a former Oregon school superintendent, "Academic rigor is one of those things you give up in this program."[172] Well, just how much academic rigor is given up? In Mr. Jenkins class there was no textbook, but his graduate students did have to write a two-page paper and give an hour-long group presentation.[173] In addition, the highly trained education professionals in his class had to demonstrate "ways of praising schoolchildren, including the 'silent cheer,' 'clam clap,' 'lobster cheer,' 'rainbow cheer,' 'butterfly clap,' and 'shake your tail feathers.'"[174]

Besides teaching methods courses, Cambridge College also helps teachers satisfy more subject matter oriented requirements. When New York required teachers to have two semesters of a foreign language, Cambridge stepped into the breach with a one-week Spanish course for which it granted one semester's worth of credit. How much Spanish can you learn in a week? Apparently the goal was to learn about twenty phrases – challenging stuff such as, "Habla Ingles?"[175]

The point here is that the school reformers might as well try to nail Jell-O to a wall. Not only are traditional school of education master's degrees of dubious educational significance, the proliferation of master's degrees from places like Cambridge College shows that state and local officials are willing collaborators in what most parents and taxpayers would consider a rank credentialing scam. The No Child Left Behind Act's demands that teachers have better grounding in subject matter areas *will* be circumvented. There aren't enough bureaucrats in Washington or anywhere else committed to true reform to monitor every course or test taken to satisfy the "highly qualified" teacher requirements. After an initial adjustment period, the state and local education establishments will simply find ways to pretend to fulfill them, and Washington will find ways to pretend that the requirements have been satisfied. Sometime thereafter, the next round of reform will begin, which will, of course, require more money.

AN ELECTION YEAR PRE-EMPTIVE SURRENDER

In fact, it may not even be necessary for state and local education establishments to worry their pretty little heads about figuring out how to circumvent the requirements of the No Child Left Behind Act. In an homage to the power of the education industry and the teachers unions, the Department of Education is preparing a pre-emptive surrender on portions of the Act's accountability provisions.[176]

Those inside the Beltway have noticed that even Republican legislators in conservative states such as Utah are in open revolt against the Act's modest effort to impose standards.[177] Seeing the political writing on the wall, in February 2004 the Department of Education announced that it was going to make it easier for schools to comply with the Act's requirements, including making it easier for all teachers to become highly qualified.[178] To save time, perhaps the Department of Education could just consult with California's board of education regarding the fastest way to make sure that all teachers are "highly qualified."

So, just as the government school hyper-monopoly hasn't reformed itself, it has also successfully resisted every effort by outsiders to reform it. Further, there are no signs that the government school system will permit itself to be reformed in the foreseeable future. Nearly $500 billion a year provides a lot of power and buys a lot of friends. Which brings us to the next question for reform-minded Christian parents.

WHY ARE YOU FIDDLING WITH THE SCHOOL BOARD WHILE YOUR CHILD'S FUTURE IS BURNING?

Many Christian and non-Christian parents have noticed or seen some of the problems endemic to government schools, and have often expended extraordinary efforts to reform their local schools. In some cases they have enjoyed a degree of success. Programs have been dropped, delayed, or modified; school districts have agreed to obtain parental consent before presenting certain kinds of information; and commitments to change teaching methods have been given. But while the motives of these parents can't be faulted, it is clear that they have failed to recognize that they are at best winning a few skirmishes in a war that they (and especially their children) are losing badly.

By now it should be apparent that the government school system as an institution is driven by interests that are largely unrelated to any meaningful conception of education. In reality, the education industry that controls government schools is a very broad *informal* coalition of groups that use the schools as a vehicle for pursuing their social, political, professional, and economic interests. The nearly $500 billion distributed every year through the government school system is the glue that binds the disparate elements of the coalition together. Are the general contractors, food vendors, and other commercial elements of the coalition necessarily opposed to parental proposals to move government schools toward more traditional academic and moral standards? Of course not. But if the teachers' unions, gender feminists, homosexual activists, and others make an issue of it, the commercial interests aren't going to jeopardize their piece of the cash that passes through the government school system by opposing more powerful elements of the coalition.

When parents do win a local skirmish, it involves considerable personal sacrifice of time and effort. Because parents don't make their living policing schools, however, there are very definite limits on what they can accomplish. On the other side are arrayed groups who do make their living through government schools. For those in the coalition who are ideologically driven, their agenda for government schools is their life. Moreover, the coalition has developed materials at taxpayer expense for teaching sophisticated techniques for dealing with dissident parents.

The best known of these is Ronald Havelock's *The Change Agents' Guide to Innovation in Education*. Havelock, a professor at the University of Michigan, wrote the guide using funding provided by the United States Office of Education. The guide is essentially a manual instructing our highly trained education professionals in methods for forcing through educational practices and curricula over the objections of parents and taxpayers. Charlotte Iserbyt, a critic of government schools who as a school board member attended a workshop based on the guide, describes her experience as follows:

> The presenter (change agent) taught us how to "manipulate" the taxpayers/parents into accepting controversial programs. He explained how to identify the "resisters" in the community and how to get around their resistance. He instructed us in how to go to the highly respected members of the community – those with the Chamber of Commerce, Rotary, Junior League, Little League, YMCA, Historical Society, etc. – to manipulate them into supporting the controversial/non-academic programs and into bad-mouthing the resisters. Advice was also given as to how to get the media to support these programs.[179]

As you might suspect, for those whose lives and livelihoods revolve around the government school system there is simply too much at stake not to have well designed strategies and tactics for preventing parents and other annoying "outsiders" from "interfering."

Havelock's guide is not the only work in this genre. The California Teachers' Association, for example, prepared and has distributed a "Primer on the Extremist Attacks on Education." Similar handbooks on coping with "extremists" have been produced by Arizona, Michigan, Florida, Texas, Nevada, and Washington State affiliates of the NEA, and the NEA's Governmental Affairs unit has developed "A Checklist for Contending with Right-wing Extremism."[180] Like Havelock's guide, the purpose of these publications is to help union affiliates and their members combat their enemies – drum roll, please – the "*extremists.*"

Who are the teachers' unions likely to try to smear as "extremists"? Well, it appears that first and foremost the "extremists" are the dreaded "Christians," especially Christian organizations such as Focus on the Family, the National Association of Christian Educators, and the Christian Coalition. Then, of course, there are the parents and taxpayers who object to such twaddle as whole language reading instruction and values clarification, anyone who might oppose a school bond issue, anyone who thinks vouchers might be a good idea, or, more generally, anyone who opposes the unions' ideological enthusiasms or their stranglehold on government schools.[181]

To keep track of all of these threats, the intrepid employees and officials of the teachers' unions and their allies regularly place themselves in harms' way by attending meetings of "Far Right" groups such as, well, just about any Christian organization that is more conservative than the World Council of Churches. In case you attend such an event in the future, you'll be able to identify the union operatives by looking for men and women wearing false noses and glued on mustaches (the women are especially conspicuous). But, of course, direct surveillance is never enough. To be sure they don't miss anything, they also get materials from Christian bookstores, radio stations, and newspapers.[182] In any event, like Koko, the Lord High Executioner in Gilbert and Sullivan's *Mikado*, teachers' unions have compiled "a little list" of people and organizations who, in their estimation, never will be missed. If you are a Christian, or even if you are just skeptical of what is going on in your local school district, you might be on it.

This brings us back to the futility of school reform efforts. All too often even a successful reform skirmish is like sticking a finger in a bucket of water. As long as the finger is there it displaces some water, although not very much. As soon as the finger is removed, the displacement vanishes without a trace. Charlotte Iserbyt describes just this experience when writing about her tenure as a dissident school board member:

Whatever good I accomplished while on the school board – ... getting values clarification banned by the board and demanding five (yes, 5!) minutes of grammar per day, etc. – was tossed out two weeks after I left office.[183]

Are you really surprised?

Attempting to reform government schools is not unlike the attempts to reform Soviet agriculture in the late, not much lamented, U.S.S.R. Government school reform is not only blocked by powerful forms of reform-resistant corruption, but the very nature of the government school system precludes transforming it into a means of providing an education appropriate to Christian children, just as the very nature of Soviet agriculture precluded the possibility of making farmers in Soviet collectives as efficient as American farmers. *For those Christians who remain dedicated to improving government schools the only effective strategy is to take our children out. Only crisis will beget change in government schools.* But please don't misunderstand me. No matter how they might be reformed, government schools cannot provide the Christian education that Christian parents are obligated to give their children. Moreover, as is discussed in the next chapter, it would be sinful for Christians even to attempt to transform the government school system into a system of Christian schools.

YOUR CHILD'S EDUCATION: YOU ONLY HAVE ONE CHANCE TO GET IT RIGHT

I have often been amazed by the extraordinary effort that some Christian parents invest in fighting a futile guerilla war for "school reform" *while their children languish in government schools.* As parents, we only get one opportunity to raise our children in the nurture and the admonition of the Lord. There are no second chances. Consider how many more Christian schools could be started or strengthened and how many more Christian children could be homeschooled if Christians would give up the delusion of "school reform" and put the same energy into creating more opportunities for giving children a Christian education. If you really want to help the children left behind in government schools, the most effective thing you can do is take your child out and urge as many other parents as you can to do the same thing. Government schools won't reform themselves or allow others to reform them in any meaningful way. They will only change if they are faced with being publicly delegitimized and defunded by a mass exodus of children.

GOVERNMENT SCHOOLS:
THE WAGES OF CHRISTIAN SIN

"A general State education is a mere contrivance
for molding people to be exactly like one another...
in proportion as it is efficient and successful,
it establishes a despotism over the mind."
John Stuart Mill, "On Liberty"

In "A Nation at Risk," the National Commission on Excellence in Education reported in 1983 on the condition of American education. Among their findings, the authors observed:

> If an unfriendly foreign power had attempted to impose on America the mediocre educational performance that exists today, we might well have viewed it as an act of war.[1]

The Commission was, of course, talking about the educational performance of government schools. Not unexpectedly, the Commission's report resulted in loud calls for reform. Many hundreds of billions of dollars of "reform" later, however, it is clear that the education industry has successfully resisted any meaningful restructuring of government schools, which continue to function as disorderly, and sometimes dangerous, factories of ignorance and bad character.

By now you may be wondering how this utterly dysfunctional system of government schooling was foisted upon America in the first place. Was it forced on Christians by anti-Christian zealots? Not quite. In fact, the government schools that today are destroying the faith, morals, and intellect of Christian children only came into existence because a majority of Protestants collaborated with Unitarians and secularists in the 19th century in the "Common School" movement.

In a sense, it would be fair to say that we Christians (at least the Protestants among us) did this to ourselves. To understand why this is so, let's take a brief look at America's early educational traditions and their sources. Then we will turn to how America's original educational traditions degenerated into our current government school hyper-monopoly. Finally, we will consider why, on a deeper, more principled level, Christians must *not* attempt to reform government schools so that they would provide an education appropriate for Christian children.

EDUCATION IN EARLY AMERICA

Government schools and compulsory schooling have not always been the norm in America. From the founding of the first colonies until well into the 19th century, young children in America were often taught at home by parents or tutors, and formal schooling constituted a far smaller part of a child's education than it does today. In many instances, schools would not accept students who did not already know how to read.[2] But, as already mentioned, there was no lack of literacy in early America, even though school attendance was sporadic by contemporary standards.

Such schools as existed before the development of today's government school system did not always fit into today's familiar, neat categories of "public" and "private."[3] Financial support for schools during that period came primarily from parents, with philanthropic and tax support also sometimes playing a role.[4] Such tax support as was provided was sometimes in the form of a "rate bill," which assessed parents a fee for the children they had in the community's school.[5] In effect, the "rate bill" could be viewed as simply a mechanism for collecting tuition from parents. Further complicating our understanding of America's early schools and their financing arrangements is the fact that some of the colonies and states – Massachusetts and Connecticut, for example – were for generations theocracies in some measure.[6] In fact, the Congregational Church did not become disestablished in Massachusetts and Connecticut until 1833 and 1818, respectively.

By today's standards, however, most schools in early America would be considered private Christian schools, even though some of them were financially heterogeneous affairs.[7] In fact, in 1831 Alexis de Tocqueville observed that almost all education in America was entrusted to Protestant clergy.[8]

By the second and third decades of the 19th century, school-based education was available to virtually everyone, including the poor. For example, in November 1817 the Boston School Committee announced the results of a survey it had commissioned to determine the extent of school attendance by children between the ages of 4 and 14. The survey showed that 96% of Boston's children were attending school.[9] According to the survey, which came to be known as the "Bullfinch Report," almost two-thirds of these students attended privately supported schools.[10] The children not attending school were largely ages 7 and under,[11] and charity schools were available if their parents wanted to send them to school but lacked the financial ability to do so.[12] More generally, in an 1823 address to the American Philosophical Society, a well-known author and Jeffersonian political leader, Charles J. Ingersoll, observed that "Nearly the whole minor population of the United States are receiving school education."[13]

Even though schooling was widely available in America at the time of Ingersoll's address, private schools still educated many more children than schools that in any contemporary sense could be considered "public." Common schools, the prototype for what we would consider public schools, were nowhere more widespread than in Massachusetts – and in Massachusetts common schools were most frequently found in the Boston area. Yet, as the Bullfinch Report showed, fully private schools were dominant even in Boston. Moreover, education historian Samuel Blumenfeld points out that in the third decade of the 19th century "the trend outside of Boston was away from the public school on the secondary level to the private academy."[14] Why? As Blumenfeld explains:

> The free market in education was clearly phasing out the public schools because the latter were not supplying the services that

more and more parents wanted. The private schools were more efficiently organized, provided better instruction, pupil supervision, and social atmosphere. They were less crowded and offered a more practical curriculum.[15]

Advocates of the common schools viewed this trend with alarm, and over time succeeded in making it increasingly burdensome to escape government schools. Nevertheless, as Henry Steele Commager, a well-known historian, has observed, as late as 1900 two-thirds of the students in American high schools were attending private schools.[16]

Partly because of ignorance of American history and partly because of propagandizing by the partisans of government schools, most people today believe that if America had no system of compulsory education dominated by government schools there would be widespread illiteracy. This is far from the truth. As already noted, well before we had anything like our current system of government schools America was perhaps the most literate society in the world. Indeed, the present system of schooling that we are apt to assume is the natural order of things is an experiment that did not fully triumph over America's original educational traditions until 1918, when Mississippi became the forty-eighth state to adopt a compulsory education law.[17]

Yet, if rampant illiteracy did not give rise to our system of government schools and compulsory education, how did it come about? The answer to this question is bound up with the early religious history of America.[18]

THE REFORMATION AND THE AMERICAN EDUCATIONAL IMPERATIVE

The Western ideal of universal education is a legacy of the Reformation. While all Protestants know that the Reformation was born of Luther's rediscovery of the principle of justification by faith alone, fewer understand how the Reformation made a high level of literacy a religious obligation for Protestants.[19]

At the time that Luther nailed his 95 Theses to the church door in Wittenberg, the Catholic Church had a hierarchical bureaucratic structure modeled on the Holy Roman Empire, and it viewed itself as the priestly mediator between God and Man. Moreover, from the Middle Ages until the Reformation, the Bible was virtually treated as the property of the Roman Catholic Church. In 1073 Pope Gregory VII prohibited translation of the Bible into the vernacular languages of the Christian laity. In the 12th century the Catholic Church officially spoke against the laity memorizing, preaching, or possessing the Bible. As a result of concern over the spread of Wycliffe's 1382 translation of the Bible into English, the Catholic Church declared in 1414 that anyone found reading the Bible in English would forfeit his property and his life.

Although the Catholic Church had often provided an exceptional education to its elite and had done much to preserve the learning of antiquity following the fall of the Roman Empire, prior to the Reformation no religious importance was attributed to having a literate Christian laity. Laymen received their knowledge of the Bible from the Roman Church through its priests, and it was through this monopolization of the Bible that the Roman Church bureaucracy regulated the beliefs and practices of Christians. If anything, literacy among the laity was seen as potentially dangerous because it could lead to questioning of the authority of Rome, particularly if that literacy permitted them to read the Bible.

The key to understanding the Protestant attitude toward education is to recognize how the Reformation changed the Protestant's understanding of his relationship to God. In addition to recovering the Biblical doctrine that we are justified by faith alone, the Reformation also swept away the unbiblical belief that a church bureaucracy or priestly class is required as an intermediary between Man and God. Instead, Protestants asserted the priesthood of all believers and understood that Man's relationship to God is direct and personal. But if Man's relationship to God was personal, so, too, were the snares laid for him by Satan. The Bible, then, was both the Christian's key to understanding God's plan of salvation and his bulwark against evil. Yet, what use was a Bible to a Christian who could not read?

Thus, in contrast to the Catholic Church *at that time*, Reformation Protestantism demanded an educated people because their salvation depended upon it. Luther and his followers, for example, strongly advocated education for all social classes and for both boys and girls. Protestants in the Reformed tradition, often called "Calvinists," were even more committed to popular education. One historian of Calvinism puts the point bluntly:

> Wherever Calvinism has gone it has carried the school with it and has given a powerful impulse to popular education…. In fact, we may say its very existence is tied up with the education of the people. Mental training is required to master the [theological] system and to trace out all it involves. It makes the strongest possible appeal to the human reason and insists that man must love God not only with his whole heart but also with his whole mind…. This Calvinistic love for learning, putting mind above money, has inspired countless members of Calvinistic families in Scotland, in England, in Holland, and in America, to pinch themselves to the bone in order to educate their children.[20]

This Protestant perspective on education was present in America from the earliest colonial times because, until at least the 19th century, the preponderance of settlers in America adhered to some version of Reformed theology.

From their first arrival, the Puritans, for example, sought to maintain the Calvinist standards of literacy they had brought with them from the Old World. As the Massachusetts Bay Colony became more firmly established and settlements became more numerous, the Puritans' General Court enacted a law in 1642 requiring that families and masters teach children and apprentices how to read English "perfectly," provide them with knowledge of the capital laws of the colony, and instruct them in orthodox catechisms.[21] Five years later, the General Court enacted the first school code in the American colonies, known as the "Old Deluder Satan" law. The preamble of this early legislation clearly reflects the Reformation view that Christianity and education are inextricably linked:

It being one chief point of that old deluder, Satan, to keep men from the knowledge of Scriptures, as in former times, by keeping them in an unknown tongue, so that in these latter times, by persuading them from the use of tongues that so at least the true sense and meaning of the original might be clouded with false glosses of saint-seeming deceivers; that learning not be buried in the grave of our fathers, in church and commonwealth, the Lord assisting our endeavors, – it is therefore ordered....[22]

This statute required every township with fifty or more families to appoint someone to teach such children (including apprentices) to read and write as were sent for an education. The teacher was to be paid by the parents and masters (of apprentices) of the children in attendance or by the inhabitants in general. The law also required that, if a town had one hundred or more families, it had to establish a grammar school.

By the time of the War for Independence, America had roughly three million free inhabitants. Of those, it is estimated that 900,000 were Presbyterians, 600,000 were Congregationalists (the spiritual descendants of the Puritans), and 400,000 were German or Dutch Reformed.[23] All of these denominations shared a form of Reformed theology. In addition, the Episcopalians, who were the American branch of the Anglican Church, also had a Calvinistic confession, and many Huguenots had fled persecution in France to settle in America.[24] Thus, the high levels of literacy in early America were an expression of American Protestant religious traditions. Not Surprisingly, of course, the influence of early America's various communities of Reformed Protestants went well beyond educational practices: the Reformed were central to the shaping of American character. As Professor Page Smith, a well-known historian, observed: "Of all those forces – physical or mental – that gave shape to the American consciousness, that created, so far as there was one, a new man, the reformed faith of Protestant Christianity was pre-eminent."[25]

Apart from efforts by Americans themselves to promote literacy, the Anglican Church sent more than three hundred missionaries to America through an organization known as the "Society for the Propagation of the Gospel in Foreign Parts." These missionaries' efforts focused heavily on teaching reading and writing to children, especially those of slaves and Indians.

The American emphasis on literacy was further reinforced by the influence of the ministry of George Whitefield in America. Through his many voyages to America, Whitefield contributed significantly to creating and sustaining the revival known as the "Great Awakening." In addition to his role in the Great Awakening, Whitefield's work was an important factor in the development of Methodism in the American colonies. Like earlier forms of American Protestantism, the Methodists emphasized education and worked effectively through their Methodist Societies to provide education to both children and adults.

By the 1790s, Baptist churches, whose membership had begun to grow rapidly as a result of the disestablishment of the Anglican and other churches in many American states, followed the example of the Methodists by urging their members not to neglect their duty to educate their children.

Given this cultural milieu, it is hardly surprising that literacy was widespread in early America. But, again, this brings us back to our earlier question: "How was a system of government schools and compulsory schooling foisted upon an America that already had all the education that free Americans of that era could need?"

THE RISE OF THE PUBLIC SCHOOL IDEOLOGY

In the very beginning, the project of promoting the system of Common Schools was pursued largely by Massachusetts Unitarians and a group of utopian socialists known as "Owenites." In time, however, as the school historian Lloyd P. Jorgenson notes, the Common School movement became one of a number of interrelated Protestant-led social reform efforts:

> Leaders of the Common School movement also served as leaders in other humanitarian causes of the day....The Common

School movement was therefore by no means an isolated phenomenon, nor is it to be understood as a merely political or civil movement....The school movement was one part – albeit an important part – of a far reaching and intertwined complex of cooperative reform efforts, all of them suffused with the spirit of evangelical Protestantism....The ensuing spiritualization of the public schools... was to have profound significance for American education.[26]

Nevertheless, even though orthodox Protestants played a decisive role in creating and sustaining the Common School movement, the real roots of the Common School movement are to be found within Unitarianism and Owenite socialism.

THE OWENITES

The "Owenites" were followers of Robert Owen, a Welshman who is mainly remembered as the father of modern socialism.[27] Owen was a successful industrialist who was convinced that an individual's character was entirely the product of the society in which he lived.[28] Moreover, Owen also believed that human evil resulted from the competitive and allegedly irrational social order created by capitalism and religion.[29]

The remedy for the social ills caused by capitalism and religion, according to Owen, was education. The educational system he envisioned included a uniform, secular, state-sponsored system of schools that all would attend. These schools were also to be augmented by a system of training colleges for teachers. Government schools would, in essence, raise children from infancy. In fact, the Owenites advocated separating children from their parents as early as age two by placing them in boarding schools.[30] The education to be provided in these schools was to focus primarily on forming a well-adjusted, obedient character instead of teaching literacy and intellectual skills. Education, as Owen saw it, should in large part form character to advance the interests of the state, and he even boasted that he had inspired the Prussians to create their new national system of education in 1819.[31]

Owen's views on education grew out of the educational experiments he undertook as manager and part owner of a mill in New

Lanark, Scotland. In 1813 and 1814 Owen published his views on society, economics, and education in three volumes titled *A New View of Society or Essays on the Formation of the Human Character*.[32] In the first of his essays, Owen stated clearly his belief that human character can be molded into any form by the "application of proper means":

> Any general character, from the best to the worst, from the most ignorant to the most enlightened, may be given to any community, even to the world at large, by the application of proper means; which means are to a great extent at the command and under the control of those who have influence in the affairs of men.[33]

The "proper means" referred to by Owen were, of course, primarily educational.

Owen's views on education influenced America's move toward a system of government schooling through two channels of influence. The first channel was the Boston Unitarians and others in America who read Owen's writings on education shortly after their publication. In fact, in 1813 John Quincy Adams, who was then Ambassador to Britain, personally asked Owen for enough copies of his writings on education to distribute to every governor in America.[34] While the Unitarians were cool to Owen's socialism, they were receptive to his belief that society could be made rational and virtuous through a national system of education because they, too, believed that Man is innately good and perfectible.[35]

The second channel of influence through which Owen's ideas moved in America grew out of Owen's attempt in 1825 to create a utopian socialist community in New Harmony, Indiana, which involved close to 1,000 Scottish and American enthusiasts. Unfortunately for Owen, the New Harmony experiment failed soon after it was begun.[36] From this failure, Owen concluded that a socialist society would only be successful if the inhabitants had first been properly educated to live in such a society.[37]

Although Owen returned to England in 1829, his son, Robert Dale Owen, and many of the participants in the New Harmony experiment, remained in America and devoted their energies to creating in America a system of education that they hoped would eventually lead to successful socialism. To this end the Owenites engaged newspaper publishing and political and labor organizing.[38] Robert Dale Owen became an American citizen and promoted Owenite ideas in various capacities, including as a member of the Indiana legislature (1836-38) and the United States Congress (1843-47).[39]

Some of the Owenites were also Unitarians. One of the more prominent among these was Orestes Brownson, a Unitarian clergyman in the Boston area. As publisher of the *Boston Quarterly Review,* Brownson was also in contact with many Unitarian intellectuals. In an autobiography written after his conversion to Catholicism, Brownson recalled his former activities as an Owenite and how the organization had become a secret society in 1829 to pursue the Owenite campaign for a national system of public education:

> The great object was to get rid of Christianity, and to convert our churches into halls of science. The plan was not to make open attacks on religion, although we might belabor the clergy and bring them into contempt where we could; but to establish a system of state, – we said national – schools, from which all religion was to be excluded, in which nothing was to be taught but such knowledge as is verifiable by the senses, and to which all parents were to be compelled by law to send their children.... The first thing to be done was to get this system of schools established. For this purpose, a secret society was formed, and the whole country was to be organized.... This organization was commenced in 1829, in the city of New York... this much I can say, the plan has been successfully pursued, the views we put forth have gained great popularity, and the whole action of the country on the subject has taken the direction we sought to give it.[40]

While the Owenites were the radicals promoting public schools, the Unitarians were, at least in the beginning, the respectable public face of the movement.

THE UNITARIANS

Unitarianism in America largely grew out of certain liberal theological tendencies that developed within Congregationalist churches in the 18th century. While the various theological views that ultimately coalesced into Unitarianism represented the beliefs of relatively few in Massachusetts at the turn of the 19th century, many who did hold those views were among the wealthy and influential living in and around Boston.[41] When the Unitarians managed to take over Harvard from the orthodox Congregationalists in 1805, Unitarianism began a process of development that in the second and third decades of the 19th century led to a final break with Congregationalism.[42] Nevertheless, it is important to recognize that, as Rousas Rushdoony has pointed out, "[E]arly 19th century Unitarianism had not yet, as it was to do subsequently, separated itself from Christianity. Rather, it presented itself as the true version of Christianity and the fulfillment of Protestantism."[43] In a sense, Unitarianism could be understood well into the 19th century as the aggregation of several anti-Calvinist theological trends within Protestant Christianity.

Although Unitarianism had several distinctive doctrines, most notably the denial of the Trinity, the theological view most relevant to their educational views was their rejection of the doctrine of original sin.[44] The Unitarians believed, instead, that Man was perfectible and that the road to salvation lay through works. Given this perspective, it was natural that they would view the establishment of a system of government schools that they controlled as the greatest of good works: these schools were to be the Unitarians' instrument for perfecting society.

Ultimately, the Massachusetts Unitarian leadership selected their fellow Unitarian, Horace Mann, as the man to implement this vision, and managed to have him made Secretary of the Massachusetts Board of Education in 1837. A lawyer and politician, Mann brought to his position a pragmatic sense of how to pursue Unitarian educational objectives covertly in a society that would have flatly rejected them if they had been pursued openly.

Typical of the Unitarians' belief in the redemptive power of education and their own righteousness were the views expressed by Catherine Beecher in a letter to Mann during his tenure as Secretary of the Massachusetts Board of Education:

> [A]ll the children at age four shall be placed, six hours a day, for twelve years, under the care of teachers having *the same views that I have*.... I have no hesitation in saying, – I do not believe that none, no, not a single one, would fail of proving a respectable and prosperous member of society; nay more, I believe that every one would, at the close of life, find admission into the world of endless peace and joy.[45] [emphasis added]

These views were not unusual among the members of the Massachusetts Unitarian social elite, who believed that they could work out their salvation through social activism and education.[46] Creating a system of schooling that would imprint their values on society was a significant way in which this theological impulse found expression. In effect, the Unitarians sought the *establishment of Unitarianism* through the system of government schools and teachers "seminaries" that they championed.

THE SINS OF THE FATHERS

Although Mann was often in conflict with orthodox Protestants in Massachusetts, through skillful muting of his own Unitarian theological views, and with the aid of the social and financial influence of his Unitarian sponsors, Mann successfully advanced the project of creating a centralized, tax financed, and state controlled system of compulsory education. After the Common School movement began to consolidate its position in the New England and Mid-Atlantic states, it began to accumulate the momentum that in time would allow it to metastasize through the entire country. Once the idea of creating a tax funded system of Common Schools began to take firm root, the reformers added compulsory attendance laws to their program, with Massachusetts being the first to enact such a law in 1852.[47]

Mann's political acumen notwithstanding, the Common School

movement probably would have failed in Massachusetts and elsewhere if a large number of orthodox Protestants had not come over to Mann's side.[48] For example, in 1840 a proposal to abolish the State Board of Education was put to a vote of the Massachusetts legislature. The measure was handily defeated only because a large number of orthodox Protestants had come to support the idea of "public education."[49]

Why did orthodox Protestants provide the decisive support for the implementation of Mann's educational vision? Because of Irish Catholic immigration. And it was concern among Protestants over Catholic immigration that sustained the momentum of the Common School movement from the 1840s onward.

As early as the 1820s, elements of American Protestantism had begun to make public their opposition to Catholic immigration.[50] By 1840 Irish Catholic immigration to Boston was rising dramatically, and the number of Catholics in America tripled during that decade.[51] In 1852 more than 6,600 of the 11,800 students in Boston's primary schools had foreign-born parents.[52] While the Irish were by no means the only Catholics immigrating to America in the late 1830s and beyond, the concentration of their arrivals in the cities of the Northeast tended to make the Irish the symbol of Catholic immigration.

"Protestanizing" Catholics

To understand the reaction of American Protestants to mass Catholic immigration it is necessary to recall that the members of the dominant Protestant denominations in America were not unaware that their forebears had suffered terrible persecution in Europe at the hands of Catholics. Moreover, not only did the historical fact of that persecution live in the memory of Protestants, but Catholicism was also associated in their minds with ignorance and monarchical forms of civil and ecclesiastical government. All these things were alien to the Protestant culture that had developed in America.

When large numbers of impoverished, Irish began arriving in the late 1830s and 1840s, historical memories of the Catholicism of the 16th century were revived. Lacking a clear awareness that the Reformation that had given birth to Protestantism had also led to needed reforms within the Catholic Church, and not understanding that the generally degraded condition of the Irish was the result of their brutalization by the English, not Catholicism, Protestants tended to see the Catholic immigration as a religious and social problem that required a firm response.[53]

This is what brought a critical mass of Protestants in Massachusetts and elsewhere over to the Common School cause. Even in far-off California, for example, John Swett, the state superintendent of public instruction during the 1860s, argued that public schools were indispensable because "Nothing can Americanize these chaotic elements, and breathe into them the spirit of our institutions... except the public schools."[54] The "chaotic elements" referred to by Swett were, of course, primarily Catholic immigrants. Like other "progressives" of his age, Swett also viewed human beings as a form of collective property: "[C]hildren arrived at the age of maturity belong, not to the parents, but to the State, to society, to the country."[55]

In sum, the public school was sold from the beginning as an instrument for coercively assimilating Catholic children into Protestantism and American culture. Concern over Catholic immigration and Catholicism was also the reason that public funding at the state level for any schools except public schools came to an end long before the issue was raised in a Constitutional context in the late 1940s.[56]

By using compulsory school laws and denying tax funds to "sectarian schools" (which was nothing but a veiled reference to Catholic schools), Protestants hoped to force Catholic children into what were essentially Protestant public schools. As Lloyd P. Jorgenson describes the strategy:

> [T]hey approached their goals by indirection. The proscription of public aid to "sectarian" schools was a widely employed method.... The most drastic method of isolating the non-public schools came in the form of compulsory attendance laws specifying that such attendance must be in state-approved schools. Not only the financial support but the very existence of non-public schools was placed in jeopardy by these laws.[57]

PROGRESSIVES, THE KLAN, AND PUBLIC SCHOOLS

By the turn of the 19th century, progressives were beginning to state openly that parents were obstacles to creating the new society that they envisioned. For example, Edward Ross, a well-known sociologist and commentator on education in his time, wrote in 1901 that schools provided the perfect opportunity to replace parental influence with that of the teacher:

> Another gain lies in the partial substitution of the teacher for the parent as the model upon which the child forms himself. Copy the child will, and the advantage of giving him his teacher instead of his father to imitate, is that the former is a picked person, while the latter is not. Childhood is, in fact, the heyday of personal influence. The position of a teacher gives him prestige, and the lad will take from him suggestions that the adult will accept only from rare and splendid personalities.[58]

By the third decade of the 20th century, however, the co-opted Protestants were hoisted on their own petard. With some exceptions, government schools by then were firmly under the control of the "progressives," who viewed their ascendancy in government schools and schools of education as the perfect opportunity to remake children and, therefore, society in their own image. Needless to say, that image did not include any form of Christianity. Government schools were now to be vehicles for liberating children from "the coercive influence of the small family or community group."[59] Of course, such an ambitious project would be better assured of success if all children were required to attend government schools.

Reminiscent of the early stages of the Common School movement, the initial impetus for forcing all children to attend government schools came largely from a coalition of atheists, spiritualists, agnostics, freethinkers, and non-Christian theists united in an organization known as the "National Liberal League," as well as some Unitarians, Reform Jews, and other theological liberals.[60] Organized in 1875 by a former Unitarian, Francis Ellingwood Abbot, the National League was devoted to what it termed the *absolute* separation of church and state.[61] The phrase "separation of church and state" had been somewhat in vogue prior to the formation of the National Liberal League and was mainly understood as standing for religious liberty and freedom of churches from the state, although for many the phrase also carried an anti-Catholic connotation.[62] As understood by the National Liberal League, however, the phrase meant that the government had to be completely secularized and have no connection with organized religion.[63] With respect to schools, a portion of the lyrics from a National Liberal League hymn succinctly expressed their program:

> We want no counsel from the priests,
> No bishop's crook or gown,
> No sanctimonious righteousness,
> No curse or godly frown.
> We want no Bibles in the schools,
> No creeds or doctrines there;
> We want no superstition's tools
> The children's minds to scare.[64]

The National Liberal League had neither many adherents nor a long life. Not surprisingly, sex turned out to be the League's Achilles heel. Professor Philip Hamburger describes the tensions within the National Liberal League over this issue: "For Abbot and his theist allies, obscenity was both morally repugnant and a distraction. In contrast, for many atheists among the Liberals, sexual freedom seemed of almost religious importance...."[65] The result was that five years after its formation, the League disintegrated over the issue of the repeal of obscenity laws.

The demise of the National Liberal League notwithstanding, its reinterpretation of the slogan "separation of church and state" continued to be influential. In the area of schooling, Professor Hamburger notes that the League eventually sided with the Klan and various other nativist groups to promote compulsory public education:

Later in the century, Liberals joined nativists in seeking compulsory public education. For example, in 1876, when pursuing separation, the National League resolved: "That universal
education is the only safeguard of universal liberty; that *no
child in the republic should be permitted to grow up without at
least a good common school education.*" Drawing upon the liberal theological ideals that had become a pronounced feature
of Americanism, the Klan argued that intellectual independence and therefore also the foundations of American liberty
depended on public education…. On such assumptions, which
sometimes came remarkably close to those of liberal intellectuals, the Klan and allied organizations, including many Masonic
lodges, joined movements for obligatory public schooling in
various states, including Alabama, Arkansas, California, Michigan, Nebraska, Ohio, Oklahoma, Oregon, Texas, Washington,
and Wyoming.[66] [emphasis added]

The nativists and the National Liberal League obviously differed
over the proper nature of government schools, with the League wanting them to be entirely secular and the nativists wanting them to be
de facto Protestant in tone, even if the Protestantism was of a heavily
diluted variety. Nevertheless, they both agreed that no child should be
permitted to be educated outside of government schools. Ultimately,
the movement's initial success in Oregon proved its undoing.

Oregon was fertile ground for beginning the state-by-state
implementation of mandatory government schooling. Why? Liberals had enjoyed great success in Oregon in planting their "churches";
there were relatively few Catholics or new immigrants; and the Oregon nativists, who included many Protestants, had also demonstrated
political strength.[67] Not surprisingly, then, in 1922 Oregon voters,
urged on by public school teachers, nativist organizations such as the
Ku Klux Klan, the Democrat nominee for governor, and elements of
the Masons, approved a referendum requiring children between the
ages of 8 and 16 to attend government schools.[68] The main object of
the referendum, of course, was to shut down Catholic schools.

The results of the referendum were vigorously denounced by a number of voices, including John Dewey, the presidents of Yale, Columbia, and the University of Texas, and the Baptists (this may be one of the few recorded instances in which Baptists and John Dewey agreed on anything).[69] Following the referendum, the Society of the Sisters of the Holy Names of Jesus and Mary and the Hill Military Academy, a secular private school, litigated the constitutionality of the Oregon law. In a 1925 ruling, the United States Supreme Court struck down the Oregon law stating:

> The fundamental theory of liberty upon which all governments in this Union repose excludes any general power of the state to standardize its children by forcing them to accept instruction from public teachers only. The child is not the mere creature of the state; those who nurture him and direct his destiny have the right coupled with the high duty to recognize and prepare him for additional obligations.[70]

Thus, the victory of the Liberal League's "progressive" heirs, the Klan, and others in Oregon was transformed into a crushing defeat that put an end to statutory efforts to prevent children from being educated outside of government schools. Nevertheless, state constitutional provisions prohibiting aid to "sectarian" schools and the political influence of the political left and the Klan, as well as other nativist groups, succeeded in making private education so financially burdensome that the vast majority of parents could only exercise their right to educate their children outside of government schools at considerable financial sacrifice, if at all.[71]

CONFLICT AND SECULAR DRIFT

If not quite Unitarianism, the Protestantism of the 19th century government schools tended toward a Christianity of the lowest common denominator. One indicator of the trend toward secularization in the government schools was the change over time in *McGuffey's Readers*.

Williams Holmes McGuffey was the initial compiler of the well-known series of 19th century readers that bore his name. McGuffey, a college professor of ancient languages and moral philosophy and a theologically conservative Presbyterian minister, was responsible for the content of the 1836 edition of the books that came to be known as *McGuffey's Readers*.[72] The 1836 edition was so successful that it created a McGuffey brand that ultimately sold an estimated 120 million readers between 1836 and 1920. In fact, *McGuffey's Readers* were so widely used that by 1890 thirty-seven states had adopted them as their schools' basic readers.[73]

McGuffey's 1836 edition incorporated a strongly theistic, Reformed worldview. But even though subsequent revisions of *McGuffey's Readers* continued to bear his name for marketing purposes, after 1857 McGuffey had no involvement in their production at all and would not have approved of the changes.[74]

The transformation of worldview from McGuffey's own 1836 edition to the McGuffey branded 1879 edition is both startling and instructive. As described by John H. Westerhoff, III, in his *McGuffey and His Readers*:

> By 1879, the theistic, Calvinist world view so dominant in the first editions had disappeared, and the prominent values of salvation, righteousness, and piety were entirely missing. All that remained were lessons affirming the morality and life-styles of the emerging middle class and those cultural beliefs, attitudes, and values that undergird American civil religion. [75]

The differences between the 1836 and 1879 editions of *McGuffey's Readers* clearly reflect the secular drift in government schools that had occurred in the space of less than fifty years. Ironically, McGuffey supported the Common School movement in his native Ohio, perhaps even before *McGuffey's Readers* were born, and the career of *McGuffey's Readers* paralleled and reflected the rise and ultimate triumph of the Common School movement.[76] In retrospect, beginning in at least the 1850's, government schools were in the incipient stages of "progressive" curricular revisions that eventually would increasingly estrange

American children from a Christian worldview.

Nevertheless, throughout the 19th century Protestants were generally in control of the schools, and the school Bible was the King James Bible, not the Catholic Douay translation of the Bible. This led to considerable strife between Catholics and Protestants, which sometimes escalated into violence and abusive behavior.[77] For example, in Philadelphia the forced use of the King James Bible in schools led to rioting and bloodshed.[78] In Boston public schools, officials inflicted physical punishment on Catholic schoolboys who refused to recite the King James translation's version of the Ten Commandments. One Catholic boy, Thomas Wall, had his hands whipped with a rattan for half an hour by the assistant principal of his Boston common school over this issue.[79]

In public debate, Catholic publications such as the *Catholic World* denounced efforts to use Common Schools to achieve "the social and religious unification of the American people by a system of universal and uniform compulsory education."[80] Moreover, this "unification" was clearly seen by Catholics as an attempt to force Americans "of European and African origin, Indians and Asiatics, Protestants and Catholics, Jews and pagans, into one homogeneous people after what may be called the New England Evangelical type."[81] Ultimately, conflicts between Catholics and Protestants over the nature of the "public" schools led to the creation of a national system of Catholic schools.

Many, mostly conservative, Protestants continued to oppose the program of "public" schools being foisted on America as a result of the earlier unlikely alliance of Unitarians, Owenites, and co-opted Protestants. One of the central objections of the Protestant opponents of the Common Schools was that the Common Schools were debasing the standard of religious doctrine being taught to children and that doctrinal disputes relating to the Common Schools were aiding those who desired to secularize them.[82] As they clearly saw, once the Common Schools were secularized, Common Schools would turn out to have been a Faustian bargain, with the net result being that Christians had traded their independent Christian educational institutions for a secularized system of government schools. This meant that eventually the vast majority of Christian children would receive a secular rather than a Christian education.

In response, some Presbyterians, Lutherans, Episcopalians, and others attempted to create their own system of private schools as the Catholics were doing. Unfortunately, the division of opinion within the Protestant denominations over the Common School issue prevented these alternative Protestant school systems from becoming widespread.

In addition to these concerns, many Protestant opponents of the Common Schools also believed that the effort to "Protestantize" Catholic children by means of the Common Schools and compulsory attendance laws was fundamentally unjust. For example, R.L. Dabney, a prominent 19th century Presbyterian theologian and no friend of Catholic theology, understood not only that state controlled education would become totally secularized, but that it would become so precisely because of the *injustice* being done by Protestants to Catholics:

> Catholics make an effective point when they argue that the State must not use the people's money to teach using the King James Version, which they... believe to be heretical.... Zealous Protestants, usually zealous advocates of public schools, try to refute this. But would they assent to the teaching of *their* children, with their money a version which says: "Except ye do penance ye shall likewise perish?" They exclaim: "That this is an erroneous version, while the King James is faithful."... But shall the State be appointed to judge whether that proposition is true?... In the public arena, our commitment is to respect the views of Catholics....Unless we admit that our might makes right, we ought not to inflict such wrongs....[83]

For Dabney and the many other 19th century Christians who understood this issue, the crux of the problem was the error of transferring responsibility for education from parents and the church to the government. As long as the government held responsibility for education there could only be one of two unacceptable outcomes. Either control of the government schools would be used in an effort to impose some form of sectarian belief, or it would be used to provide an anti-Christian secular education. It was obvious to Dabney that the latter would in fact be the result: "[The public schools'] *complete secularization is logically inevitable. Christians must prepare themselves then, for the following results: All prayers, catechisms, and Bibles will ultimately be driven out of the schools.*" [84] [Emphasis original.]

A handful of state court decisions in the late 19th century and the first decades of the 20th century began to foreshadow what was to come. While the question of Bible reading in government schools wasn't much litigated during this period, and in such cases as arose the courts generally deferred to the decisions of local school authorities, a few state court decisions began to point toward the coming secularization of government schools. By 1929 the supreme courts of "Ohio (1873), Wisconsin (1890), Nebraska (1902, modified in 1903), Illinois (1910), Louisiana (1915), Washington (1918), and South Dakota (1929)" had upheld bans on Bible reading in government schools. [85]

As discussed in Chapter 1, with Justice Hugo Black's 1947 opinion in the *Everson* case declaring that the Establishment Clause of the First Amendment applied to the states and required a "wall of separation between church and state," the foundation for the future foreseen in the late 19th century by Dabney and others was completed. Ironically, Black, who began as a liberal Baptist populist, in time departed from the Baptists and found a new home among the Unitarians at All Souls Unitarian Church in Washington, D.C. [86]

THE SNARE OF SCHOOL REFORM

This brings us back to the present and the thought that somehow government schools can be reformed to provide a proper education for Christian children. *It should be evident by now that this is neither possible nor a proper aim for Christians.* A Christian education must impart a Christian worldview in which the sovereignty of God and the central role of Jesus Christ in human history and affairs are understood by every Christian child. As Dabney put it over one hundred years ago: "Every line of true knowledge must find its completeness as it converges on God, just as every beam of daylight leads the eye to the sun."[87]

But this is not an education that Christians should desire to provide through a system of government schools. Moreover, even if it were possible to provide a Christian education through the existing system of government schools, Christians should oppose it because *it would be sin*, just as it would be sin to use the coercive power of the state to evangelize and catechize non-Christian children in some other fashion. Christ told His disciples, "Suffer little children to come unto me, and forbid them not" (Luke 18:16). He didn't tell them to hire truant officers to drag them over to Him or to beleaguer their parents with taxes, regulations, and threats of imprisonment to "encourage" them to bring their children to Him. Christian children must receive *a Christian education that is provided in a Christian manner*, and that can only be done through the family and the church.

The point here is that Christian parents must not be distracted from their duty to their children by hoping for a reform of government schools that *will not and should not happen*. Instead, Christian parents must squarely confront what is now being done to their children. *Secular humanists and New Agers are using government schools coercively to evangelize Christian children to their atheistic or pagan beliefs.* These government-sponsored evangelists are relentless, and, as the data from the Nehemiah Institute and Barna Research show, they have been very effective. If we are to be faithful stewards of the children God has given us, Christian parents must lead their children out of Pharaoh's schools now.

ARE YOUR CHILDREN UNEQUALLY YOKED?

"...and what communion hath light with darkness?...
Wherefore come out from among them."
II Corinthians 6:14, 17

You would think that parents across America would be in open revolt over what government schools are doing to their children. But they aren't. Instead, as the Horatio Alger Association poll mentioned in the third chapter shows, as far as *their* local government schools are concerned, most parents are quite content. How come?

Although there is undoubtedly more than one reason, chief among them is this: the average parent doesn't have any idea what is really going on at the local government school. In fact, the average parent probably doesn't know much more about the curricula, teachers, administrators, and other aspects of his local government schools than he does about Zamboanga. Yes, he may know the names of some of his child's teachers and perhaps a few bits of unimportant biographical information about them. But unless a teacher happens to be a neighbor or a friend, it is a virtual certainty that he knows nothing important about the teacher's moral beliefs, religious commitments, level of literacy, knowledge of subject areas, social views, and so on. Yes, the parent has a vague understanding that the local government school is ostensibly teaching mathematics, language arts, social studies, and other subjects (both real and imagined). But he has no actual idea of what is in the curriculum. Is the school teaching constructivist math and "Rainforest" algebra? He doesn't know. Is the school teaching reading by whole language or phonics? He doesn't know. Is the school teaching history or "self-esteem studies"? He doesn't know. Is the school honest in its standardized testing? He doesn't know. Does the school teach values clarification or have a Gay/Straight Alliance club? He doesn't know. And even if he has heard of any of these, you can almost bet that he doesn't know in any depth what the government school is actually doing. Not really.

Is this a sign that the average parent is indifferent to what happens to his child? No. There are two factors at work here. First, parents today (and their parents, and their parents before them) were raised in a society that unreflectively came to accept the belief that the education of children is the business of the state, not parents. Government schools, after all, employ legions of "highly trained education professionals" who have been known to remind questioning parents that they, not the parents, are the "experts." From the perspective of today's parents, why should they undertake something that is the government's job, that they haven't been "trained" for, and that they've already paid to have someone else do? Besides, being personally responsible for their children's education might cause some anxiety and force them to reorder their lives.

Second, as bad as they are at what they are supposed to be doing, government schools are pretty slick at public relations. Eighty-seven percent of children come home with above average grades on their report cards, with over 60% having nothing lower than a "B." Standardized tests also regularly show that most children and school districts are above average. Lots of bumper stickers are handed out to build the self-esteem of the parents of some absurdly high percentage of children who are on a school's "Honor Roll." Yard signs are liberally distributed so that every neighbor can know that Buffy or Bobby is involved in drill team, band, or some other activity. Local papers obediently transcribe school district press releases and print them as news, and never miss an opportunity to report on school sports and other extracurricular goings-on. In sum, with the exception of some urban school districts whose pathologies can't be concealed, parents in school districts across America unwittingly inhabit a psychological Lake Wobegon unobtrusively constructed for them by their local school district. And, of course, if they recently attended government schools, they probably wouldn't get the joke about all of the children being above average.

As for their children, they are generally reconciled to their lot. Nothing much is asked of them, they seldom confront failure, and they lack the experience and knowledge to understand what is being done to them. Once a child gets used to being institutionalized, whatever school is, that's what is normal because it's all the child has known in his short life.

But we have been talking about parents in general. What about Christian parents? Are they unequally yoking their children? To what extent are they forcing their children to walk in the counsel of the ungodly (Ps. 1:1)?

WHERE IS YOUR TREASURE?

To answer these questions we need to consider some facts. According to the 2001 American Religious Identity Survey of 113,000 adults, 76.5% of American adults identify themselves as Christians.[1] According to October 2000 U.S. Census Bureau estimates, there are almost 49 million children in the age range from 1st through 12th grade.[2] The Council for American Private Education estimates that about 11% of elementary and secondary schoolchildren attend private schools, and it appears that students in Christian private schools constitute roughly 80% of the private school total.[3] There are no hard figures on how many children are homeschooled, but private estimates indicate that the number is likely to be in the range of 1.5 million to 2 million.[4] Of homeschooled children, it is estimated that roughly 75% to 80% are from Christian families.[5] As a result, if we assume that 76.5% of schoolchildren are from Christian families and that there are 1.75 million homeschoolers, it appears that about 85% of children from Christian families are in government schools.[6] So, it seems that with respect to the education of their children the vast majority of Christian parents are not very different from their non-Christian counterparts. They, too, have fallen prey to the assumption that the education of their children is properly a government function, and they have been lulled into complacency by the education industry's public relations efforts.

While it is clear that Christians in general are not fulfilling their obligation to provide their children with a Christian education, some church denominations are being more faithful than others. Below is a table that estimates for each of several major denominations: (a) the percentage of all Christians in America that the denomination represents, (b) the percentage of all children attending Christian schools that the denomination educates, and (c) enrollment in the denomination's schools expressed as a percentage of the estimated number of the denomination's primary and secondary school-age children.[7] As indicated in the endnotes, some of these figures are based on various assumptions and estimates, but they illustrate fairly that American Christians are providing a Christian education to very few of their school-age children:[8]

Denominations	Percent of Professing Christians by Denomination[9]	Percent of All Children in Christian Schools in the Denomination's Schools[10]	Enrollment in a Denomination's Schools as a Percent of the Denomination's School-age Children[11]
Catholics	32.0%	62.5%	19.0%
Baptists	21.0%	8.0%	3.6%
Methodists	8.8%	0.4%	0.0%
Lutherans	6.0%	5.4%	8.7%
Presbyterians	3.5%	0.8%	2.2%
Church of Christ	1.6%	1.0%	6.6%
Seventh-Day Adventists	0.4%	1.6%	40.0%

This simple table demonstrates several things. First, of the major denominations, Catholics are educating a vastly disproportionate share of the children in Christian schools, including many Protestant children. Although Protestants constitute roughly two-thirds of American Christians, they educate less than 40% of the children in Christian schools. That Protestants fail to provide Christian education is clearly one of the many unfortunate consequences of the majority of 19th century Protestants embracing the Common School movement. If Protestants were to provide opportunities for a Christian education just in the same proportion as Catholics, the percentage of all school age children attending Christian schools would increase to approximately 16.5%, almost double the current level.[12] This would further mean that Christian schools would be able to educate roughly 21.5% of all Christian children.[13] Interestingly, in relation to their numbers the Seventh-Day Adventists have been the most faithful of all Christian denominations in providing opportunities for Christian education. But even in the case of the Seventh-Day Adventists, a majority of their children is likely enrolled in government schools.[14]

As noted before, if we take into account both Christian schools and homeschools it is likely that between 85% and 90% of children from Christian families are attending government schools. Why is that? For some, it is a matter of never having thought about the issue. Others, like most parents, actually think that their school district is doing a good job based on information they receive from school officials. Yet others suspect that something is genuinely wrong with sending their children to government schools, but, for various reasons, are attempting to ignore the problem or to rationalize what they are doing.

How can a Christian rationalize sending his children to the spiritually, morally, and academically corrosive environment of the government schools? There are a number of common excuses. Let's consider some of them.

THE RITUAL OF EVASION AND DENIAL

Perhaps you've discussed with Christian parents of school-age children some of the reasons why Christian children should not attend government schools. If you have, then you may also have been told that "You're right, *but*...," as in "You're right that our high school has a serious gang, drug, and alcohol problem, *but*...," or "You're right that most of the children in our schools have trouble reading and can't find Texas on a map, *but*...," or "You're right that the local schools are promoting earth-worship and homosexuality in the classroom, *but*...." Here are some of the more common "*buts*."

"BUT OUR GOVERNMENT SCHOOL IS DIFFERENT"

In a trivial sense this is true, which is why this claim has some superficial plausibility. But let's ask some relevant questions. Does your government school receive *money* from the *federal* government and is it subject to *federal laws, regulations, and court decisions* interpreting the Constitution and federal statutes? Does your government school receive money from the state government and is it subject to state laws, regulations, state court decisions interpreting your state constitution and statutes? Are teachers' unions present in your school? Did most of the teachers and administrators in your school receive training in a school of education? The answers to these questions will, of course, be "Yes."

So, in what relevant sense can your government school be different? It is subject to the same federal laws and court decisions that have driven the Bible and Christianity out of the schools, that have rendered effective discipline impossible, and that virtually force schools to have homosexual clubs. It is also as subject to the programmatic incentives and disincentives created by various forms of federal funding as any other school. For example, as noted in Chapter 2, if you are a government school administrator and you don't want a homosexual club in your middle school or high school, you aren't free to make that decision entirely on the merits. By federal legislation, your alternatives to the homosexual club are (a) giving up the roughly 8% of your budget that comes from the federal government, (b) shutting down all non-curricular clubs, or (c) spending a whole lot of money on a lawsuit that you might not win.

At the state level, your school is subject to the same statutes and court decisions as every other school in your state. If you live in California, for example, that means that your boys and girls get to choose whether for purposes of school they will be considered "boys" or "girls," or something else. The presence of the teachers' unions, which are little more than leftist political parties, and the training of the overwhelming majority of teachers and administrators in schools of education controlled by the "multicultural" left help create a government school institutional culture deeply antagonistic to Christianity, traditional morality, and intelligent approaches to teaching.

So, yes, in some superficial respects not every government school is the same. But none of them is really different enough to justify leaving a Christian child behind in the seething cauldron of spiritual, moral, and academic pathologies that government schools have become.

The truth is hard, but simple. Those who control government schools want your children and your money. They don't want you sticking your nose into what they consider to be their business, and they don't want to change. To preempt annoying parental scrutiny and demands for change, school districts make liberal use of the tools of public relations: A steady flow of glossy brochures, press releases, personal contacts, and other forms of communication are used to create an educational Potemkin Village to pacify parents. Like an illusionist's sleight of hand techniques, pictures of new buildings, reports about the fortunes of the football team, and human-interest stories about students, teachers, and administrators are used to create an undeserved wholesome image and to distract attention from the spiritual, moral, and academic rot endemic to government schools.

Yes, it is always possible for the officials of just about any school district to point to some other district – say, Philadelphia – for the purpose of convincing parents that, in comparison, things aren't so bad. In this sense, the government schools in Philadelphia, Washington, D.C., Los Angeles, New York, and a few other places play an indispensable role for the education establishment: They can always be used to persuade parents that things could be worse. Of course, this is beside the point. The question is whether the education of Christian children should be entrusted to an anti-Christian institution that is destroying our children spiritually, morally, and intellectually. By that standard, it makes no difference, for example, whether 12% or "merely" 9% of teachers were physically threatened in school in the last year. No government school is different enough to justify leaving the Christian children in them behind.[15]

"BUT MY CHILD IS SALT AND LIGHT"

Some Christian parents rationalize sending their children to government schools by claiming that their children are "salt and light," or that their children must participate in carrying out the Great Commission. In fact, it almost seems that they are trying to convince you that their 9-year-old is really a Christian evangelist with a public ministry. Of course, when Christ spoke about "salt and light" and the Great Commission he was speaking to adults. Further, He wasn't speaking to just any adults, but to His disciples, who had been with Him day and night in His ministry. In fact, by the time Christ gave the Great Commission His disciples had been with Him for about three years. Yet even then Christ told His disciples to stay in Jerusalem until after they were "endued with power from on high." Thus, despite the extensive teaching He had provided them, Christ's disciples were not ready to undertake their mission until the Holy Spirit had come to them. Plainly, they needed to have on the "whole armor of God" (Eph. 6:13) before they ventured out.

Christians really shouldn't have to be reminded that Christ was not speaking to 5-year-olds, 10-year-olds, or 15-year-olds when He gave the Great Commission, or when He described His disciples as "salt and light." Christian adults bear this responsibility, not children. In fact, the Bible is quite clear that children require nurturing, training, and, yes, even being "set apart for a season." As Psalm 144:11-12 tells us:

> Rid me, and deliver me from the hand of strange children, whose mouth speaketh vanity, and their right hand is a right hand of falsehood: That our sons may be as plants grown up in their youth; that our daughters may be as cornerstones, polished after the similitude of a palace.

Obviously, the Psalmist understood that children should be given time to grow and develop before facing a hostile and sinful world on their own. In other words, childhood is a time of discipling.

E. Ray Moore, Jr., founder of the Exodus Mandate and a retired army chaplain, describes the "salt and light" error as follows:

The salt and light of the earth theology is laudable, but misapplied in education because small children simply don't have the experience to be evangelists for the Christian faith, given the onslaught of secular humanism, political-correctness and the *demand for conformity in the public schools.* Confronting these is work for adults. Christian families should not be sending in children as surrogate evangelists before they are old enough and mature enough in their own faith to handle the pressures of the hostile environment now represented by the pagan school system.[16] [emphasis added]

Still, many parents persist in the belief that young children or teenagers should be placed in an exceptionally hostile, anti-Christian environment 35 or 40 hours a week to win 40-year-old New Agers and 16-year-old gang members to Christ. Simply stating the proposition reveals its absurdity, and what an unspeakable burden to place on a child. Even Christian adults in the workplace don't have to confront anything remotely resembling the pervasively hostile, anti-Christian environment found in government schools. Further, even if they did, they would be facing it as adults dealing with adults, not as children submerged in a pagan seminary controlled by adults with knowledge, experience, and power that children can barely begin to comprehend.

This is not to say that Christian children cannot be "salt and light" in the sense of setting a Christian example in a manner consistent with their still developing level of maturity. They can visit the elderly in nursing homes; they can involve themselves in community projects; and they can participate in a host of other constructive activities in which they display the Christian character that they are *developing.* But our children must be given a chance *to develop* – to grow and be polished. Otherwise, they are likely to fall away. If you doubt this, go back and look at the findings by the Nehemiah Institute.

For those who care to pay attention, the facts show that by sending our children to government schools we are plunging them into acid and darkness. They are losing their "saltiness" and their light is being extinguished. Government schools are evangelistic institutions for secularists, New Agers, Wiccans, and the rest. As the data also show, the anti-Christian elements within government schools are doing a remarkably effective job of evangelizing Christian children. We know *empirically* that it is simply not true that Christian children are "salt and light" in government schools. Instead, government schools are converting our children to alien creeds and infusing them with false and destructive values.

Perhaps the next time a parent tells you that his child goes to government schools to be "salt and light," you might gently ask, "Who is evangelizing whom?" But asking, "Who is kidding whom?" might be more to the point.

"BUT WE CAN'T JUST WITHDRAW FROM THE CULTURE!"

This excuse presupposes that surrendering our children to an aggressively anti-Christian institution is somehow the only or the best way to engage the "culture." *On the contrary, sending our children to government schools is in fact a pre-emptive surrender in the culture wars.*

The evidence clearly indicates that children educated in government schools overwhelmingly end up being both "in the world" and "of the world." By rescuing our children and providing them with a solid Christian education we would instead finally join the battle by declaring that the world's values and beliefs are not ours. Moreover, we can provide no better witness to others than by showing those outside the Church our commitment to our faith and children.

Further, if all Christians withdrew their children from government schools, sending children to government schools would no longer represent the cultural norm – we would have changed it. This is, in part, the point. By being faithful in the education of our children we are in fact adopting the most effective strategy for changing the culture.

"BUT OUR PASTOR HASN'T SAID IT'S A PROBLEM"

It is certainly true that very few Christians hear the truth about their government school habit from the pulpit, but this is beside the point. Our obligations as Christians are not determined by what is said from the pulpit, but instead are enjoined upon us through the Bible. Second, many churches are quite political, and pastors are often pressured to avoid some issues to maintain the cohesion and peace of the congregation. This is why sin often seems not to be much spoken about from the pulpit these days. Similarly, many pastors are reluctant to preach against sending Christian children to government schools for fear of alienating those in the congregation who make their livings directly or indirectly through the government school system. They also fear offending parents who are sending their children to government schools by telling them that they are sinning against their children and against God.

But this, too, is beside the point. The responsibility is first and foremost ours as parents, not our pastors.' Moreover, do you seriously doubt that those who raise this "*but*" would just find another excuse if their pastors *did* preach about the sin of sending Christian children to government schools?

"But Our Government School Has Some Christian Teachers"

Many parents think that their children are a getting a somewhat Christian education at their local government school because there are some Christian teachers or administrators. By now it should be apparent that this is false comfort. The law, curricula, and other factors make it impossible to provide a Christian education within any government school. In fact, most parents probably don't fully appreciate how *difficult* the position of Christian teachers and administrators within government schools is. Today, a teacher or administrator who openly affirms his faith in any significant way within the school is likely to be harassed, disciplined, or dismissed. Further, in many instances they must teach or administer curricula and participate in programs that are antithetical to their Christian beliefs. Consequently, many Christian teachers and administrators have left government schools for Christian schools or other fields. Those who remain behind struggle to find some way of reconciling their faith with their work. As Christians we should be grateful that some Christian teachers and administrators feel called to remain in government schools. This, however, is hardly an excuse for leaving our children there.

"BUT WHAT ABOUT SOCIALIZATION?"

Some Christian parents are a little schizophrenic – they want their children to be Christian *and* to be like everyone else. This is obviously impossible. Christ offended many because His words and His actions were a rebuke to sinners. His apostles knew that they would suffer because they would give offense for His sake. Christians are not commanded, "Go and be like everyone else." In 2 Corinthians 6:14 and 17 we are asked "what communion hath light with darkness?" and are then told to "come out from among them, and be ye separate... and touch not the unclean thing...." Similarly, Psalm 1:1 admonishes us not to walk in the counsel of the ungodly, stand in the way of sinners, or sit in the seat of the scornful. *So, the real question is, to which standards are we going to socialize our children* – to those of Pharaoh's schools or to those of Christ?

"BUT WHAT ABOUT EXTRACURRICULAR ACTIVITIES?"

Some children become very engaged in sports and other extracurricular activities. This can be a good thing. It's a problem from the Christian perspective, however, if we allow these sorts of activities to become an excuse for failing to provide our children with a Christian education. Christ asks us where our treasure is. What are our priorities? What is first? Christ or the football team? Christ or the school band? Christ doesn't tell us to seek first the junior high school drill team, but rather the Kingdom of God (Matt. 6:33).

Our true priorities are what we do, not what we *say* our priorities are. Christian schools, homeschool groups, and communities provide a wide variety of extracurricular activities. With the exception of some team sports such as football, baseball, and basketball, the quality of the activities sponsored through these sources is likely to be at least as good as those provided through government schools. Could there be a clearer example of misplaced priorities than leaving a child in a government school so he can participate in a more competitive sports or other extracurricular program?

"BUT WHAT WOULD MY FAMILY AND FRIENDS THINK?"

This is seldom a problem for parents who decide to send their children to a Christian school. It used to be a significant problem for those who chose to homeschool. Fortunately, to the chagrin of the teachers' unions, most people now have a favorable view of homeschooling. Parents who decide to homeschool today are far more likely to encounter curiosity than hostility. But if grandparents or others do react negatively, Chapter 8 points you toward some of the many studies and other materials available to allay their concerns. Many times, just showing worried grandparents homeschooling curriculum materials is enough to convince them that they don't need to be concerned. Homeshooling parents also have found that doubters have become believers when they have seen how their homeschooled children have flourished. In the final analysis, however, you are responsible for providing your children with a Christian education no matter what others may think.

"BUT WE WENT TO PUBLIC SCHOOLS AND WE TURNED OUT JUST FINE"

No, *we were sent* to government schools, and while we may not have developed an alcohol or drug problem, gotten pregnant out-of-wedlock, had an abortion, become Druids, experimented with homosexuality, or failed to learn that the United States is located in North America, government schools were a bad place for children even when we attended them – our nostalgic memories notwithstanding. The pathologies of government schools were just far better concealed then and not as far advanced.

Today government schools are vastly worse than they were even ten or twenty years ago. Moreover, the hazards they pose today to any child, not just Christian children, are obvious for any parent who cares to look. You wouldn't let your child play Russian Roulette, so why would you chose to give your children to an institution that is anti-Christian, that aggressively promotes anti-Christian values, that is physically dangerous, and that cripples children intellectually, and hope that your child will somehow pass through the fire unscathed?

"But We Can't Afford It"

Apart from working out our own salvation, we, as Christian parents, have no more important task on this earth than raising our children as the Bible commands us. If we are giving our children over to an anti-Christian institution for their education we are failing to be faithful, and we are harming our children spiritually, morally, and intellectually – perhaps even physically. Thus, the question for us cannot be, "Can we afford a Christian education?" Instead, it must be, "How are we going to do it?"

Those of us who are middle class Americans already have been graced with abundant means. If we ask, "Can we afford a Christian education?", what we are really asking is whether we can provide our children one without disturbing our existing material priorities. Can you give your children a Christian education in a Christian school or by homeschooling without changing how you live? I don't know, but all of us need to constantly remind ourselves that cars, boats, hobbies, clothes, vacations, large houses, and restaurant meals are all ephemera. Like our flesh, they will wither and fade. As parents we are obligated to ensure that the Word abides within our children and that they receive a Christian education.

For those of us whose material means are less than average, giving our children a truly Christian education seems a great challenge. Yet, in America we all tend to measure our material circumstances in relation to others, usually in relation to those whom we believe are doing better economically than we are. But consider our early American forebears.

In 18th and early 19th century Connecticut, for example, virtually everyone was literate, even though by today's standards the well-to-do then would be considered to be living in shocking poverty. Even the "poor" in America today enjoy things that would have been unimaginable luxuries to the wealthy of that era. Early American children living in homes without running water and without central heating or air-conditioning received a Christian education because their parents couldn't imagine having a higher priority than raising their children as God commands. They did whatever was necessary to demonstrate their faithfulness in the education of their children. If the means for doing so weren't close at hand, they figured out how to provide what was needed as a community of Christians. We need to be mindful of their witness. Acting together as a community of Christians is the single most important thing we can do to ensure that all of the children in our churches can get a Christian education.

"BUT WE CAN'T SEND OUR CHILDREN TO CHRISTIAN SCHOOL AND I DON'T THINK I AM QUALIFIED TO TEACH"

Many parents who can't afford a Christian school would consider homeschooling, but they are afraid to homeschool because they don't think they are qualified to teach. If this still bothers you, go back and re-read Chapter 5.

Many teachers in government schools, unfortunately, don't really know how to teach. In fact, they are steeped in educational theories that virtually assure that they *won't* be able to teach. The dwindling remnant of teachers who *do know how to teach* are often required to use curricula that make teaching almost impossible. For example, Matthew Clavel, a capable young math teacher in New York, found that the district-mandated "Fuzzy Math" curriculum actually prevented learning and was demoralizing his students. His solution? Civil disobedience. As he put it: "If school officials knew how far my lessons would deviate from the school district-mandated program in the months ahead, they probably would have fired me on the spot."[18] Clavel, by the way, is no longer teaching.

You actually have several advantages over those who teach in government schools: your head hasn't been stuffed full of false theories of learning by a school of education; you are free to use with your children whatever curriculum you discover works well for them; you know your pupils better than anyone else and can discipline them as needed; and you don't have to manage a classroom of 20 to 30 children or deal with government school administrative red-tape. In addition, there are many turn-key curricula available that, besides books, provide daily lesson plans, video courses, grading and testing services, transcripts, and other products and services that make it easy to homeschool. If you are still worried, take a look at the study referenced in the next chapter that found that homeschooled children substantially outperform their government school counterparts even if a parent hadn't graduated from high school.

"But We Can't Send Our Children to Christian School and Don't Have Time to Homeschool"

No time? This is almost never true. Homeschoolers finish their schoolwork on average within three to four hours, and only a part of that time involves instruction by a parent. Many families in which both parents work homeschool by teaching in the evenings. Single parents often find ways to homeschool. In fact, in my family's church there is a single mother of modest means who has successfully homeschooled her five children. If she can do it, the rest of us don't have any excuses. We may not have time to homeschool *and* watch as much television as we do now; we may not have time to homeschool *and* go out as much as we do now; we may not have time to homeschool *and* play or watch as much sports as we do now – but, we do have time. If you are worried about time, perhaps you should also ask yourself if you have the time to deal with the many problems that are likely to affect your children if you do leave them in Pharaoh's schools.

Why Are We Failing in the Education of Our Children?

Obviously, our failure to be faithful in the education of our children is *not* a denominational problem. We are *all* falling short – even denominations known to be Biblically conservative.

For example, in a 2001 address to the Southern Baptist Convention Executive Committee, T.C. Pinckney provided one of the best, most succinct statements of the reasons why we are failing to provide our children with a Christian education:

> Why have we failed our God in this critically important responsibility? We have failed because we have been willfully, blissfully ignorant… and satisfied in our ignorance. We have failed because the great majority of us have not made the effort to inform ourselves of the facts… even though there are books and articles galore readily available. *We have failed because – even when we have known the facts – we have not had the courage to point them out to our people.*[18] [Emphasis added.]

Ignorance, sloth, and a failure of courage – this is a Southern Baptist indicting his own convention for its failure to be faithful in the education of its children. Rousas J. Rushdoony long ago sounded the same alarm among Presbyterians, and similar voices have been speaking out among Lutherans, Methodists, Catholics, Pentecostals and others.

IT TAKES A CHURCH

What are we doing as a community of Christians to provide Christian education for our children? That question has been answered already – nearly nothing. Most churches have ministries of all sorts. Ironically, many of them are directed at helping with the problems of adults – for example, the consequences of crime, using drugs, and divorce – that have become commonplace because we and earlier generations have not been faithful in how we educate our children.

Somehow churches fail to recognize there is no ministry more urgent and important than helping assure that no Christian child is left behind in a government school. This doesn't mean that every church needs to start a school. But *every* church should be counseling parents whose children are in government schools to take their children out; *every* church should be discussing with parents of limited means how their children can be rescued from government schools; *every* church should be actively educating parents about homeschooling and supporting homeschooling groups; and, *every* church should be collaborating with other churches to find ways of bringing every Christian child out from government school bondage.[19]

LEADING YOUR CHILDREN INTO THE PROMISED LAND OF HOMESCHOOLING AND CHRISTIAN SCHOOLS

"And he shall turn the heart of the fathers to the children,
and the heart of the children to the fathers...."
Malachi 4:6

C hristian education isn't something to turn to reluctantly. Rather, we should embrace it with a sense of joy and hope. Our failed national experiment with government schooling over the course of a century and more has created intense conflict between Christian homes and government schools and between Christian parents and their own children. Becoming obedient to the obligations God has enjoined upon us in the education of our children allows us to eliminate that conflict. Christian education aligns the values of education with those of Christian homes and prevents schooling from alienating children from their parents. Moreover, as in all things, God has provided us with the means to do this.

Christian schools are plentiful in many parts of the country, and homeschooling resources are more widely available today than ever before. Moreover, whether you are interested in traditional Christian schools or homeschooling, the Internet provides Christian parents an astonishing amount of information regarding these alternatives to government schools. If you do not have an Internet connection, you probably have a friend who does, or a local library that can give you access to the World Wide Web. Nothing provides an easier or more comprehensive way of becoming familiar with the many opportunities for Christian education than the Internet. If you are unfamiliar with the Internet, invest a few minutes in learning how to use this powerful tool.

Christian schooling and, particularly, Christian homeschooling are growing. This chapter is devoted to an overview of a few of the practical considerations for parents interested in investigating these alternatives.[1]

CHRISTIAN SCHOOLS

Of the two approaches to Christian education, traditional Christian schools currently educate about three times as many Christian children as do homeschooling families.[2] There are roughly 20,000 Christian schools in America,[3] and not surprisingly their students clearly perform better academically, on average, than their government school counterparts as indicated by nationally-normed standardized tests.[4] What may be surprising, however, is that Christian schools achieve these results while generally charging relatively modest tuition. Census Bureau data show that in 1997, for example, 25% of church-related schools charged less than $1,385 per year, 50% charged less than $2,212 per year, and 75% charged less than $4,052 per year.[5] A 2000 study by the Center For Education Reform examining tuition costs at all private elementary and secondary schools (secular and religious) found that the average tuition nationwide was $3,116.[6] Moreover, 67% of those schools charged $2,500 or less.[7] The U.S. Department of Education's figures from the year 2000 tell a similar, though not identical, story: Average tuition for private elementary schools nationwide was $3,267, with 41% of private elementary and secondary schools costing less than $2,500 per year to attend.[8] Median private school elementary tuition has been reported in New Orleans at $2,386, in Denver at $3,528, in Charleston at $3,150, in Philadelphia at $2,504, and in Washington, D.C., at $4,500.[9]

Although this sort of general information is helpful, deciding on how and where to pursue Christian schooling requires a certain amount of detective work. Some resources for beginning that process are identified below, along with a few suggestions concerning criteria that you might want to use in your evaluation of Christian schools.

How Do You Find the Christian Schools in Your Area?

Probably the single most comprehensive tool for locating Christian schools is a searchable database available through the National Center for Educational Statistics. This database was created as a result of a national survey of Christian schools conducted in 2001 and can be found at:

http://nces.ed.gov/surveys/pss/privateschoolsearch/

Other general sources of information for Christian schools in your area include your local yellow pages. A computer searchable version of the yellow pages is available on the Internet from Yahoo!

Information about particular kinds of Christian schools is also readily available over the Internet. Here are a few resources:

- The Southern Baptist Association of Christian Schools (SBACS) assists many of the over 650 Southern Baptist schools advance a Christian worldview through providing "information, training, fellowship, and avenues of influence for pastors and educational leaders of Southern Baptist schools and churches." This organization also assists churches affiliated with the Southern Baptist Convention with starting Christian schools. The website for the Southern Baptist Association of Christian Schools can be found at www.sbacs.org. With Ed Gamble as its executive director, this organization is likely to dramatically increase support for Christian schools among Southern Baptists.
- The Association of Classical and Christian Schools (ACCS, www.accsedu.org) is an excellent source for information about classical Christian schools. ACCS's primary mission is to promote, establish, and equip schools committed to a classical approach to education based on a Christian worldview. Among other things, ACCS provides a directory of its affiliate and member schools, an accreditation program, and information on how to start a classical Christian school.

- The American Association of Christian Schools (AACS, www.aacs.org) is a federation of state associations of Bible-believing schools that cooperate in providing services to Christian schools. In addition to a directory of member schools, AACS provides accreditation and other services helpful to Christian schools.
- Christian Schools International (CSI, www.gospelcom. net/csi/) is an organization of Reformed Christian schools providing accreditation and various other services to its members. CSI's web site provides a searchable directory of its member schools.
- Directories of Lutheran schools are available through the Lutheran Church-Missouri Synod (www.lcms.org), the Wisconsin Evangelical Lutheran Synod (www.wels.net), the Church of Lutheran Brethren (www.clba.org), the Evangelical Lutheran Church in America (www.elca.org), and Lutheran Central (www.lutherancentral.com).
- A listing of Seventh-Day Adventist Schools, as well as information about many other Christian and secular private schools, can be found at About.com (http://privateschool. about.com/cs/assocna/index_3.htm). You can also get information about Adventist Schools by contacting the Seventh Day Adventist Church, 12501 Old Columbia Pike, Silver Spring, MD 20904, (301) 680 6604.
- The Association of Christian Schools International (ACSI, www.acsi.org), a provider of accreditation and other services to its some 5,000 member schools, provides a school directory.
- Catholic Online provides a wealth of information about Catholic education, including a worldwide directory of Catholic schools (www.catholic.org/cen/schoolsonweb/ school.html). Additional information is available from the National Catholic Education Association, 1077 30th Street N.W., Ste. 100, Washington, D.C., 2007, (202) 337 6232 nceaadmin@ncea.org.

- The Episcopal Church sponsors many schools, and information about them is available through the National Association of Episcopal Schools, 815 Second Ave., Ste. 313, New York, NY, 10017, (800) 334 7626, info@naes.org. You can find them on the web at http://www.naes.org/.
- Information about schools sponsored by the Church of the Nazarene can be obtained by contacting the Nazarene International Education Association, 6401 The Paseo, Kansas City, MO 64141, (816) 333 7000, gensec-hoo@nazarene. org. Visit their website at http://www.niea-online.org/.
- Schools sponsored by the Church of Christ can be found on the web at http://church-of-christ.org/schools/United_States/S_United_States.htm. Additional information is available through Church of Christ Schools, P.O. Box 336, Garland, Texas 78839, (830) 374 9130, Garcia@church-of-christ.org.

These are just some of the resources available for finding Christian schools on the Internet. For those interested in further research, the Internet provides a number of search-engines to ferret out additional information. Dogpile (www.dogpile.com) is one of the most efficient of these.

In some instances, parents may consider starting their own Christian school because no suitable Christian school is available locally. SBACS, ACCS, AACS, CSI, ACSI, Christian curriculum providers such as ABEKA, School of Tomorrow (http://www.schooloftomorrow.co.za/), Alpha Omega Publications (www.aop.com), and other organizations provide information on how to start a Christian school. About.com also is a source of helpful information for starting a school (http://privateschool.about.com/cs/startingaschool/).

WHICH CHRISTIAN SCHOOL?

Selecting a Christian school is obviously a highly individual matter requiring consideration of religious orientation, academic and non-academic programs, location, and cost. But selecting a Christian school requires weighing more than just these considerations. Unfortunately, some schools that claim to be "Christian" are not all that different from government schools. You can't just visit a campus to meet administrators, get the official tour, and make a decision. Instead, parents must spend some time observing classes and students. How do the students dress? Do you see students with tattoos or body piercings (other than girls with pierced ears)? How do the students speak and behave toward each other, faculty, and administrators? How do the students behave in class and the cafeteria? What is on the bulletin boards? If the students tend to look and behave like government school students, you should look for another school.

Similarly, parents need to know about the administration, staff, and curriculum. Does the school board allow the administration to discipline students as it determines is necessary, including expelling students who will not honor the rules of the school? Do the administrators have the power to hire and dismiss faculty? What spiritual requirements does the school have for its administrators and faculty? How is the Bible integrated into the curriculum? Does the school strive in class and outside of class to help children develop a Christian worldview?[10] Does the school pride itself on hiring teachers that attended schools of education and are certified by the state? Is it using many of the same textbooks that are used in government schools?

In sum, the commitment to Christ of any truly Christian school will be readily reflected in its students, classes, textbooks, faculty, administrators, and extracurricular activities. If you can't see it clearly, it probably isn't there.

HOMESCHOOLING

Homeschooling is the fastest-growing phenomenon in education. In 1980 homeschooling was illegal in thirty states, and in 1985 there were only about 50,000 homeschooled children.[11] But by 1993, homeschooling was legal in all fifty states,[12] and some current estimates peg the number of homeschooled students at about 2 million. All of this progress notwithstanding, many Christian parents are still unfamiliar with homeschooling and are fearful over whether they could do it themselves. What is "homeschooling"? Does it work? Where can you get more information about it? Some brief answers to these questions follow.

WHAT IS HOMESCHOOLING?

Homeschooling is a tutorial method of instruction in which parents assume responsibility for the education of their children. Homeschooling parents choose their children's curriculum, determine the schedule for their children's school day and school year, tutor their children on their school work, and evaluate their children's work and arrange for testing.

Contrary to the misconceptions of some, homeschooled students are not necessarily taught exclusively by their parents. Homeschool families typically belong to homeschool cooperatives in which parents with knowledge of specialized subjects provide instruction in those subjects to the children in the group. A number of providers of homeschool curricula offer instruction in individual subjects or entire curricula using videotapes, satellite feeds, or the Internet. In addition, tutors offer high level seminars in history, literature, and other subjects to homeschool students over the Internet using streaming video and audio. Because of the profound changes in the capabilities and cost of computers and telecommunications over the last five years, homeschooling children have access to a range of educational and social opportunities that not long ago would have been unimaginable.

Another misconception about homeschooling is the assumption that, like schoolteachers, homeschool parents must spend five or six hours a day in front of their children lecturing. In reality, the typical homeschooled child spends about three to four hours a day on "school," including homework. This reduced time commitment is possible because homeschools don't have the distractions and the time-wasting logistics typical of government schools. Moreover, of that three or four hours, only a part is devoted to the parents' coaching their child on his schoolwork. The balance of the child's time is typically spent working independently or making use of other resources for instruction. *Moreover, most homeschooling parents strive to inculcate in their children the understanding that they themselves are ultimately responsible for their education and must learn how to educate themselves.* In fact, the academic and other successes of homeschooled children undoubtedly result in large part from their efficient use of time and their greater sense of intellectual responsibility and independence.

DOES HOMESCHOOLING WORK?

It is striking that homeschooling turns common beliefs about education on their heads. Although homeschoolers don't attend classes taught by our highly trained education professionals, there is plenty of evidence that they outperform public school, hands-down. A 1999 fifty-state study by Dr. Lawrence Rudner of the University of Maryland of over 20,000 homeschooled students found, for example, that the median reading scores of the homeschoolers by grade level fell between the 82nd and 92nd percentiles in reading and were as high as the 85th percentile in mathematics.[13] Generally, homeschoolers' median test scores reported by grade were between the 75th and 85th percentiles, while the test scores of private school students were between the 65th and 75th percentiles, and government school students' median scores (by definition) were at the 50th percentile.[14] It should be noted, however, that Dr. Rudner's sample included a disproportionately large number of children from conservative Christian families. Consequently, while Dr. Rudner's results do provide good evidence of how Christian homeschoolers are doing academically, they do not provide much insight into the academic performance of non-Christian homeschoolers.[15]

While Dr. Rudner's study alone does not conclusively demonstrate that homeschool students outperform government school students academically, it obviously indicates that to be the case. When all of the academic evidence available is taken together, however, it is rather hard to escape the conclusion that homeschool students substantially outperform government school students. Some of the additional supporting evidence is described below.

In a 1997 national study conducted by Dr. Brian Ray, homeschoolers (K-12) were found to have outperformed their government school counterparts by 30 to 37 percentile points across all the areas tested.[16] In reading and mathematics, for example, homeschoolers scored in the 87th and 82nd percentiles, respectively. Moreover, the 1997 study found that by 8th grade the average homeschooled student was performing four grades ahead of the national average and that the longer a child was homeschooled the better he did academically. S.A.T. scores, for example, were on average at the 59th percentile for students who had been homeschooled for one year. But for students who had been homeschooled for seven years, the average S.A.T. score was in the 92nd percentile.

In 2001, The Fraser Institute, a Canadian public policy think tank, published a survey of the research that had been done on homeschooling. With respect to homeschoolers' academic performance, the author of the survey, Patrick Basham, summarizes as follows:

> [A]ccording to the U.S. Department of Education, "Virtually all the available data show that the group of home schooled children who are tested are above average" (Lines, 1995). Such impressive results have been observable for at least 15 years. An analysis of SAT scores since 1985 in Washington State, for example, finds that home schooled children score consistently above average (Lyman, p. 14). Dr. Howard Richman and his colleagues found that the home schooled in Pennsylvania score, on average, at the 86th percentile in reading and at the 73rd percentile in math (Richman, Girten, and Snyder, 1992). From coast to coast, and from border to border, homeschooled students in the United States surpass the national averages on both of the major college entrance tests, the ACT and the SAT.[17]

Apart from performing well on standardized tests, homeschoolers have also been winning national geography contests, national spelling bees, and gold medals in international mathematics competitions. Here are a few examples:

- In 2000 homeschoolers took the top three spots in the Scripps Howard National Spelling Bee and four of the top ten spots in the National Geography Bee.[18]
- In the 2001 International Mathematics Olympiad a Massachusetts homeschooler was one of two American students, and of only four students worldwide, to achieve a perfect score.[19]
- In 2002, a team of homeschoolers from Chattanooga, Tennessee, won the National High School Mock Trial Championship.[20]
- In 2002 almost 25% of the finalists in the National Geography Bee, including the winner, were homeschooled, as were over 10% of the finalists in the National Spelling Bee.[21]
- In 2002 two homeschoolers were among the twelve national winners in the USA Math Olympiad.[22]
- In 2003 a homeschooler won the National Geography Bee, and a homeschooler took second in the National Spelling Bee.[23]

Not surprisingly, this has been humiliating to the education industry, and, predictably, friends of government schools began to complain that homeschooled children must have some sort of "unfair advantage."[24] In fact, the clamor from the friends of government schools was so loud that Scripps Howard adopted regulations that appear to have no other purpose than to disqualify homeschoolers from its spelling competition.[25]

The studies showing the success of homeschoolers have also told us a great deal more about what matters in education. Does state regulation of homeschoolers improve their academic performance? No.[26] Does having a parent who is certified as a teacher improve homeschoolers' academic performance? No.[27] Does how much a homeschooling family pays for educational materials significantly affect academic performance? No.[28] Is the superior performance of homeschooled students limited to the United States? No. Studies in Canada and the United Kingdom also show that homeschooled students academically outperform students in government schools.[29]

Beyond all of this, homeschooling also has some other interesting effects on student achievement:

- In a review of the performance of homeschooled children in Virginia, it was found that reading scores among minority homeschoolers were not only thirty-eight points above those of minority students in government schools, they were equal to the reading scores of white homeschooled children. In mathematics, minority homeschooled children were found to outperform minority students in government schools by twenty-seven percentile points, and they were within 5 percentile points of the average score of white homeschooled children.[30] The academic success enjoyed by minority homeschoolers is undoubtedly one reason why an estimated 5% of homeschooled children in 2003 were black and why black children were five times more likely to be homeschooled in 2003 than they were in 1998.[31] In fact, black families are probably the fastest growing subgroup among homeschoolers.[32] One indication of a coming boom in minority homeschooling comes from a survey of students at Vanderbilt University and Nashville State Tech. Of the respondents, 45% of the black students and two-thirds of the non-black minorities responded "yes" or "maybe" when asked if they would homeschool their children. In contrast, less than 25% of the white students answered "yes" or "maybe."[33]
- In government schools, the average boy is in the 52nd percentile in mathematics and the 43rd percentile in reading, while the average girl is in the 48th percentile in mathematics and the 58th percentile in reading. Among homeschoolers boys and girls have virtually identical reading scores (87th percentile for boys versus 88th percentile for girls). In mathematics, boys maintain their average four percentile point advantage, but the average homeschooled girl's mathematics score is *thirty-one percentile points higher* (79th percentile) than scores for girls in government schools.[34]

- Students in government schools whose parents didn't graduate from high school scored in the 34th percentile in writing and the 28th percentile in mathematics. Students in government schools whose parents had graduated from college scored in the 61st percentile in writing and in the 63rd percentile in mathematics. In contrast, in a basic battery of tests that included writing and mathematics, homeschooled students whose mothers hadn't finished high school scored in the 83rd percentile while students whose father hadn't finished high school scored in the 79th percentile.[35]

How much is spent by homeschooling families to achieve these results? According to 2001 estimates, homeschooling families spend on average around $550 in materials per student. Because of the Internet and the availability of used materials, however, it is possible to do it for less. In fact, several web sites are devoted to helping families homeschool on a shoestring:

> **Homeschooling for Pennies** at
> http://www.universalclass.com/i/crn/2542.htm
> **Free Homeschooling** at www.gomilpitas.com
> A wealth of free resources can also be found at http://dmoz.
> org/Reference/Education/K_through_12/Home_Schooling/.

CAN HOMESCHOOLING STUDENTS GET INTO COLLEGE?

Not surprisingly, over 700 colleges and universities in the United States have admitted homeschooled students.[36] These institutions include a wide range of public and private post-secondary institutions, including prestigious schools such as Harvard, Yale, Rice, MIT, the United States Military Academy, The United States Naval Academy, and Stanford. In fact, the quality of homeschooled college students has gotten the attention of officials at some of the most selective schools. For example, Jon Reider, a Stanford University admissions officer, has remarked: "Home schoolers bring certain skills–motivation, curiosity, the capacity to be responsible for their education–that high schools don't induce very well."[37] Similarly, Joyce Reed, a dean at Brown University, observed: "Homeschoolers are the epitome of Brown Students. They are self-directed, they take risks, and they don't back off. Most importantly, home grown graduates have proven that they are well prepared for the transition, and that perceived obstacles to college entry are hurdles that research, planning, and their talents and qualifications easily overcome."[38] Not exactly the picture of homeschoolers that the NEA and the rest of the education industry promotes, is it?

WHAT ABOUT "SOCIALIZATION"?

With homeschoolers winning national spelling bees, geography contests, mock trial championships, and international mathematics competitions, and trouncing their government school counterparts in every standardized measure of academic competence, the education industry is increasingly reluctant to question the quality of home-school education for fear of embarrassment. Instead, they try to mislead parents unfamiliar with homeschooling by claiming that by not attending government schools homeschoolers are poorly "socialized." Proper "socialization" is, of course, what "progressive" educational theorists such as John Dewey saw as the most important function of government schooling. So, it is no surprise that today's highly trained education professionals would seize on this issue as a way of trying to discourage homeschooling.

In a sense, the education industry is right. What is at stake in the controversy over socialization is one of cultural and spiritual values; namely, whose values will children learn? From the perspective of our highly trained education professionals, Christian homeschooled children are not properly socialized because they are learning the values of their parents and their church, not those inculcated through government schools. This is not, of course, how the issue is presented to the public. Rather, the education industry critics of homeschooling suggest that somehow homeschoolers are socially isolated misfits because they don't attend government schools. As with nearly everything else the education industry tells the public, this is simply not true.

Fortunately there are a number of studies that have addressed these issues, and their findings should be reassuring to Christian parents considering homeschooling:

- The average homeschooled child is involved in 5.2 activities outside of the home, with 98% being involved with two or more activities. These activities involve such extracurricular pursuits as scouting, dance classes, volunteer work, community ministries, Bible clubs, 4-H, team and individual sports, music and other arts performance groups, as well as participation in academic seminars and classes outside the home through homeschool cooperatives, colleges, and tutorial services.[39] These children are obviously not hermits.
- A 1992 study assessed whether homeschooled children suffered from retarded social development.[40] The researcher found that, on the contrary, children in government schools had significantly more behavioral problems than homeschoolers and that there was no difference between children in government schools and homeschoolers with respect to self-concept development or assertiveness.
- In another 1992 study, the researcher found that homeschoolers were better socialized and more mature than children attending either government or private schools.[41]
- The results of earlier studies are also consistent with the 1992 studies: a 1989 study showed that homeschoolers were as likely to be involved with activities that predict adult leadership as private school students and more involved in such activities than government school students,[42] and 1986 studies found that homeschooled students are more independent of peer pressure than students in government schools or private schools, are as well adjusted socially and emotionally as private school students, and have higher self-esteem than government school students.[43]
- A 1991 paper presented to the American Education Research Association addressed the long-term effects of home-

schooling. The author noted, among other things, that none of the homeschooled adults were unemployed or on welfare and concluded that there was no evidence that these adults were even moderately disadvantaged.[44]

Greg Cizek, associate professor of educational research at the University of North Carolina at Chapel Hill, summarized in 2001 what researchers now know about the "socialization issue": "Its basically a non-issue... If anything, research shows that because parents are so sensitive to the charge, they expose them to so many activities."[45]

How homeschoolers are doing in the real world is also beginning to receive favorable comment. In an article in *HR Magazine*, Andy Lorenzen, a corporate employee responsible for recruiting part-time high school-age workers for a national restaurant company, describes homeschoolers, saying, "They're smart, ambitious, and very driven."[46] Similarly, another of Lorenzen's colleagues, a restaurant operator who has employed 75 homeschoolers, is dismissive of the socialization argument:

> People assume that they will be socially handicapped because they've been homebound, but it is just the opposite.... They have a good sense of humor and know how to act. Lots of kids have trouble with judgment.... Not these kids. They're stable and mature, good team players and likely to stand up for what is right.[47]

A senior scientist for the EPA, Larry Turner, described a homeschooled college intern that he had worked with as having "a level of maturity well beyond what we would expect of someone his age.... He had the ability to organize things, to think independently and to think out of the box."[48]

There are plenty of stories like these that put a face on the studies and numbers that indicate homeschoolers "work and play well with others." But a former U.S. Department of Education researcher, Patricia Lines, who is well acquainted with homeschooling, has rendered perhaps the most telling judgment on the character of homeschooled children:

If I didn't know anything about someone other than their [sic] educational background, I'd rather hop into a foxhole with a homeschool kid than one from a public school. The homeschool kid will be a little better educated and dependable. It's just the law of averages.[49]

Why should any of this be surprising to Christians? We know that "foolishness is bound up in the heart of a child" (Pr. 22:15), and every parent has seen that where there are a lot of children gathered together there is a great deal of foolishness. Because homeschooled children spend more time with their parents and other adults than do children in government schools, their natural "foolishness" is more constrained by adult examples and standards of behavior than is the "foolishness" of their government school counterparts. Homeschooled children also have fewer negative influences because they watch far less television than their government school peers. Nationally, 65% of homeschooled children watch television only one hour or less per day, while, in contrast, 25% of all students watch television one hour or less per day.[50] Similarly, it has been found that only 1.7% of homeschooled 4th graders watch television 4 hours or more per day, while 38.5% of 4th graders overall watch television more than 4 hours or more per day.[51]

WHEN HOMESCHOOLERS GROW UP

Are you still wondering what sort of adults homeschooled children become? A 2003 study by the National Home Education Research Institute of 7,000 adults who were homeschooled has found, among other things, that adults who were homeschooled are more civically involved than the general population.[52] For example, 71% participate in community service activities compared to 37% of adults of similar ages in the general population. Homeschooled adults also are more engaged politically, perhaps because only 4.2% of homeschooled adults surveyed thought politics and government were too complicated to understand, compared to 37% of adults in the general population. Homeschooled adults also reported high levels of satisfaction with their lives – 58.9% said they were "very happy," as compared with only 27.6% of the adults in the general population. In addition, homeschooled adults reported higher levels of job satisfaction and satisfaction with their financial circumstances. Only 4.4% said that they would not homeschool their own children.

If you're considering homeschooling, don't waste your time worrying about the "socialization" bogeyman. It is just one of many canards contrived by the education industry to distract parents from how government schools are failing children on every level and by every measure.

Finding Out about Homeschooling

Unlike twenty years ago, information about homeschooling is abundant and easily found today. Good ways to begin finding out about homeschooling are the Internet and local homeschooling and cooperatives and conventions.

Here are some sites that can acquaint you with homeschooling:

- Christian Homeschool Forum, http://www.gocin.com/ homeschool/ (information on how to get started in home-schooling, message boards, and other helpful features)
- Classical Christian Homeschooling, www.classicalhome-schooling.org (a comprehensive source of information on the classical Christian approach to homeschooling, together with many helpful curriculum suggestions and reviews – this is one of my favorite sites, and the art work on the site is beautiful)
- HomeSchool Headquarters (www.homeschoolheadquarters. com) is an association of Christian retail stores that provide an extensive selection of homeschooling materials. Using this site's locator map is easiest way to find Christian book-stores in your area that carry a wide range of homeschooling materials.

- Catholic Scholars Online, www.geocities.com/Athens/Academy/6823/mercy.html (links to Catholic homeschool support groups, message boards, and free online curriculum)
- Home School Central, http://homeschoolcentral.com (lots of information for new homeschoolers and links to state and local organizations)
- Home School Legal Defense Association, www.hslda.org (links to homeschooling resources, research, and information on state laws and regulations relating to homeschooling – a tremendously helpful site)
- Texas Home Schooling Coalition, www.thsc.org (many useful links to all kinds of homeschooling resources)
- You Can Homeschool, http://www.youcanhomeschool.org/starthere/default.asp?bhcp=1 (a resource for anyone wanting to learn more about the how's and why's of homeschooling)
- Homeschooling Today, http://www.homeschoolingtoday.com (The website for *Homeschooling Today Magazine*, which is an outstanding source of current news, perspectives, and practical tips on homeschooling for beginners and veteran homeschoolers. Homeschooling Today's "Homeschooling 101" link is particularly helpful for beginners.)
- The Foundation for American Christian Education (FACE), www.face.net, provides curriculum and other educational resources to Christian homeschoolers and Christian schools based on its "Principle Approach." FACE's best known curricular offering is The Noah Plan.
- The National Home Education Research Institute, founded by Dr. Brian Ray, produces research on homeschooling and also serves as a clearinghouse for information about homeschooling. Visiting NHERI's website is a great way to stay current, so visit www.nheri.org.
- Information about National Christian Home Education Conferences and Retreats can be found at www.howto-homeschool.com. These programs are very helpful to prospective and veteran homeschoolers.

- Vision Forum at www.visionforum.com provides a wealth of information regarding homeschooling *and* an online community for homeschoolers whose faith is informed by Reformed theology. In addition to homeschooling information, this site also provides cultural news and trenchant commentary.
- While there is no national clearinghouse for information on scholarships for homeschooling and private schooling, the Alliance for the Separation of School and State's web site does provide helpful information on scholarships for Christian schools and for homeschooling (http://www.sepschool. org/misc/liberate.html).
- Perhaps the single most comprehensive collection of homeschooling information on the web is found at www. geocities.com/Athens/8259 – the information on national, state, and local support groups at www.geocities.com/Athens/8259/local.html can be very useful for finding homeschoolers and homeschool cooperatives in their area.
- The National Black Home Educators Resource Association (www.nbhera.org) and Minority Homeschoolers of Texas (www.mhot.com) specialize in helping minority parents learn about homeschooling.

If these don't satisfy your curiosity, you can use Dogpile (www. dogpile.com) to expand your search, and you will quickly find more information on homeschooling (or any other subject you are interested in) than you would have believed possible.

For those who prefer books to the Internet, here are a few useful books about homeschooling that you can get through Amazon or Barnes & Noble:

- *Christian Home Educators' Curriculum Manual* by Cathy Duffy
- *Anyone Can Homeschool* by Zan Tyler and Terry Dorian, Ph.D.
- *The Complete Home Learning Source Book* by Rebecca Rupp

- *The Big Book of Home Learning* by Mary Pride
- *Homeschooling Almanac* by Mary Leppert and Michael Leppert
- *Homeschooling on a Shoestring* by Melissa L. Morgan and Judith Waite Allee
- *The Homeschooling Book of Answers: 88 Important Questions Answered by Homeschooling's Most Respected Voices* by Linda Dobson
- *The Well-Trained Mind: A Guide to Classical Education at Home* by Jessie Wise and Susan Wise Bauer.

If you have doubts about your ability to homeschool, or its legality, you could hardly do better than to read *Homeschooling: The Right Choice* by Chris Klicka, a homeschooling father and senior counsel for the Home School Legal Defense Association. *Homeschooling: The Right Choice* provides, among other things, a fascinating account of how homeschooling became legal in every state and a great deal of information regarding state homeschooling laws. Mr. Klicka also takes a careful look at the myth of state-defined teacher qualifications. *Homeschooling: The Right Choice* is available on the Home School Legal Defense Association web site (www.hslda.org), along with a number of other helpful books on homeschooling.

In addition to these sources, the Alliance for the Separation of School and State (www.sepschool.org) provides insightful analysis regarding why government schools have failed and will continue to fail. Rather than calling for school reform, the Alliance advocates the end of all government involvement in schooling. Marshall Fritz, the founder of the Alliance for the Separation of School and State, is also the president of HonestEd.com, an organization seeking to replace the "dishonest education" provided by government schools with "Honest Education." As Fritz puts it, "Honest Education" requires reintegrating into education a discussion of the "Big Questions of Life" – questions regarding God, values, truth, evil, and so on – that have been banished by government control of education to the ghetto of home and church (www.honested.com).

Once you have taken a look at some of these resources, you should get in touch with Christian homeschooling parents in your area through your local and state homeschooling associations and cooperatives. Most homeschool cooperatives have parents who are available to answer the questions of new and prospective homeschoolers. Doing a little research and talking to homeschooling parents will quickly give you a very good idea of what is involved in homeschooling. It will also provide you with a reasonable basis for comparing it with educating your children in your local Christian schools.

Some Interesting Hybrids

Although Christian schools and homeschooling are the main alternatives to government schools, some interesting hybrids are beginning to appear. For example, "University Model Schools" combine homeschooling and classroom instruction. This approach might be characterized as essentially a college preparatory Christian homeschool cooperative. The classes are taught by a faculty, and parents pay tuition for each course their child attends. A typical elementary school child would attend classes two days a week and study at home the rest of the week (the full story is available at www.naums.net).

Another interesting hybrid is PACES. PACES families follow a classical Christian homeschool curriculum, but their children spend one day a week at a PACES campus, where they receive instruction from the faculty and get to have some fun in group activities related to the curriculum (for more information go to http://www.pacesinfo. org/ClassicalSchool/ClassSchool.htm).

Neither of these hybrid models is widely available yet. Nevertheless, similar alternatives may be provided in your area under different names by different organizations. The homeschoolers in your area are likely to know what is available. You should also visit the website for the Alliance for the Separation of School and State for links to information on variations on Christian schooling and homeschooling (http://www.sepschool.org/misc/liberate.html).

WHAT'S AT STAKE

Over 100 years ago R.L. Dabney – preacher, theologian, poet, essayist, and soldier – put our responsibility as Christian parents in perspective:

> The education of children for God is the most important business done on earth. It is the one business for which the earth exists. To it all politics, all war, all literature, all money-making, ought to be subordinated; and every parent especially ought to feel every hour of the day, that, next to making his own calling and election sure, this is the end for which he is kept alive by God – this is his task on earth.[53]

Nevertheless, the overwhelming majority of Christian children head off day after day, year after year on foot, by bus, or by car to that local pagan seminary known as the "public" school. And day after day and year after year our children are increasingly alienated from Christian values, their parents, and Christianity itself. Oftentimes, the effects of the systematic anti-Christian evangelism children are subjected to in government schools are dismissed as normal youthful rebellion or aren't even noticed. Parents are shocked and brokenhearted, however, when their child graduates from high school and shortly afterward ceases to attend church and begins to conform to the standards of our anti-Christian secular culture. Many of them never return to their faith. Others do, but only after damaging themselves, their futures, and others through experimentation with drugs, broken marriages, illegitimate children, abortion, and all the other harms that can befall us when we succumb to the enticements prepared for us by the Prince of this World.

New Agers, secular humanists, and other anti-Christian forces are working to eliminate Christian influence from society by gradually eliminating Christianity. Not by extermination or forcibly shutting our churches, but by gradually euthanizing Christianity through their influence over the education of our children. We have inadvertently been accomplices in the destruction of our children, our culture, and our faith. Yet, this can all be changed in the "twinkling of an eye." We are still free to lead our children out of the Egypt of government schools and into the Promised Land of Christian schools and home-schooling. All that is required is a "fresh obedience."[54] Will we be found to have been good and faithful servants or wicked and slothful servants? We have a decision to make.

POSTSCRIPT TO TEACHERS
AND ADMINISTRATORS

"[W]hen good people are working in a bad system, the system wins."
Marshall Fritz[1]

If you're reading this, you're almost certainly part of the remnant of capable teachers and administrators trying to stick it out in government schools. I went to "public" schools from kindergarten through high school; I have taught teachers during "in-service" days and in enrichment programs; both of my grandmothers taught in public schools – one of them began teaching in a one-room schoolhouse; my mother was a school nurse; I have more than a few uncles, aunts, and cousins who have taught, or who are teaching, in government schools; I have served in a community arts organization with a number of current and retired public school teachers; and a wonderful Christian woman in our church who teaches at one of our local government schools has also taught our oldest son's Sunday school class. In sum, I have more than a passing personal acquaintance with government schools.

You, of course, live with this strange, expensive, and destructive institution daily, and the odds are that you have seen many of the problems I have discussed. Whether you are a new or experienced teacher or administrator, you probably feel trapped, beleaguered, isolated, frustrated, betrayed, and, perhaps, a bit persecuted.

You also probably feel a bit conflicted. While the right course of action for Christian parents is clear, your position is ambiguous. For some of you there are compelling reasons to stay and soldier on; for others of you it's time to move on. This is a question that each of you must weigh in light of your circumstances. There are a few things, however, that may be useful to bear in mind as you try to sort out from time to time whether your government school has simply reduced you to the role of an enabler for its many pathologies.

GETTING OUT OF DODGE

One of the recurring themes I have run across in my research is the depth of dissatisfaction with the current state of government schools among the most experienced teachers and administrators. Linda Schrock Taylor, a Michigan teacher, writer, and entrepreneur, voices eloquently why, as she puts it, seasoned teachers "are leaving the teaching profession in droves":

> [W]e began teaching when learning was valued, students were motivated, and administration was supportive of excellence in education. We then spent these thirty years observing, with no power to stop, the trashing of traditional teaching methods; the entrenching of inferior fads and materials; the lowering of expectations... the "other-world" craziness of administrative leadership. We have watched our schools be vandalized; traditional curriculum be compromised; students speak, dress, and act like the lowest of classes. We work for young bosses who are proud of never earning anything higher than a "C" in school, but who expect us to applaud their "achievements."...We have no choice but to pick up, turn in our keys, and leave....[2]

This critique is borne out by various studies. One of the most recent was produced by Public Agenda, a New York-based non-profit polling organization, by analyzing of a decade of research. Not surprisingly, Public Agenda found that even though many teachers may support higher academic standards, they also often feel that students lack the necessary work-ethic to meet those standards and that parents and administrators don't give teachers the support they need to enforce them.[3] Also not surprisingly, students and teachers report unruly students and school violence as significant problems.[4] Apart from these concerns, forty-seven percent of principals reported that *talented* teachers are most likely to leave because of "politics and bureaucracy."[5]

The day-to-day reality behind these disturbing statistics was vividly described in a 2002 report by *The Palm Beach Post*, which interviewed dozens of Palm Beach County teachers and school district officials.[6] According to the teachers interviewed, student discipline problems in the Palm Beach County schools are worse than ever. Obscene graffiti written on walls; students cursing at teachers, spitting in teachers' coffee, throwing desks at teachers and threatening to have them beaten up; and general classroom disruptions were among the problems Palm Beach County teachers have been experiencing with increasing frequency. At the same time, teachers also complained that administrators "brush aside [student] behavior problems," partly out of a desire to avoid a "negative image" for their schools, partly because they are "overwhelmed with other duties," and partly for fear of litigation if they discipline "too harshly."[7] What's a teacher to do? The answer for many teachers in Palm Beach County schools is to leave the profession. And most of those leaving are very likely those who are competent and who, therefore, can find other suitable employment.

More recently the Associated Press wrote about "disruptive student behavior" in Oklahoma City's F.D. Moon Academy, a magnet school for mass media communications and technology. On one day of 2004 alone, 120 of 147 sixth graders were suspended from school for picking up tables in the cafeteria and slamming them into the floor and mouthing-off to faculty.[8] Earlier in the week another 16 students from the same sixth grade class had been suspended for "class disruptions." At a meeting with parents, the principal, Elaine Ford, said that roughly 85% of faculty time is taken up with disciplining students. One parent at the meeting told the reporter that "she wasn't surprised by the students' behavior because some of the parents in the audience were yelling while school officials talked."[9] These are the sorts of conditions that are driving many long-time teachers and administrators out of government schools.

But it's not just the capable, experienced teachers who are being driven from the profession. Joshua Kaplowitz recounts in "My Classroom from Hell" part of his all too brief career as a fifth-grade teacher in a government school in Washington, D.C.[10] Kaplowitz, a recent Yale graduate, discovered rapidly after arriving at Emery Elementary what government schools have become. Not only were Kaplowitz's efforts to maintain classroom order not supported by the administration, the administration actually thwarted them. Honest grading? Kaplowitz was told, in effect, that it was prohibited by law, and he was cited for insubordination when he insisted on giving students the failing grades they had earned. As for trying to protect students from assaults by other students, he soon learned that his colleagues were in a survival mode and bound by what can only be considered inhumane school district rules:

> When I asked other teachers to help me stop a fight, they re-
> minded me that D.C. Public Schools banned teachers from
> laying hands on students, even to protect other children. You
> have to be made of iron to wait passively for the security guard
> while one enraged child tries to hurt another. [11]

The *coup de gras* for Kaplowitz's brief teaching career came when an emotionally disturbed child falsely alleged that Kaplowitz had injured his head and back by violently shoving him in the chest. While being acquitted on a criminal charge of misdemeanor assault, and having to endure a civil proceeding in which the boy's mother thought she would win the litigation lottery, Kaplowitz learned that the teachers' union is flooded yearly with fabricated corporal punishment charges. Needless to say, Joshua Kaplowitz is no longer a government schoolteacher.

Another first year teacher in the New York City government schools recently wrote anonymously of the sham that passes for education there.[12] Children, he quickly learned, were "often the last thing on teachers' minds." Instead, school politics, collecting free lunch forms, and otherwise figuring out how to survive in a dysfunctional institution were the order of the day. Moreover, despite the vast budget for New York City government schools, he also learned that little of it was reaching the classrooms. Getting books, chalk, and even staples was a struggle, not to mention figuring out how to teach in a building where there were dead rodents in the hallways and the air-conditioning often didn't work.

Yet another young teacher, Matthew Clavel, recently wrote of his frustrations as a math teacher required to use a "fuzzy math" curriculum that was dooming his students to a life of mathematical illiteracy.[13] How did administrators respond to complaints from teachers that the "fuzzy math" curriculum was a disaster? According to Clavel: "District officials told us that we should just keep going – *even if not a single child in our rooms understood what we were talking about.*"[Emphasis added.][14] Clavel, by the way, is also no longer teaching.

In Piper, Kansas, a second-year biology teacher, Christine Pelton, flunked 28 students who had cheated in a class project that accounted for 50% of the class grade.[15] Indignant parents lobbied the school board, and, as a result, the school board instructed Pelton to change the weighting and the scores on the project – changes that would have resulted in 27 out of the 28 students passing the course. Rather than change the grades, Pelton resigned. Afterwards, Pelton commented on the effect of the school board's irresponsible action on students' thinking: "I'd lost the kids' respect. I heard kids talking about that if they didn't like what I did in the future, they could go to the board of education and they could change that ...."[16]

There is an endless supply of stories like these, and if you've been working in a government school for a while, you probably know more than a few.

SURVIVAL OF THE "UNFITTEST"

The point here is that there are powerful forces of "adverse selection" at work in government education. Think of it as a system that encourages the "survival of the unfittest." Moreover, capable veteran teachers and administrators are not merely retiring or walking away. Linda Schrock Taylor reports that that there are now many in government school administration who are actively seeking to *drive out* teachers who haven't bought into the latest school of education fads.[17]

The 2004 winner of the National Right to Read Foundation's Teacher of the Year Award, veteran teacher Ann Edwards[18], expressed the same sentiment in her 1999 testimony before the Subcommittee

on Early Childhood Education of the U.S. House of Representatives'
Committee on Education and the Workforce:

> I have an idea now what it might have felt like for minorities
> in the South at the beginning of the Civil Rights Movement
> when one might have to sit at the back of the bus. It is now as
> though traditional teachers have to go to the back of the school
> bus. Sitting with them are students, many of whom will be mi-
> norities, that will never become proficient readers and will lack
> other skills necessary to compete in the real world in the 21st
> century. Many in the education profession today worship at the
> "shrine of change" and have a "child-centered" as opposed to a
> "subject-centered" approach to education. Disciplines needed
> to have a chance at succeeding in life have been abandoned. [19]

In addition to the loss of veteran teachers, many aspiring teachers who would be great educators never make it to the starting line
today because they are repulsed by the rank pedagogical and political
stupidities served up in the curricula of schools of education. Of the
motivated and capable aspiring teachers who actually do make it into
the classroom, many are either driven out, like Joshua Kaplowitz,
or leave because, like Matthew Clavel, they cannot stand being accomplices in the destruction of their students' futures. Beyond this,
consider that more than a million veteran teachers are nearing retirement.

Government schools are being utterly transformed by the loss
of this enormous cadre of teachers that, on the whole, tends to share
your values and standards.[20] What will it be like to be surrounded
increasingly by "teachers" who have been led to believe that academic
standards are an impediment to social justice and that the main function of schools should be to reconstruct identities, values, beliefs, and
lifestyles? What will it be like to find yourself increasingly among "colleagues" imbued with high "self-esteem," but many of whom would
have trouble passing a 10th-grade literacy test?[21] If you are candid, you
will have to admit that this process has been going on for years and is
intensifying.

The bottom line is that capable, conscientious teachers and administrators are going to be increasingly isolated. The vast bulk of the survivors are going to be those without real job skills or who are so dim that they think that gross mistakes such as "whole language" reading instruction and "fuzzy math" are just fine. For the diminishing remnant, however, government schools will become lonelier places by the year.

The situation for Christian teachers and administrators is even worse. Your faith has been virtually criminalized within government schools. For many of you, even the slightest affirmation of your Christian beliefs at school would lead to discipline or termination if found out. Further, you must cope with a system in which any pretense to upholding real academic standards has long ago disappeared; faddish curricula make effective teaching all but impossible; and much of the school day for the children in your school necessarily involves indoctrination in leftist ideology, immoral values, and New Age and other pagan theologies. Not in your class, perhaps, but it's there in your school, and the problem is metastasizing.

"Accountability" and Mission Impossible

As the failure of government schools has become more apparent, the public rightly has been demanding more accountability; that is, the public increasingly wants schools, administrators, and teachers to feel some economic or other "pain" if their students fail to learn. For many of you, the lack of discipline within your schools makes effective teaching at best a rather remote prospect. What, for example, can a principal like Elaine Ford do?

Moreover, one of the cruelest ironies you face is that you are being held accountable for achieving results while often being denied – in fact, prohibited from using – the tools you know you need to do your job. Consider the upside-down world in which Matthew Clavel found himself as a math teacher. How could he produce results if he used the mandated "fuzzy math" curriculum? And what about those who teach reading? How can you produce reading results when you are forced to use something other than a sound phonics-based curriculum? During a conversation with a principal over teachers being forced to use a poorly-conceived and ineffective new reading curriculum, Ann Edwards expressed well the frustration of a skilled teacher:

> I feel like a doctor with patients who are dying and the district... is only allowing me to treat patients with one type of medicine. The medicine that I am required to use does not work as well as the proven treatment I (and other experienced teachers) have used successfully for several years. In fact, several patients are dying with the new medicine. The old medicine works; you know it works and I know it works. *As a professional, I am now in a moral and ethical dilemma. You want me to watch my children fail at reading and not teach what I know works best.*[22] [emphasis added]

The truth is, being asked to teach and get results under the circumstances in which many of you must work is a lot like being asked to paint the Golden Gate Bridge with a hammer and a bucket of milk.

WHAT IS TO BE DONE?

Some of you have good reasons to stay in your government schools, but most of you, over time, are going to leave. But whether you stay or go, there are some things that you can and must do as *Christian* educators.

First, if you have a child in a government school, take him out. Your witness is important – both to your child and to other parents. Second, you must tell your pastors and the parents in your church the truth about what is happening in government schools – the whole truth, "with the bark off." To remain silent is to collaborate in the destruction of our children. Third, you must help your church think through ways of providing alternatives to government schools and help encourage parents afflicted with a "government school habit" to rescue their children from Pharaoh's schools. Fourth, you need to dream. What could you and others like you do if you were free to provide the kind of education that you know Christian children should have, but that you are not allowed to provide? God may be ready to open some doors for you. Finally, and most important, pray – pray that Christian parents be given wisdom in educating their children.

A NOTE ON ENDNOTES AND FINDING WEB-PAGES

If you have gotten this far, you know that this book covers a wide range of topics. You also know that many of them have been treated in great depth over the years by various writers. The endnotes that follow represent only some of the sources consulted in the preparation of this manuscript, but they are often sources that will lead the curious reader into a larger literature for any given controversy. Moreover, virtually every controversy I discuss is a subject of continuing, typically vitriolic, debate. Consequently, the internet is an invaluable tool for monitoring the current "state-of-play" with respect to any of the issues I have addressed. I hope that you will find this book a helpful introduction to the many problems of government schools. I also hope you will read at least some of the sources cited in the endnotes and make use of the internet to get a better feel for how embedded those pathologies are.

You have undoubtedly noticed that in many instances in the text and in the following endnotes I have pointed readers toward a website or a web-page. The web addresses (or "URLs") all worked at the time of final submission of this manuscript for publication. Alas, websites are sometimes discontinued or moved, and it appears that the source is lost. Never fear, however, there is always the "Wayback Machine." The Wayback Machine is the creation of the Internet Archive, which is building a digital library of Internet sites and other cultural artifacts in digital form. Access is free to researchers, historians, scholars, and the general public. The Wayback Machine gives you access to over 10 billion web-pages and can help you find just about anything. So, if you are having trouble finding a website or web-page, just go to www.archive.org and enter the url for the document you are seeking.

Finally, you will notice that we have dispensed with certain conventions typically used in notes – references such as "Id.", "Op. Cit.", etc. These conventions are still widely used, for example, in the academic press, but they are really a vestige from a time when it was important to shorten references to save typesetters' time. We believe that dispensing with these conventions makes the endnotes more accessible.

ENDNOTES

Preface

1. As quoted in Tammi Reed Ledbetter, "Christian Schools, Homeschooling Make Gains Among Southern Baptists," *BPNews*, March 12, 2003.

Introduction

1. Daniel J. Smithwick, "A 'World' of Difference in Public and Christian Schools," The Nehemiah Institute, Inc. (Lexington, Kentucky, 1998), p. 13.

2. T.C. Pinckney, "We are Losing Our Children," remarks to the Southern Baptist Convention Executive Committee, Nashville, Tennessee, September 18, 2001. Pinckney states that research indicates 70% of teenagers involved in church youth groups stop attending church within two years following high school graduation. If this seems too pessimistic, the Southern Baptist Council on Family Life reported at the Southern Baptist Convention's 2002 meeting in St. Louis that "88% of the children raised in evangelical homes leave church at the age of 18, never to return." Jon Walker, "Council Says It's Time to Bring Family Back to Life," *Southern Baptist Texan*, July 1, 2002. Even if these sources overstate the extent of the problem by thirty to forty percent, it is clear there is something very wrong in the way we are discipling our children.

3. "The Year's Most Intriguing Findings, From Barna Research Studies," Barna Research, December 17, 2001, www.barna.org. One more recent and appalling finding by Barna is that only 32% of born-again adults and 9% of born-again teenagers believe that absolute truth exists. "Americans Are Most Likely to Base Truth on Feelings," February 12, 2002, Barna Research, available at www.barna.org.

4. The American Religious Identification Survey as cited in Andy Butcher, "America Losing its Christian Faith – But Finding Others," Charisma News Service, December 28, 2001, available at www.charismanews.com.

Chapter One - *Why Are You Educating Your Children at a Pagan Seminary?*

1. Joe R. Burnett, *The Humanist*, 6 (1961), p. 347, as cited in Robert L. Waggoner, "The Humanization of America in Culture, Education, and Law," an article adapted from the second chapter of an unpublished doctoral dissertation, available at www.biblicaltheism.com/humanameri.htm.

2. The use of the term "public schools" today misleads more than it informs. "Public schools" are in fact government schools – schools that for all practical purposes are controlled by government officials outside of the communities that the schools purport to serve. One hundred years ago it was true that the communities in which public schools were located made almost all decisions regarding the operation of their schools, and those schools were in every sense fully accountable to the communities that established and supported them. Unfortunately, that sort of community control and accountability is a distant memory. What we have now are "public" schools that in all important respects are controlled by state and federal legislation, agencies, and courts. Teachers' unions and similar organizations also exert far more influence over "public schools" than local taxpayers and parents. The main role of local communities now is to supply students and money.

3. "Christian Symbols Don't Make the Grade in U.S. Schools," EWTN News (Zenit.org), December 16, 2001.

4. Mary Mostert, "The ACLU – America's Very Own Taliban Demands End of 'God Bless America'," *Banner of Liberty*, October 8, 2001, available at www.bannerofliberty.com.

5. These bullet points are based on "Religion in the Social Studies Curriculum," ERIC Digest, Risinger, C. Frederick, Publication Date: 1993-08-00, ERIC Identifier: ED363553.

6. As quoted in Jim Remsen, "Schools Risk U.S. Funds if Prayer Isn't Tolerated," *Philadelphia Inquirer*, February 15, 2003.

7. Jim Remsen, "Schools Risk U.S. Funds if Prayer Isn't Tolerated," *Philadelphia Inquirer*, February 15, 2003.

8. Chris Klicka has compiled a very helpful collection of Bible verses relating to the education of our children. Chris Klicka, "Biblical Reasons to Homeschool," National Center for Home Education, available online at http://www.hslda.org/docs/nche/000000/00000069.asp.

9. While the historical development of "humanism" in the United States is an interesting story, it is not essential to this discussion. Suffice it to say that the rise of humanism in the United States as a significant cultural force began in the 19th century, with humanism reaching its full maturity in the fourth through eighth decades of the 20th century.

10. Both the original *Humanist Manifesto* and the *Humanist Manifesto II* are available from the American Humanist Association or on the Internet at www.jcn.com/manifestos.html.

11. These bullet points are drawn from the *Humanist Manifesto*s, which are available online at www.jcn.com/manifestos.html.

12. Philip Hamburger, *Separation of Church and State* (Cambridge, MA: Harvard University Press, 2002), pp. 455 - 456. The discussion of the social aspects of *Everson* and the background of Justice Black condenses Hamburger's interesting and detailed account.

13. Philip Hamburger, *Separation of Church and State* (Cambridge, MA: Harvard University Press, 2002), p. 456.

14. Philip Hamburger, *Separation of Church and State* (Cambridge, MA: Harvard University Press, 2002), pp. 455 - 457.

15. Philip Hamburger, *Separation of Church and State* (Cambridge, MA: Harvard University Press, 2002), pp. 452 - 453.

16. Vast expansions of judicial power have resulted from this sort of "misdirection play" in which the Court declines, with apparent modesty, to set aside an action of another governmental entity, but does so by establishing a legal principle that will later allow the Court to override the actions of that entity. *Marbury v. Madison* is the best known example in which the Court created its own power of judicial review of the actions of Congress. In *Everson*, the Court bootstrapped its way into becoming the arbiter of what states could do in the area of religion.

17. Philip Hamburger, *Separation of Church and State* (Cambridge, MA: Harvard University Press, 2002), p. 462.

18. Philip Hamburger, *Separation of Church and State* (Cambridge, MA: Harvard University Press, 2002), p. 427.

19. Philip Hamburger, *Separation of Church and State* (Cambridge, MA: Harvard University Press, 2002), pp. 429 - 434.

20. Philip Hamburger, *Separation of Church and State* (Cambridge, MA: Harvard University Press, 2002), p. 463, quoting Black's son: "The Ku Klux Klan and Daddy, so far as I could tell, only had one

thing in common. He suspected the Catholic Church. He used to read all of Paul Blanshard's books exposing power abuse in the Catholic Church...."

21. Philip Hamburger, *Separation of Church and State* (Cambridge, MA: Harvard University Press, 2002), pp. 463 - 470

22. Philip Hamburger, *Separation of Church and State* (Cambridge, MA: Harvard University Press, 2002), p. 462.

23. As quoted in Philip Hamburger, *Separation of Church and State* (Cambridge, MA: Harvard University Press, 2002), p. 462.

24. There is substantial reason to believe that Black had left the Klan (though not his Klan sympathies) out of political expediency. See Philip Hamburger, *Separation of Church and State* (Cambridge, MA: Harvard University Press, 2002), pp. 422 - 434.

25. The influence on First Amendment jurisprudence of Jefferson's phrase, "a wall of separation between church and state" in his 1802 letter to the Danbury Baptist Association of Connecticut is quite remarkable considering that Jefferson was not even in the country during the Constitutional Convention and was not a member of the Congress in which the First Amendment was passed. For anyone interested in the origins of Jefferson's "wall of separation" metaphor, see Daniel L. Dreisbach, *Thomas Jefferson and the Wall of Separation Between Church and State* (New York: New York University Press, 2002).

26. Apparently, the benighted Congressmen in 1876 who debated the Blaine Amendment pro and con, many of whom had participated in the passage and ratification of the 14th Amendment, didn't realize that the 14th Amendment had already applied the religion clauses to the states. That remarkable discovery was evidently left to the superior intellects of a Supreme Court eighty years distant. It should also be noted that the Blaine Amendment was not the first attempt to amend the Constitution to apply the First Amendment's religion clauses to the states. In 1870, for example, Elisha Hurlburt introduced a Constitutional amendment that would have not only extended the First Amendment's religion clauses to the states, but would also have allowed Congress to outlaw the ecclesiastical structure of the Catholic Church. See Philip Hamburger, *Separation of Church and State* (Cambridge, MA: Harvard University Press, 2002), p. 437 and n. 113.

27. Bess Keller and Adrienne Coles, "Kansas Evolution Controversy Gives Rise to National Debate," *Education Week*, September 8, 1999.

28. "Evolution Dawns on Kansas," Associated Press, February 14, 2001, and "Kansas Votes to Restore Evolution in School Standards," CNNfyi.com, available at http://fyi.cnn.com/2001/fyi/teachers. ednews/02/14/kansas.evolution/.

29. Recently the American Humanist Association published *Humanist Manifesto III*. Although there are differences in organization and emphasis between *Manifesto III* and the earlier versions, the core beliefs remain the same (*e.g.*, "Humans are an integral part of nature, the result of unguided evolutionary change. Humanists recognize nature as self-existing."). All of the *Manifestos*, as well as other materials on secular humanism, are available online at http://www.americanhumanist.org/humanism/.

30. J. Gordon Melton, *Encyclopedic Handbook of Cults in America* (New York: Garland, 1986), p. 113.

31. Much of the following account of what went on in the Bedford schools is based on Judge Brieant's opinion in *Altman v. Bedford Central School District*, 45F. Supp. 2d. 368 (SDNY 1999).

32. *Altman v. Bedford Central School District*, 45F. Supp. 2d. 368 (SDNY 1999).

33. 245 F.3d 49 (2d Cir. 2001), cert. Denied 122 S.Ct. 68 (2001).

34. These bullet points are a condensation of information contained in Alert No. 990809, The Jefferson 21st Century Institute; "Jefferson 21st Century Institute Files Lawsuit to Obtain Records of Week-

Long Buddhist Ceremony at Park City High School, News Release," March 7, 2000; and "Threats to Separation of Religion and Government," Jefferson 21st Century Institute, www.j21c.org/threats1. htm.

35. Stephan Archer, "Public Schools teaching occult religion? Lawsuit challenges tax funding of New Age curriculum," WorldNetDaily, October 1, 1999. Eugenie C. Scott, "Waldorf Schools Teach Odd Science, Odd Evolution," National Center for Science Education, 1994, available online at www. waldorfcritics.org/active/articles/Eugenie_Scott_94.html.

36. Stephan Archer, "Public Schools teaching occult religion? Lawsuit challenges tax funding of New Age curriculum," WorldNetDaily, October 1, 1999.

37. Stephan Archer, "Public Schools teaching occult religion? Lawsuit challenges tax funding of New Age curriculum," WorldNetDaily, October 1, 1999.

38. Eugenie C. Scott, "Waldorf Schools Teach Odd Science, Odd Evolution," National Center for Science Education 1994, available online at www.waldorfcritics.org/active/articles/Eugenie_Scott_94.html.

39. Stephan Archer, "Public Schools teaching occult religion? Lawsuit challenges tax funding of New Age curriculum," WorldNetDaily, October 1, 1999.

40. Stephan Archer, "Public Schools teaching occult religion? Lawsuit challenges tax funding of New Age curriculum," WorldNetDaily, October 1, 1999.

41. The reporter is Michael Serazio. His account of his Waldorf adventure, from which this paragraph draws its facts, is "School Spirit(s)," *Houston Press*, February 5-11, 2004, pp.13-14. Serazio's report on the goings-on inside Waldorf schools is consistent with what others have found.

42. The Waldorf explanation is "…the body needs to push out the hardest force, the teeth, during the first period of physical transformation 'illnesses later in life can be traced to this premature intellectuality that comes in childhood.'" Michael Serazio, "School Spirit(s)," Houston Press, February 5-11, 2004, at p. 14. So, reading too early interferes with pushing out teeth, which in turn leads to bad health, or something like that. I'm sure it makes better sense after a couple of beers.

43. Michael Serazio, "School Spirit(s)," *Houston Press*, February 5-11, 2004, at p. 13.

44. Michael Serazio, "School Spirit(s)," *Houston Press*, February 5-11, 2004, at p. 14.

45. For example, as of fall 2000 there were roughly ten Waldorf charter schools in California and three in Arizona. Generally, promoters of the Waldorf curriculum usually tout the high test scores of students in their programs and deny that Steiner's anthroposophy is taught within their schools. While it may be true that anthroposophy is not formally presented as a part of the Waldorf curriculum, the methods, the teacher training, and the worldview involved in Waldorf education incorporate anthroposophy. A visit to www.waldorfcritics.org, a website created by teachers, administrators, and parents formerly involved in Waldorf schooling, will provide a great deal of information regarding what is really going on in Waldorf schools (some of it is hilarious). I would specifically recommend reading Eugenie C. Scott, "Waldorf Schools Teach Odd Science, Odd Evolution," National Center for Science Education 1994, available online at www.waldorfcritics.org/active/articles/Eugenie_Scott_94.html. The information regarding the number of Waldorf charters in fall 2000 in California and Arizona is taken from Claudia M. Lenart, "Waldorf Succeeds in Public Schools," *Conscious Choice*, August 2000. But note that on February 7, 2001, the Chico Unified School District Board of Education rejected a proposal to establish a Waldorf charter school on the ground that it was sectarian. www.waldorfcritics.org/articles/ChicoFindings.html.

46. This narrative is based on facts contained in an article by Jason Pierce, CNSNews.com Staff Writer, "Wicca, Ecology Debated in Michigan School Controversy," May 14, 2001.

47. Jason Pierce, CNSNews.com Staff Writer, "Wicca, Ecology Debated in Michigan School Controversy," May 14, 2001, at p. 4.

48. Improving children's "self-esteem" has long been alleged to prevent smoking, drinking, illegal drug use, and early sex, as well as improve school and job performance. These kinds of claims have become articles of faith in schools of education and among the public at large. Unfortunately, there is no evidence to support these claims. The most recent study confirming that the resources devoted to improving students' self-esteem were an investment in humbug (or worse) can be found in a monograph by a group of researchers led by Roy Baumeister in the May 2003 issue of *Psychological Science in the Public Interest*. For a discussion of the Baumeister study, see Sharon Begley, "Real Self-Esteem Builds on Achievement, Not Praise for Slackers," *The Wall Street Journal*, April 18, 2003, B1.

49. John Ankerberg, John Weldon, and Craig Branch, *Thieves of Innocence* (Eugene, OR: Harvest House Publishers, 1993), p. 111. This book was subsequently reprinted under the title *Public Schools: The Sorcerer's New Apprentice?*, which is available from the Apologetic Resource Center's website at http://www.apologeticsresctr.org/default.htm .

50. John Ankerberg, John Weldon, and Craig Branch, *Thieves of Innocence* (Eugene, OR: Harvest House Publishers, 1993), p. 111.

51. John Dewey, "My Pedagogic Creed," *The School Journal*, Volume LIV, Number 3 (January 16, 1897), pp. 77-80. Available on the Internet at www.users.globalnet.co.uk/~infed/e-texts/e-dew-pc.htm.

52. John Dunphy, "A Religion for a New Age," *The Humanist*, January/February 1983, p.26.

53. Marilyn Ferguson, *The Aquarian Conspiracy: Personal and Social Transformation in the 1980s* (Los Angeles: J.P. Tarcher, 1980), p. 420.

54. Marilyn Ferguson, *The Aquarian Conspiracy: Personal and Social Transformation in the 1980s* (Los Angeles: J.P. Tarcher, 1980), p. 420.

55. John Ankerberg, John Weldon, and Craig Branch, *Thieves of Innocence*, (Eugene, OR: Harvest House Publishers, 1993), p. 66.

56. The so-called "Hatch Amendment," Public Law 95-561, Sec. 1250, Section 439 of the General Education Provisions Act, 20 USC 1232 g, is an example of such legislation at the federal level. This legislation was designed to require government schools to obtain parental consent before they can administer psychological or psychiatric tests or treatment to children or seek information from children about private matters such as their attitudes and families. The NEA and schools strenuously resisted any enforcement of the Hatch Act, which resulted in it being amended by legislation introduced by Charles Grassley.

57. Timothy D. Crater, "The Unproclaimed Priests of Public Education," *Christianity Today*, April 10, 1981, at p. 45, quoting Sidney Simon, one of the key proponent of values clarification theory.

58. Dick Sutphen, "Infiltrating the New Age into Society," *What Is*, Summer 1986, p. 14, as quoted in John Ankerberg, John Weldon, and Craig Branch, *Thieves of Innocence* (Eugene, OR: Harvest House Publishers, 1993), p. 82.

59. For a good account of what happened to the Sisters of the Immaculate Heart of Mary, see Joyce Milton, *The Road to Malpsychia: Humanistic Psychology and its Discontents* (San Francisco: Encounter Books , 2002), pp. 138-145.

60. Joyce Milton, *The Road to Malpsychia: Humanistic Psychology and its Discontents* (San Francisco: Encounter Books , 2002), p. 235.

61. As quoted in Joyce Milton, *The Road to Malpsychia: Humanistic Psychology and its Discontents* (San Francisco: Encounter Books , 2002), p. 235.

62. *Alan B. Malnak, et al v. Maharishi Mahesh Yogi, et al*

63. Most Christians have no idea how New Age curricula have proliferated in government schools. Craig Branch, director of the Apologetics Resource Center and an expert on New Age beliefs and cults, has provided the following list representing just some of the school programs that incorporate New Age elements:

- Bridges
- Choosing Wellness (by Prentice Hall)
- Coping with Kids
- Coping with Stress
- DARE (Drug Abuse Resistance Education)
- Delphi Foundation Institute
- Discipline with Dignity
- Discovery Skills for Life
- Dungeons and Dragons
- Flexing your Test Muscles
- Flights of Fantasy
- Free the Horses (Active Parenting)
- Get Set
- Green Circle Program
- Growing Healthy
- Health: A Wellness Approach (by Merril Publishing)
- Heart to Heart
- HeartMath
- Here's Looking at You
- Holistic Learning
- Impressions
- Integrated Thematic Instruction
- Know Your Body
- Kreative Kids
- Letting Go of Stress
- Life Education Centre
- Mac's Choice
- Magick
- Michigan Model for Comprehensive Health Education
- PALS
- Peaceworks
- Positive Action
- Project Aware
- Project Rainbow
- Project Strain
- Quest
- S.O.A.R.
- Self Concept
- Small World: Chinese
- SOS (Strengthening of Skills)
- Tactics for Thinking
- TAD (Toward Affective Development)
- The Centered Student
- Visual Thinking: A Scamper Tool
- Waldorf Schools
- Whole Mind Learning

- Wizards
- Workshop Way
- YogaProgram

Anyone interested in the influence of the New Age movement in government schools and our culture can find a wealth of information at the website for the Apologetic Resource Center (http://www. apologeticsresctr.org/default.htm).

64. Christians who push for legislation making it easier to have prayers in government schools should realize that any such legislation would necessarily open the doors of government schools even wider to New Age spiritualism. This is just another example of the way in which the misguided belief that government schools can be "reformed" almost invariably leads to unintended, harmful consequences.

65. The facts on which this account is based are taken from "Students Sign Contract with Satan," *Education Reporter*, October 1995.

66. Ron Selak, Jr., "Jesus School Essay Sparks Federal Suit," *Tribune Chronicle*, July 2, 2002, available at www.tribune-chronicle.com/news/story/07202002_new05.asp.

67. "Nation: School Bans Free Bible Distribution," Associated Press, May 22, 2002. In a similar incident in the heart of the "Bible Belt," a suburban Houston middle school administrator called the police in response to Gideons standing on a public sidewalk near the school giving away Bibles.

68. Perry Beeman, "Students Fight Ban on Giving Bibles at School," *Des Moines Register*, June 6, 2002.

69. Perry Beeman, "Students Fight Ban on Giving Bibles at School," *Des Moines Register*, June 6, 2002.

70. "School District Bans Ministers' Lunches with Students," Associated Press, February 19, 2004.

71. "School District Bans Ministers' Lunches with Students," Associated Press, February 19, 2004.

72. "Students Threatened by Christmas? ACLU Warns of Lawsuit unless Principal Censors Celebration," WorldNetDaily.com, November 21, 2003.

73. This account is based on Joe Kovacs, "School Bans Saying 'Christmas,'" WorldNetDaily.com, December 13, 2002.

74. This account is based on Joe Kovacs, "School Bans Saying 'Christmas,'" WorldNetDaily.com, December 13, 2002.

75. As quoted in "Student's Pro-Life T-Shirt is Equivalent to the Swastika says School Principal," and "School Backs Off Claim that Pro-Life Message = Swastika," Thomas More Law Center, January 27, 2003 and January 29, 2003.

76. These incidents are reported in Robert B. Bluey, "Students Face Discipline for Passing Out Candy with Religious Note," CNSNews.com, January 10, 2003.

77. "Family Files Suit Against School District over Religious Speech," Associated Press, February 10, 2004.

78. This account is based on reporting by News 14 Carolina (available online at http://www. news14charlotte.com/content/special_edition/back_to_school/?ArID=48539&SecID=124) and "Counselor Suspended over 'Religious Advice'", WorldNetDaily.com, December 12, 2003.

79. Eventually, a federal judge reversed the educrats. The teacher's aide, by the way, was charged by her employers with having violated an 1895 statute prohibiting religious garb. It is almost a certainty that the law was aimed at Catholics. For an account of this incident, see "Cross-Wearing Teacher's

Aide Reinstated," *Maranatha Christian Journal*, June 25, 2003, available online at http://www.mcjonline.com/news/03a/20030627b.shtml.

80. This account is based on facts contained in Carl Campanile, "Schools OK Ramadan Prayers,*" The New York Post*, November 15, 2001, and Joseph A. D'Agostino, "New York Schools Flip-Flop on Ramadan," *Human Events*, November 26, 2001.

81. Dr. David A. Yeagley, "Schools Harass Christians, Coddle Other Faiths," FrontPageMagazine.com, June 21, 2001.

82. Joseph A. D'Agostino, "New York Schools Flip-Flop on Ramadan," *Human Events*, November 26, 2001.

83. The facts on which this account is based are taken from "Flushing Public School Discriminates Against Christians," *The Catholic League*, December 3, 2001.

84. Actually, the promoters of "Kwanzaa" claim it is not a religion. In any event, everyone would agree that it is a festival that was invented in 1966 by Ron Karenga, a Black Power activist.

85. Cory de Vera, "Prayer Room Sign Pulled," *The Columbia Daily Tribune*, October 25, 2001.

86. "Islam Studies Required in California District – Course has 7th graders Memorizing Koran Verses, Praying to Allah," WorldNetDaily, January 11, 2002, available at www.worldnetdaily.com/news/article.asp?ARTICLE_ID=25997.

87. Daniel Pipes, "Become a Muslim Warrior," *Jerusalem Post*, July 2, 2002.

88. Daniel Pipes, "Become a Muslim Warrior," *Jerusalem Post*, July 2, 2002.

89. "Islam Studies Required in California District – Course has 7th graders Memorizing Koran Verses, Praying to Allah," WorldNetDaily, January 11, 2002, available at www.worldnetdaily.com/news/article.asp?ARTICLE_ID=25997. The course is being taught using a Houghton-Mifflin textbook, Across the Centuries, that has been adopted by the California school system. References to Christianity apparently focus on events such as the Inquisition and the Salem witch-trials, and no mention is made of the long history of atrocities perpetrated by Muslims. Contrast this with a recent court ruling that a one-half hour weekly Bible class is unconstitutional. "Court Upholds Class Ban," Associated Press, June 8, 2004.

90. As quoted in Maureen Nolan, "Pupils to Pass Up Turkey: School Skips Thanksgiving for Fasts of Ramadan," *The Post-Standard*, November 26, 2002. This account is based on Miss Nolan's article.

91. "Michigan High School Discriminates Against Christians," and "High School Reverses Decision: Christian Club Allowed to Show Jesus Video," Thomas More Law Center, February 24, 2003, and March 4, 2003. The account of the controversy can be found at www.thomasmore.org.

92. This account is based on Nashiah Ahmad, "Schools Adapting to Muslim Holy Month," *Education Week*, November 27, 2002. See also, "Atlantic City Schools to Recognize Islamic Holidays," Associated Press, May 28, 2004.

93. As quoted in Suzanne Fields, "Radical Islam is Sanitized for American Textbooks," *Washington Times*, February 21, 2003. See also, Joseph Grant Swank, "Anti-Christian Muslim Brings Pro-Islam Books to American Schools," *Bushcountry*, May 4, 2004.

94. Suzanne Fields, "Radical Islam is Sanitized for American Textbooks," *Washington Times*, February 21, 2003.

95. The American Textbook Council's report, *Islam and the Textbooks*, is available free online at www.historytextbooks.org. As described on the Council's website, the principal conclusions of the report

are: "(1) world history textbooks hold Islam and other non-Western civilizations to different standards than those that apply to the West, (2) domestic educational activists, Muslim and non-Muslim, insist at once on harsh perspectives for the West while gilding the record of non-Western civilizations, (3) Islamic pressure groups and their allies seek to suppress critical analysis of Islam inside and outside classrooms, and distorted textbook content is one symptom of this phenomenon, and (4) publishers respond to pressure groups on account of political expediency and sales."

96. David Limbaugh, *Persecution: How Liberals are Waging War against Christianity* (Washington, D.C.: Regnery, 2003).

97. This information is taken from a speech by T.C. Pinckney, Second Vice President of the Southern Baptist Convention, to the Southern Baptist Convention Executive Council on September 18, 2001. A copy of the speech is available through the Alliance for the Separation of School and State (www.sepschool.org). According to a 2002 study by the Southern Baptist Convention's Council on Family Life, the situation is worse — 88% of children from evangelical families stop attending church after graduation from high school.

98. Johnathon Allen, "The Tragedy of Teen Suicide," *Teenagers Today*, available at http://teenagerstoday.com/resources/articles/teensuicide.htm, and "Estimated Arrests for Drug Abuse Violations by Age Group, 1970-2000," Bureau of Justice Statistics (www.ojp.usdoj.gov/bjs/glance/tables/drugtab.htm).

99. Stephanie J. Ventura and Christine Bachrach, "Nonmarital Childbearing in the United States, 1940-99," *National Vital Statistics Reports,* Volume 48, Number 16, October 18, 2000. Also, see "Report to Congress on Out-Of-Wedlock Childbearing," Department of Health and Human Services, September 1995.

100. Stephanie J. Ventura and Christine Bachrach, "Nonmarital Childbearing in the United States, 1940-99," *National Vital Statistics Reports,* Volume 48, Number 16, October 18, 2000. Also, see "Report to Congress on Out-Of-Wedlock Childbearing," Department of Health and Human Services, September 1995.

101. Daniel J. Smithwick, "A World of Difference in Public and Christian Schools," Nehemiah Institute, Inc., 1998.

102. Daniel J. Smithwick, "A World of Difference in Public and Christian Schools," Nehemiah Institute, Inc., 1998, p., 8.

103. "Teenagers' Beliefs Moving Farther from Biblical Perspectives," Barna Research Group Press Release, October 23, 2000, available at www.barna.org.

104. "Teenagers' Beliefs Moving Farther from Biblical Perspectives," Barna Research Group Press Release, October 23, 2000, available at www.barna.org.

105. Adolph Hitler, quoted in William L. Shirer, *The Rise and Fall of the Third Reich* (New York: Simon and Schuster, 1960), p. 343.

106. Charles F. Potter, *Humanism: A New Religion* (New York: Simon & Schuster 1930), p. 128, as cited in Robert L. Waggoner, "The Humanization of America in Culture, Education, and Law," an article adapted from the second chapter of an unpublished doctoral dissertation, available at www.biblicaltheism.com/humanameri.htm.

107. Paul Blanchard, quoted by Blair Adams and Joel Stein, *Who owns the Children?* (Waco, TX: Truth Forum, 1984).

Chapter Two - *Do You Like Your Daughter's Nose-ring and Tongue Stud?*

1. Rousas John Rushdoony, *The Philosophy of the Christian Curriculum* (Vallecito, California: Ross House Books 1981), p. 93.

2. Doug Thompson, "The Rant: Just When Did Our Daughters Start Dressing Like Hookers?," Capitol Hill Blue, July 8, 2002, and "Racy Back to School Clothes: Are Parents 'Skirting' the Issue?," Family Research Council – *Culture Facts*, August 17, 2001. Clothiers such as Abercrombie and Fitch seem to be taking the sexualization of children's clothing to new lows. It is reported that Abercrombie and Fitch is selling thong underwear for girls as young as 7 years old printed with phrases like "Eye Candy" and "Wink Wink." "Abercrombie and Fitch in Trouble Again – Wisconsin Parents Enraged Over Thongs for 7-year-old Girls," *Milwaukee Journal Sentinel*, May 17, 2002.

3. "Tongue-splitting is the Latest Controversial Trend," Associated Press, May 14, 2003. The appeal of tongue-splitting may be somewhat limited because the procedure is being performed by at least some practitioners with a scalpel heated by a blow torch without the benefit of anesthetic.

4. "'Plumber's Butt' Goes Coed," *The Clarion-Ledger* (from staff and wire reports) July 8, 2003.

5. A Michigan teacher, Linda Schrock Taylor, reports on what she now sees in her government school: "Last week a girl was squatted down, digging for something at the bottom of her backpack and the exposure was shocking. Her levis had dropped low in back, showing, not some modest underwear with "Monday" embroidered on them, but a g-string, too much of which was visible. Her skimpy blouse (I wonder if they refer to those little scraps of fabric as a "blouse"?), designed to let a few inches of flesh show, anyway, was pulled high enough as her arms stretched deep into her backpack. There in all its glory was a large, multicolored butterfly tattooed across her spine at waist level....The boys are as bad with Levis so oversized that they are in constant danger of slipping to the floor. Boys never carry books for girls these days. They can't, for already their hands are full – one carrying a pop; the other hitching up the pants as colored boxers peer from beneath the shirt. One of my new students was expelled last week because his pants dropped low enough to completely display his boxers. After he returned from the ousting, students were complaining that he was wearing the same baggy pants, minus boxers and with zipper undone." Linda Schrock Taylor, "G-Strings & Baggy Pants," LewRockwell.com, March 15, 2004. More of this veteran teacher's adventures in government schools can be found in the archive of her articles that is available online at www.lewrockwell.com.

6. From the Nehemiah Institute student questionnaire.

7. Moral relativism has a long history in philosophical writings. Plato, for example, has the sophist Protagoras state in the *Theatetus* that "The way things appear to me, in that way they exist for me, and the way things appear to you, in that way they exist for you." In fact, this could be considered a remarkably concise statement of the essential doctrine of postmodernism.

8. Before World War I, there were, of course, strains of moral relativism, pantheism, and other exotica working their way into American intellectual life – having mostly been imported through contacts with German universities. Nevertheless, these remained largely contained. The upheaval in social mores that followed the end of World War I created the social conditions for the beginnings of a true transformation in America's moral perspective.

9. The view that human nature is sinful was dominant in America from the very earliest times. Henry Steele Commager appears to view this as a particularly 18th century point of view. Henry Steele Commager, *The Commonwealth of Learning* (New York: Harper & Row, 1968), p. 20. It would be more accurate to say that it is a distinctively Christian point of view. Boas, by the way, hated Christianity.

10. The basic critique of Mead's *Coming of Age in Samoa* is Derek Freeman's 1983 book, *The Fateful Hoaxing of Margaret Mead*. Freeman argues that Mead was "hoaxed" by the teenage girls she interviewed into believing that Samoa was a paradise of equality and free love, whereas, in fact, it was quite

"puritanical," authoritarian, and unequal. Anyone familiar at all with accounts of Mead's work in Samoa and how they were produced would have to recognize that Mead's field work was utterly insubstantial and that she appears to have had something less than a commitment to getting to the facts because she already knew what she wanted to find.

11. Academic philosophers sometimes try to deny this by saying that we can argue with others about some values being better than others by giving reasons. If one denies the existence of transcendent moral values, however, this sort of moral discourse is just a sales job in which the point of the exercise is to reshape someone else's preferences.

12. It would take a book to detail the bizarre history of humanistic psychology and the people who created it as an academic and social force. Fortunately, that book exists. Joyce Milton's *The Road to Malpsychia: Humanistic Psychology and Our Discontents* (San Francisco: Encounter Books, 2002) details the development of the humanistic psychology movement, its outgrowths in popular culture, and the peculiar and destructive people who created and propagated it. Milton's book contains many fascinating accounts of the people responsible for creating much of the juvenile, neo-paganism that pervades popular culture today, as well as a clear account of the historical roots of humanistic psychology and the many forms that it has taken.

13. See W.R. Coulson, "The Role of Psychology in Current Educational Reform," presented at Empire State Taskforce for Excellence in Educational Methods, New Paltz, New York, December 13, 1997. A copy of this paper can be obtained on the Internet at www.issuesetc.org/resource/archives/coulson.htm. Dr. Coulson was a colleague of Rogers, and the discussion of Rogers' techniques and views are largely based on Dr. Coulson's facts contained in paper.

14. W.R. Coulson, "The Role of Psychology in Current Educational Reform," presented at Empire State Taskforce for Excellence in Educational Methods, New Paltz, New York, December 13, 1997, p. 1.

15. W.R. Coulson, "The Role of Psychology in Current Educational Reform," presented at Empire State Taskforce for Excellence in Educational Methods, New Paltz, New York, December 13, 1997, p.1.

16. See W.R. Coulson, "The Role of Psychology in Current Educational Reform," presented at Empire State Taskforce for Excellence in Educational Methods, New Paltz, New York, December 13, 1997, p. 3, and John Ankerberg, John Weldon, and Craig Branch, *Thieves of Innocence* (Eugene, Oregon: Harvest House Publishers, 1993), pp. 72-76.

17. W.R. Coulson, "The Role of Psychology in Current Educational Reform," presented at Empire State Taskforce for Excellence in Educational Methods, New Paltz, New York, December 13, 1997, p. 3.

18. W.R. Coulson, "The Role of Psychology in Current Educational Reform," presented at Empire State Taskforce for Excellence in Educational Methods, New Paltz, New York, December 13, 1997, p. 7.

19. W.R. Coulson, "The Role of Psychology in Current Educational Reform," presented at Empire State Taskforce for Excellence in Educational Methods, New Paltz, New York, December 13, 1997. and John Ankerberg, John Weldon, and Craig Branch, *Thieves of Innocence* (Eugene, Oregon: Harvest House Publishers, 1993), p. 75, quoting M. Amos Clifford.

20. "Is DARE Dying?," *Education Reporter*, October 2000.

21. Jacob Sullum, "Dare to Keep Your Kids Off DARE," Reasononline, August 6, 2002, and Paul Armentano, "The Truth about D.A.R.E.," Lewrockwell.com, March 31, 2003.

22. W.R. Coulson, "The Role of Psychology in Current Educational Reform," presented at Empire State Taskforce for Excellence in Educational Methods, New Paltz, New York, December 13, 1997, p. 6. See also John Ankerberg, John Weldon, and Craig Branch, *Thieves of Innocence* (Eugene, Oregon: Harvest House Publishers, 1993), p. 75.

23. Liz Reyer, as quoted in Rick Branch, "New Age in the Schools: Quest – Anti-Drug Program or Values Clarification?," *The Watchman Expositor*, p. 3, www.watchman.org/cults/quest.htm.

24. Liz Reyer, as quoted in Rick Branch, "New Age in the Schools: Quest – Anti-Drug Program or Values Clarification?," *The Watchman Expositor*, p. 3, www.watchman.org/cults/quest.htm.

25. Rick Branch, "New Age in the Schools: Quest – Anti-Drug Program or Values Clarification?," *The Watchman Expositor*, p. 3, quoting W.R. Coulson, www.watchman.org/cults/quest.htm.

26. Rick Branch, "New Age in the Schools: An Evaluation of Drug Education and Values Education," *The Watchman Expositor*, Volume 14, Number 2, 1997, p. 3 (www.watchman.org/na/valueclr.html).

27. Bill Coden, "The Mystery of the Undiscovered Values," Yale-New Haven Teachers Institute Curriculum Unit 89.04.01 (www.yale.edu/ynhti/curriculum/units/1989/4/89.04.01.x.html).

28. Louis E. Raths, Merrill Harman, and Sidney B. Simon, *Values and Teaching* (Columbus, Ohio: Charles E. Merrill Publishing Co., 1966 [2d edition, 1978]), pp. 138-39, as quoted in Richard A. Baer, Jr., "Teaching Values in the Schools," *American Education*, volume 18, no. 9, pp. 11-17, November 1982. This passage appears in both the 1966 and 1978 editions.

29. "Critical thinking" is also invoked as a slogan by a movement of democratic socialists active in government schools who are trying to recruit students as activists in their causes. One leader in the movement is a former high school social studies teacher, Alan Singer. Singer promotes his model for using schools as a way of promoting democratic socialism through workshops for teachers, assemblies, and his website (http://www.rethinkingschools.org/about/index.shtml). At the center of his model is the use of student clubs for recruiting students to various leftist causes (see Singer's article at http://www.rethinkingschools.org/archive/17_04/club174.shtml). The essence of Singer's message is that what you as a teacher may not be able to get away with in the classroom you can get away with using a "student club" as a vehicle. Moreover, under the rubric of a "student club" activists can get school funds, fund raise in school, distribute newsletters and fliers, put up posters, sell political buttons, use such taxpayer provided resources as rooms, copiers, and computers, and openly recruit students from class and encourage club members to recruit other students. Moreover, in some cases, the club members might be able to get community service credit for their activities. By creating the impression that these clubs have an educational purpose, leftist teachers are able to use taxpayer resources and a community's children to promote abortion rights, radical environmentalism, opposition to U.S. foreign policy and just about anything else that gets the typical leftist's juices flowing. But, of course, also involved is a deliberate effort to indoctrinate children that would not be permitted if it were pursued openly.

30. Ironically, the "critical thinking" genre of non-directive curricula was at least partially inspired by Lawrence Kohlberg's work on moral development. Like the advocates of values clarification, Kohlberg advocated non-directive moral education and rejected the traditional "moralizing" approach to teaching children ethics. Unlike the advocates of values clarification, Kohlberg opposed moral relativism and thought that individuals could progress through stages of moral development, with the highest being moral decision making in accordance with certain abstract universal principles of justice. As he gained experience with the application of his theories to school curricula, Kohlberg ultimately concluded that the application of his theory was not leading children to progress beyond what he considered the lower levels of moral reasoning. This, in turn, led him to renounce his condemnation of indoctrinative moral education. See Lawrence Kohlberg, "Moral Education Reappraised," *The Humanist*, November-December 1978. For a summary of Kohlberg's theory of moral development, see Robert N. Barger, "A Summary of Lawrence Kohlberg's Stages of Moral Development," available at www.nd.edu/~rbarger/kohlberg.html.

31. "13-Year-Old Tells What It's Really Like in Public School," *Education Reporter*, December 1995.

32. Matthew Cella, "Catcher in the Rye Assignment Evokes Shock," *The Washington Times*, November 26, 2003.

33. Matthew Cella, "Catcher in the Rye Assignment Evokes Shock," *The Washington Times*, November 26, 2003.

34. Jesse Ogden, "Kids and the Culture These Days," Lewrockwell.com, August 22, 2003.

35. Cathy Young, "Vaginal Discourse for Teens," Reasononline, February 24, 2004, available online at http://reason.com/cy/cy022404.shtml.

36. The description of freak dancing is based on the reporting in Nicole C. Wong, "'Freaking' Banned: Palo Alto High Principal says Dance is 'Like Pornography'," *The San Jose Mercury News*, February 20, 2003.

37. Nicole C. Wong, "'Freaking' Banned: Palo Alto High Principal says Dance is 'Like Pornography'," *The San Jose Mercury News*, February 20, 2003.

38. Nicole C. Wong, "'Freaking' Banned: Palo Alto High Principal says Dance is 'Like Pornography'," *The San Jose Mercury News*, February 20, 2003.

39. See, *e.g.,* Nurith C. Aizenman, "Sexy Dancing has Schools on Prom Patrol: Teens' Gyrations a Bit too Risqué," *Washington Post*, May 17, 2002. Almost any Internet search engine will turn up a number of stories on this subject.

40. As quoted in Nicole C. Wong, "'Freaking' Banned: Palo Alto High Principal says Dance is 'Like Pornography'," *The San Jose Mercury News*, February 20, 2003.

41. Nicole C. Wong, "'Freaking' Banned: Palo Alto High Principal says Dance is 'Like Pornography'," *The San Jose Mercury News*, February 20, 2003.

42. Nurith C. Aizenman, "Sexy Dancing has Schools on Prom Patrol: Teens' Gyrations a Bit too Risqué," *Washington Post*, May 17, 2002.

43. Nurith C. Aizenman, "Sexy Dancing has Schools on Prom Patrol: Teens' Gyrations a Bit too Risqué," *Washington Post*, May 17, 2002.

44. As quoted in Nurith C. Aizenman, "Sexy Dancing has Schools on Prom Patrol: Teens' Gyrations a Bit too Risqué," *Washington Post*, May 17, 2002.

45. As quoted in Nurith C. Aizenman, "Sexy Dancing has Schools on Prom Patrol: Teens' Gyrations a Bit too Risqué," *Washington Post*, May 17, 2002.

46. Nurith C. Aizenman, "Sexy Dancing has Schools on Prom Patrol: Teens' Gyrations a Bit too Risqué," *Washington Post*, May 17, 2002.

47. Nurith C. Aizenman, "Sexy Dancing has Schools on Prom Patrol: Teens' Gyrations a Bit too Risqué," *Washington Post*, May 17, 2002.

48. Doug Thompson, "The Rant: Just When Did Our Daughters Start Dressing Like Hookers?," *Capitol Hill Blue*, July 8, 2002.

49. For a fascinating glimpse into the mentality that allows otherwise normal girls to engage in this sort of exhibitionism, see Joe Maxwell, "Bathing Suits or Birthday Suits?" *World Magazine*, June 14, 2003. The main motivator, not surprisingly, is the desire to be "noticed" by boys. Somebody ought to tell these girls that how you bait your hook will strongly influence what you catch. Obviously, many parents with daughters are AWOL.

50. "Thong-Wearing Teens Kicked Out of Dance," TheSanDiegoChannel.com, posted April 29, 2002, updated May 1, 2002.

51. "Thong-Wearing Teens Kicked Out of Dance," TheSanDiegoChannel.com, posted April 29, 2002, updated May 1, 2002.

52. Nurith C. Aizenman, "Sexy Dancing has Schools on Prom Patrol: Teens' Gyrations a Bit too Risqué," *Washington Post*, May 17, 2002.

53. As quoted in Michelle Malkin, "The Thong Reaction," TownHall.com, May 3, 2002.

54. Eleanor Yang, "Girls Made to Show Underwear at High School Dance," SignOnSanDiego.com (*Union-Tribune*), April 30, 2002.

55. This illustrates something Christians sometimes have difficulty understanding: many, if not most, children in government schools are being raised by parents whose values are radically different from theirs. To take another jaw-dropping example, a mother sued a Pennsylvania school district for suspending her 13-year-old daughter for performing oral sex on a 13-year-old boy while riding a school bus. Her grounds for the suit? The district's written policies did not make it clear that oral sex on a school bus was unacceptable behavior. "Judge Upholds Suspension of Girl for Sex Act on School Bus," *Pittsburgh Tribune-Review* (Associated Press), September 3, 2003. In Arizona, *parents* protested an effort by the school board to fire a principal who was reported to have falsified student test scores to get incentive money for teachers, falsified enrollment reports, and failed to discipline an employee who had made "inappropriate overtures to a fifth-grade student." Anne Ryman, "Sequoya Principal Garners Support," *The Arizona Republic*, October 7, 2003, available online at http://www.azcentral.com/news/education/1007necalendar07.html. Christians need to understand that almost all of today's parents attended thoroughly paganized government schools. So, it should not be surprising that a majority of the children in government schools come from homes saturated with the values of the popular culture. The children from those homes, in turn, are passing their "family values" on to Christian children.

56. As reported in the New York Times News Service, "One in Five US Adolescents has Sex Before Turning 15," *Taipei Times*, May 21, 2003, p. 7.

57. As reported in Valarie Honeycutt Spears, "Oral-sex Issue Hits Middle Schools in Kentucky," *Lexington Herald Leader*, June 9, 2002.

58. Laura Meckler, "Teens Report Peer Pressure to Have Sex," Associated Press, May 20, 2003.

59. ABC13 Eyewitness News (Houston), "Teen Reportedly Aborts Baby at School," February 20, 2003.

60. Jim Daly, "Students Applaud School Bus Sexcapade," *The Patriot Ledger*, January 8, 2003. It should be noted that Richard Kelly, principal of the high school attended by one of the students, vigorously denied the accuracy of the story. According to Mr. Kelly, there was no "cheering ... the students were watching, laughing, making comments." Well, I suppose, the lack of cheering makes all the difference. Charles Mathewson, "Fallout Continues Over Sex on Bus," *The Brocton (MA) Enterprise*, January 9, 2003.

61. "Middle Schoolers Suspended for Sex in Class: Teacher Put on Paid Leave," TheLouisvilleChannel.com, February 12, 2003.

62. "Middle Schoolers Suspended for Sex in Class: Teacher Put on Paid Leave," TheLouisvilleChannel.com, February 12, 2003.

63. Jeff Ehling, "Middle School Students Allegedly Have Oral Sex in Classroom," ABC13 Eyewitness News, February 4, 2004.

64. Valarie Honeycutt Spears, "Oral-sex Issue Hits Middle Schools," *Lexington Herald Leader*, June 9, 2002.

65. Valarie Honeycutt Spears, "Oral-sex Issue Hits Middle Schools," *Lexington Herald Leader*, June 9, 2002.

66. As quoted in Valarie Honeycutt Spears, "Oral-sex Issue Hits Middle Schools," *Lexington Herald Leader*, June 9, 2002. The problem of sexual activity among ever younger children may be even farther advanced in Canada, where one-third of ninth grade girls report that they have engaged in oral sex. For an illuminating account of the problem north of the border, see Sara Wilson, "Mainstreaming Oral S*x Among Teens," *Canada Globe and Mail*, February 7, 2004, available online at http://209.157.64.200/focus/f-news/1075247/posts.

67. Maggie Fox, "Half of Young Americans to Get Sex Diseases – Study," Reuters, February 24, 2004, available online at http://uk.news.yahoo.com/040224/325/emux4.html.

68. Quoted in Maggie Fox, "Half of Young Americans to Get Sex Diseases – Study," Reuters, February 24, 2004, available online at http://uk.news.yahoo.com/040224/325/emux4.html.

69. Perhaps the single best article for understanding not merely what is happening to curricula in government schools, but what students and teachers are being subjected to as the curricula are implemented is Candi Cushman, "Unsafe at Any Grade," *Citizen Magazine*, December 2002, available online at http://family.org/cforum/citizenmag/coverstory/a0023411.cfm.

70. As quoted in "'Diversity' Days Define Deviance, Parents Say," *Education Reporter*, May 2001.

71. "'Diversity' Days Define Deviance, Parents Say," *Education Reporter*, May 2001.

72. As quoted in "'Diversity' Days Define Deviance, Parents Say," *Education Reporter*, May 2001.

73. John Haskins, "It's 1984 in Massachusetts – And Big Brother is Gay," *Insight Magazine*, December 17, 2001.

74. The following discussion of "Fistgate" is based on Brian Camenker and Scott Whiteman, "Kids Get Graphic Instruction In Homosexual Sex," *The Massachusetts News*, available at www.massnews.com, "Fistgate Instructor Was Paid by State," *The Massachusetts News*, January 23, 2001, and Anand Vaishnav, "Parents' Groups Faults State on Workshop," *The Boston Globe*, May 19, 2000.

75. Brian Camenker and Scott Whiteman, "Kids Get Graphic Instruction In Homosexual Sex," *The Massachusetts News*, p. 4.

76. Ed Oliver, "Fistgate II Teaches More Sexual Activity for Young 'Homosexuals,'" *The Massachusetts News*, March 26, 2001.

77. "Sex Educators Not Telling Whole Truth," Concerned Women for America, Press Release, September 26, 2000.

78. "Sex Educators Not Telling Whole Truth," Concerned Women for America, Press Release, September 26, 2000.

79. "Sex Educators Not Telling Whole Truth," Concerned Women for America, Press Release, September 26, 2000.

80. "Florida School District Forced to Alter Sex Ed Curriculum," *Education Reporter*, February 1999.

81. "Decision-Making for Kids, Not Parents," *Education Reporter*, December 1995.

82. News Briefs, Agape Press, May 31, 2002, available at www.agapepress.com.

83. News Briefs, Agape Press, May 31, 2002, available at www.agapepress.com.

84. Susan Jones, "California Democrats Refuse to Notify Parents of Sex Ed Speakers," CNSNews.com, January 8, 2004, available online at http://www.cnsnews.com/ViewPolitics.asp?Page=%5CPolitics%5Carchive%5C200401%5CPOL20040108a.html.

85. General Laws of Massachusetts, Title XII. Education. Chapter 71 Public Schools: Section 32A. Sex Education; policy regarding notice to parents, exemption.

86. Reports on this, and the following incidents, have been collected by the Parents' Rights Coalition. Its web site can be accessed at www.parentsrightscoalition.org.

87. Matt Pyeatt, "Mom Sues Over Ejection From School Assembly on Homosexuality," CNSNews. com, May 13, 2002.

88. Matt Pyeatt, "Mom Sues Over Ejection From School Assembly on Homosexuality," CNSNews. com, May 13, 2002.

89. Kelley Beaucar Vlahos, "CDC-Funded Sex Ed Programs Draw Fire," Fox News, September 9, 2003.

90. Kelley Beaucar Vlahos, "CDC-Funded Sex Ed Programs Draw Fire," Fox News, September 9, 2003.

91. Kelley Beaucar Vlahos, "CDC-Funded Sex Ed Programs Draw Fire," Fox News, September 9, 2003.

92. Kelley Beaucar Vlahos, "CDC-Funded Sex Ed Programs Draw Fire," Fox News, September 9, 2003.

93. For an overview of the history and current politics of Title X, which was established by the Family Planning Services and Population Research Act of 1970, see Paul Weyrich, "Parent's Right to Know Act of 2003," NewsMax.com, June 21, 2003.

94. See Karen Holgate, "Expanding School-Based Health Clinics: A Bad Idea," available at www.paul-revere.org/pr/holgate/ar990701.shtml.

95. "Invasive Exams Violate Civil Rights of 59 Girls: School District Held Accountable," *Education Reporter*, October 1999.

96. Paul Weyrich, "Parent's Right to Know Act of 2003," NewsMax.com, June 21, 2003.

97. Judith A. Reisman, quoted in Judith A. Reisman, *Crafting "Gay" Children, An Inquiry into the Abuse of Vulnerable Youth Via Government Schooling & Mainstream Media, A Work in Progress*, The Institute for Media Education, p. 36, available at www.rsvpamerica.org.

98. Ann McClure, "Student Survey Destroyed After Parental Complaints," *Granite State News*, January 16, 2003.

99. "Parents Outraged Over School Sex Survey of 10 Year-Olds," *Los Angeles Daily News*, June 17, 2002.

100. "School District Eyes 'Parent Report Card'," Associated Press, February 6, 2003. For an interesting discussion of how the very same highly trained education professionals who have trouble teaching children to read proficiently by 4th grade intend to grade parents on how they are raising their children, see R. Cort Kirkwood, "Public Schools Harm Parents," LewRockwell.com, October 1, 2003, available online at www.lewrockwell.com/kirkwood/kirkwood43.html.

101. Andrea Petersen, "The 'Re-Engineered' Child," *The Wall Street Journal*, April 8, 2003.

102. Keith Ervin, "Warm Embrace for Kids, or Merely 'Psycho Cry Fest'?," *Seattle Times*, April 10, 2002.

103. Keith Ervin, "Warm Embrace for Kids, or Merely 'Psycho Cry Fest'?," *Seattle Times*, April 10, 2002.

104. Lynn Vincent, "The Liberal Future," *World Magazine*, August 31, 2002.

105. This legislation is part of the legacy of the last days of Gray Davis as governor. Cal Thomas, "A New Sexual Education," available online at http://www.crosswalk.com/news/1223701.html.

106. *Drug Use in the United States*, U.S. Department of Justice, Drug Enforcement Administration, www.usdoj.gov/dea/concern/use.htm.

107. *Drug Use in the United States*, U.S. Department of Justice, Drug Enforcement Administration, www.usdoj.gov/dea/concern/use.htm.

108. *Juvenile Offenders and Victims: 1997 Update on Violence*, U.S. Department of Justice, Office of Juvenile Justice and Delinquency Prevention.

109. James G. Kahn, Claire D. Brindis and Dana A Glei, "Pregnancies Averted Among U.S. Teenagers By the Use of Contraceptives," *Family Planning Perspectives*, Volume 31, No. 1, January/February 1999, p. 2, and "Teen Sex and Pregnancy, Facts in Brief," The Alan Guttmacher Institute, September 1999, available at www.agi-usa.org/pubs/fb_teen_sex.html. The number of girls having had sexual intercourse by age 18 more than doubled between the 1950s and 1999. In considering these figures it is important to bear in mind that rates of marriage among teenagers were far higher in the 1950s than they currently are.

110. Stephanie J. Ventura and Christine Bachrach, "Nonmarital Childbearing in the United States, 1940-99," *National Vital Statistics Reports*, Volume 48, Number 16, October 18, 2000; and "Report to Congress on Out-Of-Wedlock Childbearing," Department of Health and Human Services, September 1995.

111. Stephanie J. Ventura and Christine Bachrach, "Nonmarital Childbearing in the United States, 1940-99," *National Vital Statistics Reports*, Volume 48, Number 16, October 18, 2000; and "Report to Congress on Out-Of-Wedlock Childbearing," Department of Health and Human Services, September 1995. "Care for the Illegitimate?," *The National Review (On the Right)*, March 10, 1997, and John R. Smith, "Teen Pregnancies and Kids Living in Poverty: Should Taxpayers Do More?," *Madison Op-Ed Series*, July 1996, James Madison Institute.

112. "Facts in Brief: Induced Abortion," The Alan Guttmacher Institute (February 2000), available at www.agi-usa.org/pubs/fb_induced_abortion.html.

113. Michael Fletcher, "Marriage Rate Lowest Ever," *The Washington Post*, July 2, 1999.

114. Barbara Vobejda, " 4 Million Unwed Couples Live Together," *The Washington Post*, July 27, 1998.

115. Arlene Saluter, *Marital Status and Living Arrangements: March 1994*, U.S. Bureau of the Census, March 1996; series P20-484, p. vi.

116. "Cheating and Succeeding: Record Numbers of Top High School Students Take Ethical Shortcuts: *Who's Who* Finds Troubling Trends, Some Good News in 29th Annual Survey of High Achievers." Available online at www.eci-whoswho.com/highschool/annualsurveys/29.shtml.

117. Jane Gross, "Exposing the Cheat Sheet, With the Students' Aid," *New York Times*, November 25, 2003.

118. Jane Gross, "Exposing the Cheat Sheet, With the Students' Aid," *New York Times*, November 25, 2003.

119. Jane Gross, "Exposing the Cheat Sheet, With the Students' Aid," *New York Times*, November 25, 2003.

120. Jane Gross, "Exposing the Cheat Sheet, With the Students' Aid," *New York Times*, November 25, 2003.

121. Jane Gross, "Exposing the Cheat Sheet, With the Students' Aid," *New York Times*, November 25, 2003.

122. These facts are taken from a publication of the Alan Gutmacher Institute, as quoted by John Ankerberg, John Weldon, and Craig Branch, *Thieves of Innocence* (Eugene, Oregon: Harvest House Publishers, 1993), p. 190.

123. In 1999, 18% of the students surveyed by *Who's Who* reported having had sexual intercourse, while nationally over 50% of 17 year-olds and over 65% of 18 year-olds reported having sexual intercourse. In 2000, 47% of the students surveyed by Who's Who reported having consumed alcohol, while nearly 80.3% of 12th graders nationally reported having consumed alcohol. See, "Cheating and Succeeding: Record Numbers of Top High School Students Take Ethical Shortcuts: *Who's Who* Finds Troubling Trends, Some Good News in 29th Annual Survey of High Achievers" and " Teen Sex and Pregnancy, Facts in Brief," The Alan Guttmacher Institute, September 1999, available at www.agi-usa. org/pubs/fb_teen_sex.html; and, The National Institute for Drug Abuse, at www.nida.nih.gov/Infofax/Infofaxindex.html.

124. These figures are taken from the executive summary of *Alcohol and Other Drug Use Among College Students in New York State*, a study by the New York State Office of Alcoholism and Substance Abuse Services (findings from a statewide college survey, 1996), available online at www.oasas.state.ny.us/pio/col-exec.htm.

125. As cited in Bryan Gruley, "How One University Stumbled In Its Attack on Alcohol Abuse," *The Wall Street Journal*," October 14, 2003, p. A-1. For another source with similar results, see "Survey Finds Students have Largely Accurate Perceptions of College Binge Drinking," *The Journal of American College Health*, September 8, 2000, available as a press release at www.collegebingedrinking.org/alcohol/alcoholpr9_08.shtml.

126. *Monitoring the Future Study*, National Institute for Drug Abuse, available at www.topchoice.com/~psyche/drugs/drunk9196.html.

127. Norval Glenn and Elizabeth Marquardt, *Hooking Up, Hanging Out and Hoping for Mr. Right: College Women on Dating and Mating Today*, Institute for American Values (www.americanvalues.org).

128. As quoted in "Major New Study: Hooking Up, Hanging Out, and Hoping for Mr. Right: College Women on Dating and Mating Today," Press Release, July 26, 2001, Institute for American Values.

129. "Major New Study: Hooking Up, Hanging Out, and Hoping for Mr. Right: College Women on Dating and Mating Today," Press Release, July 26, 2001, Institute for American Values.

130. As quoted in Elizabeth Marquardt, "Fathers Should Demand Changes in Coed Dorms," *The Detroit News*, November 2, 2001.

131. Laura Vanderkam, "Hookups Starve the Soul," *USA Today*, Editorial, July 25, 2001.

132. William Rasberry, "What's Love Got to Do With It," *The Washington Post* ONLINE, July 27, 2001, citing Norval Glenn and Elizabeth Marquardt, *Hooking Up, Hanging Out and Hoping for Mr. Right: College Women on Dating and Mating Today*, Institute for American Values.

133. The foregoing discussion of the NEA and "New B" is based on Phyllis Schlafly, "NEA Goals, Spin, and Concealment," Eagle Forum, August 2001.

134. The 1972 Gay Rights Platform, State positions 1 and 6 and Federal position 6, available at www.afa.net/homosexual_agenda/ha1972.htm. The homosexual effort to lower age of consent laws is international, see, e.g., Phillipe Fraser, "Age of Consent: Equality at Last," EuroGay (http://web.archive.org/web/20010210114850/http://eurogay.co.uk/article/1200/equality.html.). For an interesting ac-

count of how gay activists have worked to promote the mainstreaming of their lifestyle, see "Is There a Gay Agenda?," available at www.sphi.com and Marshall K. Kirk and Erastes Pill, "The Overhauling of Straight America," *Guide Magazine*, November 1987.

135. As reported in Richard G. Howe, "Homosexuality in America: Exposing the Myths," *The American Family Association*, 1994, p. 23. *The Advocate*, August 23, 1994, as quoted in Charles W. Socarides, M.D., *The Erosion of Heterosexuality*, originally published in *The Washington Times* and available at the American Family Association web-site, www.afa.net.

136. As reported in Richard G. Howe, "Homosexuality in America: Exposing the Myths," *The American Family Association*, 1994, p. 14.

137. As reported in Richard G. Howe, "Homosexuality in America: Exposing the Myths," *The American Family Association*, 1994, p. 14, citing a study published by the Berean League in June of 1991. A summary of the results is available through the American Family Association at its web site, www.afa.net/homosexual-agenda/resources.asp.

138. Jon Ward, "Virginia Park Now Taken Over by Gay Sex," *The Washington Times*, September 30, 2002. Mr. Ward also reports that homosexual men meet for anonymous sex in public places across the United States and that one homosexual-oriented Web site lists various locations by state where homosexuals may be able to find anonymous, public sex.

139. Jon Ward, "Virginia Park Now Taken Over by Gay Sex," *The Washington Times*, September 30, 2002.

140. Jon Ward, "Virginia Park Now Taken Over by Gay Sex," *The Washington Times*, September 30, 2002.

141. Jon Ward, "Virginia Park Now Taken Over by Gay Sex," *The Washington Times*, September 30, 2002.

142. The main sources of information for this paragraph are: Nathan C. Masters, "Christian Group Blasts 'Orgy of Depravity' at Disney's Gay Days," CNSNews.com, August 7, 2003, available online (including video link) at http://www.cnsnews.com/Culture/archive/200308/CUL20030807a.html; and Mike Schneider, "'Gay Days' Out of the Closet," Associated Press, June 2, 2000. The video clip in the Masters article is one minute out of the 12 minutes shown to Bill O'Reilly. According to CAN, the complete video shows homosexuals at Gay Days engaging in full public nudity, analingus, crotch groping, simulated sodomy, and other colorful homosexual public behavior. For the details, go to CAN's homepage at http://216.219.199.7/. According to the Schneider story, by the way, Gay Days has expanded to Disney's other theme parks and to Universal Orlando and SeaWorld Orlando.

143. Seth R. Norman, "Students Seek Sex in Campus Bathrooms," *California Patriot*, February 4, 2003.

144. Seth R. Norman, "Students Seek Sex in Campus Bathrooms," *California Patriot*, February 4, 2003.

145. As reported in "Homophobic Cops," Tongue Tied, January 13, 2003, www.tonguetied.us.

146. As reported in "Homophobic Cops," Tongue Tied, January 13, 2003, www.tonguetied.us.

147. Catherine Lucey, "5 Arrested at Gay Sex Site," Phillynews.com, February 13, 2003.

148. As quoted in "Homophobic Cops," Tongue Tied, January 13, 2003, www.tonguetied.us.

149. Karla Jay and Allen Young, *The Gay Report* (New York: Summit, 1979), p. 500. See also, Tony Marco, "Special Class Protections for Self-Alleged Gays: A Question of 'Orientation' and Consequences," available at www.leaderu.com.

150. See, e.g., Peter Tatchell, "30 Years On," EuroGay, January 12, 2000 (http://eurogay.co.uk/editorial/011200.html).

151. Gregory A. Freeman, "Bug Chasers: The Men who Long to be HIV+," *Rolling Stone*, February 6, 2003.

152. This percentage is attributed to Dr. Bob Cabaj, director of behavioral-health services for San Francisco and past president of both the Gay and Lesbian Medical Association and the Association of Gay and Lesbian Psychiatrists. Gregory A. Freeman, "Bug Chasers: The Men who Long to be HIV+," *Rolling Stone*, February 6, 2003.

153. Gregory A. Freeman, "Bug Chasers: The Men who Long to be HIV+," *Rolling Stone*, February 6, 2003.

154. Richard Roeper, "What Makes Bug Chasers, Gift Givers Do Such a Thing?," *The Chicago Sun-Times*, April 22, 2003. Some homosexuals are even more aggressive in spreading the joy of HIV. In February 2004 a man was arrested in Orlando for having homosexual sex parties in his garage during which he drugged other party-goers and injected them with HIV-tainted blood. Unfortunately for his defense lawyer, he made over 100 video-tapes of his party exploits. Some of the victims were juveniles. "Syringes of Blood, Sex Harness Found in Man's Garage," Local6.com, Februaruy 27, 2004, available online at http://www.local6.com/news/2876599/detail.html

155. Richard Roeper, "What Makes Bug Chasers, Gift Givers Do Such a Thing?," *The Chicago Sun-Times*, April 22, 2003.

156. Sabin Russell, "S.F. has Nation's Highest Syphilis Rate," *San Francisco Chronicle*, November 21, 2003.

157. Sabin Russell, "S.F. has Nation's Highest Syphilis Rate," *San Francisco Chronicle*, November 21, 2003.

158. Sabin Russell, "S.F. has Nation's Highest Syphilis Rate," *San Francisco Chronicle*, November 21, 2003.

159. Andrew Jacobs, "The Beast in the Bathhouse," *The New York Times*, January 12, 2004, available online at http://www.lgbtcenters.org/news/news_item.asp?NewsID=432.

160. Karla Jay and Allen Young, *Out of the Closets* (New York: New York University Press, 1972), pp. 338 and 365, quoted in Judith A. Reisman, "Crafting Homosexual Youth," *Regent University Law Review*, Volume 14, Number 2, Spring 2002, p. 300. The entire issue of the *Regent University Law Review* cited, which is available on the web, is devoted to articles on the behavior of homosexuals and their influence in society (http://www.regent.edu/acad/schlaw/lawreview/issues/v14n2.html). The articles contained in the Spring 2002 issue of the *Regent University Law Review* provide a far more detailed and comprehensive treatment of the issues relating to homosexuality touched upon in this chapter. Frankly, every Christian, and certainly every pastor, ought to read the issue from cover to cover. The content may be disturbing, but there is no better way to learn of the threat posed by homosexual activism to our culture. Incidentally, you should know that the articles appearing in the *Regent University Law Review* were originally solicited and written for a *Stanford Law and Policy Review* (*SLRP*) symposium on gay rights. Although the proposed *SLPR* issue was to include both pro and con perspectives on gay rights, the editorial board peremptorily decided that it would only publish the "pro" articles. Consequently, the articles critical of gay rights had to find another home. The *SLRP*'s effort to suppress arguments and evidence questioning gay rights indicates how powerful gay activists and their friends have become in colleges and universities. An account of this imbroglio at Stanford is provided in the above-cited issue of the *Regent University Law Review* in an article by Ty Clevenger titled "Gay Orthodoxy and Academic Heresy." Clevenger, by the way, was a co-editor of the issue of the *SLRP* that was censored.

161. Harris Mirkin, "The Pattern of Sexual Politics: Feminism, Homosexuality and Pedophilia," *Journal of Homosexuality*, volume 37 (2), 1999, pp. 1-24. Mirkin has grandchildren and says that he has never had sexual contact with a child. Jodi Wilogoren, "Scholar's Pedophilia Essay Stirs Outrage and Revenge," *The New York Times*, April 30, 2002.

162. Robert Stacey McCain, "Children: 'The Next Sexual Frontier!'," *The Washington Times*, April 19, 2002.

163. Jon Daughtery, "Report: Pedophilia More Common Among Gays," WorldNetDaily, April 29, 2002.

164. Heterosexual and homosexual pedophiles make the same arguments. As a general proposition, however, homosexual pedophiles appear to lead the pedophile movement. For an example of a heterosexual male rationalizing pedophilia, see Russ Flanagan, "I'm Tired of Being Forced into the Shadows by Society," *The Express-Times*, February 22, 2004, available online at http://www.nj.com/specialprojects/expresstimes/index.ssf?/news/expresstimes/stories/molesters1_otherside.html. The subject of Mr. Flanagan's story, Lindsay Ashford, "…believes it is time the public learned pedophiles are different from child molesters in that they enjoy a romantic and emotional, but not always sexual, connection with children. He also believes it is time for a child rights movement that will give kids more say in how to live their lives." Lindsay also repeats the by now well-worn line that pedophilia is a "sexual orientation" with which one is born, not a mental or moral disorder.

165. Elements of the motion picture industry are beginning to try this theme out. "L.I.E."(which stands for "Long Island Expressway"), a movie released in 2001 to favorable reviews by even some mainstream reviewers, suggests that pedophilia is not such a bad thing. For more information, see, Rev. Louis P. Sheldon, "'L.I.E.' Is Infomercial For North American Man-Boy Love Association," Toogood Reports, November 7, 2001, available at www.toogoodreports.com/column/general/sheldon/110701.htm.

166. This quote is from Rind, Tromovitch, and Bauserman, "A Meta-analytic Examination of Assumed Properties of Child Sexual Abuse Using College Samples," as cited in Nicolosi and O'Leary, "On the Pedophilia Issue: What the APA Should Have Known," Narth (www.narth.com/docs/whatapa.html).

167. Lawrence Morahan, "Psychiatric Association Debates Lifting Pedophilia Taboo," CNSNews.com, June 11, 2003.

168. Robert Stacey McCain, "Children: 'The Next Sexual Frontier!'," *The Washington Times*, April 19, 2002.

169. As quoted in Robert Stacey McCain, "Children: 'The Next Sexual Frontier!'," *The Washington Times*, April 19, 2002.

170. Robert Stacey McCain, "Children: 'The Next Sexual Frontier!'," *The Washington Times*, April 19, 2002.

171. George Archibald, "Child Sex Book Given Out at U.N. Summit," *The Washington Times*, May 10, 2002.

172. George Archibald, "Child Sex Book Given Out at U.N. Summit," *The Washington Times*, May 10, 2002.

173. George Archibald, "Child Sex Book Given Out at U.N. Summit," *The Washington Times*, May 10, 2002.

174. The National Coalition for Sexual Freedom, a pro-sadism and masochism group, is another organization that advocates the elimination of all sex-related laws.

175. Deroy Murdock, "No Boy Scouts: The ACLU Defends NAMBLA," National Review Online, February 27, 2004, available online at http://www.nationalreview.com/murdock/murdock200402270920.asp.

176. Deroy Murdock, "No Boy Scouts: The ACLU Defends NAMBLA," National Review Online, February 27, 2004, available online at http://www.nationalreview.com/murdock/murdock200402270920.asp.

177. Larry Frisoli, as quoted in Deroy Murdock, "No Boy Scouts: The ACLU Defends NAMBLA," National Review Online, February 27, 2004, available online at http://www.nationalreview.com/murdock/murdock200402270920.asp. Mr. Frisoli is an attorney arguing the case against NAMBLA in federal court. The murderers, Jaynes and Salvatore Sicari, suffocated their victim, James Curley, with a gasoline soaked rag after he resisted their sexual overtures. The murderers then took the boy's body to their apartment, where they engaged in necrophilia with the cadaver.

178. See, for example, *The Spartacus International Gay Guide*.

179. Jon Daughtery, "Report: Pedophilia More Common Among Gays," WorldNetDaily, April 29, 2002.

180. Phillipe Fraser, "Age of Consent: Equality at Last," EuroGay. http://web.archive.org/web/20010210114850/http://eurogay.co.uk/article/1200/equality.html.

181. Nicolosi and O'Leary, "On the Pedophilia Issue: What the APA should have known," Narth (www.narth.com/docs/whatapa.html). Unbeknownst to most Americans, a sitting Supreme Court Justice, Ruth Bader Ginsberg, wrote in favor of lowering the age of consent to 12 years-old in an article titled "Sex Bias in the U.S. Code" that she prepared for the U.S. Commission on Civil Rights. Steve Brown, "Fears Grow Over Academic Efforts to Normalize Pedophilia," CNSNews.com, July 10, 2003.

182. Jon Daughtery, "Report: Pedophilia More Common Among Gays," WorldNetDaily, April 29, 2002.

183. Jon Daughtery, "Report: Pedophilia More Common Among Gays," WorldNetDaily, April 29, 2002.

184. Izzy Lyman, "Little Children Featured at Northampton's 'Gay Pride'," *Massachusetts News*, May 6, 2002.

185. Karla Jay and Allen Young, *Out of the Closets* (New York: New York University Press, 1972), pp. 338 and 365, quoted in Judith A. Reisman, "Crafting Homosexual Youth," *Regent University Law Review*, Volume 14, Number 2, Spring 2002, p. 300.

186. Judith Reisman and Charles Johnson, "Partner Solicitation Characteristics as a Reflection of Male Sexual Orientation," 1994 (available online at http://www.leaderu.com), as quoted in Judith A. Reisman, "Crafting Homosexual Youth," *Regent University Law Review*, Volume 14, Number 2, Spring 2002, p. 299. A further indication of how entrenched pedophilia is among a subculture of male homosexuals is the large number of euphemisms homosexual men have developed for discussing their sexual interest in boys. Those euphemisms are collected in a homosexual lexicon titled *The Queen's Vernacular*. According to Judith Reisman, *The Queen's Vernacular* contains "254 words for boys, most of these involve men sexually abusing boys." Judith A. Reisman and Eunice Van Winkle Ray, "254 Boy Words," WorldNetDaily, November 14, 2000, available at www.worldnetdaily.com/news/article.asp?ARTICLE_ID=16461. The "Vernacular" includes such phrases as "Professional Guest" (kept boy who doesn't put out for his host) and "Poultry Dealer" (a man who pimps boys to interested homosexuals). Most of the other phrases cited in the article are too explicit to mention here. *The Queen's Vernacular*, it should be noted, is considered the foremost homosexual lexicon.

187. *Palaver 6*, for "Paedophile Awareness & Liberation," *Rising Free*, London, October 1976, pp. 2-4, as quoted in Judith A. Reisman, *Crafting "Gay" Children, An Inquiry into the Abuse of Vulnerable Youth Via Government Schooling & Mainstream Media, A Work in Progress*, The Institute for Media Education, p. 15, available at www.rsvpamerica.org.

188. Judith A. Reisman, "Crafting Homosexual Youth," *Regent University Law Review*, Volume 14, Number 2, Spring 2002, pp. 330-333.

189. Eugene Abel, *et al.*, "Self Reported Sex Crimes of Non-Incarcerated Paraphiliacs," *Journal of Interpersonal Violence*, Volume 2, No. 1, March 1997, pp. 5-25, as cited in Judith A. Reisman, "Crafting Homosexual Youth," *Regent University Law Review*, Volume 14, Number 2, Spring 2002, p. 299.

190. Judith A. Reisman, "Crafting Homosexual Youth," *Regent University Law Review*, Volume 14, Number 2, Spring 2002, pp. 302-303, and the sources cited therein.

191. The claim that 10% of the population is homosexual, which is often repeated in the press and by homosexual activists, is a myth. Homosexuals constitute no more than between 1% and 3% of the population, with it probably being in a range of 1.5% to 2%. See Judith A. Reisman, "Crafting Homosexual Youth," *Regent University Law Review*, Volume 14, Number 2, Spring 2002, p. 302. "Your Neighbors May Be Gay? It's Only a 1 in 2000 Chance," *Culture Facts*, September 7, 2001, Family Research Council, available at www.frc.org; and, "Nonmarital Childbearing in the United States, 1940-99," *National Vital Statistics Reports* Volume 48, Number 16, October 18, 2000, by Stephanie J. Ventura, NCHS, and Christine Bachrach, National Institute for Child Health and Human Development, National Institutes of Health, and "Report to Congress on Out-Of-Wedlock Childbearing," Department of Health and Human Services, September 1995, pp. 9-10.

192. "The Commercial Sexual Exploitation of Children in the U.S., Canada, and Mexico," Center for the Study of Youth Policy, as cited in Steve Aiken, "New Study Says 95% of Sexually-Abused Boys Are Molested by Homosexuals," *Traditional Values Coalition*, September 10, 2001.

193. Judith A. Reisman, "Crafting Homosexual Youth," *Regent University Law Review*, Volume 14, Number 2, Spring 2002, p. 303.

194. Steve Aiken, "New Study Says 95% of Sexually-Abused Boys Are Molested by Homosexuals," *Traditional Values Coalition*, September 10, 2001.

195. Peter Wood, "Sex & Consequences," *The American Conservative*, June 28, 2003, available online at http://www.amconmag.com/07_28_03/cover.html. Wood also discusses the anthropological findings regarding the consequences to society of polygamy.

196. Peter Wood, "Sex & Consequences," *The American Conservative*, June 28, 2003, available online at http://www.amconmag.com/07_28_03/cover.html.

197. Peter Wood, "Sex & Consequences," *The American Conservative*, June 28, 2003, available online at http://www.amconmag.com/07_28_03/cover.html.

198. From records compiled by *The Wall Street Journal* and reported in Richard G. Howe, "Homosexuality in America: Exposing the Myths," *The American Family Association*, 1994, p. 12.

199. Reported in Richard G. Howe, "Homosexuality in America: Exposing the Myths," *The American Family Association*, 1994, p. 8.

200. Homosexual activists often claim that suicides by homosexual teens represent 30% of teen suicides. This "fact" can be traced by to a report by homosexual activist Paul Gibson. Gibson's claim has been shown to be a myth. In 1997, two studies were cited by Peter Muehrer of the National Institute of Mental Health that had found that 2.5% to 5% of the suicides in their samples were by people *believed* to be "gay." A Columbia University study of teen suicides indicated that of 107 teen suicides

6% were by teens who were or *who might have been* homosexual. A University of Minnesota study has shown that there are many risk factors such as substance abuse and family dysfunction associated with suicides by homosexual teenagers, not simply "homophobia." See "AMA Criticizes 'Exclusionary' Organizations, Culture Facts," Family Research Council, June 28, 2001. Similarly, studies claiming to find that 30% of gay adolescents have attempted suicide have been found to grossly exaggerate the prevalence of suicide attempts by gay adolescents, because they failed to distinguish between thoughts of suicide and suicide attempts, and because they drew their samples disproportionately from support groups and shelters, where the most troubled gay teens tend to congregate. More careful studies have shown gay adolescents to be only slightly more likely than normal teens to attempt suicide. See Marilyn Elias, "Gay Teens Less Suicidal Than Thought, Report says," *USA Today*, November 26, 2001.

201. The information in the bullet-points is taken from the following sources: Hogg, Strathdee, Craib, O'Shaughnessy, Montaner, and Schechter, "Modeling the Impact of HIV Disease on Mortality in Gay and Bisexual Men," *International Journal of Epidemiology*, Volume 26, 657-661 (1997); Gary Glenn, "Compassionate Society Should Deter Deadly Homosexual Behavior," *The American Family Association*, March 19, 2001, available at www.afa.net; Judith A. Reisman, *Crafting "Gay" Children, An Inquiry into the Abuse of Vulnerable Youth Via Government Schooling & Mainstream Media, A Work in Progress*, The Institute for Media Education, p. 33, available at www.rsvpamerica.org; and, Jon Garbo, "Reports of LGBT Domestic Violence on the Rise," *Gay Health*, November 8, 2001. R. Morgan Griffin, "Breaking the Silence: Sociologist Studies Woman-to-Woman Sexual Violence," *Gay Health*, February 1997. For a bibliography of Lesbian Domestic Violence, go to www.lib.jjay.cuny.edu/research/DomesticViolence/v.html. For a summary of studies on homosexual domestic violence, see Timothy J. Dailey, "Homosexual Parenting: Placing Children at Risk," Family Research Council, available at www.frc.org/get/is01j3.cfm. The *American Journal of Public Health* has also published a detailed study of domestic violence among male homosexuals (December 2002, Vol. 92, No. 12). The rate of physical abuse between homosexual male "partners" was much higher than for heterosexual men or heterosexual women.

202. "Homosexual Activists Solidify Hold on School, Sex at State Expense," *American Family Journal*, November/December 2000, available at www.afa.net.

203. "Homosexual Activists Solidify Hold on School, Sex at State Expense," *American Family Journal*, November/December 2000, available at www.afa.net.

204. For a description of how "AIDS education" ultimately morphs into homosexual advocacy within government schools, see "First AIDS Education, Then 'Safe Schools,' Then Gay Advocacy," available at www.leaderu.com/orgs/narth/firstaids.html.

205. Tal Brooke, "Education: Capturing Hearts and Minds for a New World," in John Ankerberg, John Weldon, Craig Branch, *Thieves of Innocence*, (Eugene, OR: Harvest House Publishers, 1993), p. 230.

206. As reported in "Teens back Marriage By Gays, A Poll Finds," *The New York Daily News*, August 28, 2001, Stuart Shepard, "Students' Views Markedly Pro-Gay," Family News in Focus, September 19, 2001, available online at http://family.org/cforum/fnif/news/a0017727.cfm, and "Q&A: Media Skews Study on Views About Homosexuality," *Culture Facts*, Family Research Council, September 21, 2001, available from the Family Research Council.

207. Here are a few of the others: Parents, Friends, and Families of Lesbians and Gays (PFLAG); Lambda Legal Defense Education Fund (LLDEF); Gay and Lesbian Alliance Against Discrimination (GLAAD); and, Gay, Lesbian, and Straight Teacher's Network (GLSTN).

208. This language can be found at http://www.glsen.org/templates/student/record.html?section=48&record=145

209. Robert B. Bluey, "Same-Sex Marriage Debate Moves into Schools," CNSNews.com, February 9, 2004, available online at http://www.cnsnews.com//ViewCulture.asp?Page=\Culture\archive\200402\CUL20040209a.html.

210. For those without ready access to the *New England Journal of Medicine*, a chapter from a 1989 Centers for Disease Control report gives similar information regarding the adverse effects of smoking on life expectancy (as well as other adverse health effects) and is available online at http://www.cdc.gov/tobacco/sgr/sgr_1989/1989SGRChapter1.pdf .

211. For a recent summary of many of the health problems associated with homosexual behavior, "Homosexual Behavior Fuels Aids and STD Epidemic," Traditional Values Coalition, available at http://www.traditionalvalues.org/pdf_files/Diseases.pdf.

212. Much of this senario can be found in Phyllis Schlafly, "NEA Goals, Spin, and Concealment," Eagle Forum, August 2001. One source for keeping track of these trends is People for the Way, Truth, and Life at http://myweb.ecomplanet.com/TPFT8634/mycustompage0015.htm. Of course, the same information can be gleaned from NEA, GLSEN, general news, and other sources. For information on speech code controversies, see Jennifer Mrozowski, "Vote Delayed on Gay Slurs in School," *The Cincinnati Enquirer*, August 14, 2001, and "To Avoid Lawsuit, Traverse City Schools Agree Not to Promote Homosexual Agenda or Enforce Unconstitutional Speech Code," American Family Association, Press Release, March 14, 2001, available at www.massnews.com/apmich.htm.

213. See "GLSEN's Gay Lesson Plans for Elementary Schoolchildren," *Education Reporter*, January 2001, "Pro-Gay Curricula: Coming Soon to a School Near You," *Education Reporter*, November 2001, and "NEA Fights Critics of Gay History," *Education Reporter*, November 1995. For a particularly well written and shocking discussion of the progress homosexual activists are making in schools, see Marjorie King, "Queering the Schools," *City Journal*, May 29, 2003, available at http://www.city-journal.org/html/13_2_queering_the_schools.html. This article is relatively short, but provides an excellent overview.

214. Fermin Leal, "School Board Defying California Rules on Gender," *Orange Register*, March 9, 2004, available online at http://209.157.64.200/focus/f-news/1096993/posts.

215. McKay, Hill, and Buckler, *A History of Western Society* (Boston/New York: Houghton Mifflin Company 1999, 6th Edition), p. 209. Three sentences before this quotation the text states that according to a "controversial study" Christians had the same attitudes regarding homosexuality as pagans for 300 or 400 years after the birth of Christ. It is unclear from the context on page 209 how much of the text reader is supposed to attribute to the "controversial study." On page 349, however, the authors remove any doubt about what they intend for students and teachers to take away from the passage on page 209: "Early Christians, as we have seen (page 209), displayed no special prejudice against homosexuals." Moreover, according to the authors, "prejudice against homosexuals" didn't emerge until the late twelfth century. While there is a great deal that could be said about the treatment of homosexuality and Christianity and other issues in this textbook, it is notable that the text presupposes that the proper categories for analyzing social phenomena are race, class, and gender. This, of course, is the analytical framework of cultural Marxism. Moreover, it is obvious from the text that regarding homosexuality as a sin is merely "prejudice."

216. GLSEN press release, as quoted in "Homosexual Activists Solidify Hold on School," *American Family Journal*, November/December 2000.

217. GLSEN press release, as quoted in "Homosexual Activists Solidify Hold on School," *American Family Journal*, November/December 2000.

218. See, *e.g.*, Lawrence Morahan, "Parents Protest 'Homosexual Rights' in Virginia School District," CNSNews.com, July 26, 2002.

219. Julie Foster, "California Schools' New Homosexual Curriculum – 2 bills take 'diversity' training to the classroom," WorldNetDaily, December 26, 2000, available at www.worldnetdaily.com/news/article.asp?ARTICLE_ID=21132.

220. Paul Likoudis, "NY Legislator Pilloried for Opposition to 'Safe Schools' Bill," *The Wanderer Press*, July 3, 2003.

221. The issue goes far beyond schools. Using *Lawrence* to advance homosexual marriage is the matter uppermost in the minds of homosexual activists and their opponents at the moment. The end game of the homosexuals, however, is really the criminalization of *criticism* of homosexuality. If you think that this is far-fetched, you should be aware that some European countries have adopted statutes that could make criticizing homosexuality a crime, including preaching the parts of the Bible that point out that homosexuality is a sin. Canada is already far down this path. For examples of some of these developments in Canada, see Jim Brown, "'Heterosexism' under Attack in Canada," *American Family Association*, January 13, 2003, "Teacher to be Suspended One Month without Pay for Writing Against Homosexual Agenda in Schools: Penalty is More than that Given to Teachers Guilty of Criminal Acts," *LifeSite Daily News*, April 16, 2003, available online at www.lifesite.net/Idn/2003/apr/03041603.html. Art Moore, "The Bible as 'Hate Literature'?," WorldNet Daily, October 21, 2002, available online at http://www.worldnetdaily.com/news/article.asp?ARTICLE_ID=29328 . According to Rabbi David Eidensohn, an opponent of New York's Sexual Orientation Nondiscrimination Act ("SONDA"), SONDA is drafted so that it could be used to "force all religious schools to teach that homosexuality and cross-dressing… is acceptable." Apparently, the religious exemptions included in the bill are far weaker and more ambiguous than represented to the public. Consequently, the SONDA exemptions are likely to be interpreted as very limited by New York courts. Further, the ambiguity of the exemptions makes SONDA a perfect tool for litigation by homosexual activists against individuals and small religious organizations that cannot afford the cost of defending themselves. Paul Likoudis, "NY Legislator Pilloried for Opposition to 'Safe Schools' Bill," *The Wanderer Press*, July 3, 2003. Mark Steyn has written an essay detailing how homosexual activists have succeeded in chilling speech critical of homosexuality in Europe, America, and elsewhere. Mark Steyn, "Is Banning the Bible Next?," *Jerusalem Post*, August 13, 2003.

222. Elvia Diaz, "Gays in Arizona Now Feel Free to 'Pursue Agenda'," *The Arizona Republic*, June 27, 2003.

223. Surely even the most benighted souls should be able to see from *Lawrence, Goodridge, Roe v. Wade, McConnell v. FEC,* and a host of other decisions that the "rule of law" exists in the United States vestigially at best. The power of the courts, like the power of Congress and the power of the executive branch, is no longer restrained by meaningful state or federal constitutional moorings. Liberal courts will continue to do whatever they think they can get away with. Among the unpleasant truths that Christians seem so eager to avoid is that the American Republic today is nearly as dead as the Roman Republic in the days of Caesar Augustus.

224. Robert B. Bluey, "Same-Sex Marriage Debate Moves into Schools," CNSNews.com, February 9, 2004, available online at http://www.cnsnews.com//ViewCulture.asp?Page=\Culture\archive\200402\CUL20040209a.html.

Chapter Three - *My Child Is On the Honor Roll*

1. Thomas Sowell, "Artificial Stupidity," *Capitalism Magazine*, March 25, 2003, available at www.capmag.com/article.asp?ID=2607.

2. The information regarding the Horatio Alger Association survey is drawn from Richard Matthews, "Students are Happy: Survey shows teens blind to failure of their schools," *Atlanta-Journal Constitution*, August 9, 2001. For an account of how grades have inflated as S.A.T. scores have declined, see William H. Honan, "S.A.T. Scores Decline Even as Grades Rise," *The New York Times*, September 2, 1998.

3. Jean Johnson, Ann Duffett, Jackie Vine, and Leslie Moye, "Where We Are Now: 12 Things You Need to know about Public Opinion and Public Schools," *Public Agenda 2003*, p. 20.

4. Anne Marie Chaker, "Why Colleges Scoff at Your Kid's GPA," *The Wall Street Journal*, July 24, 2003.

5. Anne Marie Chaker, "Why Colleges Scoff at Your Kid's GPA," *The Wall Street Journal*, July 24, 2003.

6. Daniel Henninger, "A School is for: a) Diversity b) Learning to Read," *The Wall Street Journal*, January 24, 2003. The source of the information is Jay P. Greene and Marcus A. Winters, "Public School Graduation Rates in the United States," Manhattan Institute for Policy Research, *Civic Report 31*, November 2002.

7. Daniel Henninger, "A School is for: a) Diversity b) Learning to Read," *The Wall Street Journal*, January 24, 2003. An additional source of the information is Jay P. Greene and Marcus A. Winters, "Public School Graduation Rates in the United States," Manhattan Institute for Policy Research, *Civic Report 31*, November 2002. Some of the "non-graduating" students may eventually obtain G.E.D.s or complete a high school diploma. It is unlikely, however, that this represents a large percentage of the "non-graduating" students. Note that NCES claims that the graduation rate is 86.5%, but NCES relies upon accurate self-reporting from education officials and also counts G.E.D. students. The problem with public school officials misrepresenting or falsifying dropout data is well known. See, for example, Salatheia Bryant, "Hoping to Quell Controversy, Agency Revamps Dropout Rate," *Houston Chronicle*, March 7, 2003; Mike Snyder, "HISD Insists Dropout Error Unintentional," *Houston Chronicle*, February 11, 2003; Jane Elliot, "Numbers Central to Dropout Fight: Critics Say State Jiggers Data to 'Define Away' the Problem," *Houston Chronicle*, September 13, 2002.

8. Jay P. Greene and Marcus A. Winters, "Public School Graduation Rates in the United States," Manhattan Institute for Policy Research, *Civic Report 31*, November 2002.

9. Vin Suprynowicz, "High Schools Fail Thanks to Grade Inflation and Social Promotion," Toogood Reports, December 5, 2001, available at http:/toogoodreports.com/column/general/suprynowicz/120501.htm.

10. "The Pilgrims' Magna Carta," *The Wall Street Journal* (editorial), November 23, 2001.

11. Craig R. Barrett, "Education SOS," *The Wall Street Journal*, March 4, 2004.

12. As quoted in Declan McCullagh, "US 'Risks Losing No. 1 Ranking' – Barrett," CNET News.com, March 16, 2004, available online at http://news.zdnet.co.uk/business/management/0,39020654,39149313,00.htm.

13. Declan McCullagh, "US 'Risks Losing No. 1 Ranking' – Barrett," CNET News.com, March 16, 2004, available online at http://news.zdnet.co.uk/business/management/0,39020654,39149313,00.htm.

14. A concise account of the transformation of American Christianity referred to in the text can be found in Donald Scott, "Evangelicalism, Revivalism, and the Second Great Awakening," National Humanities Center, available at www.nhc.rtp.nc.us:8080/tserve/nineteen/nkeyinfo/nevanrev.htm.

15. John Adams, *A Dissertation on the Canon and Feudal Law*, available online at www.ashbrook.org/library/18/adams/canonlaw.html. This essay by Adams is well worth reading on many accounts, not least of which is its statement of the objections of Reformed Christians to the Roman Catholicism that existed in the preceding centuries.

16. Page Smith, *The History of America* (Norwich, Conn.: Easton Press, 1976), Vol.I, p.72.

17. Daniel Webster, speaking at Plymouth, Massachusetts in 1820. *The Works of Daniel Webster*, Volumes I and II, Boston, 1851, as cited in John Eidsmoe, *The Christian Legal Advisor* (Milford, Michigan: Mott Media, 1984), p. 289.

18. John Taylor Gatto, *The Underground History of American Education* (Oxford, NY: Oxford Village Press, 2000/2001), p. 57.

19. DuPont de Nemours, *National Education in the United States of America* (Newark: University of Delaware Press, 1923), pp. 3-5, cited by Rousas John Rushdoony, *The Messianic Character of American Education: Studies in the History of the Philosophy of Education* (Nutley, New Jersey: Craig Press, 1963), pp. 329-330.

20. Henry Steele Commager, *The Commonwealth of Learning* (New York: Harper & Row, 1968), pp. 23-24.

21. Lawrence A. Cremin, *American Education: The Colonial Experience 1607-1783* (New York: Harper & Row, 1970), p. 544, as cited in Samuel L. Blumenfeld, *Is Public Education Necessary?* (Boise Idaho: The Paradigm Company, 1985), p. 20.

22. Andrew J. Coulson, *Market Education: The Unknown History* (New Brunswick: Transaction Publishers, 1999), p. 84, citing Carl F. Kaestle, "Studying the History of Literacy," in Kaestle *et al.*, *Literacy in the United States* (New Haven: Yale University Press, 1991), pp. 24-25. With respect to colonial literacy, Coulson cites somewhat lower levels of literacy than other sources and colonial writers, relying on a single source. Nevertheless, Coulson is clear that the advent of compulsory education and our system of government schools did not result from a crisis in literacy or educational opportunity. For anyone with an interest in a broad and analytical treatment of the history of education, Coulson's book is an excellent choice.

23. John Taylor Gatto, *The Underground History of American Education* (Oxford, NY: Oxford Village Press, 2000/2001), p. 52.

24. Page Smith, *The History of America* (Norwich, Conn.: Easton Press, 1976), Vol.I, p.64.

25. For more information on the history of homeschooling, see Patrick Basham, "Home Schooling: From the Extreme to the Mainstream," The Fraser Institute, 2001, pp. 5-6. Among other things, Basham reports that homeschooling was widespread in North America until the 1870s.

26. John Taylor Gatto's *The Underground History of American Education* (Oxford, NY: Oxford Village Press, 2000/2001), and Samuel L. Blumenfeld's *Is Public Education Necessary?* (Boise Idaho: The Paradigm Company, 1985), 1995 edition, provide two informative and highly readable accounts of the history of American education.

27. U.S. Department of Education, National Center for Education Statistics, *Projections of Education Statistics to 2011*, Table 3. Enrollment in public elementary and secondary schools, available at www.nces.ed.gov/pubs2001/proj01/tables/table03.asp.

28. The actual number of schools is probably somewhat higher than 91,000 because that figure comes from 1998-99 data contained in the U.S. Department of Education, National Center for Education Statistics, *Digest of Education Statistics*, Chapter 2, Elementary and Secondary Education, Table 87. Public school districts and public and private elementary and secondary schools: 1929-1930 to 1998-99, available at www.nces.ed.gov/pubs2001/digest/dt087.html.

29. With the exception of (a) the approximation of the total amount currently spent nationally on K-12 education, which is my estimate for the 2003-2004 school year based on projections by the National Center for Educational Statistics, (b) the information cited in note 22 above, and (c) the reference to the amount that it cost to educate a child in New York, which is taken from Gatto at p. xiv, the information in the bullet points come from Kirk A. Johnson and Krista Kafer, "Why Money Will Not Solve America's Education Crisis," *Heritage Foundation Backgrounder,* No. 1448, June 11, 2001, and the U.S. Department of Education, National Center for Education Statistics. Pete Du Pont reports that the aggregate national expenditure for primary and secondary education in 2002-2003 was $480 billion. Pete Du Pont, "Two Decades of Mediocrity: America's Public Schools Still Risky After All These Years," *The Wall Street Journal*, May 5, 2003.

30. Jay P. Greene and Greg Forster, "Widespread Exploitation," *National Review*, February 10, 2003. The authors are quoting spending statistics from the U.S. Department of Education.

31. Stephen Coleman, "Debunking the Manufactured Crisis: Dispelling Myths about Public Education," Center for Market Based Education (1998/1999), p. 4.

32. The information regarding the pupils in long-ago Kansas is taken from Thomas Sowell, *Inside American Education* (New York: The Free Press, 1993), pp. 7-8.

33. Looking back at the *McGuffey's Readers* in 1962 – a full two generations after reading instruction was transformed by "progressive educators" and *McGuffey* was displaced by "Dick and Jane" – Henry Steele Commager observed: "What is striking about the Readers… was that they made so few conscious concessions to immaturity. There was no nonsense about limiting the vocabulary to familiar words, for example. There was no effort always to be entertaining, and no policy of easy familiarity between young and old. There was no drawing back from many of the harsher experiences of the grownup world." Henry Steele Commager, *The Commonwealth of Learning* (New York: Harper & Row, 1968), p. 98. Commager was, by the way, a rather conventional New Deal liberal and was generally disdainful of much of the value-system taught by *McGuffey's Readers*.

34. Students who completed *Ray's Higher Arithmetic* had not only a thorough understanding of the general principles of arithmetic, geometry, and progressions, but were also thoroughly familiar with their application. Thus, *Ray's* requires, for example, that students be able to work with actuarial tables, perform complicated bond payment calculations, and develop a facility for moving among various systems of measurement. Here are a couple of examples from *Ray's New Higher Arithmetic*:

> Q. Find the present value of a perpetuity of $250, deferred 8yr., allowing 6% interest.

> Q. I took a risk of $45000; re-insured at the same rate, $10000 each, in three offices, and $5000 in another; my share of the premium was $262.50: what was the rate?

These examples can be found in *Ray's Higher New Arithmetic* (Milford, Michigan: Mott Media, 1985), pp. 310 and 231. Contrast these problems with the following problems from the 2003 TAKS test, a state-wide accountability test to ensure that Texas children have a world-class education:

> Q. A jeweler bought 2 meters of silver chain. She used 20 centimeters to make a bracelet and 60 centimeters to make a necklace. How many meters of silver chain did she have left?

> F) 1,200 m
> G) 120 m
> H) 1.2 m
> J) 0.12 m

> Q. The results of a random survey showed that 42 out of 80 people plan to vote for Mr. Vu for city council. Which is the best prediction of the total number of votes he will receive if 2,000 people vote?

> F) 25
> G) 50
> H) 120
> J) 1,000

The TAKS questions can be found at www.tea.state.tx.us/student/assessment/resources/release/taks/2003/gr8taks.pdf, pp. 18 and 11. While any number of complaints could be lodged against this comparison, I think that most would be utterly tendentious. To cut through the pettifogging, I suggest you compare *Ray's Arithmetics* to curricula such as *Everyday Math* (currently used in New York City schools) and the many other "connected math," "constructivist math," and "new-new math," curricula widely in use.

35. The facts on the LEX test are reported in Maribel Villalva, "The Science of Reading," *USA Today*, February 23, 2000.

36. Diane Ravitch, "Dumb Students? Or Dumb Textbooks?," *Forbes*, December 16,1996.

37. The facts on the literacy survey are reported in John Taylor Gatto, *The Underground History of American Education*, (Oxford, NY: Oxford Village Press, 2000/2001), pp. 61-62.

38. Craig R. Barrett, "Education SOS," *The Wall Street Journal*, March 4, 2004. Barrett also points out that even though students may take courses called "Algebra II," for example, there is no assurance that the course content actually measures up to the course title.

39. Jackie Hallifax, "Study: High School Tests no too Demanding," Associated Press, June 10, 2004.

40. Karen Arenson, "Study Says U.S. Should Replace States' High School Standards," *The New York Times*, February 10, 2004.

41. The 2000 NAEP results appear to be a continuation of a trend. In the 1990s NAEP results showed that 54% of black high school seniors and 48% of Hispanic seniors could not read at a basic level. When school dropouts are factored in, it is likely that in the 1990s a substantial majority of black and Hispanic teenagers coming out of government schools were illiterate or functionally illiterate. Morton Kondracke, "Turnaround in Test Scores is a Mirage," *Dallas Morning News* (from Roll Call), September 5, 1995.

42. *Education Statistics*, a Heritage Foundation Supplement, May 15, 2001, pp. 1-2. A report by Abigail Thernstrom ("The Racial Gap in Academic Achievement") notes that black 12th grade students' skill in solving scientific problems is at the level of 6th grade whites; the average black high school senior has the math skills of a typical white student half way through ninth grade; and black 17-year-olds read at the level of a white student who isn't quite 13-years-old. As quoted in Walter E. Williams, "The Inferior Education of Black Americans," CNSNews.com, February 5, 2003. See, also, "Achievement Gap," *Education Week*, May 22, 2003.

43. *The Economist*, July 14, 2001, p. 84.

44. These survey results are reported in Sonja Barisic, "U.S. Teens Struggle With History," Associated Press, July 2, 2001.

45. As reported in Karl Zinsmeister, "The 60s Rules in Public Schools," *American Enterprise*, May-June, 1997.

46. As reported in Karl Zinsmeister, "The 60s Rules in Public Schools," *American Enterprise*, May-June, 1997.

47. Paul Recer, "Young Americans Flunk Geography, According to National Geographic Quiz Survey," Associated Press, November 20, 2002.

48. U.S. Department of Education, Office of Educational Research and Improvement, National Center for Educational Statistics. *The Nation's Report Card: U.S. History 2001*, NCES 2002-483, by M.S. Lapp, W.S. Grigg, & Brenda S. H. Tay-Lim. Washington, DC: 2002, Figures 3.12a,b, and c, pp. 42-44. See, also, Diana Jean Schemo, "Students, Especially 12th Graders, Do Poorly on History Tests," *The New York Times*, May 10, 2002.

49. U.S. Department of Education, Office of Educational Research and Improvement, National Center for Educational Statistics. *The Nation's Report Card: U.S. History 2001*, NCES 2002-483, by M.S. Lapp, W.S. Grigg, & Brenda S. H. Tay-Lim. Washington, DC: 2002, Figures 3.6a, b, and c, pp. 29-31. Not surprisingly, the data also show that children in private schools significantly out-perform their government school counterparts. The results among the private school students are divided into two categories: those of Catholic schools and those of non-Catholic private schools (which category

includes both secular private schools and non-Catholic religious private schools). Catholic schools slightly out-performed the non-Catholic private schools overall. The authors of the study attempt to avoid conclusions about the relative educational performance of government and private schools by stating that socioeconomic and sociological factors *may* affect student performance, and should be considered when interpreting the results (p. 40). The results from the Catholic schools, which educate many inner-city and Hispanic immigrant children for a fraction of the money available to government schools, however indicate that the authors' concerns about interpretation may be as much a reflection of their concern over offending the government education lobby as a concern about the use of statistics.

50. U.S. Department of Education, Office of Educational Research and Improvement, National Center for Educational Statistics. *The Nation's Report Card: U.S. History 2001*, NCES 2002-483, by M.S. Lapp, W.S. Grigg, and Brenda S. H. Tay-Lim. Washington, DC: 2002, see Chapter 3 for various comparisons of performance for selected subgroups.

51. George Archibald, "Ignorance of U.S. History Called Threat to Security," *The Washington Times*, April 11, 2003.

52. George Archibald, "Ignorance of U.S. History Called Threat to Security," *The Washington Times*, April 11, 2003.

53. George Archibald, "Ignorance of U.S. History Called Threat to Security," *The Washington Times*, April 11, 2003. For similar observations from Emory University professors, see Jim Wooten, "Students Need a Grasp of the Past," *Atlanta Journal-Constitution*, October 7, 2003.

54. As deficient as American students' knowledge of history is, it appears that some who control government schools think that it needs to be reduced yet further. In January 2004 the Georgia Department of Education announced the changes it is planning to make in the state's history curriculum. Under the proposed standards, high school students' study of world history will be limited to the period from 1500 to the present, instead of from antiquity to the present, as is the case under the existing curriculum. The proposed revision to the 11th grade U.S. history course would allocate two weeks or so to the founding of America and then jump to 1876. This means that everything between the founding of America and the election of Rutherford B. Hayes as President goes down the memory hole. No more teaching about the Louisiana Purchase, the Lewis and Clark Expedition, the War of 1812, the Texas Revolution, the Mexican War, the War Between the States, Reconstruction, or the people associated with them. Yes, that means the Georgia Department of Education is quite content to have Andrew Jackson, Abraham Lincoln, Jefferson Davis, Ulysses S. Grant, Robert E. Lee, William T. Sherman, "Stonewall" Jackson, Stephen Douglas, Henry Clay, and a host of other Americans who profoundly influenced the course of American history disappear from our historical memory. Instead, according to a Georgia history teacher familiar with the proposed standards, the new curriculum encourages teachers to "…have their students write a 1920s radio drama. Teachers are also encouraged to assign essays about dating in the Jazz Age and show segments from 'All in the Family,' 'Good Times', and 'Chico and the Man.'" Well, whatever else can be said about Georgia's proposed U.S. history curriculum, it will be good for the residuals paid to aging actors who performed in old sitcoms. For a more complete account of the Georgia Department of Education's proposed change to the history curriculum, see Joseph Jarrell, "History Curriculum – Dumbing Down Our Past Doesn't Serve Our Future," *Atlanta Journal-Constitution*, January 25, 2004, available online at http://www.ajc.com/opinion/content/opinion/0104/25history.html.

55. The results and contents of the Zogby poll discussed in this section are as reported by Scott Hogenson, "College Seniors No More Knowledgeable than 1950's High School Grads," CNSNews.com, December 18, 2002.

56. Harold W. Stevenson, "A TIMSS Primer: Lessons and Implications for U.S. Education," Thomas B. Fordham Foundation, available at www.edexcellence.net/library/timss.html. Some try to claim that the performance disparity of U.S. fourth graders and twelfth graders is attributable to the adoption in

the primary grades of standards published by the National Council of Teachers of Mathematics, but Stevenson points out that "there is little concrete evidence showing a relationship between the adoption of the standards and students' performance." Stevenson's overall conclusion is that the TIMSS shows that "despite a high financial investment in education, U.S. schools are clearly not among the world's most successful." Stevenson, by the way, is a professor of psychology at the University of Michigan and is considered the foremost U.S. authority on international K-12 education.

57. Herbert J. Walberg, "Spending More While Learning Less: U.S. School Productivity in International Perspective," Thomas B. Fordham Foundation, July 1998, available at www.edexcellence. net/library/timss.html. In a more recent OECD study (known as "PISA") evaluating the ability of 15-year-old students from 32 industrialized countries to apply their reading, mathematics, science skills and knowledge in a "real-world context" the students from the United States were found to be average. Rod Paige, the U.S. Secretary of Education, expressed disappointment with the results. "U.S. Students Average Among International Peers," U.S. Department of Education Press Release, December 4, 2001. The study's results can be found at http://nces.ed.gov/surveys/pisa. It is also notable that PISA is a test designed by the governments of the member countries of the OECD. Perhaps it isn't surprising, then, that the test design resulted in a relatively tight clustering of scores.

58. Herbert J. Walberg, "Spending More While Learning Less: U.S. School Productivity in International Perspective," Thomas B. Fordham Foundation, July 1998, available at www.edexcellence. net/library/timss.html.

59. Jane Margolies, "Move Over, Steinbeck," *The Wall Street Journal*, June 27, 2003, p. W-1.

60. Jane Margolies, "Move Over, Steinbeck," *The Wall Street Journal*, June 27, 2003, p. W-1.

61. Jane Margolies, "Move Over, Steinbeck," *The Wall Street Journal*, June 27, 2003, p. W-1.

62. Earl A. VanDorien, Jr., "Much Ado About a Little Common Sense," *The Seattle Times*, April 5, 2002, p. B-7.

63. Earl A. VanDorien, Jr., "Much Ado About a Little Common Sense," *The Seattle Times*, April 5, 2002, p. B-7.

64. Earl A. VanDorien, Jr., "Much Ado About a Little Common Sense," *The Seattle Times*, April 5, 2002, p. B-7.

65. Earl A. VanDorien, Jr., "Much Ado About a Little Common Sense," *The Seattle Times*, April 5, 2002, p. B-7.

66. Keith Swanson, "Movies Help Explain an R-Rated World," *The Seatttle Times*, April 5, 2002, p. B-7.

67. For a review of the 2000 NAEP science assessment, go to http://nces.ed.gov/nationsreportcard/ science/results/.

68. As reported in Linda Bowles, "Time for Outrage," WorldNetDaily, November 27, 2001.

69. This brief survey of the history of the S.A.T. is based on facts reported by the ETS (which provides a history of the SAT at it website, www.collegeboard.com), Diane Ravitch, "Defining Literacy Downward," *The New York Times*, August 28, 1996, and an interview with Nicholas Lemann by PBS, which is available at http://www.pbs.org/wgbh/pages/frontline/shows/sats/interviews/lemann.html. Lemann is a journalist and the author of *The Big Test – The Secret History of the American Meritocracy*, which examines, among other things, the role the S.A.T. has played in America since the end of World War II.

70. Also embarrassing to the K-12 education industry is the way in which S.A.T. scores have persistently showcased how poorly American schools – the government schools, really – have prepared

blacks and Hispanics for college. This has placed the S.A.T. and ETS squarely in the middle of one of the most poisonous controversies in America – the debate over "affirmative action."

71. For a fairly comprehensive refutation of the education establishment's evasions regarding test results, see Lawrence C. Stedman, "Respecting the Evidence: The Achievement Crisis Remains Real," *Education Policy Analysis*, Volume 4, Number 7, April 4, 1996, available at http://olam.ed.asu.edu/epaa/v4n7.html.

72. Thomas Sowell, *Inside American Education* (New York: The Free Press, 1993), pp. 8-9.

73. Thomas Sowell, *Inside American Education* (New York: The Free Press, 1993), pp. 8-9.

74. John Taylor Gatto, *The Underground History of American Education* (Oxford, NY: Oxford Village Press, 2000/2001), p. 55.

75. Diane Ravitch, "Defining Literacy Downward," *The New York Times*, August 28, 1996.

76. Diane Ravitch, "Defining Literacy Downward," *The New York Times*, August 28, 1996.

77. Diane Ravitch, "Defining Literacy Downward," *The New York Times*, August 28, 1996.

78. "Math SAT Scores Reach 36-Year High," Associated Press, August 26, 2003.

79. Diane Ravitch, "Defining Literacy Downward," *The New York Times*, August 28, 1996.

80. Editorial, "National Testing is No Magic Bullet," *Investor's Business Daily*, September 3, 1997.

81. Tamar Lewin, "Abuse is Feared as SAT Test Changes Disability Policy," *The New York Times*, July 15, 2002.

82. Tamar Lewin, "Abuse is Feared as SAT Test Changes Disability Policy," *The New York Times*, July 15, 2002.

83. Peter Wood, "The SAT Asterisk," *National Review* Online, October 7, 2002.

84. Jane Gross, "Paying for a Disability Diagnosis to Gain Time on College Boards," *The New York Times*, September 25, 2002.

85. Michelle Healy, "Boys Citing Disabilities May Be Skirting SAT Rules," *USA Today*, January 11, 2000.

86. Standardized testing is also under political assault by various racial, ethnic, and gender-oriented special interest groups. In 1997 the Preliminary Scholastic Achievement Test (PSAT) was again changed to improve the scores of girls. See "PSAT Altered to Appease Critics," *Education Reporter*, December 1996. For a detailed account of the various efforts underway to eliminate the S.A.T. and similar "high stakes" tests, see Chris Patterson, "Losing the Race: The SAT & College Admissions," *Veritas Reprint*, Vol. 2, No. 2, available from www.tppf.org.

87. Mark Goldblatt, "The S.A.T. is the Thing: It is a Reliable Measure," *National Review* Online, May 22, 2002.

88. Mark Goldblatt, "The S.A.T. is the Thing: It is a Reliable Measure," *National Review* Online, May 22, 2002.

89. The redesigned S.A.T. verbal test will also include a written essay, while the math test will cover some subjects from algebra II in addition to geometry and algebra I. While it is unclear whether the change in the math test will really amount to requiring an increase in mathematical competence, it is unlikely that the addition of the essay requirement is anything other than a way of trying to obscure the decline in rigor in the verbal test. For a perspective on the redesigned exam from the point of view of the minority community, see "How Changes in the S.A.T. will Affect College-Bound Blacks," *The Journal of Blacks in Higher Education*, August 28, 2003. For another view on the changes to the

S.A.T., see Peter Wood, "The SAT Asterisk," *National Review* Online, October 7, 2002. The bottom line for the redesign, however, is making the exam more acceptable to the university left – especially dropping the analogy portions of the verbal test, which is partly responsible for the large gap in S.A.T. verbal scores between blacks and Hispanics, on the one hand, and whites and Asians, on the other (in 2003 the combined scores for whites were 206 points higher than for blacks and 158 points higher than for Hispanics). The desire to eliminate the portions of the S.A.T. verbal test that demonstrate skills in verbal reasoning is significantly influenced by the need to conceal the damage government schools are doing to these minorities. Unlike mathematics, where necessary skills for the S.A.T. can often be sharpened relatively rapidly through taking a few additional courses, the highly nuanced verbal reasoning skills measured by the pre-1994 S.A.T. verbal test are developed over a long period of time. Given what has happened to the quality of the preparation of teachers, the proliferation of anti-intellectual education fads in schools, and the racism of low expectations prevalent in government schools, it is no surprise that black and Hispanic students in general are struggling. Both Thomas Sowell and Walter Williams have written of how lowering of standards in inner city schools has harmed black children. Sowell, for example, points out that the test scores of black students in Harlem in the 1940s were comparable to the test scores of white working class students on the lower east side of New York. The IQ tests given during World War I disclosed that black soldiers from New York, Pennsylvania, Illinois, and Ohio scored higher than white soldiers from Georgia, Arkansas, Kentucky, and Mississippi. Clearly, as Sowell points out, the problem today is not that blacks cannot perform; it is that their "friends" (read "liberal elites") do not expect them to perform. Even today, Walter Williams notes that at the Fredrick Douglass Academy in Harlem, a predominantly black government school, high standards of performance are required and the children deliver. Ninety-eight percent of Fredrick Douglass's students graduate with Regents diplomas, 95% go on to college, and the students' performance on Advanced Placement tests has led *Newsweek* to include the school on its list of the best public schools in the country. Thomas Sowell, "Friends of Blacks," *Jewish World Review*, September 4, 2002, and Walter Williams, "Affirmative Action or Racism II," www.townhall.com, February 5, 2003. Some upper middle-class white parents have also been jumping on the anti-testing bandwagon. It appears that they don't like tests that disclose how little their children really know, and they especially don't want their children's failure to master various skills and knowledge to have consequences. Anyone interested in this phenomenon should visit the website for an organization known as "Fairtest" (www.fairtest.org). Not surprisingly, Fairtest and the NEA have similar views regarding "high-stakes" testing, as a visit to the NEA's website will plainly show (www.nea.org).

90. Charles Murray, "SAT Reform Fails the Needy," *The Wall Street Journal*, July 3, 2002, p. A10.

91. See Charles Murray, "SAT Reform Fails the Needy," *The Wall Street Journal*, July 3, 2002, p. A10.

92. Steve Giegerich, "Math Scores on ACT, SAT Diverge," HoustonChronicle.com (Associated Press), September 7, 2003. Available online at http:/www.chron.com/cs/CDA/ssistory.mpl/nation/2087135.

93. Steve Giegerich, "Math Scores on ACT, SAT Diverge," HoustonChronicle.com (Associated Press), September 7, 2003. Available online at http:/www.chron.com/cs/CDA/ssistory.mpl/nation/2087135.

94. Steve Giegerich, "Math Scores on ACT, SAT Diverge," HoustonChronicle.com (Associated Press), September 7, 2003. Available online at http:/www.chron.com/cs/CDA/ssistory.mpl/nation/2087135.

95. Steve Giegerich, "Math Scores on ACT, SAT Diverge," HoustonChronicle.com (Associated Press), September 7, 2003. Available online at http:/www.chron.com/cs/CDA/ssistory.mpl/nation/2087135.

96. John Jacob Cannell, *Nationally Normed Elementary Achievement Testing in America's Public Schools: How All Fifty States Are Above the National Average* (Daniels, W.Va.: Friends for Education, 1987), pp. 1-2. For a discussion of the controversy created by Cannell's work, see Myron Lieberman, *Public Education: An Autopsy* (Harvard Press: 1993), pp. 82-83. According to a conversation I had with Robert L. Linn, it appears that Cannell's investigation of standardized testing data grew out of the disconnect he noticed between the academic skills of teenagers he observed and his state's reported standardized test results.

97. See, *e.g.*, Myron Lieberman, *Public Education: An Autopsy* (Cambridge, Ma.: Harvard University Press, 1993), pp. 82-83.

98. Thomas Toch and Betsy Wagner, "Schools for Scandal," *U.S. News & World Report*, April 27, 1992.

99. Robert L. Linn, "Assessments and Accountability," *ER* Online, Vol. 29, Number 2, March 2000, p. 6.

100. Thomas Toch; Betsy Wagner, "Schools for Scandal," *U.S. News & World Report*, April 27, 1992.

101. Robert L. Linn, "Assessments and Accountability," *ER* Online, Vol. 29, Number 2, March 2000, at p. 4.

102. Richard Innes, "The NAEP is Losing Credibility," *Education Reporter*, July 2000, and "Exclusions Mar 2000 NAEP Math Gains," *Education Reporter*, October 2001.

103. Richard Innes, "The NAEP is Losing Credibility," *Education Reporter*, July 2000.

104. Another technique for manipulating scores upward is through the use of "accommodations." "Accommodations" give disabled students special treatment in taking the test – extra time, for example. The score inflating potential of granting accommodations is obvious. Still, there is reason for parents and taxpayers to take heart that the integrity of NAEP results is being protected vigilantly against abusive accommodations. In a rare demonstration of bureaucratic courage in demanding accountability in testing, those in charge of the NAEP have prohibited having "its reading assessment read aloud to a student." Lynn Olson, "NAEP Board Worries States Excluding too Many from Tests," *Education Week*, March 19, 2003. As early as 1999 the Commissioner of Education Statistics, Pascal D. Forgione, Jr., expressed concern over exclusion rates in connection with the 1998 NAEP reading assessment. As Forgione observed: "jurisdictions with larger increases in total exclusion percentages also tended to have larger score increases." "NAEP State Reading Scores and Exclusion Rates," *Commissioner's Statement*, May 14, 1999, available from the National Center for Educational Statistics online at http://nces.ed.gov/Pressrelease/naep599.asp.

105. Richard Innes, "The NAEP is Losing Credibility," *Education Reporter*, July 2000.

106. Richard Innes as quoted in "Exclusions Mar 2000 NAEP Math Gains," *Education Reporter*, October 2001.

107. "Exclusions Mar 2000 NAEP Math Gains," *Education Reporter*, October 2001.

108. "Exclusions Mar 2000 NAEP Math Gains," *Education Reporter*, October 2001.

109. Kathleen Kennedy Manzo, "NAEP Reading Scores: Progress Mixed with Decline," *Education Week*, June 20, 2003.

110. Kathleen Kennedy Manzo, "NAEP Reading Scores: Progress Mixed with Decline," *Education Week*, June 20, 2003. Also reported by Manzo is that officials from the Department of Education have been looking into a possible relationship between Delaware's improved NAEP reading scores and its dramatically increased exclusion rates. Those officials told Manzo that "there is *currently* no indication… that exclusion rates had significantly affected the scores." (emphasis added). Well, I suppose it all depends on the definition of "significantly" and "currently." More to the point, it is obvious that the additional 7% of students were excluded because they would do badly on the test and that excluding so many poor performers is bound to move the test results in a favorable direction. The unwillingness of the Department of Education to confront the obvious abuse of exclusions and accommodations squarely and forcefully illustrates how inbred the education industry is and why it has taken outsiders such as Dr. Cannell to point out what a fraud testing "for accountability" has become. For more on the exclusions from the 2002 NAEP reading assessment, see Lynn Olson, "NAEP Exclusion Rates Continue to Bedevil Policymakers," *Education Week*, May 28, 2003.

111. Lynn Olson, "NAEP Board Worries States Excluding too Many from Tests," *Education Week*, March 19, 2003.

112. Lynn Olson, "NAEP Board Worries States Excluding too Many from Tests," *Education Week*, March 19, 2003.

113. Thomas Toch and Betsy Wagner, "Schools for Scandal," *U.S. News & World Report*, April 27, 1992.

114. "NAEP Targeted for Change," *Education Reporter*, May 1997.

115. Apart from trying to manipulate test results, the main response of the education industry to the dismal story told by standardized tests has been to wage a public relations war against testing itself. That public relations effort has so misrepresented the facts that the president of the National Council on Measurement in Education felt it necessary to appeal to the organization's members to assist in counteracting the misleading stories and reporting about testing. John Fremer, "A Message from Your President," *NCME Newsletter*, December 2000, Volume 8, Number 4.

116. For examples of this type of reporting on the TAAS, see Janet Elliott, "Sophomores Soar in TAAS Exit Exam,"www.HoustonChronicle.com, April 18, 2002, and "Texas Students Pass Spring TAAS Test at the Highest Rate Ever: 82%," www.HoustonChronicle.com, May 23, 2001.

117. Janet Elliot and Salatheia Bryant, "With Scoring Standards Lowered, More Passing TAAS," HoustonChronicle.com, May 16, 2002. According to state officials, of course, the standards were lowered because the test was made "harder." Some familiar with the TAAS say, however, that it was not made more difficult. The decline of SAT and ACT scores while TAAS pass rates "soared" make it quite unlikely, however, that the TAAS was testing harder material.

118. Melanie Markley, "TAAS Scores Rose as SATs Fell," *Houston Chronicle*, June 5, 2004. For a good summary of how Texas educators are deceiving the public about academic performance in Texas schools, see Rick Casey, "Texas Schools are Like Enron, " *Houston Chronicle*, June 1, 2004.

119. Eric Hanson, "TAAS Scheme Investigation Leads to School Officials' Resignations," *Houston Chronicle*, June 19, 2002.

120. Janet Elliott, "TAKS Passing Scores May Be Lowered: Board Aims to Toughen Passing Scores after '03," *Houston Chronicle*, November 15, 2002.

121. Connie Mabin, "Questions, Answers About TAKS," Associated Press, December 2, 2002. Having preemptively lowered the passing standards for the 2003 administration of the TAKS, which was billed as a temporary expedient, the State Board of Education appears likely to continue the lower standards for the 2004 TAKS. Jane Elliott, "Tougher Standards for TAKS May Wait: State Officials Fear Rise in Failure Rates," *Houston Chronicle*, September 12, 2003.

122. Janet Elliott, "Perry Defends TAKS Against Rising Concern," *Houston Chronicle*, January 25, 2003.

123. Janet Elliott, "Perry Defends TAKS Against Rising Concern," *Houston Chronicle*, January 25, 2003.

124. Janet Elliott, "Perry Defends TAKS Against Rising Concern," *Houston Chronicle*, January 25, 2003.

125. Rebecca Miller, "N.C. Education Officials Throw Out Low Test Scores, Say Test to Blame," *Tampa Bay* Online, July 11, 2002.

126. Heather Hare, "Mills Stands by Regents Standards," *Rochester Democrat and Chronicle*, July 30, 2003. Apparently only 28% of the seniors taking the exam passed (excluding seniors in the NYC schools). Joe Williams, "39 = 55 in Regent Math Test," *The New York Daily News*, August 30, 2003.

127. Joe Williams, "39 = 55 in Regents' Math Test," *The New York Daily News*, August 30, 2003.

128. Joe Williams, "39 = 55 in Regents' Math Test," *The New York Daily News*, August 30, 2003.

129. Karen W. Arenson, "New York to Lower the Bar for High School Graduation," *The New York Times*, October 8, 2003.

130. Karen W. Arenson, "New York to Lower the Bar for High School Graduation," *The New York Times*, October 8, 2003.

131. Joe Williams, "39 = 55 in Regents' Math Test," *The New York Daily News*, August 30, 2003.

132. As quoted in Rick Karlin, "Regents' Diplomas Remain in Reach," *Albany Times Union*, July 9, 2003. Another reason education bureaucrats lowered the passing standards is that non-Asian minority students flunk the Regents' exams at much higher rates than white and Asian students. This bigotry of low expectations has been criticized by Barbara Clark, a black Assemblywoman from Queens. Speaking against the dilution of standards, Assemblywoman Clark stated: "When a majority of the students in the New York City public school system were white, we expected high standards.... Why is it that high standards shouldn't be the norm when 85 percent of the students are children of color? That they should achieve less than anyone else? I reject that argument." Carl Campanile, "Lowering Academic Standards Is Bigoted: POL," *New York Post*, October 16, 2003.

133. This account of the *Times'* story is based on "N.Y. City Teachers Helped Students Cheat on Tests," *Education Reporter*, January 2000. See also, "Teachers Accused of Cheating on Students' Tests," *School Board News*, January 11, 2000.

134. Jodi Wilgoren, "Cheating on Statewide Tests Is Reported in Massachusetts," *The New York Times*, February 25, 2000. The account of the cheating scandal in Massachusetts is based on Wilogren's article.

135. Aimee Edmondson, "Model school cheated, officials say - Test scandal ousts Caldwell principal," www.GoMemphis.com, March 13, 2003.

136. Aimee Edmondson, "Model school cheated, officials say - Test scandal ousts Caldwell principal," www.GoMemphis.com, March 13, 2003.

137. Aimee Edmondson, "Model school cheated, officials say - Test scandal ousts Caldwell principal," www.GoMemphis.com, March 13, 2003.

138. Aimee Edmondson, "Model school cheated, officials say - Test scandal ousts Caldwell principal," www.GoMemphis.com, March 13 2003.

139. Manuel Perez-Rivas, "Accused Teachers Discuss Actions," *The Washington Post*, May 12, 2001.

140. Manuel Perez-Rivas, "Accused Teachers Discuss Actions," *The Washington Post*, May 12, 2001.

141. Barbara Kantrowitz and Daniel McGinn, "When Teachers are Cheaters," and Evan Thomas and Pat Wingert, "Bitter Lessons," *Newsweek*, June 19, 2000.

142. Barbara Kantrowitz and Daniel McGinn, "When Teachers are Cheaters," and Evan Thomas and Pat Wingert, "Bitter Lessons," *Newsweek*, June 19, 2000, and Robert C. Johnson and Michelle Galley, "Austin District Charged with Test Tampering," *Education Week*, April 14, 1999.

143. Rosalind Rossi and Anne Sweeney, "Teachers Face Firing in Cheating Scandal," *Chicago Sun Times*, October 2, 2002.

144. Rosalind Rossi and Anne Sweeney, "Teachers Face Firing in Cheating Scandal," *Chicago Sun Times*, October 2, 2002.

145. Rosalind Rossi and Anne Sweeney, "Teachers Face Firing in Cheating Scandal," *Chicago Sun Times*, October 2, 2002.

146. Rosalind Rossi and Anne Sweeney, "Teachers Face Firing in Cheating Scandal," *Chicago Sun Times*, October 2, 2002.

147. For example, officials in California, according to Levitt, have not responded to requests to use his statistical analysis there. Rosalind Rossi and Anne Sweeney, "Teachers Face Firing in Cheating Scandal," *Chicago Sun Times*, October 2, 2002.

148. Thomas Toch and Betsy Wagner, "Schools for Scandal," *U.S. News & World Report*, April 27, 1992.

149. Daniel Golden, "With Eye on Scores, Schools Fight Over Gifted Kids," *The Wall Street Journal*, February 4, 2004, A-1. My account of these goings-on in Iowa, Missouri , and Ohio is based on the facts reported in Mr. Golden's story.

150. As quoted in Daniel Golden, "With Eye on Scores, Schools Fight Over Gifted Kids," *The Wall Street Journal*, February 4, 2004, A-1.

151. Maria Cougras Pappas characterized these actions as "sabotage." See, Daniel Golden, "With Eye on Scores, Schools Fight Over Gifted Kids," *The Wall Street Journal*, February 4, 2004, A-1.

152. As quoted in Daniel Golden, "With Eye on Scores, Schools Fight Over Gifted Kids," *The Wall Street Journal*, February 4, 2004, A-1.

153. Robert L. Linn, "Assessments and Accountability," *ER* Online, Vol. 29, Number 2, March 2000, at p. 4.

154. Jessica L. Sandham, "Exam-Testing Breaches Put Focus on Security," *Education Week*, April 7, 1999.

155. This second proposal was discussed in the Sandham article in *Education Week* cited above. In that article the director of the Council of Chief State School Officers, Wayne Martin, expressed concern that "student absences, uncertain weather, and district-level scheduling conflicts" would make administration of the tests on a given day difficult. He was also concerned that third-party administration would be cost prohibitive. What Mr. Martin seems to be overlooking is that school districts have long managed to schedule third-party administered tests such as the S.A.T. and the ACT and that the cost of third-party administration, according to Stephen Klein, is approximately $1.00 per student, which is hardly prohibitive. The response to the third-party administration proposal that most clearly indicates what is wrong with the education establishment came from Lisa Graham Keegan, who is in charge of Arizona's government schools. According to Keegan, third-party administration of standardized tests is bad idea because it might hurt educators feelings… it says that they can't be trusted. Inexplicably, Keegan also thinks it would be a sin against the postmodern virtue of inclusiveness: "I feel strongly that [educators] own this test, and I would rather err or the side of inclusion." Well, maybe Keegan's point is this: We can't adopt testing procedures that would show what a bad job our highly trained education professionals are doing because it would hurt their feelings and it might result in their "exclusion" – as in getting fired.

156. "Disconnecting Children from 'Connected' Math," *Education Reporter*, October 1999. See, also, Lynne V. Cheney, "The Latest Education Disaster: Whole Math," *The Weekly Standard*, August 4, 1997.

157. Marianne M. Jennings, "'Rainforest' Algebra Course Teaches Everything But Algebra," *Christian Science Monitor*, April 2, 1996. Anemona Hartocollis, "The New Flexible Math Meets Parental Rebellion," *The New York Times*, April 27, 2000.

158. "Disconnecting Children from 'Connected' Math," *Education Reporter*, October 1999.

159. "Disconnecting Children from 'Connected' Math," *Education Reporter*, October 1999.

160. Matthew Clavel, "How not to Teach Math: New York Chancellor Klein's Plan Doesn't Compute," *City Journal*, Winter 2003, Vol. 13, No. 1. This article, which chronicles the experience of a

young math teacher in the New York City schools, is well worth seeking out for its concrete account of just what this approach to math does to children and classrooms. With respect to reading instruction, the New York City schools discontinued "Success for All," a strong phonics-based reading curriculum whose effectiveness has been shown in over a dozen controlled studies, in favor of a "balanced literacy" curriculum called "Month by Month Phonics." "Balanced literacy" is educrat-speak for a whole language curriculum that has been repackaged by adding a little phonics. Sol Stern, "NYC Schools: Aiming for Illiteracy," *New York Post*, April 4, 2003.

161. John Ankerberg, Craig Branch, and John Weldon, *Thieves of Innocence* (Eugene, OR: Harvest House Publishers, 1993), p. 121. See also, Joyce Milton, *The Road to Malpsychia: Humanistic Psychology and our Discontents* (San Francisco: Encounter Books, 2002), Chapter 8 "The Malpsychian Classroom."

162. John Ankerberg, Craig Branch, and John Weldon, *Thieves of Innocence* (Eugene OR: Harvest House Publishers, 1993), p. 121.

163. The Nashville government schools recently provided an example of how some of our highly trained education professionals and parents obsess over student "self-esteem." As reported by Matt Gouras of the Associated Press, it seems that the Nashville school district will no longer allow its schools to post their honor rolls. After receiving a few complaints from parents allegedly concerned that their children would be ridiculed for not being on the honor roll, the school district banned public disclosure of the honor roll. Then, the district lawyers got into the act, advising the district that disclosing who was on the honor roll without student permission might violate state privacy laws. Now the Nashville school district is considering banning spelling bees, academic pep rallies, and hanging good work by students in the hallways. Schools across Tennessee are also considering following suit. For some inside the Nashville schools, this is a progressive move. According to one Nashville elementary school principal, Steven Baum, it would be better to get rid of the honor roll, spelling bees, and publicly graded events altogether. He also doesn't like competitive games: "They just don't fit my world view." As quoted in Matt Gouras, "Nashville Schools to Stop Honor Roll, Embarrass Underachievers," *Chicago Sun-Times*, January 25, 2004, available online at http://www.suntimes.com/output/education/cst-nws-honor25.html.

164. *Newsweek*, cover article, Feb. 17, 1992, pp. 46-48.

165. Thomas Sowell, *Inside American Education* (New York: The Free Press, 1993), p.3.

166. Thomas Sowell, *Inside American Education* (New York: The Free Press, 1993), p. 5.

167. James Traub, "Multiple Intelligence Disorder," *New Republic*, October 26,1998. In *The Schools We Need*, E.D. Hirsch, Jr., points out that Gardner's theory is not widely accepted by psychologists. See E.D. Hirsch, Jr., *The Schools We Need*, (New York: Doubleday, 1996), pp.105; 260-61.

168. For an interesting account of how schools in China's cities are developing a generation of exceptionally well-educated children, see Nicholas D. Kristof, "China's Super Kids," *The New York Times*, November 22, 2002.

169. "The Trouble with Self-Esteem," *U.S. News & World Report*, April 1, 1990, p. 16.

170. "The Trouble with Self-Esteem," *U.S. News & World Report*, April 1, 1990, p. 16.

171. *Newsweek*, cover article, Feb. 17, 1992, pp. 46-48.

172. "Beliefs About Low Self-Esteem Are Myths," *Independent* ONLINE, November 28, 2001, available at www.iol.co.za/index.php?click_id=31&art_id=qw1006926841898S322&set_id=1.

173. W.R. Coulson, "Sex, Drugs, and Schoolchildren: What Went Wrong?," included as Chapter 15 in John Ankerberg, Craig Branch, and John Weldon, *Thieves of Innocence* (Eugene, OR: Harvest House Publishers, 1993), pp. 123, 268-271.

174. W.R. Coulson, "Sex, Drugs, and Schoolchildren: What Went Wrong?," included as Chapter 15 in John Ankerberg, Craig Branch, and John Weldon, *Thieves of Innocence* (Eugene, OR: Harvest House Publishers, 1993), p. 268.

175. Discussions of this controversy can be found in Karen Diegmueller, "Revise History Standards, Two Panels Advise," *Education Week*, October 18, 1995; Jim Morris, "How Not to Set National History Standards," [journal] (sic), March-April 1998, Volume 2, Number 2, available at http://civnet. org/journal/issue6/revjmorr.htm, and Christopher Bates, "'History on Trial' Littered with Sloppy Contradictions," *The Daily Bruin*, November 20, 1997.

176. Lynne Cheney, "The End of History," *The Wall Street Journal*, October 24, 1994.

177. The following description of the history standards is largely based on Jim Morris, "How Not to Set National History Standards," [journal] (sic), March-April 1998, Volume 2, Number 2, available online at http://civnet.org/journal/issue6/revjmorr.htm, Lynne Cheney, "The End of History," *The Wall Street Journal*, October 24, 1994, and Diane Ravitch and Arthur Schlesinger, Jr., "The New Improved History Standards," Thomas R. Fordham Foundation, available online at www.edexcellence. net/fordham/foreports.html.

178. The National Council for Social Studies is a 26,000-member organization of history, sociology, geography, political science, psychology, and economics teachers. Kay S. Hymowitz describes the far-left orientation of this organization in "Anti-Social Studies: So Many Ideas for Improving the Curriculum – All of Them Bad," *The Weekly Standard*, Vol. 007, Issue 33, May 6, 2002.

179. Kay S. Hymowitz "Anti-Social Studies: So Many Ideas for Improving the Curriculum – All of Them Bad," *The Weekly Standard*, Vol. 007, Issue 33, May 6, 2002.

180. For an in-depth look at "Afrocentrism," see Mary Leftowitz, *Not Out of Africa: How Afrocentrism Became an Excuse to Teach Myth as History* (New York: Basic Books, 1996). One of the more bizarre theories of some Afrocentrists is that black children should be taught "ebonics" – black street slang – in school. Apparently, many educators are too intimidated by the threat of being denounced as a "racist" to object vocally. See Nicoholas Stix, "Students Hooked on 'Ebonics' are being Groomed for Failure," *Insight Magazine*, June 3, 2002, available online at http://www.insightmag.com/main. cfm?include=detail&storyid=254234.

181. Debra Viadero, "A School of Their Own," *Education Week*, October 16, 1996.

182. Kathleen Kennedy Manzo, "Proposal to Scuttle Afrocentric Curricula Sparks Protest," *Education Week*, January 15, 1997.

183. Kathleen Kennedy Manzo, "Proposal to Scuttle Afrocentric Curricula Sparks Protest," *Education Week*, January 15, 1997.

184. Kathleen Kennedy Manzo, "Proposal to Scuttle Afrocentric Curricula Sparks Protest," *Education Week*, January 15, 1997.

185. Douglas Kennedy, "Texas History Gets New Mexican Twist," Fox News, May 30, 2002, and Michael Quinn Sullivan, "Texans' Way of Life at Stake in Textbook Hearings," *Houston Chronicle*, August 11, 2002.

186. Henry Lamb has written a fascinating piece on how Holt, Rinehart and Winston has allowed its middle-school vocabulary text, *Vocabulary Workshop*, to become a "Green" propaganda vehicle. The lesson titles include "Balancing society and the environment: Global warming," "Jean of the Environment," and "What is the forecast for Brazil's rain forest?," as well as other environmentally-themed lessons. In the lesson on global warming, for example, the children are instructed in environmentalism through sentences demonstrating correct word usage. For example: "Urge people to support a candidate running for public office who has a concern about the environment...." The study word is

"candidate." Lamb points out that there are many examples like this, and that what is ostensibly an English workbook has "a strong anti-capitalist, anti-corporate and anti-human tone." Henry Lamb, "Green Zombies: Henry Lamb Explains Eco-Propaganda Immersion Plan," WorldNetDaily.com, June 15, 2002.

187. George Neumayr, "Dumbed Down and Dumber Still," TheAmericanProwler.org, January 15, 2003, and Michelle Malkin, "Hip Hop Hogwash in the Schools," Vdare.com January 14, 2003. Apart from its being an utter waste of time, there are additional reasons to be concerned about the influence of hip-hop and rap "music." By now most are aware that hip-hop and rap are violent, misogenistic, and utterly obscene. One black researcher, Ronald Ferguson of the Kennedy School of Government, however, also claims that hip-hop and rap have negatively affected academic achievement by black students. In 1988, 35% of black children read daily for pleasure. By 1992, that percentage had declined to 14%. Moreover, during that period the progress black students had made in standardized test results began to be reversed. Ferguson argues that hip-hop is one factor contributing to this decline in reading and test results. "Study Ties Hip-Hop, Rap Music to Drop in Test Scores," *UPI*, June 26, 2000. Nicole Martin, "Fears Over Lure of Rap's Violence and Obscenity," *The Daily Telegraph*, August 21, 2000. Of course, hip-hop and rap are now part of the mainstream youth culture, and there is every reason to believe that it has the same negative influence on any child who listens to it regularly.

188. "Policing the Vocabulary: Textbook Sensitivity Goes Fanatic," *The Sacramento Bee*, February 27, 2003; Anita Vogel, "Calif. Offers Textbook Case of Political Correctness," Fox News, April 30, 2003.

189. N.R. Kleinfeld, "The Elderly Man and the Sea? Test Sanitizes Literary Texts," *The New York Times*, June 2, 2002.

190. Diane Ravitch, "Cut on the Bias," *The Wall Street Journal*, July 1, 2003, p. A-10.

191. Underlying all of these distortions of curricular standards is cultural Marxism, a form of Marxism developed by such radical leftists as Antonio Gramsci, Theodor Adorno, Max Horkeimer, and the more familiar Herbert Marcuse. These Marxists realized that Marxism could not overcome the West militarily or economically because of the strength of Western Civilization. Instead, they and those influenced by them have pursued a strategy of capturing institutions and using those institutions to transform Western societies. This is why government schools are now so dangerous. It is not simply that they make our children ignorant; they are creating a "false consciousness" – a delusional view of reality – in our children and inculcating them with anti-Christian, destructive values. Of course, most of the people helping to implement this "Gramscian vision," including those who work in government schools, have no idea what they are doing. They are simply carrying out the imperatives of the institutions for which they work, but that work is increasingly defined and structured to implement a version of cultural Marxism. Research by organizations such as the Nehemiah Institute show how effectively our children are being proselytized by the cultural Marxists.

192. Saul K. Padover, *Thomas Jefferson on Democracy*, (New York: Appleton-Century Company, Inc., 1939), p. 89.

Chapter Four - *A Blackboard Jungle*

1. Thomas Toch, *et al.*, "Violence in the Schools," *U.S. News & World Report*, November 8, 1993, pp. 31-37.

2. P. Kaufman, X. Chen, S.P. Choy, S.A. Ruddy, A.K. Miller, K.A. Chandler, C.D. Chapman, M.R. Rand, and P. Klaus, *Indicators of School Crime and Safety*, 1999. U.S. Departments of Education and Justice. NCES 1999-057/NCJ-178906 Washington, D.C.: 1999, figure 1.2. "Serious violent crimes" are defined as including rape, sexual assault, robbery, and aggravated assault. The statistics reported in figure 1.2 appear to include the data for students ages 12 through 18 in both government and private

schools, and represent the combined incidence of serious violent crimes at school and on the way to and from school (for example, on school buses). The rate of victimization is reported as 10 per 1,000 for boys and 5 per 1,000 for girls. Note that in figure 2.1, however, the data show that in a six-month period of 1995 students ages 12 through 19 in government schools were 100% more likely to be victims of "violent crime" at school than students in private schools. In this case, a "violent crime" includes physical attacks or taking property from a student directly by force, weapons, or threats. Thus, this category is broader than the category of "serious violent crimes" reported in figure 1.2, but there is no reason to think that "serious violent crimes" are a larger proportion of "violent crimes" reported by private school students than they are among government school students. Further, there is no reason to think private school students suffer higher rates of victimization going to and from school than government school students. As a result, using the data shown in figure 1.2 as representing the rate at which government school students suffer serious violent crimes probably *understates* the rate at which government school students are victimized because the data from the private schools tend to pull down the average. The data in both figures 1.2 and 2.1 were collected by the Bureau of Justice Statistics in 1995 and 1997 National Crime Victimization Surveys.

3. The data on assaults on inmates in U.S. federal prisons are taken from James J. Stephan, *Census of State and Federal Correctional Facilities, 1995*, U.S. Department of Justice, Bureau of Justice Statistics, August 1997, Table 16, p. 13, NCJ-164266. The "assaults" cited in the 1995 Census were reported in response to the question: "Between July 1, 1989, and June 30, 1990, were there any inmate-inflicted physical or sexual assaults on inmates?" Arguably, this is a lower threshold for reporting than the "serious violent crimes" category reported in the schools data. Consequently, it may be that "serious violent crimes" would only be a subset of "assaults on inmates" if that data were collected for purposes of the prisons' census, whereas, on the other hand, "serious violent crimes" might involve the reporting of a broader range of incidents than the "major assault" category used in reporting by Canadian authorities (as discussed in the footnote below).

4. "Violence and Suicide in Canadian Institutions: Some Recent Statistics," Volume 4, Number 3, 1992 – *Prison Violence and Inmate Suicide and Self-Injury*. A "major assault" is defined as a deliberate attack causing grievous bodily harm (examples are unconsciousness, broken bones, knife wounds, etc.). While "serious violent crimes" reported concerning American students appears to be a broader category than "major assaults," the victimization rate for "serious violent crimes" is more than three times that for "major assaults." Consequently, it could still well be that the rate of what the Canadians refer to as "major assaults" is higher among American students in urban middle and high schools than among inmates in Canadian prisons.

5. By 1995, the rate of "assaults on inmates" in federal prisons had risen to 12.4 per 1,000. James J. Stephan, *Census of State and Federal Correctional Facilities, 1995*, U.S. Department of Justice, Bureau of Justice Statistics, August 1997, Table 16, p. 13, NCJ-164266. No data exist for the federal prisons for 1997.

6. P. Kaufman, X. Chen, S.P. Choy, S.A. Ruddy, A.K. Miller, K. A. Chandler, C.D. Chapman, M.R. Rand, and P. Klaus, *Indicators of School Crime and Safety*, 1999. U.S. Departments of Education and Justice. NCES 1999-057/NCJ-178906 Washington, D.C.: 1999, figure 1.2.

7. Given that the prison population is overwhelmingly male, the higher rates of victimization for boys in government schools arguably would be a better measure for comparing the rates of violence in prison and government schools. P. Kaufman, X. Chen, S.P. Choy, S.A. Ruddy, A.K. Miller, K.A. Chandler, C.D. Chapman, M.R. Rand, and P. Klaus, *Indicators of School Crime and Safety*, 1999. U.S. Departments of Education and Justice. NCES 1999-057/NCJ-178906 Washington, D.C.: 1999, figure 1.2.

8. This information can be found in the Executive Summary and in figures 2.1, 3.1, 10.1, 12.1, 12.2, 13.1, and 14.1 to P. Kaufman, X. Chen, S.P. Choy, S.A. Ruddy, A.K. Miller, K.A. Chandler, C.D. Chapman, M.R. Rand, and P. Klaus, *Indicators of School Crime and Safety*, 1999. U.S. Departments of Education and Justice. NCES 1999-057/NCJ-178906 Washington, D.C.: 1999.

9. This data appears to include public and private school students. Because students at private schools report victimization by violent crimes at a substantially lower rate than do students at government schools, students in government schools in 1997 were very probably being threatened or injured with a weapon at school at a rate *higher* than 7%.

10. These percentages appear to be based on aggregate data from both government and private schools. Consequently, because private school students are victimized at lower rates than students in government schools, the aggregate data probably understate the severity of the problem in government schools. Research by Alex Alvarez and Ronet Bachman also confirms that students at public schools have a higher level of fear of assault than students at private schools. Alex Alvarez and Ronet Bachman, "Predicting the Fear of Assault at School and While Going to and from School in an Adolescent Population," *Violence and Victims*, 12 (1) (1997), pp. 69-86.

11. Notably, during the same time period teachers in private schools reported that they were threatened with physical injury by students at a rate *less than one-third* that of teachers in government schools, and teachers in private schools were only one-half as likely to be physically attacked by a student.

12. If you think that this is strictly an inner city phenomenon, think again. Teachers in rural public schools reported being attacked by students physically 50% more often than their private school counter-parts.

13. Devoe, J.F., Peter, K., Kaufman, P., Ruddy, S.A., Miller, A.K., Planty, M., Snyder, T.D., and Rand, M.R. *Indicators of School Crime and Safety:2003*. NCES 2004-004/NCJ 201257. U.S. Departments of Education and Justice. Washington, D.C.: 2003.

14. Devoe, J.F., Peter, K., Kaufman, P., Ruddy, S.A., Miller, A.K., Planty, M., Snyder, T.D., and Rand, M.R. *Indicators of School Crime and Safety:2003*. NCES 2004-004/NCJ 201257. U.S. Departments of Education and Justice. Washington, D.C.: 2003, p. 10. In 2001, street gangs were reported as present at lower levels in both public and private schools, although, as in the 1999 report, gangs were more than four times more likely to be reported in public than private schools (22% versus 5%). Devoe, J.F., Peter, K., Kaufman, P., Ruddy, S.A., Miller, A.K., Planty, M., Snyder, T.D., and Rand, M.R. *Indicators of School Crime and Safety:2003*. NCES 2004-004/NCJ 201257. U.S. Departments of Education and Justice. Washington, D.C.: 2003, pp. 42, 43.

15. Those familiar with the politics of Washington, D.C., know that "executive summaries" for government reports often are exercises in managing the news for some political agenda. The "big news" in the executive summary of the 2003 *Indicators of School Crime and Safety* is a decline in some rates of violent crime and theft in schools. Plainly, as is discussed elsewhere, schools have become more prison-like in their security arrangements and rules. This could well account for some or all of the reported decline in some rates of victimization. On the other hand, the researchers who compile the report have to work with the data they are provided. Ample incentive exists for those in the education industry to manage the reporting of crime in schools to maintain a positive image. This temptation, as is now apparent, is particularly acute, and is becoming more so, because of state and federal legislation designed to hold schools accountable for high levels of crime and disorder. Consequently, when one sees claims that the annual rate of physical threats against teachers has dropped from 12% to 9%, but that rate of acts of violence against teachers is unchanged, one becomes a bit suspicious. It's rather like trying to persuade someone that pit bulls are biting people at the same rate as before, but barking less. Similarly, the fact that there has been no decline in the rate of threats and injuries to students involving guns, knives, and clubs also makes one wonder about the claimed reduction in the rates of school violence. Some of the apparent anomalies in the 2003 *Indicators of School Crime and Safety* may also reflect the fact that the reports are compilations of data from several sources. The moral of the story, if there is one, however, is that accurate statistics regarding social phenomena are hard to come by under the best of circumstances. When the statistics could affect the funding of powerful special interest groups, as education statistics do, it is a virtual certainty that efforts will be made to

"corrupt the indicators." In sum, it is likely that the data regarding school crime are subject to kinds of manipulation similar to those seen in connection with the reporting of standardized testing scores and dropout rates. By the way, just as the authors of the 2003 version of *Indicators of School Crime and Safety* were reporting somewhat lower levels of crime in government schools, the newspapers were reporting that the 2003-2004 school year was off to a deadly start. By mid-October, 18 violent deaths had occurred in government schools – more than in either of the two preceding school years. This was particularly worrisome because, according to school safety experts, school violence is normally at its worst in the spring. Greg Toppo, "Violent Deaths Surge Across U.S.," *USA Today*, October 21, 2003.

16. Greg Toppo, "School Violence Hits Lower Grades," *USA Today*, January 13, 2003.

17. Greg Toppo, "School Violence Hits Lower Grades," *USA Today*, January 13, 2003.

18. The 2003 results from the survey conducted by the National Association of School Resource Officers (NASRO) can be found online at http://www.ecs.org/html/offsite.asp?document=http%3A%2F%2Fwww%2Eschoolsecurity%2Eorg%2F .

19. Brooke Adams, "Study Links Aggression and Time in Day Care," *Salt Lake Tribune*, August 17, 2003. A review of the evidence indicating that time in day care correlates with aggressiveness is provided in Brian Robertson, *Day Care Deception: What the Child Care Establishment Isn't Telling Us* (San Francisco: Encounter Books, 2003).

20. Greg Toppo, "Webcams in All Classrooms," *USA Today*, August 11, 2003.

21. Walter E. Williams, "How Much We Tolerate," *Human Events*, June 25, 2003. Williams' account is based on an article by Marc Epstein, a dean at Jamaica High School. As Williams puts it: "If an American who passed away as late as 1960 were somehow resurrected, he'd probably think Epstein fabricated the story." Epstein's article appeared in the Summer 2003 issue of *Education Next*.

22. Thomas Caywood, "Drug Czar: Test Kids," *Boston Herald*, October 9, 2003. Apparently, Colombian drug traffickers are marketing heroin to children directly and at prices as cheap as $4 per bag. "White House Drug Czar Recommends Drug Testing in Schools," Associated Press, October 8, 2003. The *Boston Herald* article notes that local educators, politicians, the ACLU, and some others are reluctant to implement, or are opposed to implementing, a regime of school-based random drug testing, citing such concerns as cost and violations of Constitutional rights of privacy. One also suspects, however, that among the politicians and educators some of the "concern" stems from a worry that such testing might make it more apparent to the public how serious the drug problem is in their schools. According to John Walters, the federal Drug Czar, 8% of New England children between 12 and 17 years old are drug abusers or drug dependent.

23. Here is a portion of Justice White's opinion in *Goss* in which he describes the activities of the offending students: "The proof below established that the suspensions arose out of a period of widespread student unrest in the CPSS [Columbus Public School System] during February and March 1971. Six of the named plaintiffs, Rudolph Sutton, Tyrone Washington, Susan Cooper, Deborah Fox, Clarence Byars, and Bruce Harris, were students at the Marion-Franklin High School and were each suspended for 10 days on account of disruptive or disobedient conduct committed in the presence of the school administrator who ordered the suspension. One of these, Tyrone Washington, was among a group of students demonstrating in the school auditorium while a class was being conducted there. He was ordered by the school principal to leave, refused to do so, and was suspended. Rudolph Sutton, in the presence of the principal, physically attacked a police officer who was attempting to remove Tyrone Washington from the auditorium. He was immediately suspended. The other four Marion-Franklin students were suspended for similar conduct. None was given a hearing to determine the operative facts underlying the suspension, but each, together with his or her parents, was offered the opportunity to attend a conference, subsequent to the effective date of the suspension, to discuss the student's future. Two named plaintiffs, Dwight Lopez and Betty Crome, were students at the

Central High School and McGuffey Junior High School, respectively. The former was suspended in connection with a disturbance in the lunchroom that involved some physical damage to school property. Lopez testified that at least 75 other students were suspended from his school on the same day. He also testified below that he was not a party to the destructive conduct but was instead an innocent bystander. Because no one from the school testified with regard to this incident, there is no evidence in the record indicating the official basis for concluding otherwise. Lopez never had a hearing. Betty Crome was present at a demonstration at a high school other than the one she was attending. There she was arrested together with others, taken to the police station, and released without being formally charged. Before she went to school on the following day, she was notified that she had been suspended for a 10-day period. Because no one from the school testified with respect to this incident, the record does not disclose how the McGuffey Junior High School principal went about making the decision to suspend Crome, nor does it disclose on what information the decision was based. It is clear from the record that no hearing was ever held."

24. John Taylor Gatto, *The Underground History of American Education*, (New York: The Oxford Village Press, 2000), p. 41.

25. Joe Matthews, Erika Hayasaki, and Duke Helfand, "School Called 'Out of Control'," *Los Angeles Times*, November 21, 2002. The account of the situation at Washington Prep is based on this article.

26. As quoted in Joe Matthews, Erika Hayasaki, and Duke Helfand, "School Called 'Out of Control'," *Los Angeles Times*, November 21, 2002.

27. The odors permeating Washington Prep's halls may have been more than just marijuana. Following years of complaints, the Los Angeles' school district has adopted a pilot program of surprise health inspections. What's the problem? Apparently the district's restrooms are often filthy (described as "contaminated with excrement and [having] dirty or clogged toilets") or closed, and there is also a lack of sanitation in the cafeterias. According to testimony to the Board of Supervisors by Los Angeles City Attorney, Rocky Delgado, "There are children in our schools today who can't use the restrooms, who have ceiling tiles falling on them and who have to deal with vermin in their cafeterias.... *But every prisoner has their own restroom and a cafeteria with health standards.*" (Oh dear, there's another one of those disturbing, over-the-top comparisons of government schools with prisons). For the rest of the story, see Troy Anderson and James Nash, "Supervisors OK Inspections of School Restrooms," *LA Daily*, November 19, 2003.

28. Carl Campanile, "Thugs Run Wild in Troubled HS," *New York Post*, December 16, 2003.

29. As quoted in Carl Campanile, "Thugs Run Wild in Troubled HS," *New York Post*, December 16, 2003.

30. Carl Campanile, "Thugs Run Wild in Troubled HS," *New York Post*, December 16, 2003. Campanile's article also reports on the disorder and violence in New York City's Far Rockaway High School. The conditions there were succinctly described by a 10th- grader, Jolena Favor:"It sucks. No one is learning. Too many kids are running around the building and fighting. Teachers and security don't have control of the kids."

31. Jim Kirksey, "Harassment Chases Teen from School," *Denver Post*, February 7, 2003.

32. "School Bus Video Shows Several Kids Beating 12-Year-Old," WJXT News4Jax.com, February 11, 2004.

33. As quoted in "School Bus Video Shows Several Kids Beating 12-Year-Old," WJXT News4Jax.com, February 11, 2004.

34. As quoted in "School Bus Video Shows Several Kids Beating 12-Year-Old," WJXT News4Jax.com, February 11, 2004.

35. This account is based on the facts reported in Tony Plohetski, "5 Teens Charged in Taped Assault," *The Austin American-Statesman*, January 16, 2003.

36. Tony Plohetski, "5 Teens Charged in Taped Assault," *The Austin American-Statesman*, January 16, 2003.

37. Susannah Meadows and Dirk Johnson, "Girl Fight: Savagery in the Chicago Suburbs," *Newsweek*, May 19, 2003.

38. Susannah Meadows and Dirk Johnson, "Girl Fight: Savagery in the Chicago Suburbs," *Newsweek*, May 19, 2003.

39. As quoted in Bryan Smith and Janet Rausa Fuller, "Tape of Local High School Hazing Becomes World News," *The Chicago Sun-Times*, May 8 2003.

40. "Students Fear 'Lesbian Gang' at School," NBC10.com, February 19, 2004.

41. "Students Fear 'Lesbian Gang' at School," NBC10.com, February 19, 2004.

42. As quoted in "Students Fear 'Lesbian Gang' at School," NBC10.com, February 19, 2004.

43. "Students Fear 'Lesbian Gang' at School," NBC10.com, February 19, 2004.

44. D. Aileen Dodd, "Gwinnet (Atlanta) Schools Now Report 48,501 Incidents (Had reported 4,258)," *Atlanta Journal-Constitution*, June 10, 2003.

45. D. Aileen Dodd, "Gwinnet (Atlanta) Schools Now Report 48,501 Incidents (Had reported 4,258)," *Atlanta Journal-Constitution*, June 10, 2003.

46. D. Aileen Dodd, "Gwinnet (Atlanta) Schools Now Report 48,501 Incidents (Had reported 4,258)," *Atlanta Journal-Constitution*, June 10, 2003.

47. D. Aileen Dodd, "Gwinnet (Atlanta) Schools Now Report 48,501 Incidents (Had reported 4,258)," *Atlanta Journal-Constitution*, June 10, 2003.

48. D. Aileen Dodd, "Gwinnet (Atlanta) Schools Now Report 48,501 Incidents (Had reported 4,258)," *Atlanta Journal-Constitution*, June 10, 2003.

49. Sam Dillon, "School Violence Under a Cloud in Houston," *The New York Times*, November 7, 2003, available online at http://www.nytimes.com/2003/11/07/education/07HOUS.html?ex=1384 232400&en=bd1e58f9da23d450&ei=5007&partner=USERLAND and Lindsey Nair, "Va. Schools Have Incentive to Underreport Crime Data," *The Roanoke Times*, August 31, 2003, available online at http://www.roanoke.com/roatimes/news/story154544.html.

50. Sam Dillon, "School Violence Under a Cloud in Houston," *The New York Times*, November 7, 2003, available online at http://www.nytimes.com/2003/11/07/education/07HOUS.html?ex=138423 2400&en=bd1e58f9da23d450&ei=5007&partner=USERLAND.

51. Sam Dillon, "School Violence Under a Cloud in Houston," *The New York Times*, November 7, 2003, available online at http://www.nytimes.com/2003/11/07/education/07HOUS.html?ex=138423 2400&en=bd1e58f9da23d450&ei=5007&partner=USERLAND.

52. "Houston School District Official Defends Action," *The New York Times*, November 8, 2003. See, also, "HISD Denies Report it Held Back Data on School Crime," *Houston Chronicle*, November 7, 2003.

53. Sam Dillon, "School Violence Under a Cloud in Houston," *The New York Times*, November 7, 2003, available online at http://www.nytimes.com/2003/11/07/education/07HOUS.html?ex=138423 2400&en=bd1e58f9da23d450&ei=5007&partner=USERLAND.

54. Sam Dillon, "School Violence Under a Cloud in Houston," *The New York Times*, November 7, 2003, available online at http://www.nytimes.com/2003/11/07/education/07HOUS.html?ex=138423 2400&en=bd1e58f9da23d450&ei=5007&partner=USERLAND.

55. Sam Dillon, "School Violence Under a Cloud in Houston," *The New York Times*, November 7, 2003, available online at http://www.nytimes.com/2003/11/07/education/07HOUS.html?ex=138423 2400&en=bd1e58f9da23d450&ei=5007&partner=USERLAND.

56. "Teachers Union Says HISD Fudges Assault Reports," Associated Press, November 11, 2003.

57. Sam Dillon, "School Violence Under a Cloud in Houston," *The New York Times*, November 7, 2003, available online at http://www.nytimes.com/2003/11/07/education/07HOUS.html?ex=138423 2400&en=bd1e58f9da23d450&ei=5007&partner=USERLAND.

58. Sam Dillon, "School Violence Under a Cloud in Houston," *The New York Times*, November 7, 2003, available online at http://www.nytimes.com/2003/11/07/education/07HOUS.html?ex=138423 2400&en=bd1e58f9da23d450&ei=5007&partner=USERLAND.

59. Melanie Markley, "Teachers Group Says Principals Failing to Reassign Violent Kids," *Houston Chronicle*, November 12, 2003.

60. Lindsey Nair, "Va. Schools Have Incentive to Underreport Crime Data," *The Roanoke Times*, August 31, 2003, available online at http://www.roanoke.com/roatimes/news/story154544.html.

61. The 2003 results from the survey conducted by the National Association of School Resource Officers (NASRO) can be found online at http://www.ecs.org/html/offsite.asp?document=http%3A %2F%2Fwww%2Eschoolsecurity%2Eorg%2F . NASRO's 2002 survey results are available online at http://www.ecs.org/html/offsite.asp?document=http%3A%2F%2Fwww%2Eschoolsecurity%2Eo rg%2F. See, also, Noel C. Paul, "'Persistently Dangerous' – School-safety Rankings – Or Just Black Marks?", *Christian Science Monitor*, August 20, 2003.

62. This figure is from the 2003 NASRO survey, which can be found online at http://www.ecs.org/ html/offsite.asp?document=http%3A%2F%2Fwww%2Eschoolsecurity%2Eorg%2F. The 2003 NAS-RO survey also indicates that 90% of school-based police officers believe that schools are "soft targets" for terrorists, and 76% believe their schools are not prepared to respond to such an attack.

63. Noel C. Paul, "'Persistently Dangerous' – School-safety Rankings – Or Just Black Marks?", *Christian Science Monitor*, August 20, 2003, quoting Kenneth Trump of National School Safety and Security Services, a consulting firm.

64. As quoted in Erik W. Robelen, "States Report Few Schools as Dangerous," *Education Week*, September 24, 2003.

65. As quoted in Erik W. Robelen, "States Report Few Schools as Dangerous," *Education Week*, September 24, 2003.

66. See, for example, Texas and New Jersey educators' responses in Noel C. Paul, "'Persistently Dangerous' – School-safety Rankings – Or Just Black Marks?", *Christian Science Monitor*, August 20, 2003, and Erik W. Robelen, "States Report Few Schools as Dangerous," *Education Week*, September 24, 2003.

67. Kim Cobb, "Citing Flawed Data, TEA Takes Schools Off 'Dangerous' List," *Houston Chronicle*, October 11, 2003.

68. As quoted in Erik W. Robelen, "States Report Few Schools as Dangerous," *Education Week*, September 24, 2003.

69. Noel C. Paul, "'Persistently Dangerous' – School-safety Rankings – Or Just Black Marks?", *Christian Science Monitor*, August 20, 2003, quoting Ronald Stephens, executive director of the National School Safety Center, and other unnamed experts for the proposition that schools and administrators "are ignoring – or simply not reporting – all the mayhem in their hallways."

70. Caroline Hendrie, "Sexual Abuse by Educators is Scrutinized," *Education Week*, March 10, 2004, available online at http://www.edweek.org/ew/ewstory.cfm?slug=26Abuse.h23. *Education Week* itself has investigated the issue of the sexual abuse of students by teachers and other school employees for some years. An archive of some of *Education Week's* work on this subject is available online at http://www.edweek.org/sreports/abuse98.htm.

71. As might be expected, the response of the NEA *has not been,* "It looks as if there is a serious problem, and we owe it to America's schoolchildren to devote the necessary resources to get to the bottom of it immediately." Instead, Kathleen Lyons, a spokeswoman for the NEA, responded in the NEA's typical self-absorbed, defensive, the facts-be-damned, ostrich-like fashion: "[It is] a misuse of data to imply the public schools and the Catholic Church have experienced the same level of abuse cases...I take great umbrage at that suggestion...That just seems like someone is reaching conclusions based on half the data that is needed." As quoted in Caroline Hendrie, "Sexual Abuse by Educators is Scrutinized," *Education Week*, March 10, 2004, available online at http://www.edweek.org/ew/ewstory.cfm?slug=26Abuse.h23.

72. As quoted in Caroline Hendrie, "Sexual Abuse by Educators is Scrutinized," *Education Week*, March 10, 2004, available online at http://www.edweek.org/ew/ewstory.cfm?slug=26Abuse.h23.

73. Caroline Hendrie, "Sexual Abuse by Educators is Scrutinized," *Education Week*, March 10, 2004, available online at http://www.edweek.org/ew/ewstory.cfm?slug=26Abuse.h23.

74. Caroline Hendrie, "Sexual Abuse by Educators is Scrutinized," *Education Week*, March 10, 2004, available online at http://www.edweek.org/ew/ewstory.cfm?slug=26Abuse.h23.

75. Caroline Hendrie, "Sexual Abuse by Educators is Scrutinized," *Education Week*, March 10, 2004, available online at http://www.edweek.org/ew/ewstory.cfm?slug=26Abuse.h23.

76. As quoted in Caroline Hendrie, "Sexual Abuse by Educators is Scrutinized," *Education Week*, March 10, 2004, available online at http://www.edweek.org/ew/ewstory.cfm?slug=26Abuse.h23.

77. As quoted in Caroline Hendrie, "Sexual Abuse by Educators is Scrutinized," *Education Week*, March 10, 2004, available online at http://www.edweek.org/ew/ewstory.cfm?slug=26Abuse.h23.

78. As quoted in Caroline Hendrie, "Sexual Abuse by Educators is Scrutinized," *Education Week*, March 10, 2004, available online at http://www.edweek.org/ew/ewstory.cfm?slug=26Abuse.h23.

79. Caroline Hendrie, "Sexual Abuse by Educators is Scrutinized," *Education Week*, March 10, 2004, available online at http://www.edweek.org/ew/ewstory.cfm?slug=26Abuse.h23.

80. Caroline Hendrie, "Sexual Abuse by Educators is Scrutinized," *Education Week*, March 10, 2004, available online at http://www.edweek.org/ew/ewstory.cfm?slug=26Abuse.h23.

81. Jane Elizabeth Zemel and Steve Twedt, "Dirty Secrets: Why Sexually Abusive Teachers Aren't Stopped," *Pittsburgh Post-Gazette*, October 31, 1999, available online at http://www.post-gazette.com/regionstate/19991031newabuse1.asp.

82. Jane Elizabeth Zemel, "Dirty Secrets: Research on Abuse Limited, but Indicates a Pervasive Problem," *Pittsburgh Post-Gazette*, November 1, 1999, available online at http://www.post-gazette.com/regionstate/19991101studies2.asp.

83. Michael Gurian, as quoted in Kate Zernike, "Focusing on Boys, Schools Not Meeting Needs, Studies Say," *The Boston Globe*, January 6, 1997, page A1.

84. Francine Prose, "Confident at 11, Confused at 16," *New York Times Magazine*, January 7, 1990, p. 23.

85. As quoted in Christina Hoff Sommers, *The War Against Boys* (New York: Simon & Schuster, 2000), p. 20. For a more detailed account of how gender equity feminists invaded government and

other schools, see Chapter 1 of Sommers' book. The account in this section relating to the AAUW's studies and the media's reaction to it are based on the facts reported in Sommers' Chapter 1.

86. Women's Educational Equity Act of 1994, Section 5201.

87. Women's Educational Equity Act of 1994, Section 5203.

88. No attempt will be made to pursue the unrewarding task of elaborating the differences among "difference feminism," "equity feminism," "postmodern feminism," and the other varieties of "feminism."

89. These claims of Katherine Harris are quoted in Christina Hoff Sommers, *The War Against Boys* (New York: Simon & Schuster, 2000), p. 48.

90. Christina Hoff Sommers, *The War Against Boys* (New York: Simon & Schuster, 2000), p. 49.

91. Christina Hoff Sommers, *The War Against Boys* (New York: Simon & Schuster, 2000), p. 49.

92. See the Women's Education Equity Act Equity Resource Center's web-site at www.edc.org/WomensEquity/about.htm.

93. Christina Hoff Sommers, *The War Against Boys* (New York: Simon & Schuster, 2000), p. 47.

94. Christina Hoff Sommers, *The War Against Boys* (New York: Simon & Schuster, 2000), p. 47.

95. Education Equity Concepts and Wellesley College Center for Research on Women, *Quit It!: A Teacher's Guide on Teasing and Bullying for Use with Students in Grades K-3* (New York and Wellesley, Mass.: Education Equity Concepts and Wellesley College Center for Research on Women, 1998). The discussion of *Quit It!* is based on information contained in Christina Hoff Sommers, *The War Against Boys* (New York: Simon & Schuster, 2000), pp. 52-53.

96. Christina Hoff Sommers, *The War Against Boys* (New York: Simon & Schuster, 2000), p. 53.

97. Department of Children, Families and Learning, *Girls and Boys Getting Along: Teaching Sexual Harassment Prevention in the Elementary Classroom* (St. Paul, Minn.: Department of Children, Families, and Learning, 1997), as quoted in Christina Hoff Sommers, *The War Against Boys* (New York: Simon & Schuster, 2000), p. 53.

98. Department of Children, Families and Learning, *Girls and Boys Getting Along: Teaching Sexual Harassment Prevention in the Elementary Classroom* (St. Paul, Minn.: Department of Children, Families, and Learning, 1997), p. 55, as quoted in Christina Hoff Sommers, *The War Against Boys* (New York: Simon & Schuster, 2000), p. 53.

99. Richard Zoglin, "A Kiss Isn't Just a Kiss," *Time Magazine*, October 7, 1996.

100. Richard Zoglin, "A Kiss Isn't Just a Kiss," *Time Magazine*, October 7, 1996.

101. John Leo, "Expel Georgie Porgie Now!", *U.S. News and World Report*, October 7, 1996.

102. Christina Hoff Sommers, *The War Against Boys* (New York: Simon & Schuster, 2000), pp. 54-55.

103. John Leo, "Expel Georgie Porgie Now!", *U.S. News and World Report*, October 7, 1996.

104. John Leo, "Expel Georgie Porgie Now!", *U.S. News and World Report*, October 7, 1996.

105. Linda Chavez, "Feminist Kiss Patrol is on the March," *USA Today*, October 2, 1996.

106. For further information on these programs and, particularly, the people involved in promoting them, see Stanley Kurtz, "Silencing Sommers," *National Review*, December 5, 2001, available at www.

national review.com/contributors/kurtz120501.shtml and Sally Satel, "The Sorry CSAP Flap: It's Worse Than It Looks," *American Enterprise Institute*, December 7, 2001.

107. For a discussion by a feminist of how anti-male bias in our society appears to be contributing to a decline in men's willingness to marry, see Wendy McElroy, "The Marriage Strike – Why Reluctant Males Just Say No!," August 12, 2003, available at http://mensnewsdaily.com/archive/m-n/mcelroy/03/mcelroy081203.htm.

108. Nan Stein commenting in an antiharassment video produced by the National Education Association, as quoted in Christina Hoff Sommers, *The War Against Boys* (New York: Simon & Schuster, 2000), p. 54.

109. Christina Hoff Sommers, *The War Against Boys* (New York: Simon & Schuster, 2000), p. 19.

110. Christina Hoff Sommers, *The War Against Boys* (New York: Simon & Schuster, 2000), p. 21.

111. Tamar Lewin, "How Boys Lost Out to Girl Power," *The New York Times*, December 12, 1998, section 4, p. 1, as quoted in Christina Hoff Sommers, *The War Against Boys* (New York: Simon & Schuster, 2000), p. 22.

112. This information is taken from the *AAUW/Greenberg-Lake Full Data Report: Expectations and Aspirations: Gender Roles and Self-Esteem* (Washington, D.C.: American Association of University Women, 1990), p. 18, as quoted in Christina Hoff Sommers, *The War Against Boys* (New York: Simon & Schuster, 2000), p. 42.

113. Judith Kleinfeld, as quoted in Kim Asch, "Girls Overtake Boys in School Performance," *The Washington Times*, January 13, 1999.

114. Michelle Conlin, "The New Gender Gap," *BusinessWeek*, May 26, 2003. Anne Marie Owens, "Schools Conspire Against Boys: Educator," *National Post*, June 30, 2002.

115. Kim Asch, "Girls Overtake Boys in School Performance," *The Washington Times*, January 13, 1999.

116. U.S. Department of Education, *The Condition of Education 2001* (Washington D.C.: U.S. Department of Education, 2001), section 1, p. 10.

117. U.S. Department of Education, *The Condition of Education 2001* (Washington D.C.: U.S. Department of Education, 2001), section 1, p. 10 and Supplemental Table 5-1 and Supplemental Note 10 and the sources cited therein.

118. U.S. Department of Education, National Center for Educational Statistics, "Fall Enollments in Colleges and Universities," August 1998, as quoted in Christina Hoff Sommers, *The War Against Boys* (New York: Simon & Schuster, 2000), p. 14.

119. Ted Byfield, "School is Now Just a 'Girl Thing'," *The Edmonton Sun*, August 4, 2002.

120. Ted Byfield, "School is Now Just a 'Girl Thing'," *The Edmonton Sun*, August 4, 2002.

121. Kamal Ahmed and Mark Townsend, "Poor White Boys Flounder Under 'Feminised' Teaching," *The Observer*, August 17, 2003.

122. Kamal Ahmed and Mark Townsend, "Poor White Boys Flounder Under 'Feminised' Teaching," *The Observer*, August 17, 2003.

123. Kamal Ahmed and Mark Townsend, "Poor White Boys Flounder Under 'Feminised' Teaching," *The Observer*, August 17, 2003.

124. Kamal Ahmed and Mark Townsend, "Poor White Boys Flounder Under 'Feminised' Teaching," *The Observer*, August 17, 2003.

125. The lyrics, in part, go like this: "Kids are different today / I hear ev'ry mother say / Mother needs something today to calm her down / And though she's not really ill / There's a little yellow pill / She goes running for the shelter of a mother's little helper / And it helps her on her way, gets her through her busy day."

126. Psychotropic drugs are a class of drugs that act on the central nervous system to produce changes in thinking, feeling, and behaving. Jonathan Leo and David Cohen, "Broken Brains or Flawed Studies? A Critical Review of ADHD Neuroimaging Research," *The Journal of Mind and Behavior*, Winter 2003, Volume 24, Number 1, p. 32, available online at http://psychrights.org/Research/Digest/NLPs/criticalreviewofadhd.pdf

127. Because historically Ritalin has been the psychotropic drug prescribed in the vast majority of ADHD cases, the discussion of the general problem of schools drugging schoolchildren is discussed in terms of Ritalin, although the same or similar issues exist with respect to the use of other psychotropic drugs in connection with diagnoses of ADHD.

128. Ephrat Livni, "A Diagnosis Excess? A Lawsuit Alleges Attention Deficit Disorder is Over-Diagnosed," ABCNews.com, December 17, 2000. CHADD (Children and Adults with Attention Deficit/Hyperactivity Disorder), a non-profit organization of parents whose children are labeled with ADHD and which receives substantial funding from makers of Ritalin and similar drugs, promotes estimates that only 1.5 million schoolchildren take drugs for ADHD and seems to support the position that these drugs are generally under-prescribed. See, Russell A. Barkley, Ph.D., *ADHD, Ritalin, and Conspiracies: Talking Back to Peter Breggin*, March 4, 1999, available at www.chadd.org/news/Russ-review.htm. Critics of the use of Ritalin-type drugs and ADHD as a medical diagnosis, such as Dr. Peter Breggin, argue that 8 million schoolchildren a year are being drugged.

129. This is based on a study conducted by Dr. Jerry Rushton of the University of Michigan, as quoted in "Ritalin and Prozac Combination used by more Children," *Reuters*, May 15, 2000.

130. "Ritalin: Violence Against Boys, Drug is Being Used to Sedate Active Young Boys," *The Massachusetts News*, November 1, 2000, available at www.massnews.com/vioboy.htm.

131. Jane Marcus, "Schools Need To Crack Down on Ritalin Use," *The Baltimore Sun*, February 20, 2001.

132. "House Told Schools Overuse Mood Drugs," 7am.com News, June 16, 2003.

133. "House Told Schools Overuse Mood Drugs," 7am.com News, June 16, 2003.

134. Kelly Patricia O'Meara, "Doping Kids," *Insight Magazine*, June 28, 1999.

135. Kelly Patricia O'Meara, "Doping Kids," *Insight Magazine*, June 28, 1999.

136. Peter R. Breggin, M.D. and Ginger Ross Breggin, "The Hazards of Treating 'Attention-Deficit/Hyperactivity Disorder' with Methylphenidate (Ritalin)," *The Journal of College Student Psychotherapy*, Volume 10 (2,) 1995, pp. 55-72.

137. Peter R. Breggin, M.D. and Ginger Ross Breggin, "The Hazards of Treating 'Attention-Deficit/Hyperactivity Disorder' with Methylphenidate (Ritalin)," *The Journal of College Student Psychotherapy*, Volume 10 (2), 1995, pp. 55-72.

138. Kelly Patricia O'Meara, "Doping Kids," *Insight Magazine*, June 28, 1999, and Peter R. Breggin, M.D. and Ginger Ross Breggin, "The Hazards of Treating 'Attention-Deficit/Hyperactivity Disorder' with Methylphenidate (Ritalin)," *The Journal of College Student Psychotherapy*, Volume 10 (2), 1995, pp. 55-72.

139. Jane Marcus, "Schools Need To Crack Down on Ritalin Use," *The Baltimore Sun*, February 20, 2001.

140. As quoted in "Ritalin: Violence Against Boys, Drug is Being Used to Sedate Active Young Boys," *The Massachusetts News*, November 1, 2000, available at www.massnews.com/vioboy.htm.

141. Jane Marcus, "Schools Need To Crack Down on Ritalin Use," *The Baltimore Sun*, February 20, 2001.

142. Jane Marcus, "Schools Need To Crack Down on Ritalin Use," *The Baltimore Sun*, February 20, 2001.

143. Jane Marcus, "Schools Need To Crack Down on Ritalin Use," *The Baltimore Sun*, February 20, 2001.

144. "Dealing and Stealing Ritalin," *Education Reporter*, February 2001.

145. Jonathan Riskind, "Schools Push Ritalin Panel Told," *The Columbus Dispatch*, May 17, 2000.

146. "Ritalin: Violence Against Boys, Drug is Being Used to Sedate Active Young Boys," *The Massachusetts News*, November 1, 2000, available at www.massnews.com/vioboy.htm.

147. Nadine Lambert, as quoted in "Ritalin: Violence Against Boys, Drug is Being Used to Sedate Active Young Boys," *The Massachusetts News*, November 1, 2000, available at www.massnews.com/vioboy.htm.

148. Kelly Patricia O'Meara, "Doping Kids," *Insight Magazine*, June 28, 1999.

149. Kelly Patricia O'Meara, "Doping Kids," *Insight Magazine*, June 28, 1999.

150. As set forth in *Diagnostic and Statistical Manual of Mental Disorders*. For a discussion, see Peter R. Breggin, M.D. and Ginger Ross Breggin, "The Hazards of Treating 'Attention-Deficit/Hyperactivity Disorder' with Methylphenidate (Ritalin)," *The Journal of College Student Psychotherapy*, Volume 10 (2), 1995, pp. 55-72.

151. As set forth in *Diagnostic and Statistical Manual of Mental Disorders*. For a discussion of these symptoms, see Peter R. Breggin, M.D. and Ginger Ross Breggin, "The Hazards of Treating 'Attention-Deficit/Hyperactivity Disorder with Methylphenidate (Ritalin)," *The Journal of College Student Psychotherapy*, Volume 10 (2), 1995, pp. 55-72.

152. As set forth in *Diagnostic and Statistical Manual of Mental Disorders*. For a discussion of these symptoms see Peter R. Breggin, M.D. and Ginger Ross Breggin, "The Hazards of Treating 'Attention-Deficit/Hyperactivity Disorder' with Methylphenidate (Ritalin)," *The Journal of College Student Psychotherapy*, Volume 10 (2) ,1995, pp. 55-72.

153. Peter R. Breggin, M.D. and Ginger Ross Breggin, "The Hazards of Treating 'Attention-Deficit/Hyperactivity Disorder' with Methylphenidate (Ritalin)," *The Journal of College Student Psychotherapy*, Volume 10 (2) 1995, pp. 55-72.

154. Kristin Leutwyler, "Paying Attention – The Controversy Over ADHD and the Drug Ritalin is Obscuring a Real Look at the Disorder and its Underpinnings," *Scientific American*, August 1996.

155. Kristin Leutwyler, "Paying Attention – The Controversy Over ADHD and the Drug Ritalin is Obscuring a Real Look at the Disorder and its Underpinnings," *Scientific American*, August 1996.

156. Kristin Leutwyler, "Paying Attention – The Controversy Over ADHD and the Drug Ritalin is Obscuring a Real Look at the Disorder and its Underpinnings," *Scientific American*, August 1996.

157. See, *e.g.*, Kristin Leutwyler, "Paying Attention – The Controversy Over ADHD and the Drug Ritalin is Obscuring a Real Look at the Disorder and its Underpinnings," *Scientific American*, August 1996, and Russell A. Barkley, Ph.D., "ADHD, Ritalin, and Conspiracies: Talking Back to Peter Breggin," March 4, 1999, available at www.chadd.org/news/Russ-review.htm.

158. These articles are: "Ritalin is Safe – and It Works," *The Detroit Daily News*, December 12, 2002; Robert McGough, "Attention-Deficit Gene is Located," *The Wall Street Journal*, October 22, 2002, D-3. Michael Fumento, "Trick Question: A Liberal Hoax Turns Out to be True," *The New Republic*, February 2, 2003.

159. See, *e.g.*, Dr. Richard Bromfield, "Is Ritalin Overprescribed? Yes," drkoop.com, September 10, 1999, available at www.drkoop.com/news/focus/september/ritalin_yes.html; George Will, "Boys Will Be Boys Or You Can Just Drug Them," *The Washington Post*, December 2, 1999.

160. Dr. Richard Bromfield, "Is Ritalin Overprescribed? Yes," drkoop.com, September 10, 1999, available at www.drkoop.com/news/focus/september/ritalin_yes.html;

161. In America, at least, the makers of drugs for ADHD are now beginning to market them to adults. As Sally Satel points out in a *Wall Street Journal* Op-Ed, there is a new epidemic of Attention-Deficit disorder on the way. Satel believes that, although medical professionals will be "finding" that many adults are clinically mentally ill with ADD, much of the demand for these drugs will in fact be a demand for what Peter Kramer (author of *Listening to Prozac*) calls "cosmetic psychopharmacology." The object of cosmetic psychopharmacology is to make people who do not suffer from a mental disorder feel "better than well." Sally Satel, "ADD Overdose?," *The Wall Street Journal*, July 24, 2003, A-14. Satel does, by the way, accept the validity of the ADHD diagnosis. Adult ADHD is diagnosed using a test in which the patient is asked how often he (1) has trouble wrapping up the final details of a project, (2) has difficulty getting things in order, (3) has trouble remembering appointments or obligations, (4) avoids or delays starting tasks that require a lot of thought, (5) fidgets or squirms with his hands or feet when he has to sit for a long time, and (6) feels overly active and compelled to do things, like he is driven by a motor. If you answer "sometimes" with respect to (1), (2), and (3), and answer "often" to any of (4), (5), and (6), "It may be beneficial for you to talk with your healthcare provider about an evaluation." In other words, you can probably get a medical professional to write you a prescription for Ritalin, Adderall, or some other psychotropic drug. Given that Ritalin, like caffeine, will help most people concentrate, and if Walter Kirn's "inside view" of what it is like to be on Ritalin is correct (see the end of the discussion of Ritalin in the text), we can expect that adult ADHD will bcome a growth industry. Popularizing the adult ADHD diagnosis presumably will also allow pharmaceutical companies to keep at least some of the children diagnosed with ADHD as customers for life. The test for adult ADHD is published by the World Health Organization. A copy of the test and an account of how adult ADHD is gaining ground as a diagnosis are provided in Robert McGough and Patricia Callahan, "An Illness That's not Just for Kids Anymore," *The Wall Street Journal*, November 26, 2003, D1.

162. Peter R. Breggin, M.D., and Ginger Ross Breggin, "The Hazards of Treating 'Attention-Deficit/Hyperactivity Disorder' with Methylphenidate (Ritalin)," *The Journal of College Student Psychotherapy*, Volume 10 (2), 1995, pp. 55-72.

163. Jay Joseph, "Problems in Psychiatric Genetic Research: A Reply to Faraone and Biederman," *Developmental Review* 20, pp. 582-593, p. 587.

164. Harvey McConnell, "ADHD Just Doesn't Add Up to Brit Psych Society," *The Medical Post*, January 21, 1997.

165. As quoted in Harvey McConnell, "ADHD Just Doesn't Add Up to Brit Psych Society," *The Medical Post*, January 21, 1997.

166. Harvey McConnell, "ADHD Just Doesn't Add Up to Brit Psych Society," *The Medical Post*, January 21, 1997.

167. The *DSM-IV* does not say that ADHD is due to brain malfunction. Journals and textbooks do, however, express this view. See Fred Baughman, "The ADHD Consensus Conference: End of the Epidemic," quoting W.B. Carey (NIH), *Consensus Development Conference on ADHD*, November 16-18, 1998, available at www.home.att.net/~Fred-Alden/Es39.html.

168. Dr. Fred Baughman, as quoted in Kelly Patricia O'Meara, "Doping Kids," *Insight Magazine*, June 28, 1999.

169. Dr. Peter Breggin, as quoted in Kelly Patricia O'Meara, "Doping Kids," *Insight Magazine*, June 28, 1999.

170. This view has been expressed, for example, by the president of The Citizens Commission on Human Rights, Bruce Wiseman. See Kelly Patricia O'Meara, "Doping Kids," *Insight Magazine*, June 28, 1999.

171. As quoted in Kelly Patricia O'Meara, "Doping Kids," *Insight Magazine*, June 28, 1999.

172. Dr. Russell Barkley headed the group that produced the letter, which is on the CHADD website.

173. Peter R. Breggin, M.D., and Ginger Ross Breggin, "The Hazards of Treating 'Attention-Deficit/Hyperactivity Disorder' with Methylphenidate (Ritalin)," *The Journal of College Student Psychotherapy*, Volume 10 (2), 1995, pp. 55-72.

174. Fred A. Baughman, Jr., M.D., "The Totality of the ADD/ADHD Fraud," February 4, 1998, available at www.home.att.net/~Fred-Alden/Es5.html. The earlier work by Nashrallah *et al.* is referred to in Peter R. Breggin, M.D., and Ginger Ross Breggin, "The Hazards of Treating 'Attention-Deficit/Hyperactivity Disorder' with Methylphenidate (Ritalin)," *The Journal of College Student Psychotherapy*, Volume 10 (2), 1995, pp. 55-72.

175. Castellanos, Lee, Sharp, Jeffries, Greenstein, Clasen, *et al.*, "Developmental Trajectories of Brain Volume Abnormalities in Children and Adolescents with Attention-Deficit Hyperactivity Disorder," *Journal of the American Medical Association* (2002), p. 288, 1740-1748.

176. For Castellanos' views on the significance of his study regarding Ritalin and brain growth, see Jonathan Leo and David Cohen, "Broken Brains or Flawed Studies? A Critical Review of ADHD Neuroimaging Research," *The Journal of Mind and Behavior*, Winter 2003, Volume 24, Number 1, p. 48, and the sources cited therein. Castellanos is also quoted in the *Detroit Daily News* story as saying "It is possible that medication may promote brain maturation." Given this quote from Castellanos in the story itself, it is hard to understand how the journalists believed they were justified in tarting up Castellanos' views into a story suggesting something far less tentative regarding brain growth. Moreover, given the disparity in the ages, heights and weights between the control group and the children diagnosed with ADHD, is hard to see how increases in brain size over time could be attributed to Ritalin as opposed to the natural process of maturation on the basis of Castellanos' study. In addition, because most studies indicate that the long-term use of stimulants correlates with brain atrophy, it would be odd, to say the least, for the powerful stimulant methylphenidate (Ritalin) to cause brain growth. Further, an increase in the size of the brain is not in itself evidence of a physiological improvement. In any event, the Castellanos study as it was designed simply does not establish anything at all regarding the effects of Ritalin on brain development.

177. Jonathan Leo and David Cohen, "Broken Brains or Flawed Studies? A Critical Review of ADHD Neuroimaging Research," *The Journal of Mind and Behavior*, Winter 2003, Volume 24, Number 1, p. 45, available online at http://psychrights.org/Research/Digest/NLPs/criticalreviewofadhd.pdf

178. Jonathan Leo and David Cohen, "Broken Brains or Flawed Studies? A Critical Review of ADHD Neuroimaging Research," *The Journal of Mind and Behavior*, Winter 2003, Volume 24, Number 1, available online at http://psychrights.org/Research/Digest/NLPs/criticalreviewofadhd.pdf.

179. Jonathan Leo and David Cohen, "Broken Brains or Flawed Studies? A Critical Review of ADHD Neuroimaging Research," *The Journal of Mind and Behavior*, Winter 2003, Volume 24, Number 1, p. 51, available online at http://psychrights.org/Research/Digest/NLPs/criticalreviewofadhd.pdf.

180. For a very readable summary of this controversy of brain-imaging studies, see Kelly Patricia O'Meara, "In ADHD Studies, Pictures May Lie," *Insight Magazine*, August 19, 2003. Researchers, by the way, explain the lack of studies using unmedicated children who have been diagnosed with ADHD as resulting from the difficulty of finding children with the diagnosis who have not been medicated. Yet, when Castellanos had the opportunity to do this, he chose an inappropriate control group.

181. Robert McGough, "Attention-Deficit Gene is Located," *The Wall Street Journal*, October 22, 2002, D-3. An additional 2003 story in the popular press defending the ADHD diagnosis is Michael Fumento, "Trick Question: A Liberal Hoax Turns Out to be True," *The New Republic*, February 2, 2003. This article, though entertainingly written, appears to be the product of uncritical discussions with advocates of the ADHD diagnosis. One bizarre element in the Fumento article is his apparently approving quotation of Dr. Russell Barkley's statement that the lack of any physiological evidence of ADHD is not problematic: "Where are the lab tests for headaches and multiple sclerosis and Alzheimer's…? Such a standard would virtually eliminate all mental disorders." Fumento and Barkley should know that multiple sclerosis is often verifiable with a brain scan that shows white matter lesions, although the procedure is not 100% accurate. This is so well known that insurance companies will pay for MRI's to detect multiple sclerosis, but no insurance company will pay for any sort of brain scan to confirm a diagnosis of ADHD. At the time Fumento's article was written, Alzheimer's was not detectable through a lab test on living individuals, but was identifiable through the presence of pathological lesions on the patient's brain discoverable in a post mortem examination. It has been reported recently that Positron Emission Tomography brain scans can now diagnose Alzheimer's with about 90% accuracy. Laura Johannes, "Finding Alzheimer's Early," *The Wall Street Journal*, October 16, 2003, B-1. Brain scans and lab tests also can identify physical causes of some headaches. Moreover, the symptoms of Alzheimer's and multiple sclerosis are models of diagnostic clarity compared to the symptoms defining the ADHD diagnosis. As for Barkley's *reductio ad absurdam* argument, either a diagnosis satisfies a reasonable scientific standard or it doesn't. Fumento also writes that "often the best diagnostic test for an ailment is how it responds to treatment." This is odd because he cites Dr. Judith Rapoport in support when her work, in fact, has shown, as others know, that Ritalin will help *anyone* pay attention. By Fumento's treatment-response standard of diagnosis, then, every human on the planet has ADHD. Fumento's article makes other claims in favor of the ADHD diagnosis, which, in my view, are more polemical and confused than substantive.

182. Jay Joseph, "Not in Their Genes: A Critical View of the Genetics of Attention-Deficit Hyperactivity Disorder," *Developmental Review* 20, pp. 539-567. Joseph's article drew a response, Stephen V. Faraone and Joseph Biederman, "Nature, Nurture, and Attention Deficit Hyperactivity Disorder," *Developmental Review 20*, pp. 568-581, to which Joseph responded, "Problems in Psychiatric Genetic Research: A Reply to Faraone and Biederman," *Developmental Review 20*, pp. 582-593.

183. Sharon Begley, "Diet During Pregnancy Could Have Effects that Last to Adulthood," *The Wall Street Journal*, August 22, 2003, B1. According to Begley's sources, sequence variations don't correlate well with diseases. Consequently, attention is increasingly being given to what is known as "epigenetics," which studies the pattern of gene silencing and activation.

184. Stephen Faraone, as quoted in Jay Joseph, "Problems in Psychiatric Genetic Research: A Reply to Faraone and Biederman," *Developmental Review 20*, pp. 582-593.

185. The belief that many mental illnesses result from biological causes that are genetic in origin seems to be broadly accepted as justifying treating mental illnesses with medications. This belief, in turn, appears to rest largely on a body of research purporting to have found a 50% concordance rate for schizophrenia for identical twins, but only a 15% concordance rate for fraternal twins. In essence, it appears that many, if not most, psychiatrists believe explicitly or implicitly that these twin studies prove that biological deficits are the primary source of mental illnesses. This view, along with the validity of the schizophrenia twin studies, is challenged by Jay Joseph in *The Gene Illusion* (Ross-on-

Wye, United Kingdom: PCCS Books, 2003). Jonathan Leo provides an informative essay-review of *The Gene Illusion* in *Human Nature Review* 3 (2003), pp. 406-415.

186. For a discussion of the questions of medical ethics raised by the use of psychotropic drugs in connection with ADHD, see "The Ethics and Science of Medicating Children," by Jacqueline A. Sparks, Ph.D., Center for Family Services and Barry L. Duncan, Psy.D., Institute for the Study of Therapeutic Change, available online at http://psychrights.org/Research/Digest/ADHD/Medicating-Kids.pdf.

187. Peter R. Breggin, M.D., and Ginger Ross Breggin, "The Hazards of Treating 'Attention-Deficit/Hyperactivity Disorder' with Methylphenidate (Ritalin)," *The Journal of College Student Psychotherapy*, Volume 10 (2,) 1995, pp. 55-72.

188. Peter R. Breggin, M.D., and Ginger Ross Breggin, "The Hazards of Treating 'Attention-Deficit/Hyperactivity Disorder' with Methylphenidate (Ritalin)," *The Journal of College Student Psychotherapy*, Volume 10 (2), 1995, pp. 55-72.

189. Peter R. Breggin, M.D., and Ginger Ross Breggin, "The Hazards of Treating 'Attention-Deficit/Hyperactivity Disorder' with Methylphenidate (Ritalin)," *The Journal of College Student Psychotherapy*, Volume 10 (2), 1995, pp. 55-72.

190. A January 2004 story in the *Harvard Crimson* reports on students' use of prescription drugs such as Ritalin and Adderall as "study drugs." According to the *Crimson*, many students believe that these drugs are far better than caffeine for enhancing study performance. According to one student interviewed by the *Crimson*, "It's helped me a lot…I can sit down for three hours and it feels like ten minutes….You don't necessarily have to have ADD for it to do something to you…. Especially if you snort it…The thing with coffee is that your head is awake but your body isn't – it doesn't feel all that natural…Ritalin is more like an all-over buzz." As quoted in David B. Rochelson, "Students Turn to Drugs to Study," *Harvard Crimson*, January 26, 2004.

191. Gottlieb, D.J., *et al.*, "Symptoms of Sleep Disordered Breathing in 5-year-old children are Associated with Sleepiness and Problem Behaviors," *Pediatrics*, October 2003, 112:870-877. This study involved a fairly large sample – 3019 children.

192. See, *e.g.*, *The Physician's Desk Reference*, "ADHD May be Overdiagnosed, Study Says," CNN. com, September 1, 1999, and Kristin Leutwyler, "Paying Attention – The Controversy Over ADHD and the Drug Ritalin is Obscuring a Real Look at the Disorder and its Underpinnings," *Scientific American*, August 1996.

193. "Ritalin: Violence Against Boys, Drug is Being Used to Sedate Active Young Boys," *The Massachusetts News*, November 1, 2000, available at www.massnews.com/vioboy.htm.

194. Kelly Patricia O'Meara, "Doping Kids," *Insight Magazine*, June 28, 1999.

195. Kelly Patricia O'Meara, "Doping Kids," *Insight Magazine*, June 28, 1999.

196. As quoted in Ephrat Livni, "A Diagnosis Excess? A Lawsuit Alleges Attention Deficit Disorder if Over-Diagnosed," ABCNEWS.com, December 17, 2000, available at http://abcnews.go.com/sections/living/DailyNews/ritalin_lawsuit0808.html.

197. Peter R. Breggin, M.D., and Ginger Ross Breggin, "The Hazards of Treating 'Attention-Deficit/Hyperactivity Disorder' with Methylphenidate (Ritalin)," *The Journal of College Student Psychotherapy*, Volume 10 (2), 1995, pp. 55-72.

198. "Ritalin May Change Brain Long-Term, Study Shows," Reuters News Service, November 11, 2001. See, also, Brendan McGarry, "UB Researcher's Findings on Ritalin Attract National Attention," *The Spectrum*, November 28, 2001.

199. "Ritalin May Change Brain Long-Term, Study Shows," Reuters News Service, November 11, 2001.

200. Dr. Jerry Rushton as quoted in "Ritalin and Prozac Combination Used by More Children," Reuters, May 15, 2000.

201. As quoted in Kelly Patricia O'Meara, "New Research Indicts Ritalin," *Insight Magazine*, July 22, 2003.

202. Kelly Patricia O'Meara, "New Research Indicts Ritalin," *Insight Magazine*, July 22, 2003.

203. Kelly Patricia O'Meara, "New Research Indicts Ritalin," *Insight Magazine*, July 22, 2003.

204. As quoted in Kelly Patricia O'Meara, "New Research Indicts Ritalin," *Insight Magazine*, July 22, 2003.

205. Robert McGough, "Brain Structure May Make Teens Addiction-Prone," *The Wall Street Journal*, June 6, 2003.

206. Robert McGough, "Brain Structure May Make Teens Addiction-Prone," *The Wall Street Journal*, June 6, 2003.

207. Robert McGough, "Brain Structure May Make Teens Addiction-Prone," *The Wall Street Journal*, June 6, 2003.

208. The Carlezon study should be available online sometime in 2004 at Biological Psychiatry's homepage: http://www-east.elsevier.com/bps/.

209. As quoted in "Ritalin Use During Childhood May Increase Depression, Decrease Cocaine Sensitivity in Adults," Press Release by McClean Hospital, December 8, 2003, available online at http://www.mcleanhospital.org/PublicAffairs/ritmod20031208.html.

210. "Ritalin Use During Childhood May Increase Depression, Decrease Cocaine Sensitivity in Adults," Press Release by McClean Hospital, December 8, 2003, available online at http://www.mcleanhospital.org/PublicAffairs/ritmod20031208.html.

211. It must also be noted that the study also found that the rats that had been given Ritalin demonstrated a lower level of interest in cocaine than the rats in the control group. Note, however, that the University of California and University of Buffalo studies mentioned indicate that Ritalin may be a "gateway" drug for humans. Obviously, the differences in human and rodent biology may be such that all, some, or none, of the findings from Carlezon's study may be applicable to humans.

212. Lauran Neergaard, "FDA Cites Possible Suicide Link in Paxil," Associated Press, June 19, 2003.

213. Kelly Patricia O'Meara, "Doping Kids," *Insight Magazine*, June 28, 1999.

214. The American Psychiatric Association sponsored a symposium at its 2003 annual convention to debate whether pedophilia, exhibitionism, fetishism, transvestism, voyeurism, and sadomasochism should continue to be considered mental illnesses. Some believe that the ultimate goal of those pushing for such changes is the decriminalization of the activities of pedophiles. See Lawrence Morahan, "Psychiatric Association Debates Reclassifying Pedophilia," CNSNews.com, June 11, 2003.

215. Ephrat Livni, "A Diagnosis Excess? A Lawsuit Alleges Attention Deficit Disorder is Over-Diagnosed," ABCNews.com, December 17, 2000.

216. Ephrat Livni, "A Diagnosis Excess? A Lawsuit Alleges Attention Deficit Disorder is Over-Diagnosed," ABCNews.com, December 17, 2000.

217. Lawrence H. Diller, M.D., "Just Say Yes to Ritalin," Salon.com, September 25, 2000.

218. Douglas Montero, "Ritalin Pusher Changes His Tune on Schools," *The New York Post*, September 27, 2002.

219. Douglas Montero, "Ritalin Pusher Changes His Tune on Schools," *The New York Post*, September 27, 2002.

220. Douglas Montero, "Ritalin Pusher Changes His Tune on Schools," *The New York Post*, September 27, 2002.

221. "ADHD May Be Overdiagnosed, Study Says," CNN.com, September 1, 1999.

222. Gretchen B. LeFever, Ph.D., "Ritalin Alert," compiled by Dee Dickinson from material sent to New Horizons for Learning by Gretchen B. LeFever, Ph.D., available at www.newhorizons.org/spneeds_lefever.html. To read Dr. LeFever's own work on the subject, see "ADHD among American Schoolchildren: Evidence of Overdiagnosis and Overuse of Medication," by Gretchen B. LeFever and Andrea P. Arcona - Center for Pediatric Research, Eastern Virginia Medical School and Children's Hospital of the King's Daughters David O. Antonuccio - University of Nevada School of Medicine, Veterans Affairs Sierra Nevada Health Care System, *The Scientific Review of Mental Health Practice*, Spring/Summer 2003, Vol.2, No.1, available online at http://psychrights.org/Research/Digest/ADHD/Overdxrx.htm.

223. "ADHD May Be Overdiagnosed, Study Says," CNN.com, September 1, 1999.

224. Rick Karlin, "Ritalin Use Splits Parents, School," *Times Union* (Albany, New York), May 7, 2000.

225. Rick Karlin, "Ritalin Use Splits Parents, School," *Times Union* (Albany, New York), May 7, 2000.

226. David Lansner, as quoted in Rick Karlin, "Ritalin Use Splits Parents, School," *Times Union* (Albany, New York), May 7, 2000.

227. Lawrence H. Diller, M.D., "Just Say Yes to Ritalin," Salon.com, September 25, 2000.

228. Jonathan Riskind, "Schools Push Ritalin Panel Told," *The Columbus Dispatch*, May 17, 2000.

229. "Reading, Writing, and Ritalin? Back to School, Back to Ritalin," ABCNews.com, August 31, 1998, available at www.abcnews.go.com/onair/GoodMorningAmerica/GMA000831Ritalin.html.

230. The Bill is SB 1390, and it is known as The Child Medication Safety Act.

231. It is estimated that Ritalin alone has added about $10 Billion to the market capitalization of Novartis since 1991. See Kelly Patricia O'Meara, "New Research Indicts Ritalin," *Insight Magazine*, July 22, 2003.

232. "Into the Mouths of Babes – The Drugging of Preschoolers is on the Rise, Study Shows," *Education Reporter*, April 2000.

233. Douglas Montero, "Studies on Ritalin are 'Child Abuse'," NYPost.com, December 3, 2001.

234. "Into the Mouths of Babes – The Drugging of Preschoolers is on the Rise, Study Shows," *Education Reporter*, April 2000.

235. It appears that those who have prescribed Ritalin and similar drugs to children and adolescents have consistently done so without research to support their use. In an editorial in the January 2003 issue of *Archives of Pediatrics and Adolescent Medicine* Dr. Michael Jellinek, commenting on a study in the same issue indicating dramatically increased use of Ritalin and other psychiatric drugs by children and adolescents between 1987 and 1996, expresses concern over increased prescription of psychiatric drugs to children *at a time when there was little research to support the use of these drugs with children*.

236. Douglas Montero, "Studies on Ritalin are 'Child Abuse'," NYPost.com, December 3, 2001.

237. Douglas Montero, "Studies on Ritalin are 'Child Abuse'," NYPost.com, December 3, 2001.

238. Douglas Montero, "Studies on Ritalin are 'Child Abuse'," NYPost.com, December 3, 2001.

239. Douglas Montero, "Studies on Ritalin are 'Child Abuse'," NYPOST.COM, December 3, 2001.

240. Julie Magno Zito, as quoted in "Into the Mouths of Babes – The Drugging of Preschoolers is on the Rise, Study Shows," *Education Reporter*, April 2000.

241. Julie Magno Zito, *et al.*, "Trends in Prescribing of Psychotropic Medications to Preschoolers," *The Journal of American Medical Association*, 2000, p. 283.

242. This admittedly hard to believe estimate is from Kelly Patricia O'Meara, "New Research Indicts Ritalin," *Insight Magazine*, July 22, 2003.

243. For example, in a recent article it is reported that some geriatric specialists believe that Ritalin may relieve lethargy and depression in the elderly. Ritalin also has been used to combat the effects of strokes and brain injuries. Still, it appears that there are serious concerns about side effects. Christopher Windham, "Ritalin Shows Promise in Treating Lethargy, Depression in Elderly," *The Wall Street Journal*, July 17, 2003, D-1.

244. Walter Kirn, "Inside Ritalin," *GQ*, December 2000, pp. 297-301, at p. 300.

245. Walter Kirn, "Inside Ritalin," *GQ*, December 2000, pp. 297-301, at p. 300. Kirn also notes that if he had been given Ritalin in junior high he wouldn't have missed one dose. Why? As he explains: "They're uppers. Get it? Uppers. They act like downers on kids who truly need them, according to the experts, but what do they know? The experts are on the outside, looking in, monitoring behavior, not emotion. All they see are rows of little heads sitting obediently at little desks. The kids are the ones on the inside. It's different there – stranger, hotter, faster. I know...." At p. 301.

246. Fred A. Baughman, M.D., Jr., "The Totality of the ADD/ADHD Fraud," February 4, 1998, available at http://home.att.net/~Fred-Alden/Es5.html. A more recent work by Dr. Baughman on this subject is "Attention-Deficit Hyperactivity Disorder (ADHD) As Fraud," by Fred A. Baughman Jr., M. D., Neurologist, Pediatric Neurology, published *La Catarsis de Quiron. Revista de Psicologia* 2(1), 2002, available online at http://psychrights.org/Research/Digest/ADHD/ADHDAsFraud.htm

247. Terri Williams, "Report Challenges School Rules, But Educators Defend 'Zero Tolerance' Policy," *The Dallas Morning News*, February 24, 2001.

248. Ralph Reiland, "Zero Tolerance Makes Zero Sense," WorldNetDaily, May 11, 2001, available at www.worldnetdaily.com/news/article.asp?ARTICLE_ID=22787.

249. "'Patriotic' Stick Figure Drawing Troubles School," NYPost.com, October 29, 2003. The quoted language in the description of the incident is also from the same source.

250. Ralph Reiland, "Zero Tolerance Makes Zero Sense," WorldNetDaily, May 11, 2001, available at www.worldnetdaily.com/news/article.asp?ARTICLE_ID=22787.

251. Michelle Norris, "Schools Enforce the Rules with No Exceptions," ABCNews.com, February 8, 2000, available at http://more.abcnews.go.com/onair/closerlook/wnt_000208_cl_zerotolerance_feature.html.

252. Dean L. Kalahar, "Zero Tolerance or Hidden Agenda," EducationNews.org., November 26, 2001, available at www.educationnews.org/inside_the_classroom.htm.

253. Jesse Katz, "Taking Zero Tolerance to the Limit," *Los Angeles Times*, March 1, 1998.

254. Dean L. Kalahar, "Zero Tolerance or Hidden Agenda," EducationNews.org., November 26, 2001, available at www.educationnews.org/inside_the_classroom.htm.

255. Michelle Norris, "Schools Enforce the Rules with No Exceptions," ABCNews.com, February 8, 2000, available at http://more.abcnews.go.com/onair/closerlook/wnt_000208_cl_zerotolerance_feature.html.

256. Dean L. Kalahar, "Zero Tolerance or Hidden Agenda," EducationNews.org., November 26, 2001, available at www.educationnews.org/inside_the_classroom.htm.

257. Dean L. Kalahar, "Zero Tolerance or Hidden Agenda," EducationNews.org., November 26, 2001, available at www.educationnews.org/inside_the_classroom.htm.

258. Dean L. Kalahar, "Zero Tolerance or Hidden Agenda," EducationNews.org., November 26, 2001, available at www.educationnews.org/inside_the_classroom.htm.

259. "Third-Grader Suspended for Taking Vitamin at School," Associated Press, January 30, 2003.

260. Jesse Katz, "Taking Zero Tolerance to the Limit," *Los Angeles Times*, March 1, 1998.

261. "Middle School Puts Lid on Bathroom Breaks," Associated Press, February 16, 2004.

262. As quoted in "Middle School Puts Lid on Bathroom Breaks," Associated Press, February 16, 2004.

263. As quoted in "Middle School Puts Lid on Bathroom Breaks," Associated Press, February 16, 2004.

264. Ralph Reiland, "Zero Tolerance Makes Zero Sense," WorldNetDaily, May 11, 2001, available at www.worldnetdaily.com/news/article.asp?ARTICLE_ID=22787.

Chapter Five - *School Reform: A Popular Delusion*

1. As quoted in Chester Finn, *We Must Take Charge: Our Schools and Our Future* (New York: The Free Press, 1991), p. 44, cited in Andrew J. Coulson, *Market Education: The Unknown History* (New Brunswick: Transaction Publishers 1999), footnote 23 to Chapter 5.

2. Mike Antonucci, "One Yard Below, II. Teacher Salaries and Benefits," The Education Intelligence Agency, available at www.calnews.com/Archives/1YB_II_sal.htm. According to a recent study by the Hoover Institution that surveyed education policy analysts from a cross-section of think-tanks, teachers are not "underpaid." The report instead concluded that when compared with professionals in professions that might be viewed as "comparable," such as civil engineers, architects, biological and life scientists, and statisticians, and after adjusting for the number of hours worked, government school teachers are earning about what they should be earning. Christian Bourge, "Teachers Not Underpaid," *UPI*, May 21, 2003. As will be evident from the discussion in this chapter concerning who becomes a teacher and how teachers are trained, it is risible to claim that the current population of government schoolteachers is somehow comparable to civil engineers, statisticians, or any of the other occupations used for benchmarking the adequacy of teacher compensation. Very few of today's government schoolteachers would even qualify for entrance into a school of engineering, for example.

3. In light of the widespread dishonesty by the education establishment in conducting standardized tests such as the NAEP, it is highly probable that the skills measured by the NAEP have deteriorated rather than remaining unchanged.

4. Eric A. Hanushek, "Assessing the Effects of School Resources on Student Performance: An Update," *Educational Evaluation and Policy Analysis*, University of Rochester, Summer 1997, pp. 141-164. For a brief and incisive look at this issue with respect to New York City's government schools,

see Emanuel Tobier, "NewYork City's Public Schools: The Facts about Spending and Performance," Manhattan Institute for Policy Research, Civic Bulletin 26, available online at http://www.manhattan-institute.org/html/cb_26.htm. Tobier, now deceased, was a professor emeritus of economics and planning at NYU. His paper points out, among other things, that New York City's government schools educate roughly the same number of students today as they did fifty years ago, but they do it today at vastly greater cost and student achievement has deteriorated. To illustrate, in the 1950s there were roughly 35,000 teachers (resulting in a student-teacher ratio of 30:1) and 200 central office administrators in the City's schools. Today there are 90,000 teachers (resulting in a student-teacher ratio of 12:1) and 4,900 central and district office administrators. Yet, only 50% of students graduate with a high school diploma within four years after entering 9th grade. Only 58% receive a diploma within 7 years. Annual spending on K-12 education increased by 50% from 1997 to 2002 – $8 billion to $12 billion.

5. Rod Paige, "It's Not About the Money," *The Wall Street Journal*, October 30, 2003, A-16. The education establishment's rejoinder to Paige is that if you want the No Child Left Behind Act implemented, you have to give us even more money. By the way, the national averages for sources of funding for K-12 education are: 50% from income taxes, corporate taxes, sales taxes, and fees; 43% from local property taxes; and 7% from the federal government. Of course, these percentages vary somewhat from state to state.

6. Even now the teachers' unions continue to claim that government schools are "chronically under funded" and "starved" for resources. See, *e.g.*, Sandra Feldman, "A Better Way," December 2001, available at www.aft.org/stand/index.html.

7. The Heritage Foundation illustrates the point in a non-technical way with a chart that is easily accessible: http://www.heritage.org/research/features/issues/education/Education_14.pdf . The following link will point you toward further information on this subject: http://www.mnplan.state.mn.us/issues/scan.htm?Id=696.

8. For an interesting account of the Kansas City desegregation lawsuit written from the point of view of the plaintiffs' lawyer, see Arthur Benson, "School Segregation and Desegregation in Kansas City," available at www.bensonlaw.com/deseg/deseg_history.htm. More information on the Kansas City experiment and its results can be found in Paul Ciotti, "Money and School Performance: Lessons from the Kansas City Desegregation Experiment," Policy Analysis No. 298, March 16, 1998; Cato Institute, and Phillip O'Connor, "Kansas City School District Ponders Fate of Magnet Schools," *The Kansas City Star*, January 4, 2001.

9. Deann Smith, "Superintendent Wants to Pay District Students for Higher Test Scores," *The Kansas City Star*, March 13, 2003. www.KansasCity.com. The idea that economic incentives will somehow make children in government schools academically successful is also contradicted by a rather bold experiment. In 1987 George and Diane Weiss told the sixth grade pupils and their parents of Philadelphia's Belmont Elementary School that the Weiss's would pay for the college education of each child who graduated from high school. The Weiss's also poured $5 million dollars into an effort to help the children reach that goal. The results are as follows: roughly 50% graduated from high school; thirty of those were admitted to college and about half of them didn't attend or dropped out; and twenty of those that didn't graduate are convicted felons. David D. Perlmutter, "Education Reform only Works with Self-Motivation," *Atlanta-Journal Constitution*, April 2, 2002.

10. In case you're thinking that perhaps the failure in Kansas City was somehow mainly attributable to "troubled inner-city youth," you're deluding yourself. In 1997 the NEA teamed up with Disney and Stetson University to create a model school for Disney's new town of Celebration, Florida. Here the NEA and its partners started with a clean slate, no impediments from Disney, adequate funding, and a middle to upper-middle class clientele. The "Celebration Teaching Academy" was described by NEA President, Bob Chase, in a national Press Club Speech as follows: "It will be for educators what a teaching hospital is for doctors. A place where teachers can come to sharpen their skills and

be exposed to the best 'practices.' NEA professionals on site will help to shape the curriculum and to direct the academy's Master Teacher Institute." The Celebration Teaching Academy liberally indulged the hot-house educational theories dear to professors of education – cooperative learning, multiple intelligences, assessing students on "social responsibility," etc. – with predictable results. The school was quickly recognized as a disaster. Students were removed in large numbers, almost a third of the teachers left, and the principal quit even before Bob Chase gave his speech to the National Press Club. Because of the Academy's collapse, the NEA terminated its relationship with the Academy within two years after it opened. Tellingly, parents complained that while at the Academy their children regressed academically and behaviorally. Just think what teachers' unions and schools of education could do for American education as a whole if they had a free hand. A frightening thought. For a fascinating, more detailed account of the debacle in Celebration, Florida, and the NEA's involvement in charter schools of its own, see Peter Brimelow, *The Worm in the Apple: How the Teacher Unions are Destroying American Education* (New York: Harper Collins, 2003), pp. 185-193. The above quote from Bob Chase's National Press club speech can be found on p. 191 of Brimelow's book. Even when a school board attempts to take rational measures to stave off imminent collapse, opposition to virtually any change is encountered. Faced with a financial meltdown, a 50% dropout rate, and fewer than 7% of juniors scoring "proficient" on a state test of reading and writing, the St. Louis school board brought in a corporate turn-around company in an attempt to prevent the district from self-destructing. Egged-on by community leaders and the local teachers' unions, many parents were so infuriated by the changes that had to be made that they urged a boycott of school on the first day – even though the restructuring of the district had not involved laying off even one teacher. Stephanie Simon, "St. Louis Parents Hit School Overhaul," *The Boston Globe*, September 8, 2003.

11. For an account of waste in the California government school system, see Carl Brody and Dr. Alan Bonsteel. "CA: Schools a Swamp of Waste," OC Register, January 16, 2004, available online at http://209.157.64.200/focus/f-news/1059358/posts. Of course, where there are copious amounts of money, there are also crooks. For an account of the thieving endemic to the public school system, see Lydia G. Segal, *Battling Corruption in America's Public Schools,* (Northeaster University Press).

12. Laura Bird, "Cafeteria Food Fight: Nation's Kids Get Fatter While School Lunch Programs Battle Fast-Food and Soda," *The Wall Street Journal*, June 14, 2002, B-1.

13. Laura Bird, "Cafeteria Food Fight: Nation's Kids Get Fatter While School Lunch Programs Battle Fast-Food and Soda," *The Wall Street Journal*, June 14, 2002, B-1.

14. Laura Bird, "Cafeteria Food Fight: Nation's Kids Get Fatter While School Lunch Programs Battle Fast-Food and Soda," *The Wall Street Journal*, June 14, 2002, B-1.

15. "Bill to Cut Snack Machines Leads Instead to New Panel," Associated Press, May 7, 2003.

16. "Bill to Cut Snack Machines Leads Instead to New Panel," Associated Press, May 7, 2003.

17. As quoted in "Bill to Cut Snack Machines Leads Instead to New Panel," Associated Press, May 7, 2003.

18. The American Pediatrics Academy has issued a policy statement making clear the connection between soft drink consumption and obesity and other health problems in children and has recommended removing sweetened drinks from schools. *The Seattle Times* took the policy announcement as an opportunity to lend its support to the proposal. "Skip the Soda," *The Seattle Times*, January 12, 2004.

19. This information has been gleaned from the NEA's and the AFT's websites and various other sources, including Myron Lieberman, "Liberating Teachers Toward Market Competition in Teacher Representation," Cato Institute, Analysis 450, August 28, 2002. Lieberman's very interesting paper is available online at http://www.cato.org/pubs/pas/pa450.pdf .

20. See Peter Brimelow and Leslie Spencer, "The National Extortion Association?", *Forbes Magazine*, June 7, 1993.

21. Myron Lieberman and David Salisbury, "Teacher Unions vs. Good Schools," *New York Post*, April 19, 2003 (Online Edition).

22. "Where the NEA Gets its Power," HSLDA, October 17, 2002, quoting Bob Williams of the Evergreen Freedom Foundation.

23. As quoted in "Where the NEA Gets its Power," HSLDA, October 17, 2002.

24. See Jami Lund, "Evergreen Freedom Foundation Takes Teachers Union to Court," Capital Research Center, June 1999, available at www.capitalresearch.org/LaborWatch/lw-0699.htm.

25. Despite the obviously massive expenditures by the NEA and its affiliates to influence elections, it blatantly ignores IRS reporting rules and has been getting away with it. The teachers' unions are required to report on their tax returns whether they have spent any money or provided any other form of support directly or indirectly to political campaigns. According to Mark Levin of the Landmark Legal Foundation, however, the NEA has reported to the IRS that it has not spent even one cent on politics since at least 1994. Needless to say, it is a measure of the power of the teachers' unions that the IRS has somehow neglected to challenge transparently false statements on the NEA's tax reports. See Christine Hall, "NEA Called 'School Yard Bullies' in America's Political System," CNSNEWS. com, October 2, 2002.

26. Andrew Jacobs and Robert Hanley, "Anger Grows in Middleton Over Teachers' Strike," *The New York Times*, December 7, 2001.

27. Ellen Sorokin, "NEA Ordered to End Hassles Over Religion," *The Washington Times*, May 21, 2002.

28. Stefan Gleason, vice president of the National Right to Work Legal Defense Foundation, as quoted in Ellen Sorokin, "NEA Ordered to End Hassles Over Religion," *The Washington Times*, May 21, 2002.

29. "Landmark Unleashes Major Complaint Against NEA," Press Release, September 4, 2003, available on line at http://www.landmarklegal.org/latest_developments.cfm?webpage_id=549. For a commentary on Landmark's request for an investigation see"The NEA's Dubious Expenditure's," *The Washington Times*, September 10, 2003.

30. "Landmark Unleashes Major Complaint Against NEA," Press Release, September 4, 2003, available on line at http://www.landmarklegal.org/latest_developments.cfm?webpage_id=549.

31. "IRS Auditing National Education Association," Associated Press, November 25, 2003.

32. "The NEA's Dubious Expenditure's," *The Washington Times*, September 10, 2003.

33. "Landmark Unleashes Major Complaint Against NEA," Press Release, September 4, 2003, available on line at http://www.landmarklegal.org/latest_developments.cfm?webpage_id=549.

34. If the NEA is not called to account for its tax evasion, that will tell us a great deal about how dangerous the power of the teachers' unions has become.

35. This discussion of the WEA is based in part on information that can be found in Jami Lund, "Evergreen Freedom Foundation Takes Teachers Union to Court," Capital Research Center, June 1999, available at www.capitalresearch.org/LaborWatch/lw-0699.htm.

36. Under the Supreme Court's *Beck* decision union members are not supposed to be forced to contribute money used for political purposes. *Beck* has never been fully enforced and is routinely violated by the unions. As previously noted, unions regularly ignore or obstruct a worker's right to divert to charities of the worker's choosing funds that the unions would otherwise use for a purpose that would violate the worker's sincerely held religious beliefs. In Washington State, for example, a pastor who was also a part-time public-school bus driver told the union that he wanted his dues sent to a food bank. Instead, the union informed him that it had decided to send his dues to the ACLU. See "Give Teachers Their Due(s)," *The Wall Street Journal*, June 11, 2002, A-14.

37. Scheduling elections also gives the hyper-monopolists a notable advantage in passing revenue measures. To illustrate, a large suburban Houston school district with an enrollment of roughly 67,300 students set a $470 million (!) bond election for December 8, 2001. In addition to renovating schools, the funds were ear-marked for an agricultural farm, a second athletic stadium (of a caliber previously seen only at universities), an "educational support center" to hold more than 9,000 people, a transportation center, the expansion of food services, and who knows what else. As reported in the local paper, the measure passed by a landside, getting 85.1 percent of the vote. Of course, fewer than 5,000 voters out of well over a hundred thousand in the district voted. This means that the votes of school district employees alone could have carried the election. This sort of low turnout was undoubtedly what the district had in mind when it set the election. For more information, see Paris Achen, "Voters Approve Cy-Fair ISD's $470.5 million Bond," *The 1960 Sun*, December 12, 2001.

38. The leadership of the teachers' unions generally has had radical political views, so forming overt alliances with leftwing organizations is congenial to the leadership. Pointing out that additional political power would further economic and other traditional union interests, however, was undoubtedly the way this strategy was sold to many of the rank-and-file members, who tend to be substantially less radical than the leadership.

39. Robert B. Bluey, "Dems Get Nearly All Teacher Union Contributions, Report Says," CNS.com, October 2, 2002.

40. As quoted in Robert B. Bluey, "Dems Get Nearly All Teacher Union Contributions, Report Says," CNS.com, October 2, 2002.

41. Sean R. Sedam, "Schools to Give Students Credit for Attending Thornton Rally," *The Gazette*, February 4, 2004. Of course, students are also increasingly being used for political purposes by some teachers in government schools through "assignments" requiring students to write letters to political figures in support of positions advocated by the teachers.

42. Robert Tanner,"Rod Paige Criticizes Teachers Union," Associate Press, February 23, 2003.

43. As quoted in Ben Feller, "NEA Asks Bush to Fire Education Secretary," Associated Press, February 24, 2004.

44. Ben Feller, "NEA Asks Bush to Fire Education Secretary," Associated Press, February 24, 2004.

45. Dave McKinney and Leslie Griffey, "Gov Drops 'Bomb' on Board of Ed," *The Sun-Times*, January 16, 2004.

46. "Judge Orders Kansas Public Schools Closed," Associated Press, May 11, 2004.

47. Peter Brimelow, *The Worm in the Apple: How the Teacher Unions are Destroying American Education* (New York: Harper Collins, 2003), Chapter 7.

48. Michelle Malkin, "The Looters Liberals Ignore," WorldnetDaily, May 2, 2003, available at www.worldnetdaily.com. The amount stolen is about $1,000 per union member. Nicholas Stix, "Washington, D.C.: America's Scandal Capital," *Middle American News*, March 2003.

49. This partial list of the ill-gotten goods was compiled from Nicholas Stix, "Washington, D.C.: America's Scandal Capital," *Middle American News*, March 2003, and Michelle Malkin, "The Looters Liberals Ignore," WorldNet Daily, May 2, 2003.

50. "Union Doozy," *The Wall Street Journal*, A-24. This article also discusses how lax teachers' unions financial reporting obligations have been.

51. Nicholas Stix, "Washington, D.C.: America's Scandal Capital," *Middle American News*, March 2003.

52. Nicholas Stix, "Washington, D.C.: America's Scandal Capital," *Middle American News*, March 2003.

53. Nicholas Stix, "Washington, D.C.: America's Scandal Capital," *Middle American News*, March 2003.

54. Nicholas Stix, "Washington, D.C.: America's Scandal Capital," *Middle American News*, March 2003.

55. As quoted in Michelle Malkin, "The Looters Liberals Ignore," WorldnetDaily, May 2, 2003.

56. Joe Mozingo and Larry Lebowitz, "Teachers' Union Raided in Miami-Dade," *The Miami Herald*, April 30, 2003, www.herald.com.

57. Joe Mozingo and Larry Lebowitz, "Teachers' Union Raided in Miami-Dade," *The Miami Herald*, April 30, 2003.

58. As quoted in Joe Mozingo and Larry Lebowitz, "Teachers' Union Raided in Miami-Dade," *The Miami Herald*, April 30, 2003.

59. The FBI's press release on Tornillo's guilty plea can be found at http://miami.fbi.gov/press-rel/2003/mm082503.htm.

60. Dave Wedge, "MTA Thief Hits Jackpot in Court, *Boston Herald*, December 16, 2003.

61. This has been reported by various sources. Mike Antonucci's "Education Intelligence Agency" provides a quick summary that is available online at http://home.earthlink.net/~mantonucci/ar-chives/20030218.htm.

62. One interesting account of how the teachers' unions are trying to defuse this issue using a chimerical peer review assistance program while at the same time providing nearly absolute job security is found in Peter Brimelow, *The Worm in the Apple: How the Teacher Unions are Destroying American Education* (New York: Harper Collins, 2003), pp. 181-184.

63. Martin L. Gross, *The Conspiracy of Ignorance: The Failure of American Schools* (New York: Harper Collins, 1999), p. 214.

64. As quoted in Richard Whitmire, "Scrutiny Falls on Teacher Testing," *The Seattle Times*, July 6, 1998.

65. Richard Whitmire, "Scrutiny Falls on Teacher Testing," *The Seattle Times*, July 6, 1998.

66. Richard Whitmire, "Scrutiny Falls on Teacher Testing," *The Seattle Times*, July 6, 1998.

67. "Teacher Testing – Recent Developments," National Council on Teacher Quality, July 19, 2001, available at www.nctq.org/issues/testing.html. The salary information is a modest extrapolation from a 1996 average, and the benefits information is from Mike Antonucci, "One Yard Below, II. Teacher Salaries and Benefits," The Education Intelligence Agency, available at www.calnews.com/Archives/1YB_II_sal.htm.

68. "Teacher Testing – Recent Developments," National Council on Teacher Quality, July 27, 2000, available at www.nctq.org/issues/testing.html.

69. Glori Chaika, "Testing Teachers Makes Teachers Testy," *Education World*, September 26, 2000.

70. As quoted in Walter Williams, "What's Wrong with Education?," *The Washington Times*, October 29, 2001.

71. Glori Chaika, "Testing Teachers Makes Teachers Testy," *Education World*, September 26, 2000, and Richard Whitmire, "Scrutiny Falls on Teacher Testing," *The Seattle Times*, July 6, 1998. Accord-

ing to Drew Gitomer, vice president of research with Educational Testing Service, even raising standards a little on teacher tests could reduce the group of teachers who make it into the classroom by 25%. Glori Chaika, "Testing Teachers Makes Teachers Testy," *Education World*, September 26, 2000. Remember, we are discussing raising the standard "a little" on a tenth-grade test. Moreover, as low as the standards are, teachers are cheating on these tests. See, for example, "Teachers in 5 States Accused of Paying Bribes to Cheat on Tests," CNN.com, August 17, 2000, available online at http://www.cnn.com/2000/US/08/17/testing.scandal.ap/, and a follow-up article "Dozen Mississippi Teachers Lose Licenses in Testing Scandal," *Jefferson City New Tribune*, March 3, 2001, available online at http://www.newstribune.com/stories/030301/wor_0303010023.asp .

72. "Teacher Testing – Recent Developments," National Council on Teacher Quality, March 15, 2001, available at www.nctq.org/issues/testing.html.

73. "Teacher Testing – Recent Developments," National Council on Teacher Quality, September 6, 2001, available at www.nctq.org/issues/testing.html.

74. Rod Paige, "Meeting the Highly Qualified Teachers Challenge: The Secretary's Annual Report on Teacher Quality," available at www.title2.org and www.nochildleftbehind.gov . For a summary of the report, see "A Better Class of Teachers," *The Wall Street Journal*, July 5, 2002, p. A12.

75. Rod Paige, "Meeting the Highly Qualified Teachers Challenge: The Secretary's Annual Report on Teacher Quality," available at www.title2.org and www.nochildleftbehind.gov . For a summary of the report, see "A Better Class of Teachers," *The Wall Street Journal*, July 5, 2002, p. A12.

76. Rod Paige, "Meeting the Highly Qualified Teachers Challenge: The Secretary's Annual Report on Teacher Quality," available at www.title2.org and www.nochildleftbehind.gov . For a summary of the report, see "A Better Class of Teachers," *The Wall Street Journal*, July 5, 2002, p. A12.

77. Rod Paige, "Meeting the Highly Qualified Teachers Challenge: The Secretary's Annual Report on Teacher Quality," available at www.title2.org and www.nochildleftbehind.gov . For a summary of the report, see "A Better Class of Teachers," *The Wall Street Journal*, July 5, 2002, p. A12.

78. Rod Paige, "Meeting the Highly Qualified Teachers Challenge: The Secretary's Annual Report on Teacher Quality," available at www.title2.org and www.nochildleftbehind.gov. For a summary of the report, see "A Better Class of Teachers," *The Wall Street Journal*, July 5, 2002, p. A12.

79. Rod Paige, "Meeting the Highly Qualified Teachers Challenge: The Secretary's Annual Report on Teacher Quality," available at www.title2.org and www.nochildleftbehind.gov.

80. Kelly Patricia O'Meara, "When Teachers Flunk the Test: 40 States allow Districts to Hire Educators without Basic Skills," WorldNetDaily.com, September 23, 2003, available online at http://www.worldnetdaily.com/news/printer-friendly.asp?ARTICLE_ID=34727. The O'Meara article provides a good summary of the current state of teacher competency testing.

81. In fairness, administrators, who are often drawn from the ranks of coaches, are notorious for being on average even less intellectually distinguished than the teachers they manage. One of the more noteworthy examples is the superintendent of the Lawrence, Massachusetts, government schools, Wilfredo T. Laboy. Laboy, it turns out, failed a mandatory Communications Skills and Literacy Test three times. Passing the test is required for licensure in Massachusetts, and before his short-comings came to light, Laboy had put 24 teachers on unpaid administrative leave for failing the same test that he had failed repeatedly. Unlike the teachers he suspended without pay, Laboy continued to draw his salary of $156,560 and benefits even after his third failure. Laboy claims that he was stumped by the test's questions on rules of grammar and punctuation. Imagine someone in charge of an institution responsible for teaching punctuation and rules of grammar who cannot himself demonstrate a modest grasp of these same simple matters, yet he earns a six-figure salary, and can, in effect, fire others for not meeting that same standard. Worse, those responsible for recruiting Laboy as superintendent

had reason to know that he could not pass the mandatory Communications Skills and Literacy Test. They evidently felt that Laboy's status as a Hispanic minority trumped all other considerations. The situation with Laboy illustrates why government schools are both expensive and ineffective. For more details, see, for example, Ken McGuire, "School Leader Under Pressure to Pass Literacy Exam," Associated Press, August 4, 2003.

82. For a discussion of the academic characteristics of education majors and school of education faculty, see, *e.g.*, Thomas Sowell, *Inside American Education* (New York: The Free Press, 1993), pp. 21-34, Robert P. Strauss, "Who Gets Hired to Teach? The Case of Pennsylvania," Thomas B. Fordham Foundation, available at www.edexcellence.net/better/tchrs/10.htm; and "Prospective Teachers' SAT scores Higher than Believed, Study Finds," *Education Week – Reporter's Notebook*, March 10, 1999. Peter Brimelow also provides an interesting discussion regarding how the NEA has tried to spin the facts about teachers and student performance on standardized tests. See, Peter Brimelow, *The Worm in the Apple: How the Teacher Unions are Destroying American Education* (New York: Harper Collins, 2003), p. 39-40.

83. Samuel Blumenfeld, *Is Public Education Necessary?* (Boise: The Paradigm Company, 1985), pp. 66-69.

84. As quoted in Thomas Sowell, *Inside American Education* (New York: The Free Press, 1993), p. 24.

85. As quoted in Peter Brimelow, *The Worm in the Apple: How the Teacher Unions are Destroying American Education* (New York: Harper Collins, 2003), p. 47.

86. Thomas Sowell, *Inside American Education* (New York: The Free Press, 1993), p. 24.

87. For an entertaining first-hand account of the strange brew of politics and inanity ladled out by schools of education, read Rita Kramer's *Ed School Follies: The Miseducation of America's Teachers.* Kramer's book reports on what she found as she traveled around the country sitting in on classes in 15 schools of education — both public and private, and ranging from those thought to be "prestigious" to those regarded as pedestrian. No matter what the reputation of the school, Kramer concludes that what is happening inside is appalling.

88. This is taken from a conversation Charles J. Sykes had with a Colorado principal as reported in Martin L. Gross, *The Conspiracy of Ignorance: The Failure of American Schools* (New York: Harper Collins, 1999), p. 60.

89. In summary, the NCES found that 13% of those teaching foreign language, 17% of those teaching social studies, 25% of those teaching English, 34% of those teaching mathematics, and 40% of those teaching science had neither a major nor a minor in the subjects they were teaching. "Confronting the Crisis: Who's Teaching Our Children," November 3, 1999, available at www.nea.org/teaching/quality/facts.html. For a survey of state certification and licensure requirements prepared by the U.S. Department of Education, go to http://www.ed.gov/offices/OPE/News/teacherprep/initialreport4.pdf .

90. For an example from Texas, see Diana Reinhart, "Leaders of Teacher Groups Protest Certification Proposal," *Express-News*, February 23, 2004.

91. David Saxe of Pennsylvania State University performed the study. His words appear in the text as quoted in George C. Leef, "The Trouble with Teacher Training," *Ideas on Liberty* (published by the Foundation for Economic Education), November 2001, Volume 51, Number 11, p. 38.

92. As quoted in George C. Leef, "The Trouble with Teacher Training," *Ideas on Liberty* (published by the Foundation for Economic Education), November 2001, Volume 51, Number 11, p. 40.

93. Bess Keller, "Education School Courses Faulted as Intellectually Thin," *Education Week*, November 12, 2003.

94. Bess Keller, "Education School Courses Faulted as Intellectually Thin," *Education Week*, November 12, 2003.

95. Bess Keller, "Education School Courses Faulted as Intellectually Thin," *Education Week*, November 12, 2003.

96. Bess Keller, "Education School Courses Faulted as Intellectually Thin," *Education Week*, November 12, 2003.

97. E.D. Hirsch, Jr., *The Schools We Need: Why We Don't Have Them*, (New York: Doubleday , 1996).

98. I would strongly recommend that anyone who is skeptical of my argument concerning the deplorable influence of schools of education take the time to read chapters 3, 4, and 5 of E.D. Hirsch's *The Schools We Need: Why We Don't Have Them*. Chapter 6 also discusses many of the same issues I raise in my chapter 3 regarding the determined efforts by the education establishment to evade being held accountable through testing.

99. E.D. Hirsch, Jr., *The Schools We Need: Why We Don't Have Them*, (New York: Doubleday, 1996), p. 68.

100. As quoted in Peter Brimelow, *The Worm in the Apple: How the Teacher Unions are Destroying American Education* (New York: Harper Collins, 2003), p. 47.

101. Thomas Sowell, "Unsettling School Data," *The Washington Times*, July 31, 2002.

102. Martin L. Gross, *The Conspiracy of Ignorance: The Failure of American Schools* (New York: Harper Collins, 1999), pp. 99-101.

103. This discussion emphasizes the social and political dimensions to NCATE's ideology, but NCATE also enforces conformity with various "child-centered" or "progressive" theories of education.

104. Robert Holland, "New Teachers Face NCATE Litmus Test on Diversity Educators Must Exhibit," *School Reform News*, Heartland Institute, January 1, 2002, available online at http://www.heartland.org/Article.cfm?artId=202.

105. As quoted in Robert Holland, "New Teachers Face NCATE Litmus Test on Diversity Educators Must Exhibit," *School Reform News*, Heartland Institute, January 1, 2002, available online at http://www.heartland.org/Article.cfm?artId=202.

106. John E. Stone, "The National Council for the Accreditation of Teacher Education: Whose Standards?," Education Consumers ClearingHouse, available online at http://www.education-consumers.com/articles/whose_standards.shtm. This article thoroughly examines NCATE's standards and the mentality of the educators who support them.

107. As quoted in John E. Stone, "The National Council for the Accreditation of Teacher Education: Whose Standards?," Education Consumers ClearingHouse, available online at http://www.education-consumers.com/articles/whose_standards.shtm.

108. As quoted in John E. Stone, "The National Council for the Accreditation of Teacher Education: Whose Standards?," Education Consumers ClearingHouse, available online at http://www.education-consumers.com/articles/whose_standards.shtm.

109. The figures concerning the number of schools of education accredited by NCATE are from Martin L. Gross, *The Conspiracy of Ignorance: The Failure of American Schools* (New York: Harper Collins, 1999), pp. 100-101. Mr. Gross's views about the political nature of NCATE are more tentative than mine.

110. Martin L. Gross, *The Conspiracy of Ignorance: The Failure of American Schools* (New York: Harper Collins 1999), p. 100.

111. Some private schools, especially those that are academically elite, prefer not to hire teachers who come from the school of education gene pool.

112. Jean Johnson, Ann Duffett, Jackie Vine, and Leslie Moye, *Where We are Now: 12 Things You Need to know About Public Opinion and Public Schools* (Public Agenda, 2003), pp. 16, 17. The report is available at www.publicagenda.org.

113. Jean Johnson, Ann Duffett, Jackie Vine, and Leslie Moye, *Where We are Now: 12 Things You Need to know About Public Opinion and Public Schools,* (Public Agenda, 2003), p. 28.

114. This quip circulating among teachers is reported by Heather MacDonald in "Unsafe at Any Grade," *The Wall Street Journal*, March 25, 2004, D6, a book review of Richard Arum's *Judging School Discipline* (Harvard University Press), and Elizabeth Gold's *Brief Intervals of Horrible Sanity* (Tarcher Penguin). Both books document the severity and the sources of today's levels of public school violence.

115. Seth Stern, "The Great Escape," *The Christian Science Monitor*, October 7, 2003.

116. Seth Stern, "The Great Escape," *The Christian Science Monitor*, October 7, 2003.

117. Seth Stern, "The Great Escape," *The Christian Science Monitor*, October 7, 2003.

118. Martin L. Gross, *The Conspiracy of Ignorance: The Failure of American Schools* (New York: Harper Collins, 1999), p. 170.

119. The estimates of the number of charter schools and their enrollment vary somewhat. See, Robert Tomsho, "Charter Schools are Falling Short in Aiding the Neediest," *The Wall Street Journal*, April 8, 2003, D-8, and Robert Tomsho, "Charter-School Movement Sputters," *The Wall Street Journal*, January 21, 2003, A-3. John Fund, "Will Terror Leave Us No Choice? Teachers' Unions Try to Use September 11 as Excuse for Bad Schools," *John Fund's Political Diary*, May 1, 2002.

120. For examples of the kinds of restrictions that the teachers' unions would impose on charter schools, see the AFT's web site.

121. Martin L. Gross, *The Conspiracy of Ignorance: The Failure of American Schools* (New York: Harper Collins, 1999), p.171.

122. See Paul Strand, "Fighting a Failing System: Education in America," Christianity.com, available at www.christianity.com/partner/Article_Display_ Page/1,1183,PTID1000/CHID209188/C., and Mark Walsh, "San Francisco Moves to Revoke Edison's Contract," *Education Week*, April 4, 2001.

123. John Fund, "Will Terror Leave Us No Choice? Teachers' Unions Try to Use September 11 as Excuse for Bad Schools," *John Fund's Political Diary*, May 1, 2002.

124. John Fund, "Will Terror Leave Us No Choice? Teachers' Unions Try to Use September 11 as Excuse for Bad Schools," *John Fund's Political Diary*, May 1, 2002.

125. Marjorie Coeyman, "Charter Schools Build on a Decade of Experimentation," *The Christian Science Monitor*, January 7, 2003.

126. Marjorie Coeyman, "Charter Schools Build on a Decade of Experimentation," *The Christian Science Monitor*, January 7, 2003.

127. Robert Tomsho, "Charter-School Movement Sputters," *The Wall Street Journal*, January 21, 2003, A-3.

128. Robert Tomsho, "Charter-School Movement Sputters," *The Wall Street Journal*, January 21, 2003, A-3.

129. Robert Tomsho, "Charter-School Movement Sputters," *The Wall Street Journal*, January 21, 2003, A-3.

130. "UNT Drops Plans for Virtual School," *Houston Chronicle* (Associated Press), November 5, 2003. Teachers' unions and their allies become particularly hysterical over virtual charter schools. Online education – in essence a form of homeschooling – would dramatically reduce the need for teachers, classrooms, staffing at schools of education, and personnel and services of every kind associated with traditional government schooling. Virtual charter schools also diminish the access to children now enjoyed by the sundry ideologues currently influencing curricula and programs. They know that, for example, even if a contest to see who can put a condom on a banana fastest is included in the virtual school curriculum, moms will skip that part of the lesson plan.

131. Robert Tomsho, "Charter-School Movement Sputters," *The Wall Street Journal*, January 21, 2003, A-3.

132. As quoted in Robert Tomsho, "Charter-School Movement Sputters," *The Wall Street Journal*, January 21, 2003, A-3. More recently, the editorial page writers for *The Wall Street Journal* have sounded more upbeat about the prospects for charter schools. "The Charter Boom," *The Wall Street Journal*, November 3, 2003, A14. Unfortunately, their optimism is unsupported by signs of substantial progress. They also do not acknowledge how easily charter schools can be co-opted or sabotaged.

133. Peter Brimelow, *The Worm in the Apple: How the Teacher Unions are Destroying American Education* (New York: Harper Collins, 2003), p. 55.

134. As quoted in Peter Brimelow, *The Worm in the Apple: How the Teacher Unions are Destroying American Education* (New York: Harper Collins, 2003), p. 55.

135. Matthew Miller, "A Bold Experiment to Fix City Schools," *Atlantic Monthly*, July 1999, as quoted in Peter Brimelow, *The Worm in the Apple: How the Teacher Unions are Destroying American Education* (New York: Harper Collins, 2003), p. 140.

136. "Statement of Bob Chase, President of the National Education Association on the U.S. Supreme Court Decision on Private School Tuition Vouchers," June 27, 2002 (Press Release), www.nea.org.

137. Another potential legal problem for vouchers arose when the Supreme Court let stand in *Locke v. Davey* a Washington State law excluding students who wish to pursue theological studies from a scholarship program available to all other students. Voucher opponents see *Locke* as a major win, while proponents claim that it should not have a broad impact. For a brief commentary from the pro-voucher Institute for Justice, visit their website at http://www.ij.org/cases/school/.

138. "The Next Voucher Battleground," *The Wall Street Journal*, August 7, 2002, A-14.

139. David Royse, "Florida Judge Strikes Down Voucher Law," Associated Press Online, August 5, 2002.

140. Jon Sarche, "Colorado Supreme Court Strikes School Vouchers," Associated Press, June 28, 2004.

141. "The Empire Strikes Back," *The Wall Street Journal*, March 25, 2004, A16.

142. George Archibald, "School Vouchers Start by Fall," *The Washington Times*, January 29, 2004, available online at http://www.washingtontimes.com/functions/print.php?StoryID=20040129-122047-3274r

143. The Institute for Justice provides a very helpful summary of existing voucher programs, their characteristics, and their enrollments at http://www.ij.org/cases/school/.

144. As is plain, I think that vouchers are a dangerous distraction for Christian parents. It is a profound mistake to be waiting for a "voucher cavalry" that may never come, and that, under the best of circumstances, will not arrive in the foreseeable future. This is not meant, however, to demean the motives or the efforts of the many people and institutions that are pushing for vouchers. Even if they

ultimately don't enjoy the success for which they are striving, their activities have done a great deal to bring much needed attention to the educational disaster known as "public schools."

145. For a good discussion of the political dynamics of vouchers, see Peter Brimelow, *The Worm in the Apple: How the Teacher Unions are Destroying American Education* (New York: Harper Collins, 2003), pp. 129-140.

146. The Left opposes vouchers because vouchers threaten the monopoly position and the cash flow enjoyed by an institution the Left dominates. Some Christians and others are concerned about vouchers because they believe vouchers may pose a risk to the autonomy of private schools. Consequently, Christian educational organizations such as the Association of Classical and Christian Schools, the American Association of Christian Schools, and the Foundation for American Christian Education oppose vouchers out of fear that they will lead to government control. Similarly, some libertarians have argued that vouchers pose a serious threat of expanding rather than reducing the influence of government and the government school industry in American education. See, *e.g.*, Dwight R. Lee, "The Political Economy of Educational Vouchers," *The Freeman*, February 1987, p. 244. See also, Marshall S. Smith and Jennifer O'Day, *Systemic School Reform, Politics of Education Association Yearbook 1990*, p.259. Other Christian educational organizations such as the Association of Christian Schools International support vouchers with reservations.

147. Vouchers and school-choice programs have been very useful in making public the depth of dissatisfaction inner-city parents have with government schools. For example, according to the *Chicago Sun-Times* 250,000 students are "vying" for transfers to "higher performing" schools under the choice provisions of the No Child Left Behind Act. The problem is that there are only 5,000 places available under the program. Rosalind Rossi, "Choice Program Could Overwhelm Schools," *Chicago Sun-Times*, August 7, 2003.

148. This account of the secession effort by the Carson schools is based on facts reported by Jean Merl and Massie Ritsch, "Lessons of Secession Bid Failure," *Los Angeles Times*, November 8, 2001.

149. Michael A. Fletcher, "Philadelphia's Schools to be Privately Run Under Pa. Plan," *The Washington Post*, November 6, 2001, and "City of Brotherly Thugs," *The Wall Street Journal* (Editorial), December 3, 2001.

150. Michael A. Fletcher, "Philadelphia's Schools to be Privately Run Under Pa. Plan," *The Washington Post*, November 6, 2001.

151. "City of Brotherly Thugs," *The Wall Street Journal* (Editorial), December 3, 2001.

152. "Government Takes Over Philly Schools," Associated Press, December 22, 2001.

153. "Street Justice," *The Wall Street Journal* (Editorial), December 18, 2002.

154. "Street Justice," *The Wall Street Journal* (Editorial), December 18, 2002.

155. "Philadelphia's Loss," *The Wall Street Journal*, April 19, 2002, A-18.

156. Daniel Golden, "Boston School Severs its Ties with Edison, Citing Test Scores," *The Wall Street Journal*, May 16, 2002, B-12.

157. David Limbaugh, "Dumbing Down Schools to Please the Feds," WorldNetDaily.com, June 14, 2002, Richard Rothstein, "How U.S. Punishes States with Higher Standards," *The New York Times*, September 18, 2002.

158. Sam Dillon, "States are Relaxing Standards on Tests to Avoid Sanctions," *New York Times*, May 22, 2003. Although everything Mr. Finn says is correct, you would think this is his first rodeo. No one should be surprised that school reform will not work, least of all an old education hand like Mr. Finn.

159. Peter Schrag, "California's 40,000 New 'Highly Qualified' Teachers," *The Sacramento Bee*, August 7, 2002.

160. Peter Schrag, "California's 40,000 New 'Highly Qualified' Teachers," *The Sacramento Bee*, August 7, 2002.

161. As quoted in Peter Schrag, "California's 40,000 New 'Highly Qualified' Teachers," *The Sacramento Bee*, August 7, 2002.

162. Peter Schrag, "California's 40,000 New 'Highly Qualified' Teachers," *The Sacramento Bee*, August 7, 2002.

163. Peter Schrag, "California's 40,000 New 'Highly Qualified' Teachers," *The Sacramento Bee*, August 7, 2002.

164. Bill Lindelof, "State Schools to Delay Exit Exam 2 Years," *The Sacramento Bee*, July 10, 2003.

165. Bill Lindelof, "State Schools to Delay Exit Exam 2 Years," *The Sacramento Bee*, July 10, 2003, and Dan Walters, "Exit Exam Results Demonstrate California's Two-Tier School System," *The Sacramento Bee*, October 2, 2002.

166. The federal definition of a highly qualified teacher has three parts:

- The teacher must have at least a bachelor's degree;
- The teacher must demonstrate subject matter knowledge in the subjects taught; and
- The teacher must have full state certification.

For a speech given to educators by a Department of Education official (Associate Deputy Undersecretary Petrilli) regarding these requirements go to http://www.ed.gov/news/speeches/2003/04/04082003.html.

167. The NEA doesn't care whether it is possible or not to implement the "highly qualified" teacher standards. It plans to sue to stop their implementation. Why? The reason given publicly is that it wants more money for education before any changes are made. While it is certainly true that the NEA always wants more money for the education monopoly, it is also undoubtedly hostile to the "highly qualified" teacher standards because the NEA also always opposes higher standards and efforts to hold its membership accountable. Birds gotta fly, fish gotta swim, etc.

168. Daniel Golden, "Colleges Ease Way for Teachers to Get Advanced Degrees," *The Wall Street Journal*, September 22, 2003, A-1.

169. The increased emphasis on obtaining graduate degrees, the proliferation of teacher standards boards, and other trappings designed to create the impression of greater professionalism on the part of teachers got its initial impetus from the 1983 report, "A Nation at Risk," and the Carnegie Corporation's "A Nation Prepared: Teachers for the 21st Century." But like a Potemkin village, what has been delivered is appearance rather than substance. As Chester E. Finn, Jr., has put it: "[W]hat started as an effort to improve the teaching profession has turned instead into professionalizing teacher improvement, with little to show in the way of improved schools performance." Finn refers to this as "results-free professionalism." See Chester E. Finn, Jr., "Professionalizing Teachers versus Improving the Profession," *The Hoover Institution*, September 15, 2003.

170. Daniel Golden, "Colleges Ease Way for Teachers to Get Advanced Degrees," *The Wall Street Journal*, September 22, 2003, A-1.

171. Daniel Golden, "Colleges Ease Way for Teachers to Get Advanced Degrees," *The Wall Street Journal*, September 22, 2003, A-1.

172. Daniel Golden, "Colleges Ease Way for Teachers to Get Advanced Degrees," *The Wall Street Journal*, September 22, 2003, A-1.

173. Daniel Golden, "Colleges Ease Way for Teachers to Get Advanced Degrees," *The Wall Street Journal*, September 22, 2003, A-1.

174. Daniel Golden, "Colleges Ease Way for Teachers to Get Advanced Degrees," *The Wall Street Journal*, September 22, 2003, A-1. If the likes of Cambridge College prove too rigorous, teachers might consider getting their master's degrees from St. Regis University, an online university located in Liberia that offers degrees based on "life experience"...oh, yes, and for a payment of $995 (doctorates are $1,500). "Teachers in Georgia Got Raises for Fake Degrees," Fox News/Associated Press, March 24, 2004. Apparently, Gwinnett County, Georgia, discovered that it was paying some of its highly trained education professionals higher salaries because of their St. Regis University "degrees."

175. Daniel Golden, "Colleges Ease Way for Teachers to Get Advanced Degrees," *The Wall Street Journal*, September 22, 2003, A-1.

176. Robert Dodge, "Administration to Modify No Child Left Behind Act," *Seattle Times*, February 20, 2004. The standard complaint by state politicians is that the Act is an underfunded mandate. This is not exactly true. The Act requires states to establish their own tests and progress standards. Once they have set those standards, the Act requires them to meet them. This is, in fact, one of the weaknesses of the Act, and, as noted previously, states have been lowering standards to make sure that no federal dollar gets away. Obviously, the states have the leeway to set standards at a level they can fund. For more on this see "No Politician Left Behind," *The Wall Street Journal*, February 12, 2004, A12.

177. Ronnie Lynn, "'No Child' Rebellion Picking up Momentum," *The Salt Lake Tribune*, February 5, 2004.

178. Robert Dodge, "Administration to Modify No Child Left Behind Act," *Seattle Times*, February 20, 2004.

179. Charlotte Thompson Iserbyt, *The Deliberate Dumbing Down of America* (Ravenna, Ohio: Conscience Press, 1999), p. xvii.

180. Peter Brimelow, *The Worm in the Apple: How the Teacher Unions are Destroying American Education* (New York: Harper Collins, 2003), p. 151.

181. Peter Brimelow, *The Worm in the Apple: How the Teacher Unions are Destroying American Education* (New York: Harper Collins, 2003), p. 145-158.

182. Peter Brimelow, *The Worm in the Apple: How the Teacher Unions are Destroying American Education* (New York: Harper Collins, 2003), p. 152-154.

183. Charlotte Thompson Iserbyt, *The Deliberate Dumbing Down of America* (Ravenna, Ohio: Conscience Press, 1999), p. xvi.

Chapter Six - *Government Schools: The Wages of Christian Sin*

1. *A Nation at Risk: The Imperative for Educational Reform*, National Commission on Excellence in Education, April 1983, available online at http://www.goalline.org/Goal%20Line/NatAtRisk.html. It is well worth the effort to compare the commision's risk factors indicating the educational failure of government schools with the more recent evidence of their educational failure set forth in Chapter 3.

2. See John Taylor Gatto, *An Underground History of American Education* (New York: The Oxford Village Press, 2000/2001), p. 31, and Samuel L. Blumenfeld, *Is Public Education Necessary?* (Boise: The Paradigm Company, 1985), p. 42.

3. Lloyd P. Jorgenson, *The State and the Non-Public School 1825 – 1925* (Columbia: The University of Missouri Press, 1987), pp. 4-7.

4. Samuel L. Blumenfeld, *Is Public Education Necessary?* (Boise: The Paradigm Company, 1985), pp. 27-28.

5. Martin Morse Wooster, *Angry Classrooms, Vacant Minds: What's Happened to our High Schools?* (San Francisco: Pacific Research Institute, 1994), p. 2. Some schools in Connecticut, for example, were at least partially supported by rate bills. Common School proponents viewed this form of funding in which the government was essentially doing little more than collecting tuition from parents on behalf of schools as an obstacle to their plans and were instrumental in having this school financing mechanism repealed.

6. For an interesting account of the methods of public finance in 17th century New England, see Herbert L. Osgood, "New England Colonial Finance in the Seventeenth Century," *Political Science Quarterly* 19 (March 1904): 80-106, available online at http://www.dinsdoc.com/osgood-1.htm. As already noted, church and government were intertwined in early colonial New England: "In the Puritan colonies the support of the ministry, the building and repair of churches and the support of schools, were regular objects of public expenditure. This burden, with the building and repair of roads and bridges, the building and repair of jails, the care of the poor and the support of local officials and courts, rested mainly on the localities. Laws making such expenditures obligatory abound. But on occasion supplementary grants were made from the colony treasury" (Osgood, p. 100). The primary object of public expenditure, however, was defense. (Osgood, pp. 92-93) With respect to early efforts by the (corporate) colonial and local governments to provide financing for schools, Osgood writes: "Under the act of 1642 the towns of Massachusetts began their expenditures for elementary and grammar schools, the same policy being followed in the other three colonies. Special efforts were made for the founding of a colony grammar school at New Haven, the general court conditionally appropriating £100 for the purpose. But this scheme did not prosper. Massachusetts occasionally made grants of land for the endowment of grammar schools, and Connecticut, in 1672, set apart six hundred acres of land in each to be used for this purpose. In 1671 the general court of Plymouth voted to devote the revenue which arose from fishing at the Cape to the support of a free grammar school at the town of Plymouth. With this fund a school was soon started. In 1678 a grant of £10 was made toward the support of a school at Rehoboth. Grants came regularly to be made out of the fund from the fishery, both to the schools in these towns and to one in Duxbury. The support of both the grammar and the elementary schools continued to be mainly a local charge. Towns that failed to maintain them, as required by law, were liable to fine. Of activity on the part of the colony government in Rhode Island in support of education, we hear nothing." (Osgood, pp. 100-101). Osgood's article also points out the many difficulties involved in collecting revenues under the relatively primitive conditions that existed in 17th century New England, not the least of which was the inadequate supply of coins, which resulted in collections often having to be taken in-kind. In South Carolina, which became a royal province in 1719, the General Assembly authorized the construction of a free school in each county that would provide instruction to 10 poor children free of charge. In 1811 South Carolina enacted a further free school law to provide free elementary education to all, but with a preference for orphans and the children of the poor. See "A Brief History of Public Education in South Carolina," available online at http://www.sde.state.sc.us/publicinformation/history.htm.

7. From the time of the ratification of the Constitution until *Everson* the Establishment Clause was viewed as a constraint on the powers of the federal government. Consequently, state and local support of Christian schools during that period did not raise Constitutional issues. In fact, the Congregational Church was the established religion in Massachusetts until 1833, a state of affairs that was understood at that time to be outside the reach of the Establishment Clause.

8. Lloyd P. Jorgenson, *The State and the Non-Public School 1825 – 1925* (Columbia: The University of Missouri Press, 1987), p. 31.

9. Samuel L. Blumenfeld, *Is Public Education Necessary?* (Boise: The Paradigm Company, 1985), pp. 42-43.

10. Samuel L. Blumenfeld, *Is Public Education Necessary?* (Boise: The Paradigm Company, 1985), pp. 42-43.

11. Samuel L. Blumenfeld, *Is Public Education Necessary?* (Boise: The Paradigm Company, 1985), pp. 42-43.

12. Samuel L. Blumenfeld, *Is Public Education Necessary?* (Boise: The Paradigm Company, 1985), pp. 42-43.

13. Charles Jared Ingersoll, *North American Review*, January 1824, p. 159, as quoted in Samuel L. Blumenfeld, *Is Public Education Necessary?* (Boise: The Paradigm Company, 1985), pp. 57-58.

14. Samuel L. Blumenfeld, *Is Public Education Necessary?* (Boise: The Paradigm Company, 1985), p. 58.

15. Samuel L. Blumenfeld, *Is Public Education Necessary?* (Boise: The Paradigm Company, 1985), p. 66.

16. Henry Steele Commager, *The Commonwealth of Learning* (New York: Harper & Row, 1968), p. 46.

17. John Taylor Gatto, *An Underground History of American Education* (New York: The Oxford Village Press, 2000/2001), p. 102.

18. In Chapter 3, I remarked that government schools are inducing a form of historical amnesia. This progressive loss of historical memory has, of course, been going on for decades and permeates academia as well as the public sphere. One small, but telling, example of this even among tenured professors at the most prestigious universities cropped up in an article titled "A Schism Averted" by Harvey Cox (Hollis Professor of Divinity at Harvard) in the August 12, 2003, edition of *The Wall Street Journal*. In the course of lauding the confirmation of Gene Robinson, a homosexual, as a Bishop in the Episcopalian Church, Professor Cox made reference to "the Pilgrim fathers (who were of course Anglicans)." Despite the authoritative and perhaps somewhat condescending tone of Professor Cox's parenthetical comment, the Pilgrim fathers were, "of course," not Anglicans. Even most 5th graders into the 1960s knew that the Pilgrims were separatists who had had broken with the Church of England. This bit of American history was often taught around Thanksgiving, for obvious reasons. Now, it appears that one can hold a tenured chair in a divinity school and have only a foggy notion of who the Pilgrims were and without the faintest idea how it was that some of the Pilgrims had moved to Holland from England before coming to America. It is also instructive that this bit of nonsense made it past the *Journal's* editorial page editors – something that would not have happened under Vermont Royster's leadership. For some basic background on the subject available online, see http://en.wikipedia.org/wiki/Pilgrims. Those interested in more detail, including how contact with the Pilgrim separatists in fairly short order led the Puritans of the Massachusetts Bay Colony to take their leave of the Anglican Church, should see Peter Y. De Jong, *The Covenant Idea in New England Theology, 1620-1847* (Grand Rapids: Eerdmans, 1945); Leonard Bacon, *The Genesis of the New England Churches* (Harper & Brothers, 1874); and John A. Goodwin, *The Pilgrim Republic* (Ticknor & Co., 1888). The lack of knowledge of the history of Christianity and of America's Christian heritage among today's Christians is both profoundly disturbing and dangerous. As Marcus Tullius Cicero once remarked: "To be ignorant of what happened before you were born is to be ever a child." The price of being "ever a child" is vulnerability to being easily mislead. Moreover, a Christian ignorant of history, including church history, is also, like a child, defenseless. This is why, in part, the church is in such disarray and on the defensive today. For those interested in learning more about the role of Christianity in early America, chapter 11 ("America's Christian Roots") of David Limbaugh's *Persecution: How Liberals are Waging War against Christianity* (Regnery Books, 2003) is a good place to start. Another interesting read is M. Stanton Evans, *The Theme Is Freedom: Religion, Politics, and the American Tradition* (Regnery Books, 1994). The late M.E. Bradford's *Founding Fathers* (University of Kansas Press, 1994) provides reliable

information on the religious views of those present at the Constitutional convention in Philadelphia in 1787. Of course, the portion of Lorraine Boettner's *The Reformed Doctrine of Predestination* devoted to the history and social characteristics of Calvinism is an important source for understanding the early development of America and the War of Independence. Michael Novak's *On Two Wings: Humble Faith and Common Sense At the American Founding* (Encounter Books, 2003) provides a great deal of material regarding the views of a large number of those important to the founding of America.

19. For those wishing additional background on the Reformation and the conditions that led to it, see the following website: http://www.newgenevacenter.org/west/reformation.htm. This site provides an extraordinary range of information on the Reformation and church history.

20. Lorraine Boettner, *The Reformed Doctrine of Predestination* (Phillipsburg, New Jersey: Presbyterian and Reformed Publishing Company, 1932), p. 396.

21. In its early years, the Massachusetts Bay Colony was inhabited almost exclusively by Puritans. Until the Colony's charter was changed in 1691, only members of the Congregationalist church could vote. Consequently, at least until 1691 the Bay Colony was in some sense a theocracy.

22. *The Cambridge History of English and American Literature*, Volume XVII, Later National Literature, Part II, XXIII, Education, Section 6. New England; The Massachusetts Law of 1647, available at www.bartleby.com/227/1606.html.

23. Lorraine Boettner, *The Reformed Doctrine of Predestination* (Phillipsburg, New Jersey: Presbyterian and Reformed Publishing Company, 1932), pp. 382-383.

24. Lorraine Boettner, *The Reformed Doctrine of Predestination* (Phillipsburg, New Jersey: Presbyterian and Reformed Publishing Company, 1932), pp. 382-383.

25. Page Smith, *The History of America* (Norwalk, Conn.: Easton Press 1976), Vol. I, p.153.

26. Lloyd P. Jorgenson, *The State and the Non-Public School 1825 – 1925* (Columbia: The University of Missouri Press, 1987), pp. 27-28. On the role of 19th century Christians in abolitionism and other social reform movements of the 19th century, Page Smith comments: "The battle fought by the abolitionists against slavery was fought unequivocally in the name of Christian brotherhood. Granted that the anti-slavery warriors ranged from such marginal Christians as Unitarians and transcendentalists to Baptists and hard-line Presbyterians, I have found no prominent abolitionist, black or white, who was an avowed freethinker, atheist, or agnostic....The point to be stressed is that the motivation behind all the great reform movements of the first half of the 19th century was the Protestant Passion, which might or might not have been made evident through the organized churches." Page Smith, *The History of America* (Norwalk, Conn.: Easton Press, 1976), Vol.XII, pp. 554-555. By "Protestant Passion" Smith means "the insatiable desire to redeem mankind from sin and error."

27. Frederick Engels recognized the importance of Owen to the development of communism in his tract "Socialism: Utopian and Scientific." Owen was a fascinating 19th century personality who was at once an autodidact, a shrewd and successful business man, a sympathetic character in many respects, and a bit of a crank.

28. Samuel L. Blumenfeld, *Is Public Education Necessary?* (Boise: The Paradigm Company, 1985), p. 37.

29. Samuel L. Blumenfeld, *Is Public Education Necessary?* (Boise: The Paradigm Company, 1985), p. 37.

30. Samuel L. Blumenfeld, *Is Public Education Necessary?* (Boise: The Paradigm Company, 1985), p. 83.

31. Samuel L. Blumenfeld, *Is Public Education Necessary?* (Boise: The Paradigm Company, 1985), pp. 41-42.

32. Owen also published a *Report to the County of Lanark* in 1821 and his autobiography in 1857 and 1858. A brief, but useful, account of Owen's life is available at www.spartacus.schoolnet.co.uk. A very

sympathetic account of Owen's life can be found in "Robert Owen: Atheist, Philanthropist, Labor Reformer" at www.atheists.org/Atheism/roots/robertowen/.

33. Robert Owen, *A New View of Society and Other Writings* (New York: E.P. Dutton & Co., 1927), pp. 14-17.

34. Samuel L. Blumenfeld, *Is Public Education Necessary?* (Boise: The Paradigm Company, 1985), p. 42.

35. Samuel L. Blumenfeld, *Is Public Education Necessary?* (Boise: The Paradigm Company, 1985), p. 42.

36. Ironically, Owen bought the property that he named "New Harmony" from a German religious dissenter, George Rapp, who had previously established a successful religious community on the property.

37. Samuel L. Blumenfeld, *Is Public Education Necessary?* (Boise: The Paradigm Company, 1985), pp. 71-77.

38. Samuel L. Blumenfeld, *Is Public Education Necessary?* (Boise: The Paradigm Company, 1985), pp. 79-93.

39. Toward the end of his life Robert Dale Owen became a spiritualist and published *Footfalls on the Boundary of Another World*. A sketch of his life and information on his writings can be found at http:// faculty.evansville.edu/ck6/bstud/rdowen.html.

40. Orestes A. Brownson in *The Works of Orestes A. Brownson*, collected and arranged by Henry F. Brownson (New York: AMS Press Inc., 1966), Volume XIX, pp. 442-43, as quoted in Samuel L. Blumenfeld, *Is Public Education Necessary?* (Boise: The Paradigm Company, 1985), pp. 95-96.

41. Outside of Boston, the final separation of Unitarians from Congregationists did not result in the loss of many Congregational churches between 1817 and 1840. In Boston, however, twelve of fourteen Congregational churches became Unitarian. Consequently, by 1840 the Unitarians had achieved ascendancy in Boston. Angus Stewart, "The Decline and Fall of New England Congregationalism," *Protestant Reformed Theological Journal,* April 1999, pp. 88-89, available online at http://www.prca. org/prtj/apr99.html#Congregationalism.

42. The American Unitarian Association was formed in 1825, although it was probably evident to some as much as a decade earlier that the Unitarian tendency within the Congregational Church constituted a new denomination. Some claim that William Ellery Channing's sermon delivered at the ordination of Jared Sparks in the First Independent Church of Baltimore on May 5, 1819, represented the public break of Unitarians from the Congregational Church. Channing's sermon contains a defense of the then distinctive Unitarian doctrines and can be found at http://www.transcendental-ists.com/unitarian_christianity.htm. The texts of the essential theological writings of the 19th century Unitarians can be found at http://www.biblicalunitarian.com/html/modules.php?name=News&file=c ategories&op=newindex&catid=14 and http://www.abc-coggc.org/COGGC/cogarchives.htm.

43. Rousas J. Rushdoony, *The Messianic Character of American Education* (Nutley, New Jersey: The Craig Press, 1963), p. 19.

44. The reference to "Unitarianism" is in the past tense because the modern Unitarian Universalist Association would not be recognizable doctrinally to the Unitarians of the early and mid 19th century. For an overview of contemporary Unitarian Universalism, see the discussion at http://www. religioustolerance.org/u-u4.htm. One measure of the departure of the Unitarian Universalist Association from traditional Unitarianism is the recent formation of the American Unitarian Conference by a dissident group of Unitarian Universalist theists, primarily Unitarian "Christians." This group claims to represent the traditional Unitarian faith, although it is not clear that it has more than a few dozen adherents. There is a website, however, for "Biblical Unitarianism" at http://www.biblicalunitarian. com/html/index.php. Although the Unitarianism of this site may or may not be as conservative as the

Unitarianism of the first two decades of the 19th century, it is obviously something very different from today's Unitarian Universalism that is so often confused with historic Unitarianism.

45. As quoted in Charles Leslie Glenn, Jr., *The Myth of the Common School* (Amherst: The University of Massachusetts Press, 1988), p. 167.

46. For example, another of Mann's correspondents assured him that 95% of the "immoralities that afflict society" could be eradicated through a proper system of education. See Charles Leslie Glenn, Jr., *The Myth of the Common School* (Amherst: The University of Massachusetts Press, 1988), p. 167.

47. John Taylor Gatto, *An Underground History of American Education* (New York: The Oxford Village Press, 2000/2001), p. 102.

48. One of the most influential of these was Dr. Heman Humphrey, president of Amherst College.

49. Samuel L. Blumenfeld, *Is Public Education Necessary?* (Boise: The Paradigm Company, 1985), 1995 edition, pp. 228-230. In addition to political support, Mann's Protestant allies made other contributions to the Common School project. The method for financing government schools is one example. Plainly, early American public funding mechanisms such as rate bills would not support the grandiose educational empire envisioned by the advocates of Common Schools, and invited far too much parental scrutiny. Not surprisingly, a Common School proponent and a Methodist minister, the Reverend Birdsley Grant Northrup, found a way to fund the empire – or, rather, a way to force others to fund it. The Reverend Northrup's scheme is familiar to us all: the property tax. Incidentally, like many other Protestant ministers of his day, Reverend Northrup became a public school administrator, serving as superintendent of Connecticut schools in the 1850s.

50. Lloyd P. Jorgenson, *The State and the Non-Public School, 1825 – 1925* (Columbia: The University of Missouri Press, 1987), pp. 28-30.

51. Lloyd P. Jorgenson, *The State and the Non-Public School 1825 – 1925* (Columbia: The University of Missouri Press, 1987), pp. 69-70. See, also, Charles Leslie Glenn, Jr., *The Myth of the Common School* (Amherst: The University of Massachusetts Press, 1988), pp. 63-85, and Samuel L. Blumenfeld, *Is Public Education Necessary?* (Boise: The Paradigm Company, 1985), pp. 228-229.

52. Charles Leslie Glenn, Jr., *The Myth of the Common School* (Amherst: The University of Massachusetts Press, 1988), p. 84.

53. Contrary to the facile and false ideology that underlies the current predilection always to view "majorities" as villains and "minorities" as virtuous victims, there was an "Irish problem"; it was serious, and something needed to be done about it. As Thomas Sowell points out, cleanliness was not a cultural value of the Irish immigrants, and as a result cities such as Boston and New York began experiencing outbreaks of cholera, a very deadly disease that had previously been absent. Moreover, the Irish reputation for drinking, fighting, and crime was, as a general proposition, not undeserved. For a detailed account of the Irish immigration, see Thomas Sowell, *Ethnic America: A History* (New York: Basic Books, 1981), pp. 17-42. Nevertheless, orthodox Protestants harmed both the Irish and American culture by combining with the Unitarian and socialist promoters of Common Schools to use a system of government education and compulsory schooling as a means of dealing with the problems brought about by immigration.

54. As quoted in Murray N. Rothbard, "The Progressive Era and the Family," first printed in Joseph R. Peden and Fred R. Glahe (eds.), *The American Family and the State* (San Francisco: Pacific Research Institute, 1986), available online at www.lewrockwell.com, quotation from p. 8 of the online version.

55. As quoted in Murray N. Rothbard, "The Progressive Era and the Family," first printed in Joseph R. Peden and Fred R. Glahe (eds.), *The American Family and the State* (San Francisco: Pacific Research Institute, 1986), available online at www.lewrockwell.com, quotation from p. 8 of the online version, citing Rousas John Rushdoony, "John Swett: The Self-Preservation of the State," In *The Messianic*

Character of American Education: Studies in the History of the Philosophy of Education (Nutley, New Jersey: Craig Press, 1963), pp. 70-80.

56. Charles Leslie Glenn, Jr., *The Myth of the Common School* (Amherst: The University of Massachusetts Press, 1988), pp. 250-256.

57. Lloyd P. Jorgenson, *The State and the Non-Public School, 1825 – 1925* (Columbia: The University of Missouri Press, 1987), p. 70.

58. This excerpt is from Edward A. Ross, *Social Control*, as quoted in Andrew J. Coulson, *Market Education: The Unknown History* (New Brunswick: Transaction Publishers, 1999), p. 108.

59. George S. Counts, an influential member of the Progressive Education Association, as quoted in Andrew J. Coulson, *Market Education: The Unknown History* (New Brunswick: Transaction Publishers, 1999), p. 109, citing Herbert M. Kliebard, *The Struggle for the American Curriculum* (New York: Routledge, 1995), p. 80.

60. For the detailed account of the origins and activities of National Liberal League from which my summary is drawn, see Philip Hamburger, *Separation of Church and State* (Cambridge, Mass.: Harvard University Press, 2002), pp. 287-334, 392-393.

61. See Philip Hamburger, *Separation of Church and State* (Cambridge, Mass.: Harvard University Press, 2002), pp. 287-334.

62. Philip Hamburger, *Separation of Church and State* (Cambridge, Mass.: Harvard University Press, 2002), pp. 287-334.

63. Philip Hamburger, *Separation of Church and State* (Cambridge, Mass.: Harvard University Press, 2002), pp. 287-334.

64. "A Song for Liberals," in *The Truth Seeker Collection of Forms, Hymns, and Recitations. Original and Selected – For the Use of Liberals,* pp. 377-378 (New York: D.M. Bennett, Liberal & Scientific Publishing House, 1877), as quoted in Philip Hamburger, *Separation of Church and State* (Cambridge, Massachusetts: Harvard University Press, 2002), p. 315.

65. Philip Hamburger, *Separation of Church and State* (Cambridge, Massachusetts: Harvard University Press, 2002), p. 331.

66. Philip Hamburger, *Separation of Church and State* (Cambridge, Mass.: Harvard University Press, 2002), pp. 413-414.

67. Philip Hamburger, *Separation of Church and State* (Cambridge, Mass.: Harvard University Press, 2002), pp. 412-413.

68. Jackie Orsi, "The KKK's Attempt at Thought Control in Oregon Schools," *Education Liberator*, Vol. 1, No. 4, December 1995/January 1996, and Philip Hamburger, *Separation of Church and State* (Cambridge, Mass.: Harvard University Press, 2002), pp. 412-418. Interestingly, women voters, who had just obtained the vote, contributed significantly to the referendum's success. Masons, it appears, were deeply divided on this issue, as were Protestants.

69. Martin Morse Wooster, *Angry Classrooms, Vacant Minds: What's Happened to our High Schools?* (San Francisco: Pacific Research Institute, 1994), p. 7.

70. *Pierce v. Society of Sisters of Holy Names of Jesus and Mary*, 268 U.S. 510 (1925).

71. The anti-Catholicism of liberals continues today. As already noted, liberal antagonism against Catholics in the post-World War II period was largely motivated by the "sectarian" nature and anti-Communism of the Catholic Church. Today, liberal hatred of the Catholic Church appears to be

mainly a reaction to its conservative teachings on sexual matters – particularly with respect to birth control, abortion, and homosexuality. The line of attack, however, has been indirect. Lately, the Left has been working to delegitimize Catholicism though allegations of anti-Semitism and complicity in the Holocaust. The Left's antipathy toward Catholicism has recently been manifested in a spate of books such as John Cornwell's *Hitler's Pope*. Another example is the January 21, 2002, cover story of *The New Republic* (http://www.spectator.co.uk/article.php3?table=old&section=current&issue=2002-02-16&id=1582, by Daniel Jonah Goldhagen), a particularly scurrilous piece in which the author not only engages in calumnies against the Catholic Church that might have come out of a nativist publication, but in which the author also claims that the New Testament and the symbol of the Cross are anti-Semitic. For a review of the Goldhagen article, see Harry W. Crocker, III, "Liberal Lies and the War Against Religion," available online at http://www.lewrockwell.com/orig2/crocker3.html. Similarly, Paul Gottfried, a Jewish scholar, has few kind things to say about the scholarship and motives of Cornwell, Goldhagen, and their ilk in his February 16, 2002, article in *The Spectator* ("The Church and the Holocaust"), available online at http://www.spectator.co.uk/article.php3?table=old&section=current&issue=2002-02-16&id=1582. Michael Novak has also provided an interesting review of Goldhagen's article, "Bigotry's New Low," in the January 28, 2002, National Review Online, which is available online at http://www.nationalreview.com/contributors/novak012802.shtml. I concur with Crocker's assessment of the broader significance of the Goldhagen article: "That a mainstream magazine would print such a piece – and apparently take pride in it and think it important – is ominous. It is ominous for what it says about intellectual standards on the Left, ominous for what it shows about the Left's disregard for truth, and ominous for its announcement of a new Left-wing Kulturkampf against Christianity." You may also want to read Crocker's *Triumph: The Power and the Glory of the Catholic Church, A 2,000-Year History* (New York: Random House, 2002).

72. For an overview of McGuffey's life and the career of *McGuffey's Readers*, see John H. Westerhoff, III, *McGuffey and His Readers* (Milford, Mich.: Mott Media, Inc., 1982).

73. John H. Westerhoff, III, *McGuffey and His Readers* (Milford, Mich.: Mott Media, 1982), p. 15.

74. John H. Westerhoff, III, *McGuffey and His Readers* (Milford, Mich.: Mott Media, 1982), p. 17.

75. John H. Westerhoff, III, *McGuffey and His Readers* (Milford, Mich.: Mott Media, 1982), p. 19.

76. John H. Westerhoff, III, *McGuffey and His Readers* (Milford, Mich.: Mott Media, 1982), pp. 49-52.

77. Charles Leslie Glenn, Jr., *The Myth of the Common School* (Amherst: The University of Massachusetts Press, 1988), pp. 69-110.

78. Lloyd P. Jorgenson, *The State and the Non-Public School 1825 – 1925* (Columbia: The University of Missouri Press, 1987), pp. 76-83. In part, the effort made by those in control of the Common Schools to make them "nonsectarian" was the problem. The Catholic leadership believed that education should be "sectarian"; that is, it should include the teaching of a specific religious tradition. For a discussion of this aspect of the struggle over Common Schools, see Charles Leslie Glenn, Jr., *The Myth of the Common School* (Amherst: The University of Massachusetts Press, 1988), pp. 200-202.

79. Lloyd P. Jorgenson, *The State and the Non-Public School 1825 – 1925* (Columbia: The University of Missouri Press, 1987), pp. 90-93. See, also, Charles Leslie Glenn, Jr., *The Myth of the Common School* (Amherst: The University of Massachusetts Press 1988), pp. 202-204.

80. As quoted in Lloyd P. Jorgenson, *The State and the Non-Public School 1825 – 1925* (Columbia: The University of Missouri Press, 1987), p. 138.

81. From *Catholic World* as quoted in Lloyd P. Jorgenson, *The State and the Non-Public School 1825 – 1925* (Columbia: The University of Missouri Press, 1987), p. 138.

82. Charles Leslie Glenn, Jr., *The Myth of the Common School* (Amherst: The University of Massachusetts Press, 1988), pp. 179-196.

83. R.L. Dabney, *On Secular Education,* Douglas Wilson, ed. (Moscow, Idaho: Canon Press, 1996), pp. 9-10. The fact that Dabney opposed using government schools as an instrument for attempting to "Protestantize" Catholic children does not mean that he had a favorable view of the Catholic Church. Rather, his opposition was in spite of his deep disapproval of Catholic theology and institutions.

84. R.L. Dabney, *On Secular Education,* Douglas Wilson, ed. (Moscow Idaho: Canon Press 1996), pp. 26-27. The Massachusetts Protestants who supported the Common School movement had little appreciation of the risks involved in embracing a system of government schools. In an 1849 report supporting participation in the Common School program by the Protestant Association of Massachusetts, the authors offered the following "cost/benefit" analysis:

"The benefits of this system, in offering instruction to all, are so many and so great that its religious deficiencies, especially since they can be otherwise supplied, do not seem to be a sufficient reason for abandoning it, and adopting it in place of it, a system of denominational parochial schools....On the whole, it seems to be the wisest course, at least for the present, to do all in our power to perfect so far as it can be done, not only its intellectual, but also its moral and religious character. If after a full and faithful experiment, it should at last be seen that fidelity to the religious interests of our children forbids a further patronage of the system, we can unite with the Evangelical Christians in the establishment of private schools, in which more full doctrinal religious instruction may be possible." (See *Common School Journal*, Vol. II, No. 14, July 15, 1849, 212-213, as quoted in Samuel L. Blumenfeld, "Education and the Church," *The Chalcedon Report*, May 2004.)

The authors' belief that, having once established a government controlled and funded system of schools, they could simply reverse course if the institution proved unsatisfactory betrays a remarkable combination of naiveté and hubris.

85. Lloyd P. Jorgenson, *The State and the Non-Public School 1825 – 1925* (Columbia: The University of Missouri Press, 1987), p. 133-135.

86. Philip Hamburger, *Separation of Church and State* (Cambridge, Mass.: Harvard University Press, 2002), p. 464 n.182 and the sources cited therein.

87. R.L. Dabney, *On Secular Education*, Douglas Wilson, ed. (Moscow, Idaho: Canon Press, 1996), p. 17.

Chapter Seven - *Are Your Children Unequally Yoked?*

1. A survey conducted in February-March 2002 by the Pew Research Council found that 82% of the adults surveyed identified themselves as Christian. This information can be found at www.adherents. com.

2. This information is taken from the website of the U.S. Census Bureau and is available at http:// www.census.gov/population/socdemo/school/ppl-148/tab01.txt.

3. It is hard to find definitive current data for the number of students attending Christian schools or private schools generally. One useful source of information is U.S. Department of Education, National Center for Educational Statistics, *Private School Universe Survey, 1997-98*, NCES 1999-319, by Stephen P. Broughman and Lenore A. Colaciello, Washington, DC: 1999. Unfortunately, the *Private School Universe Survey* covers only the 1997-1998 period.

4. The National Home Education Research Institute (NHERI), for example, estimates that in 2003 between 1.7 million and 2.3 million children were homeschooled. This estimate and other information on homeschooling is available from NHERI online at http://www.nheri.org/modules.php?name= Content&pa=showpage&pid=21.

5. Because of the lack of firm data on the number of homeschoolers, there are various estimates of the

percentage of homeschoolers who are Christian. Dr. Brian Ray, president of the National Home Education Research Institute, estimates that Christians constitute 75% of homeschoolers (as cited in Ephrat Livni, "Keeping the Faith – More and More Muslim Americans are Choosing to Home-School," abcNEWS.com, December 17, 2000). Other estimates are 80% and higher.

6. The calculation is made by adding the percentage of schoolchildren attending Christian schools (11% x .8 = 8.8%) to the hypothesized percentage of children being homeschooled by Christian families (3.57% x .8 = 2.857%) and then dividing that percentage by the percentage of self-identified Christians in the population (11.657% / 76.5% = 15.23%). Obviously, this assumes, among other things, that all children in Christian private schools are from Christian families and that no children in secular private schools are from Christian families. These assumptions are almost certainly not true, but they should not materially affect the accuracy of the estimates.

7. This percentage shows how much educational "capacity" a denomination is providing in relation to an estimate of its own children. Thus, for example, even though Catholic schools provide nearly two-thirds of the *existing* opportunities for Christian schooling, they only have enough capacity to educate roughly 19% of all Catholic children. Of course, enrollments in any denomination's schools include children from outside that denomination, but this percentage illustrates how many more Christian schools are needed.

8. Please note that these columns will not sum to 100% because the chart does not include all denominations and it does not include data concerning children attending nondenominational Christian schools.

9. These numbers show the percentage a given denomination represents of all Christians in America. They have been arrived at by dividing the percentage of the adult population that identified itself with the specified denomination by the percentage of the population identifying itself as "Christian" (76.5%). All of the data are from the 2001 American Religious Identity Survey, as reported at www. adherents.com.

10. These numbers show the percentage of the total number of children enrolled in Christian schools that are enrolled in schools maintained by the specified denomination. They have been calculated by dividing the number of students enrolled in the specified denomination's schools by the estimated total number of students enrolled in Christian schools (4,026,403). The data are taken from Table 2 of the U.S. Department of Education, National Center for Educational Statistics, *Private School Universe Survey, 1997-98*, NCES 1999-319, by Stephen P. Broughman and Lenore A. Colaciello.

11. These numbers show how many students are enrolled in the specified denomination's schools expressed as a percentage of an estimate of the total number of the denomination's primary and secondary school-age children. The estimate of the denomination's total number of school-age children ("Denomination's Children") is calculated by multiplying the percentage of self-identified members of that denomination in the total population by 53.4 million, which is an estimate that assumes 46.9 million children enrolled in public schools, 5 million children enrolled in private schools (secular and Christian), and 1.5 million homeschooled children. The data on the percentage that the denomination constitutes of the total population is from the 2001 American Religious Identity Survey, while the data on the number of children enrolled in schools (public and private) are estimates from the National Center For Education Statistics for the 1999-2000 school year. Then the number of children enrolled in the denomination's schools (using the data from Table 2 of the *Private School Universe Survey*) is divided by the Denomination's Children to arrive at the percentage shown. Obviously, I am assuming for this calculation, among other things, that each denomination has a number of school-age children proportionate to the denomination's percentage of the population. In addition, the data for the number of children attending Christian schools and the data regarding the denomination's percentage of the population are for slightly different periods. The number of homeschooled children is not exactly known. Consequently, the number used is an estimate for the 1999-2000 school year and is based on estimates from various sources. It is extremely unlikely that any of these issues would

be material, however, for the purpose of illustrating how small the *enrollment capacity* of Christian schools is in relation to the number of Christian children.

12. This estimate assumes that 8.8% (80% of the 11% typically estimated to be attending private schools) of 51.9 million schoolchildren (1999-2000 school-year enrollment figures) attend Christian schools and that Catholics continue to enroll 62.5% of all children attending Christian schools.

13. This estimate results from dividing 16.5% by 76.5%.

14. Interestingly, for Orthodox Jews it is the norm to send their children to Jewish day schools, and there is a growing trend toward educating Jewish children in Jewish schools among non-Orthodox Jews. See Heidi J. Schrager, "Keepers of the Faith, Jewish Day Schools Spread in the U.S.," *The Wall Street Journal*, May 20, 2002, p. B1.

15. One of the greatest delusions parents suffer from is thinking that somehow "top-rated" suburban schools are just fine. The parents of the girls injured and humiliated at Glenbrook North High School (see Chapter 4) probably believed that too. While it is true that, even if we had honest reporting on government school crime, the level of *violence* is probably somewhat higher in the average inner-city school than the average suburban school, there are other sorts of problems that may be worse in wealthier schools than in inner-city schools – *drugs*, for example. Children from wealthier homes, after all, tend to have more spending money. This is born out, in part, by the findings of the 2003 *Indicators of School Crime and Safety* (see Chapter 4), in which approximately 25% more white students than black students (28% versus 22%) reported in 2001 that drugs had been made available to them on school property within the last 12 months (see Figure 19.2).

16. E. Ray Moore, Jr., *Let My Children Go: Why Parents Must Remove Their Children from Public Schools Now* (Columbia, S.C.: Gilead Media, 2002), p. 55.

17. Matthew Clavel, "How Not to Teach Math: New York's Chancellor Klein's Plan Doesn't Compute," *City Magazine*, March 7, 2003.

18. T.C. Pinckney, "Remarks to the Southern Baptist Convention Executive Committee," September 18, 2001, available online at www.sepschool.org. Mr. Pinckney is a retired U.S. Air Force Brigadier General, a former 2nd Vice President of the Southern Baptist Convention, and the editor of *The Baptist Banner*.

19. E. Ray Moore, Jr., founder of the Exodus Mandate and retired Army chaplain, provides some excellent advice for pastors and other church leaders on how to understand and approach the schooling issue in his *Let My Children Go: Why Parents Must Remove Their Children from Public Schools Now*, particularly in Chapters 3 and 5. Moore has a wealth of experience in addressing the government school issue in churches, and, frankly, *Let My Children Go* should be required reading for all pastors, elders, and deacons.

Chapter Eight - *Leading Your Children into the Promised Land of Homeschooling and Christian Schools*

1. Because homeschooling is a relatively new concept to most parents, my discussion of homeschooling is longer than my discussion of traditional Christian schools.

2. At the current rate of growth of homeschooling, homeschooled Christian students may outnumber children educated in traditional Christian schools within five to seven years.

3. See Table 2 of the U.S. Department of Education, National Center for Educational Statistics, *Private School Universe Survey, 1997-98*, NCES 1999-319, by Stephen P. Broughman and Lenore A. Colaciello, Washington, D.C.: 1999.

4. See, *e.g.*, Martin L. Gross, *The Conspiracy of Ignorance: The Failure of American Public Schools* (New York: HarperCollins Publishers, Inc., 1999), pp. 149-174. This is also true of students in private

secular schools. In addition, Gross debunks the excuses that government school officials give for this state of affairs. His analysis indicates persuasively that the key factor accounting for the difference in performance is the nature of the schools.

5. These costs are expressed in 1998 dollars and are taken from U.S. Department of Education, National Center for Educational Statistics, *The Condition of Education 1999*, Washington D.C.: U.S. Government Printing Office, 1999, Supplemental Table 28-4.

6. Kirk A. Johnson and Krista Kafer, "Why More Money Will Not Solve America's Education Crisis," *The Heritage Foundation*, June 11, 2001, pp.8-9.

7. Kirk A. Johnson and Krista Kafer, "Why More Money Will Not Solve America's Education Crisis," *The Heritage Foundation*, June 11, 2001, pp.8-9.

8. For data on average tuition and other information, see U.S. Department of Education, National Center for Education Statistics, Schools and Staffing Survey, "Private School Questionaire," 1999-2000, table 61 (http://nces.ed.gov/programs/digest/d02/tables/PDF/table61.pdf).

9. The information regarding median tuition in various cities is from David Salisbury, "Private Schools Cost Less Than You Think," Cato Insitute, September 8, 2003, available online at http://www.cato.org/dailys/09-08-03.html.

10. If you are unfamiliar with the term "worldview," visit http://www.christianworldview.net/. In a nutshell, the Christian worldview movement assists Christians in developing a Christian understanding of all aspects of life, including culture, politics, history, economics, etc.

11. Patrick Basham, "Home Schooling: From the Extreme to the Mainstream," *Fraser Institute Occasional Paper*, Number 51 (Fraser Institute, 2001), pp. 3-6. This is by far the best survey available regarding research on homeschooling. It is available online from The Fraser Institute at http://www.fraserinstitute.ca/admin/books/files/homeschool.pdf. In 1999, The National Center for Educational Statistics published a brief study on homeschooling, *Homeschooling in the United States in 1999*. This study primarily explores such questions as the number of homeschoolers, their family characteristics,and their reasons for homeschooling. (available online in PDF at http://nces.ed.gov/pubs2001/2001033.pdf).

12. Patrick Basham, "Home Schooling: From the Extreme to the Mainstream," *Fraser Institute Occasional Paper*, Number 51 (Fraser Institute, 2001), p. 3.

13. Lawrence M. Rudner, "Scholastic Achievement and Demographic Characteristics of Home School Students in 1998," *Educational Policy Analysis Archives*, Volume 7, Number 8 (March 23, 1999), available at http://epaa.asu.edu/epaa/v7n8/.

14. Lawrence M. Rudner, "Scholastic Achievement and Demographic Characteristics of Home School Students in 1998," *Educational Policy Analysis Archives*, Volume 7, Number 8 (March 23, 1999), available at http://epaa.asu.edu/epaa/v7n8/.

15. Christians are variously estimated to comprise 70% to 80% of homeschoolers. The bulk of the remaining homeschoolers are sometimes referred to as "unschoolers." Unschoolers typically reject government schooling for reasons of educational philosophy and tend to subscribe to the views of education critics such as John Holt, A.S. Neill, and Paul Goodman. For a description of "Unschooling" see Earl Stevens, "What is Unschooling," available online at http://www.naturalchild.com/guest/earl_stevens.html. The Family Unschoolers Network (http://www.unschooling.org/) provides a great deal of information on unschooling as an approach to education. Because of the overrepresentation of Christians in his sample, Dr. Rudner's study does not provide strong evidence regarding how unschoolers are doing academically.

16. Brian D. Ray, "Strengths of Their Own – Home Schoolers Across America: Academic Achievement, Family Characteristics, and Longitudinal Traits," National Home Education Research Institute, available at www.nheri.org.

17. Patrick Basham, "Home Schooling: From the Extreme to the Mainstream," *Fraser Institute Occasional Paper*, Number 51 (Fraser Institute, 2001), p. 11. Basham's survey is available online in PDF format at http://www.fraserinstitute.ca/admin/books/files/homeschool.pdf.

18. Noreen S. Ahmed-Ullah, "Parents Thrilled that Homeschoolers are Busy as Bees," *The Bergen Record*, May 19, 2001.

19. The student is Reid Barton, a native of Massachusetts. Barton has also won many other honors in mathematics competitions. See "Int'l Math Olympiad 2001 Medalists Announced by Wolfram Research," available at http://mathforum.org/epigone/geometry-pecollege/chexswexsang.

20. "Home Improvement," *The Wall Street Journal*, May 17, 2002, W 15.

21. Vaishali Honawar, "National Bees 'Buzz' with Home Schoolers," *The Washington Times*, May 21, 2002; Amy White, "Homework," *St. Louis Post-Dispatch*, August 15, 2002.

22. Amy White, "Homework," *St. Louis Post-Dispatch*, August 15, 2002.

23. Darlene Superville, "Eighth Grader Wins National Spelling Bee," Associated Press, May 29, 2003; Randolph E. Schmid, "Youngsters Square Off in Geographic Bee," Associated Press, May 21, 2003.

24. Helen Cordes, "Sour Grapes, Anyone?", ParentCenter.com, available at www.parentcenter.com.

25. Helen Cordes, "Sour Grapes, Anyone?", ParentCenter.com, available at www.parentcenter.com.

26. Lawrence M. Rudner, "Scholastic Achievement and Demographic Characteristics of Home School Students in 1998," *Educational Policy Analysis Archives*, Volume 7, Number 8 (March 23, 1999), available at http://epaa.asu.edu/epaa/v7n8/.

27. Lawrence M. Rudner, "Scholastic Achievement and Demographic Characteristics of Home School Students in 1998," *Educational Policy Analysis Archives*, Volume 7, Number 8 (March 23, 1999), available at http://epaa.asu.edu/epaa/v7n8/.

28. Lawrence M. Rudner, "Scholastic Achievement and Demographic Characteristics of Home School Students in 1998," *Educational Policy Analysis Archives*, Volume 7, Number 8 (March 23, 1999), available at http://epaa.asu.edu/epaa/v7n8/. Families of 4th grade homeschoolers who spent from $0 to $199 on average had a composite score on the battery of standardized tests in the 79th percentile while homeschoolers whose families spent $600 or more scored in the 84th percentile. For 8th grade homeschoolers the average composite score for students whose families spent $0 to $199 was in the 80th percentile, while homeschoolers whose families spent $600 or more had average composite scores in the 83rd percentile.

29. Patrick Basham, "Home Schooling: From the Extreme to the Mainstream," *Fraser Institute Occasional Paper*, Number 51 (Fraser Institute, 2001), pp. 12-13.

30. Brian D. Ray, "Strengths of Their Own – Home Schoolers Across America: Academic Achievement, Family Characteristics, and Longitudinal Traits," National Home Education Research Institute, available at http://www.nheri.org/modules.php?name=Content&pa=showpage&pid=20.

31. Krista Pierce, "More Black Families Choose Homeschooling of their Kids," *The Item*, September 1, 2003, (www.theitem.com). The fact that tennis stars Venus and Serena Williams were homeschooled has also made homeschooling much more visible within the black community. Apart from the increased visibility of homeschooling among minorities, much of the impetus for minority parents to take their children out of government schools comes from the increasing recognition that

government schools are destroying their children's futures. For a well-written survey of how minority students are sinking rather than swimming in the government schools, see Abigail and Stephen Thernstrom, *No Excuses: Closing the Racial Gap in Learning* (New York: Simon & Schuster, 2003). The Thernstroms point out, for example, that the NAEP shows 70% of black students score "Below Basic" in math, while 75% score "Below Basic" in science. "Below Basic" means that the students can't show even partial mastery of their subjects at their grade level. In reading and history the average black high school student is less proficient than the average white 8th grader. It is well known, however, that black and other minority children achieve well in Catholic schools and a handful of rigorous schools such as the Frederick Douglass Academy in New York City. It is less well known that homeschooling appears to eliminate that achievement gap between whites and minorities. As Dr. Brian Ray has observed: "Homeschoolers have been able to substantially eliminate the disparity between white and minority scores, even when the samples are adjusted to reflect the same proportion of American Indians, Asians, blacks and Hispanics (as that found in the public schools)." [As quoted by Lee Safley (President of South Carolina Home Educators Association) in "Homeschooling Helps Minorities," available online at http://www.iche.org/articles/homeschooling_helps_minorities.htm]. The Thernstroms urge school reform, but as already noted, "reform" has not been a successful strategy and is not likely to be no matter how much money is poured into government schools. Minority parents shouldn't wait for a reform that will never come. Instead, they should simply get their children out of the toxic culture of government schools – their children aren't the problem, the schools are.

32. Minority Homeschoolers of Texas is one example of the organizations springing up to support minority homeschooling families. You can visit their website at http://www.mhot.org/index.html. Another example is The National Black Home Educators Resource Association (website at http://www.nbhera.org/).

33. These survey results are cited in Michael Smith, "Homeschooling Grows in the Black Community," HSLDA News, June 13, 2003, available online at http://www.hslda.org/docs/news/hslda/200306/200306130.asp.

34. Brian D. Ray, "Strengths of Their Own – Home Schoolers Across America: Academic Achievement, Family Characteristics, and Longitudinal Traits," National Home Education Research Institute, available at http://www.nheri.org/modules.php?name=Content&pa=showpage&pid=20.

35. Brian D. Ray, "Strengths of Their Own – Home Schoolers Across America: Academic Achievement, Family Characteristics, and Longitudinal Traits," National Home Education Research Institute, available at http://www.nheri.org/modules.php?name=Content&pa=showpage&pid=20.

36. Patrick Basham, "Home Schooling: From the Extreme to the Mainstream," *Fraser Institute Occasional Paper*, Number 51 (Fraser Institute, 2001), p. 13. A very comprehensive list of selective colleges that have admitted homeschoolers is available online at http://learninfreedom.org/colleges_4_hmsc.html.

37. Jon Reider, as quoted in Patrick Basham, "Home Schooling: From the Extreme to the Mainstream," *Fraser Institute Occasional Paper*, Number 51 (Fraser Institute, 2001), p. 13.

38. As quoted in the *Brown University Alumni Magazine*, January/February 2002. See, also, "Home Improvement," *The Wall Street Journal*, May 17, 2002, W 15.

39. Brian D. Ray, "Strengths of Their Own – Home Schoolers Across America: Academic Achievement, Family Characteristics, and Longitudinal Traits," National Home Education Research Institute, available at http://www.nheri.org/modules.php?name=Content&pa=showpage&pid=20.

40. Larry Shyers, *Comparison of Social Adjustment Between Home and Traditionally Schooled Students*, Ph.D. Dissertation, University of Florida, as cited in Patrick Basham, "Home Schooling: From the Extreme to the Mainstream," *Fraser Institute Occasional Paper*, Number 51 (Fraser Institute, 2001), p. 14.

41. Thomas C. Smedley, "Socialization of Home Schooled Children: A Communication Approach," unpublished Master of Science thesis, Radford, Virginia: Radford University, as cited in Patrick Basham, "Home Schooling: From the Extreme to the Mainstream," *Fraser Institute Occasional Paper*, Number 51 (Fraser Institute, 2001), p. 14.

42. Linda Montgomery, "The Effect of Home Schooling on Leadership Skills of Home Schooled Students," *Home School Researcher* (1989), Volume 5, Number 1, as cited in Patrick Basham, "Home Schooling: From the Extreme to the Mainstream," *Fraser Institute Occasional Paper*, Number 51 (Fraser Institute, 2001), p. 14.

43. Raymond Moore, "Research on Sociability," *The Parent Educator and Family Report* (1986), Volume 4, Number 1, as cited in Patrick Basham, "Home Schooling: From the Extreme to the Mainstream," *Fraser Institute Occasional Paper*, Number 51 (Fraser Institute, 2001), p. 14; Mona Delahooke, "Home Educated Children's Social/Emotional Adjustment and Academic Achievements: A Comparative Study," unpublished doctoral dissertation, Los Angeles, California: California School of Professional Psychology (1986); and John Taylor, *Self Concept in Home Schooling Children*, Ann Arbor, Michigan: University Microfilms International (1986), as cited in Patrick Basham, "Home Schooling: From the Extreme to the Mainstream," *Fraser Institute Occasional Paper*, Number 51 (Fraser Institute, 2001), p. 14.

44. Gary J. Knowles, *Now We Are Adults: Attitudes, Beliefs, and Status of Adults Who Were Home-educated as Children*, paper presented at the annual meeting of the American Educational Research Association, Chicago, April 3-7, as cited in Patrick Basham, "Home Schooling: From the Extreme to the Mainstream," *Fraser Institute Occasional Paper*, Number 51 (Fraser Institute, 2001), p. 14.

45. As quoted in Robert J. Grossman, "Home Is Where the School Is," *HR Magazine*, December 3, 2001.

46. As quoted in Robert J. Grossman, "Home Is Where the School Is," *HR Magazine*, December 3, 2001.

47. As quoted in Robert J. Grossman, "Home Is Where the School Is," *HR Magazine*, December 3, 2001.

48. As quoted in Robert J. Grossman, "Home Is Where the School Is," *HR Magazine*, December 3, 2001.

49. As quoted in Robert J. Grossman, "Home Is Where the School Is," *HR Magazine*, December 3, 2001.

50. Lawrence M. Rudner, "Scholastic Achievement and Demographic Characteristics of Home School Students in 1998," *Educational Policy Analysis Archives*, Volume 7, Number 8 (March 23, 1999), available at http://epaa.asu.edu/epaa/v7n8/.

51. Lawrence M. Rudner, "Scholastic Achievement and Demographic Characteristics of Home School Students in 1998," *Educational Policy Analysis Archives*, Volume 7, Number 8 (March 23, 1999), available at http://epaa.asu.edu/epaa/v7n8/.

52. The information regarding the results of the 2003 National Home Education Research Institute (NHERI) study is taken from the Home School Legal Defense Association's (HSLDA) synopsis "Homeschooling Grows Up," available online at http://www.hslda.org/research/ray2003/default.asp. The full report can be obtained from NHERI at http://www.nheri.org/. HSLDA's website, by the way, is an excellent source of information on homeschooling.

53. Robert Louis Dabney, *On Secular Education*, Douglas Wilson, ed. (Moscow, Idaho: Canon Press, 1996).

54. This phrase and the call for an "exodus" from government schools are borrowed from E. Ray Moore, Jr., the founder of the Exodus Mandate ministry.

Postscript

1. Marshall Fritz, "The Cement Canoe," available at www.sepschool.org.

2. Linda Schrock Taylor, "Twilight Years or Twilight Zone: Seasoned Teachers Leave Public Schools in Droves," Lewrockwell.com, January 24, 2003, available at www.lewrockwell.com.

3. Jean Johnson and Ann Duffett, with Jackie Vine and Leslie Moye, "Where We Are Now: 12 Things You Need To Know About Public Opinion and Public Schools," Public Agenda 2003, available at www.publicagenda.org.

4. Jean Johnson and Ann Duffett, with Jackie Vine and Leslie Moye, "Where We Are Now: 12 Things You Need To Know About Public Opinion and Public Schools," Public Agenda 2003, available at www.publicagenda.org.

5. Jean Johnson and Ann Duffett, with Jackie Vine and Leslie Moye, "Where We Are Now: 12 Things You Need To Know About Public Opinion and Public Schools," Public Agenda 2003, available at www.publicagenda.org.

6. Shannon Colavecchio and Kimberly Miller, "Palm Beach Teachers: 'We Leave Teaching Because of Kids' Bad Behavior,'" *The Palm Beach Post*, April 14, 2002.

7. Shannon Colavecchio and Kimberly Miller, "Palm Beach Teachers: 'We Leave Teaching Because of Kids' Bad Behavior,'" *The Palm Beach Post*, April 14, 2002.

8. "School Suspends Most Sixth-Graders for Mass Rowdiness; 'You'd be Shocked,' Principal Says," Associated Press, available online at http://www.sfgate.com/cgi-bin/article.cgi?file=/news/archive/2004/03/26/national1146EST0561.DTL.

9. "School Suspends Most Sixth-Graders for Mass Rowdiness; 'You'd be Shocked,' Principal Says," Associated Press, available online at http://www.sfgate.com/cgi-bin/article.cgi?file=/news/archive/2004/03/26/national1146EST0561.DTL.

10. Joshua Kaplowitz, "My Classroom from Hell," *The Wall Street Journal*, January 24, 2003.

11. Joshua Kaplowitz, "My Classroom from Hell," *The Wall Street Journal*, January 24, 2003.

12. Anonymous, "The System's Failing Grades," *New York Press*, Vol. 15, Issue 16 (2002).

13.. Matthew Clavel, "How Not to Teach Math: New York's Chancellor Klein's Plan Doesn't Compute," *City Magazine*, March 7. 2003.

14. Matthew Clavel, "How Not to Teach Math: New York's Chancellor Klein's Plan Doesn't Compute," *City Magazine*, March 7. 2003.

15. Andrew Trotter, "Plagiarism Controversy Engulfs Kansas School," *Education Week*, April 3, 2002.

16. Andrew Trotter, "Plagiarism Controversy Engulfs Kansas School," *Education Week*, April 3, 2002.

17. Linda Schrock Taylor, "Twilight Years or Twilight Zone: Seasoned Teachers Leave Public Schools in Droves," Lewrockwell.com, January 24, 2003, available at www.lewrockwell.com.

18. Ann Edwards has taught for twenty-four years in grades K-9. Currently, Mrs. Edwards teaches at Litel Elementary School in Chino Hills, California. The National Right to Read Foundation describes its mission as follows: "… our mission is to return scientific research based, explicit, systematic phonics instruction along with good literature to every elementary school in America." For more information about this organization, visit its website at http://www.nrrf.org/index.html.

19. Written Testimony of Ann Edwards before the Subcommittee on Early Childhood, Youth and Families of the Committee on Education and the Workforce of the House of Representatives, One Hundred Sixth Congress, First Session, Hearing held in Anaheim, California, July 6, 1999, written testimony dated Thursday, July 22, 1999, Serial No. 106-57.

20. The estimate of teachers that will shortly retire is from the NEA, "Attracting and Keeping Qualified Teachers," available at www.nea.org/teachershortage/. The NEA also estimates that more than 2 million new teachers will be needed in the next decade.

21. You may recall from Chapter 5 that in the 1998 administration of Massachusetts teacher certification test 59% of 1,800 recent school of education graduates flunked. The test was described as being at about an 8th to 10th-grade level. In 1997, 75% of teacher candidates in Suffolk County, New York, flunked an 11th-grade level reading comprehension test. In 2001, The *Chicago Sun-Times* gave 10 9th to 11th-grade students the same test of "Basic Skills" used to qualify teachers. The students finished in 11 to 23 minutes, all but two passed the math and grammar portions, and half passed the reading comprehension part of the test. There are many, many stories like this, as well as many, many stories about how the education industry has worked to delegitimize testing or to lower standards to the point of making it almost impossible for someone to fail.

22. Written Testimony of Ann Edwards before the Subcommittee on Early Childhood, Youth and Families of the Committee on Education and the Workforce of the House of Representatives, One Hundred Sixth Congress, First Session, Hearing held in Anaheim, California, July 6, 1999, written testimony dated Thursday, July 22, 1999, Serial No. 106-57.

INDEX

More Educational Titles From Chalcedon

The Victims of Dick and Jane

By Samuel L. Blumenfeld. America's most effective critic of public education shows us how America's public schools were remade by educators who used curriculum to create citizens suitable for their own vision of a utopian socialist society. This collection of essays will show you how and why America's public education declined. You will see the educator-engineered decline of reading skills. The author describes the causes for the decline and the way back to competent education methodologies that will result in a self-educated, competent, and freedom-loving populace.

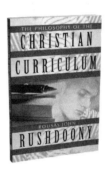

Paperback, 266 pages, index, $22.00

The Philosophy of the Christian Curriculum

By R.J. Rushdoony. The Christian School represents a break with humanistic education, but, too often, in leaving the state school, the Christian educator has carried the state's humanism with him. A curriculum is not neutral: it is either a course in humanism or training in a God-centered faith and life. The liberal arts curriculum means literally that course which trains students in the arts of freedom. This raises the key question: is freedom in and of man or Christ? The Christian art of freedom, that is, the Christian liberal arts curriculum, is emphatically not the same as the humanistic one. It is urgently necessary for Christian educators to rethink the meaning and nature of the curriculum.

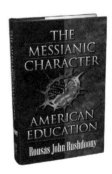

Paperback, 190 pages, index, $16.00

The Messianic Character of American Education

By R.J. Rushdoony. Rushdoony's study tells us an important part of American history: exactly what has public education been trying to accomplish? Before the 1830s and Horace Mann, no schools in the U.S. were state supported or state controlled. They were local, parent-teacher enterprises, supported without taxes, and taking care of all children. They were remarkably high in standard and were Christian. From Mann to the present, the state has used education to socialize the child. The school's basic purpose, according to its own philosophers, is not education in the traditional sense of the 3 R's. Instead, it is to promote "democracy" and "equality," not in their legal or civic sense, but in terms of the engineering of a socialized citizenry. Public education became the means of creating a social order of the educator's design. Such men saw themselves and the school in messianic terms. This book was instrumental in launching the Christian school and homeschool movements.

Hardback, 410 pages, index, $20.00

Purchase online at www.chalcedonstore.com

Intellectual Schizophrenia

By R.J. Rushdoony. When this brilliant and prophetic book was first published in 1961, the Christian homeschool movement was years away and even Christian day schools were hardly considered a viable educational alternative. But this book and the author's later Messianic Character of American Education were a resolute call to arms for Christian's to get their children out of the pagan public schools and provide them with a genuine Christian education. Dr. Rushdoony had predicted that the humanist system, based on anti-Christian premises of the Enlightenment, could only get worse. Rushdoony was indeed a prophet. He knew that education divorced from God and from all transcendental standards would produce the educational disaster and moral barbarism we have  today. The title of this book is particularly significant in that Dr. Rushdoony was able to identify the basic contradiction that pervades a secular society that rejects God's sovereignty but still needs law and order, justice, science, and meaning to life. As Dr. Rushdoony writes, "there is no law, no society, no justice, no structure, no design, no meaning apart from God." And so, modern man has become schizophrenic because of his rebellion against God.

Paperback, 150 pages, index, $17.00

Mathematics: Is God Silent?

By James Nickel. This book revolutionizes the prevailing understanding and teaching of math. The addition of this book is a must for all upper-level Christian school curricula and for college students and adults interested in math or related fields of science and religion. It will serve as a solid refutation for the claim, often made in court, that mathematics is one subject, which cannot be taught from a distinctively Biblical perspective.
Revised and enlarged 2001 edition,
Paperback, 408 pages, $22.00

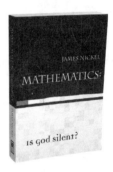

The Foundations of Christian Scholarship

Edited by Gary North. These are essays developing the implications and meaning of the philosophy of Dr. Cornelius Van Til for every area of life. The chapters explore the implications of Biblical faith for a variety of disciplines.
Paperback, 355 pages, indices, $24.00

Purchase online at www.chalcedonstore.com

The Chalcedon Foundation

Chalcedon labors to articulate in the clearest possible terms a distinctly Christian and explicitly Biblical solution to the prevalent evils of the modern world. Our objective is nothing short of setting forth the vision and program for rebuilding the theological fortifications of Christian civilization. These fortifications have been eroded by the forces of humanism and secularism over the past three centuries. We are not committed, though, merely to reproducing a glorious Christian past. We work to press the claims of historic Christianity as the Biblical pattern of life everywhere. We work for godly cultural change across the entire spectrum of life. We strive to accomplish this objective by two principal methods.

First, Chalcedon is committed to recovering the intellectual foundations of Christian civilization. We do this in two main ways, negatively, we expose the bankruptcy of all non-Christian (and alleged but compromising Christian) systems of thought and practices. Positively, we propose an explicitly Biblical system of thought and action as the exclusive basis for civilization. Only by restoring the Christian Faith and Biblical law as the standard of all of life can Christians hope to re-establish Christian civilizations.

Second, Chalcedon is dedicated to providing the tools for rebuilding this Christian civilization. We work to assist individuals, families, and institutions by offering explicitly Biblical alternatives to anti-Christian ideas and practices. In the way we guide Christians in the task of governing their own spheres of life in terms of the entire Bible: in family, church, school, vocation, arts, economics, business, media, the state, and all other areas of modern life.

We believe that the source of godly change is regeneration by the Holy Spirit, not revolution by the violence of man. As God regenerates more and more individuals, and as they reorient their lives and areas of personal influence to the teachings of the Bible, He employs them to advance His kingdom and establish Christian civilization. We believe that God's law is the divine pattern of sanctification in every area of life, but it is not the means of justification; man is saved by grace, not by law. The role of every earthly government—including family government, church government, school government, vocational government, and civil government—is to submit to Biblical law. No government in any form can make men Christians or truly obedient; this is the work of God' sovereign grace. Much less should civil government try to impose Biblical law on an unbelieving society. Biblical law cannot be imposed; it must be embraced.

A guiding principle of Chalcedon, in fact, is its devotion to maximum individual freedom under God's law. Chalcedon derives its name from the great ecclesiastical council of Chalcedon (A.D. 451), which produced the crucial Christological definition of Jesus Christ as God of very God and Man of very man, a formula directly challenging every false claim of divinity by any human institution: state, church, cult, schools, or human assembly. Christ alone is both God and man, the unique link between heaven and earth. All human power is therefore derivative; only Christ may announce that "All power [authority] is given unto me in heaven and earth" (Matthew 28:18). Historically, therefore, the Chalcedonian creed is the foundation of Western liberty, setting limits on all authoritarian human institutions by acknowledging the validity of the claims of the One who is the source of all human freedom (Galatians 5:1). Consequently, we oppose top-heavy, authoritarian systems of government which are, by definition, non-Christian. We advocate instead a series of independent but cooperative institutions and a highly decentralized social order.

Chalcedon is an educational institution. It supports the efforts of Christians and Christian organizations to implement the vision of Christian civilization. Though unapologetically Reformed, Chalcedon supports the kingdom work of all orthodox denominations and churches. Chalcedon is an independent Christian foundation governed by a board of trustees, Christian men in accord with Chalcedon's vision statement. The foundation is not subordinate to the authority of any particular denomination or ecclesiastical body.